PARENTING
AND
CHILD CARE

REVISED AND UPDATED

PARENTING
AND
CHILD CARE

A Guide for Christian Parents

WILLIAM SEARS, M.D.
Author of THE BABY BOOK

THOMAS NELSON PUBLISHERS
Nashville

Published in Nashville, Tennessee, by Janet Thoma books, a division
of Thomas Nelson, Inc., and distributed in Canada by
Word Communications, Ltd.

Unless otherwise noted Scripture quotations are from the NEW KING
JAMES VERSION of the Bible. Copyright © 1979, 1980, 1982,
Thomas Nelson Publishers, Inc.

Scripture quotations marked (NIV) are taken from the Holy Bible, New
International Version. Copyright © 1973, 1978, International Bible
Society. Used by permission of Zondervan Bible Publishers.

Scripture quotations marked (TLB) are taken from *The Living Bible*
(Wheaton, Illinois: Tyndale House Publishers, 1971)
and are used by permission.

ISBN 0-8407-4847-7

Printed in the United States of America

Dedicated to my family

Martha
James
Robert
Peter
Hayden
Erin
Matthew
Stephen
Lauren

Your wife shall be like a fruitful vine
In the very heart of your house,
Your children like olive plants
All around your table.

(Psalm 128:3)

CONTENTS

Prologue

The main purpose of *Parenting and Child Care* is to help parents achieve what I believe are the three primary goals of Christian parenting:

1. To know your child,
2. To help your child feel right, and
3. To lead your child to Christ.

Each child comes wired with a unique set of characteristics called *temperament*. No two children come wired the same. Each child also has a certain level of needs which, if met, will enable him to reach his fullest potential. Some children have higher needs than others.

Each parent is endowed with a natural ability to nurture. Some children require more nurturing than others, and some parents have a higher level of giving than others. Implied in the concept of a loving Creator is that God would not give to parents a child they could not handle. God's matching program is perfect; His law of supply and demand will work if people practice a style of parenting that allows the divine design for the parent-child relationship to develop.

The term *parenting style* means "a way of caring for your child." Restrained parenting is one parenting style which is earmarked by phrases like, "Let your baby cry it out," "What, you're still nursing?" "Don't let him sleep with you," "Get him on a schedule," "You're making him too dependent," and "You're going to spoil her." These common admonitions from trusted advisors to vulnerable new parents keep them from fully enjoying their child.

The style of parenting I believe God designed for the care and feeding of His children is what I call "attachment parenting," which encourages new parents to respond to their child's cues without restraint. The fundamentals of attachment parenting include:

1. Prenatal bonding—praying for and communicating with your unborn child during pregnancy;

2. Prenatal preparation—learning how to prepare your body to give birth according to God's design;

3. Positive birthing experience—following the dictates of your own body so that you will not fear your birthing experience;

4. Birth bonding—immediate physical contact with your baby at birth;

5. Unrestricted breastfeeding—allowing you and your baby to develop harmony with each other;

6. Infant-led weaning—letting your baby, not someone else, determine when to be weaned;

7. Prompt response to crying—developing sensitivity to your baby's needs before he or she has to cry for them;

8. Sleep sharing—welcoming your baby into your family bed and not banishing him to a place alone;

9. Father involvement—creating an environment for the father of the infant to take an active role in attachment parenting; and

10. Christian emphasis—building your home on the foundation, promises, and leadership of Christ.

I arrived at these principles of attachment parenting not only from parenting seven children with my wife Martha, but also from observing my patients for twenty years. I also have been encouraged by organizations, such as the La Leche League, that advocate similar parenting principles.

Practicing these principles can help you have a realistic expectation of childhood behavior. You will be more observant of your infant's cues and will be able to respond intuitively. As you become more confident in your ability to meet your baby's needs you will enjoy parenting more and more.

Because of the great variability in family situations, some parents may not be able to practice all of these disciplines all of the time. I just want to make the point that the more these styles of parenting are practiced, the greater is their opportunity of truly enjoying their child and of claiming the promise, "Train up a child in the way he should go, and when he is old he will not depart from it" (Prov. 22:6).

What attachment parenting does for you may be summed up in one word—*harmony*. You and your baby will be more in sync with each other; you will become sensitive to your baby.

Mothers also undergo a chemical change when they have this harmony. Because they are breastfeeding and interacting with their babies, they receive more of the hormone prolactin. I call prolactin "the mothering hormone" because it gives mothers the added boost they need during those trying times. I suspect this hormone is part of the divine design of mother's intuition.

Attachment parenting also gives your child a model to follow when he or she becomes a parent. Remember, you are parenting someone else's future husband, wife, father, or mother. How your child was parented may influence how he or she parents. The lack of a definite model is what causes confusion in many young parents today.

The principles of attachment parenting are especially rewarding for the parents of "fussy" or "demanding" children whom I like to call "high-need babies." We will be discussing the traits of high-need children and how to parent these special blessings.

There is a parallel between a child's relationship with his parents and his relationship with God. The parental relationship a child has in his early formative years has a direct bearing on his eventual relationship with God. If a child has learned trust, discipline, and love from his parents, he will be prepared to transfer these concepts to God. As you study the tenets of attachment parenting, you will see how to apply them to the spiritual training of your child.

In the following chapters, each of the disciplines of attachment parenting are covered in great detail. For parents who wish to get the most out of this book, read the entire book through once, and you will see how all these attachment tips fit together. By the end of the book I hope parents will perceive these biblical concepts to be a Christian parenting style that is in accordance with God's design.

Introduction

My dear Christian parents, this book arose out of my own deep love and concern for children as one of God's greatest gifts to us. A child is a gift for us to love, to nurture, and ultimately to return to Him a finished person.

Because they are such a precious gift, I feel that our Creator has given us a divine design for the care and feeding of His children. Over the past decade and a half, I have been increasingly concerned that this design is not being followed. As a result, parents are having difficulty training their children who are departing from the way they should go. In *Parenting and Child Care* I want to convey what I believe is God's design for parenting, and I will offer practical suggestions on how to follow that design.

During my past twenty years in pediatric practice I have carefully observed what parenting styles work for most parents most of the time. Besides learning from my patients, I have been blessed with a wonderful wife, Martha, who is a professional mother. During the revision of this book God blessed us with our seventh child, and we have recently adopted baby number eight. If, after reading this book, you are more able to achieve the three goals of parenting which are to know your child, to help your child feel right, and to lead your child to Christ, then I will have served my Lord in writing this book.

William P. Sears, M.D.
San Clemente, California

CHAPTER 1

LAYING THE FOUNDATION

There are three basic building blocks that form the foundation of a successful Christian family: (1) commitment to a God-centered life, (2) a stable and fulfilled Christian marriage, and (3) spiritual leadership.

COMMITMENT TO A GOD-CENTERED LIFE

The first and most important step toward successful Christian parenting is defining sincerely your degree of *commitment* to being a Christian parent. Dwell upon this for a moment because, unless your commitment is uncompromising, you may have an unfruitful struggle.

Throughout this book, Deuteronomy 6:5–9 will be the master verse for this commitment.

You shall love the LORD your God with all your heart, with all your soul, and with all your might. And these words which I command you today shall be in your heart; you shall teach them diligently to your children, and shall talk of them when you sit in your house, when you walk by the way, when you lie down, and when you rise up. You shall bind them as a sign on your hand, and they shall be as frontlets between your eyes. You shall write them on the doorposts of your house and on your gates.

The most important ingredient in any relationship is commitment. The more you are committed to making a relationship work, the more successful the relationship will be. Parenting is a relationship between parent and child. It is the strongest of all human bonds. One of the joys of being a pediatrician is seeing how strongly most parents are committed to their children. This commitment is strong because your love for your children is strong. Loving your children is easy because you know them so well. For most parents, commitment to God does not come as easily as commitment to their children because their love of Him is weak and their knowledge of Him is scanty. Knowledge of a person helps the commitment to that person. This was illustrated very simply by our four-year-old daughter, Hayden, who one day said, "The reason children love Mommy and Daddy more than God is because they know Mommy and Daddy better than God."

God anticipated the difficulty parents would have making a full commitment to Him; He knew that you would need help loving and knowing Him and rearing your children according to His plan. For this reason He gave you specific details of what He wants, what you should do, and what your children will become if you follow His instructions. He gave you His Word, or what I call a "Manufacturer's Handbook," to accompany the child that He and we have made. This handbook is like the owner's manual that often accompanies a car, telling how to start it up and what fuel it needs and giving a regular maintenance schedule for years of trouble-free driving—if the manufacturer's instructions are followed. The manufacturer also admonishes you to expect failure if these instructions are not followed.

The Bible is God's timeless Handbook for parents. It is the inspired Word of God talking to us through the men He chose to write His Book. In it God told people to make personal commitments to Jesus as Lord and Savior. "I am the vine, you are the branches. He who abides in Me, and I in him, bears much fruit; for without Me you can do nothing" (John 15:5). Having committed yourselves to God and to your children, you must examine what He expects of you as parents. Deuteronomy and Proverbs outline the basic instructions that you are to follow.

1. To love God (Deut. 6:5);
2. To fear Him (Deut. 10:12);
3. To walk in His ways, to be an example (Deut. 10:12);
4. To know Him, to have a knowledge and an application of His Word (Deut. 10:13);
5. To teach His Word to your children (Deut. 6:7; 11:19);

6. To discipline your children (Prov. 19:18); and

7. To avoid provoking your children to anger (Eph. 6:4).

In this sequence of God's communication to parents, one clear message emerges: before you can instruct your children, you must understand His Word yourselves. First you must know, love, and fear God and live according to His teaching. Then you can impart these concepts to your children.

To Love God

It is significant that God's first message to parents, and the message occurring most frequently in the Old and New Testaments, is to love Him. In any person-to-person relationship where there is genuine love, all else automatically follows.

There are three Greek words for love: *eros,* meaning "passionate love"; *phileo,* meaning "demonstrated natural affection"; and *agape,* meaning an "unconditional love." Most of the time when the word *love* is mentioned in the Bible's Greek text, it is agape love, which is the love God expects from Christians. Agape love takes you out of your preoccupation with yourself and into a commitment with others. When the text uses *phileo,* it means it is not enough to love your child unconditionally. You must express your love to the child in a way that he or she can experience being loved, through the things you say and do to and for that child every day.

I tell parents that the best way for a child to learn agape and phileo love is to witness it being expressed by his or her parents. The same concept holds true in helping your child love God. If he or she sees true love between you as parents, and between you and God, your child has a head start toward a relationship with God. Parents, remember that a child sees what you do, not how you feel. How you show signs of your commitment is more meaningful to a child than what you say or what you feel.

Before reading any further, take a few minutes to dwell upon your commitment to God, for this is the basis from which all parenting begins. Consider the message of John 3:16: "For God so loved the world that He gave His only begotten Son, that whoever believes in Him should not perish but have everlasting life."

To Fear the Lord

God tells us to fear Him: "What does the LORD your God require of you, but to fear the LORD your God" (Deut. 10:12). The concepts of love and fear coexist inseparably throughout the Bible. The term *fear* in the Bible implies an awesome respect for the power and wisdom of God. In the book of Proverbs (perhaps the best child psychology book ever written), Solomon said that "the fear of the LORD is the beginning of knowledge" (Prov. 1:7). As a Christian parent, when I think about this concept of the fear of the Lord, the first thought I have is of my accountability to God for rearing my children according to His plan (Matt. 18:6; Rom. 14:12; 2 Cor. 5:10). I urge you, parents, to keep this concept of accountability always before you. Dwell upon it by the day, by the hour; think about it as you go to bed and as you get up. Fathers, you especially must have a constant awareness of your accountability to your Father that you are to be the effective spiritual leaders in your families. I sincerely feel that if a home is without spiritual leadership, the father will be called on the carpet first.

To Walk in His Ways and Know Him

After God tells you to love Him and fear Him, He says you should "walk in all his ways" (Deut. 10:12 NIV). Then He adds: "With all your heart and with all your soul" (Deut. 10:12 NIV). He says further, "Fix these words of mine in your hearts and minds; tie them as symbols on your hands and bind them on your foreheads" (Deut. 11:18 NIV). These passages are the earliest and clearest messages that God does not want lukewarm Christian parents. There is an underlying depth of commitment to this message. Your love and fear of Him should be more than superficial lip service, but should be a knowing of Him in your innermost being, an inner commitment that dictates your daily living.

To Teach Your Children

In the passages in Deuteronomy, God follows His main theme of parenting: "Teach them to your children . . . impress them on your children" (Deut. 11:19; 6:7 NIV). These verses are some of the earliest and most compelling biblical mandates to parents to teach their children. They tell parents not only *to* teach but *how* to teach.

Saturate your child's environment with His words, "Talk about them when you sit at home and when you walk along the road, when you lie down and when you get up. Tie them as symbols on your hands and bind them on your foreheads. Write them on the doorframes of your houses and on your gates" (Deut. 6:7–9 NIV). In case you are a slow learner, God gives this message twice—in Deuteronomy 6:5–9 and 11:18–20. Christian parents should read these passages over and over again and attach them to their foreheads and to their doorposts. These are verses of commitment. It is clear that God expects more than Sunday-only Christian teaching. Not only are you to know God's commandments, but you are to obey them.

These passages in Deuteronomy also tell parents to teach by example, giving your children models to observe rather than commandments to obey. You must show your children that you are walking in the way of the Lord by saturating your environment with His teachings. Parents are always on stage in front of their children—a fact that makes their accountability for Christian living an awesome responsibility.

But your witness is not limited to your children. You are told to "write them on the doorposts of *your* house and on *your* gates." It seems that God is laying down specific guidelines for Christian families; they are to be examples to all who enter their homes. There should be no doubt who is the central figure in your household. We have a sign in our home that reads: "As for me and my house, we will serve the LORD" (Josh. 24:15).

To Discipline Your Children

In addition to telling you to teach your children His Word, God tells you to discipline them: "Discipline your son, for in that there is hope" (Prov. 19:18 NIV). *Teach* and *discipline* are similar terms, but as used in the Bible, they differ in degree. Discipline implies more than teaching God's Word to your children. Discipline means training their inner behavior and modifying their tendencies so that they are guided by inner rules that give them direction.

In His book of Proverbs, spoken through Solomon, God emphatically tells you how to discipline your children and what kind of inner rules to impart. Proverbs is the best portion of God's handbook for parents who wish to discipline their children according to God's plan. Discipline will be discussed in a subsequent chapter, but consider the following important points.

In Proverbs, God gives the same message He gives in Deuteronomy: before parents can impart wisdom and discipline to their children, they must be wise and disciplined themselves. In Proverbs the central theme of Deuteronomy is repeated: "The fear of the LORD is the beginning of knowledge" (Prov. 1:7) and "of wisdom" (Prov. 9:10). In order to discipline your children effectively, you must first fear the Lord and discipline yourself to overcome your inner tendencies toward evil and then fill yourself with Christ-centered living. In this way your children will see that those in charge, their parents, are disciplined according to God's plan. They will rebel against having something imposed on them that their parents are unwilling to accept for themselves.

An important concept for you to derive from the study of Proverbs is the continuum concept of Christian parenting. (*Continuum* means "a series of interrelated steps, a chain of events.") Proverbs 22:6 is called the master verse of discipline: "Train up a child in the way he should go, And when he is old he will not depart from it." A child who is disciplined according to Proverbs will most likely impart the same discipline to his or her own children and so on throughout the continuum of successive generations, for "a good man leaves an inheritance to his children's children" (Prov. 13:22). Parents will therefore be held accountable for a long-standing Christian heritage, or lack of it, to their grandchildren, great-grandchildren, and beyond.

COMMITMENT TO A HUSBAND-WIFE RELATIONSHIP

In the first section you read that your individual commitment to God is the first step toward Christian parenting. In this section this commitment is taken one step further—committing to your marital relationship. This dual commitment—your personal commitment to God plus your commitment of your marriage to Him—forms the foundation for the third step: committing to Him as parents. Each step in this relationship continuum is interrelated to the other steps.

Two important ingredients for marriage are stability and fulfillment. Marriages can have both of these ingredients, in spite of the world's messages to the contrary.

A Lifelong Commitment

The master concept in each Christian marriage is that it be a lifelong commitment: "What God has joined together, let not man separate" (Matt. 19:6). The commitment to stay married means that divorce is not an option, and this commitment is increasingly threatened in a world seducing Christians into alternative lifestyles and the path of least resistance. Let me now share with you some ways to help you keep this commitment foremost in your marriage.

Acknowledge God as the head of this relationship. Earlier you read about the Christian's individual, personal relationship with God. In this step you are to take God's Word literally, "what God has joined together" (Matt. 19:6), and the relationship evolves into a triangle. In this divine plan, husband and wife are committed to each other; both are committed to God. As husband and wife each grows closer to God, they also grow closer to each other.

You may feel you can keep your marriage commitment without God's help; however, the spirit is willing but the flesh is weak. A Christian who marries accepts a different standard of commitment to that relationship from that of a non-Christian. Acknowledging God as the cornerstone of your marriage is not just a nice, pious thought or an addendum that may make your marriage work better; it is an absolute necessity for a stable and fulfilled Christian marriage. Throughout many years of pediatric practice I have seen couples who acknowledge this triangle weather the storms of marriage crises more successfully than those going at it alone.

Pray for your marriage. Having sincerely acknowledged God's order for the committed marriage relationship, you must pray continuously asking God to strengthen this relationship. Each day, preferably upon awakening or upon retiring, kneel before your Lord, joining hands and arms. Invite God into your marriage and ask Him to bless your relationship.

By praying for your marriage you accomplish at least two things. First, the more you pray, the more deeply rooted becomes your faith that God will strengthen what He has joined together. This marriage prayer should be such an integral part of your daily living that without it your day feels incomplete. Second, your communication with each other improves. The more you communicate with God, the more you communicate with each other. During the marriage prayer, besides talking to God, you are indirectly giving your spouse the following message: "I value our relationship enough to ask continually God's blessing on our marriage [no one prays for something he doesn't want]. I acknowledge God as the foundation of our marriage, and I reaffirm my commitment to a lasting marriage."

As you reaffirm your commitment to God you are naturally reaffirming your commitment to your spouse. Your spouse cannot help feeling your sincerity. While you pray, he or she is stimulated to convey the same sincerity and commitment in his or her prayer to God. You both emerge from the marriage prayer feeling more secure in your relationship with each other and with your God, and the entire marriage relationship operates at a higher level.

Be vigilant! After acknowledging God as the Author of your marriage and praying unceasingly for its success, the next aid to a stable marriage is being vigilant against the many temptations that may weaken your relationship. Having God as part of your marriage triangle will certainly give you more strength to ward off attacks on your happiness, but you still need to stand firm against temptations (Phil.

4:1). I am firmly convinced that a marriage without God as the chief Counselor will eventually succumb to the mandates of the world to explore other options and alternatives. Why am I so convinced of this? Very simply because marriage is between two humans.

A Fulfilling Relationship

Ideally, a three-way commitment should be enough to keep a Christian couple together for a lifetime; however, this is seldom the case. A relationship that is not fulfilling has a high risk of eventually dissolving. I believe God intends Christian couples to be fulfilled in their marriages.

The concept of fulfillment may be more important for Christian than for non-Christian marriages because, for many Christians, divorce is not an option. As a result they put stability and commitment first. Therefore, a Christian couple may remain married but be unfulfilled.

A humanist viewpoint of marriage puts fulfillment before, or in place of, commitment. The humanist says that as long as both parties are fulfilled, they remain committed to their relationship. If one of the parties becomes unfulfilled, the commitment weakens. As a consequence, in this humanist view of marriage, a non-believing couple may actually work harder to fulfill each other than would the Christian couple. The humanist's commitment has strings attached; the Christian viewpoint of marriage has an unconditional commitment.

Many couples may not realize that the concept of mutual fulfillment is biblical (1 Cor. 7:3–5). An exceptionally good source for additional reading on this subject is found in Helen Wessel's book, *Under the Apple Tree*.

What are some of the ingredients that go into creating a fulfilled marriage? Mutual esteem is one ingredient. One of the primary goals of child rearing is to develop your children's self-esteem. Throughout childhood, adolescence, and the adult single life a person is preoccupied with his or her own self-image. Most daily living is dedicated to what makes a person feel right. However, when people marry, that emphasis shifts from self to outside self. Instead of being totally egocentric, they direct some of that energy toward meeting the needs of their mates. The more energy that is directed out of one's self and into fulfilling the needs of the mate, the more fulfilled a person is in marriage. At first glance this may seem self-defeating. You wonder if you are being unfair to yourself when you continually strive to meet your mate's needs. You have needs, too! How are your needs met?

As has already been discussed, if you have made an unconditional commitment to a lifelong marriage and acknowledge God as the Author of your union and if you pray continuously for God's blessing on your relationship, you are on your way toward a fulfilled marriage. Having made this unconditional commitment to another person and acknowledging your need for an outside Counselor, you have consciously come out of yourself. Perhaps for the first time in your life you have sincerely acknowledged that someone else is as important or even more important to you than yourself. This acknowledgment is the first step toward mutual esteem.

As you direct your energies toward your mate, being more tuned in to him or her and becoming more sensitive to his or her needs, your mate feels two things: (1) His or her self-esteem is boosted—he or she feels better as a person and consequently more fulfilled, and (2) he or she feels your unconditional giving. The result (not the purpose) of these two feelings is stimulating your mate to redirect his or her energy toward you. You usually get more than you give, and the result is that you wind up feeling more fulfilled than if you had selfishly directed all your energies toward yourself in the first place. Instead of having two cups half full, you wind up having two cups completely full and, perhaps, even larger cups.

The humanistic viewpoint of marriage is, "What do I *get* from this relationship?" The Christian viewpoint of marriage is, "What can I *give* to this relationship?" Marriages that are based on getting rather than giving, fail. Once they have gotten all they can out of their partners, they are back to the old song "Is That All There Is?" You are more in control when you give because giving depends only on yourself, whom you can control; however, getting depends on other people, whom you can't control.

Couples who practice this concept of mutual esteem-building seem to have developed a mirror-image radar system. Each partner's system is constantly in tune with the other's.

Mutual love is another ingredient for a fulfilled marriage. What is true love in marriage? A marriage based primarily on eros love will wear out just as soon as those physical attributes which stimulated the eros love wear out. Marriage based on agape love has a much greater likelihood of success. True agape love implies being able to release the other person when necessary. It is giving yourself to the other person and allowing him or her the freedom to be himself or herself.

Allow me to share a concept with which I have struggled for years. Where in marriage does love fit? Must I first have agape love to have a successful marriage, or must I first have a successful marriage and agape love will naturally follow?

I have come to the conclusion that if couples are unconditionally committed to their partners, if they acknowledge God as the Author of their relationships and strive to build mutual esteem, it doesn't make too much difference which comes first. Some couples begin their relationships with eros love that matures into agape love. Then they make unconditional commitments to their marriages and eventually invite God into their homes; they strive for mutual esteem to keep the flame of agape love burning. Others may not reach agape love until late in their marriages but use their unconditional and God-centered commitments for a permanence and a stability that allows love to mature into full agape love.

Mutual submission is a third ingredient for a fulfilled marriage. Ephesians 5:21–33 sets forth the marriage relationship as it was designed by God.

> *Submitting to one another in the fear of God. Wives, submit to your own husbands, as to the Lord. For the husband is head of the wife, as also Christ is head of the church; and He is the Savior of the body. Therefore, just as the church is subject to Christ, so let the wives be to their own husbands in everything.*
>
> *Husbands, love your wives, just as Christ also loved the church and gave Himself for it, that He might sanctify and cleanse it with the washing of water by the word, that He might present it to Himself a glorious church, not having spot or wrinkle or any such thing, but that it should be holy and without blemish. So husbands ought to love their own wives as their own bodies; he who loves his wife loves himself.*
>
> *For no one ever hated his own flesh, but nourishes and cherishes it, just as the Lord does the church. For we are members of His body, of His flesh and of His bones. "For this reason a man shall leave his father and mother and be joined to his wife, and the two shall become one flesh."*
>
> *This is a great mystery, but I speak concerning Christ and the church. Nevertheless let each one of you in particular so love his own wife as himself, and let the wife see that she respects her husband.*

Pediatricians become marriage counselors because of the effect of the marriage relationship on the child. In counseling couples with marital problems and in observing fulfilled Christian marriages, I have noticed that God's design for the marriage relationship really works. It would be good for both husband and wife to pray and meditate on this passage and to discuss the true meaning of the words of God concerning the sacred relationship of marriage which He designed. The Scripture is not a judgment on who is better; it is not a rating on the superiority of one sex over another. It is a teaching about a relationship. It is a doctrine of each person's role in the relationship so that the entire relationship can work.

Ephesians 5:22–25 also teaches marital responsibilities. Each member of the marriage relationship should consider first his or her responsibilities before considering his or her rights and privileges. (This principle also holds for the parent-child relationship.) This scriptural passage has three important messages: (1) Christians submit to one another; (2) wives submit to your husbands; (3) husbands love your wives as Christ loved His church.

In my experience, the ultimate destiny of every marriage depends on the success or failure of applying these principles. Because of the importance of these verses in Ephesians, they should be analyzed thoroughly.

The first point to consider is the "marriage continuum": love, submission, and commitment need to occur simultaneously in order for the entire marriage relationship to work. In order for a wife to submit to her husband, she must know she is loved by her husband; in order for a husband to love his wife continually to the degree she expects, he must know that his wife respects him; in order for both of them to maintain this relationship consistently, it must be founded on Christ. If this marriage continuum is weak in any of the three steps, the marriage is weakened.

Because God has given the husband the prime responsibility for making the marriage relationship work, the husband's role will be examined first. "Husbands, love your wives, just as Christ also loved the church and gave Himself for it. . . . Husbands ought to love their own wives as their own bodies; he who loves his wife loves himself." These are words of deep love. This is love as Christ loves His church; a sacrificial love, and an unselfish, unconditional love; a love strong enough that a husband would give up his life for his wife.

A husband may say, "Of course I love my wife." Implied in his concept of love is that not only does he feel love for his wife but he also conveys his love for her so often and to such a degree that she knows she is loved. Love is primarily an act of the will. If a husband genuinely loves his wife and has a strong commitment to their relationship, he will show signs of that love and commitment toward her. A woman who truly feels her husband's love and commitment will take great delight in submitting to him. A husband who truly feels that his wife respects him increases his love and commitment, and as a result the marriage continuum operates at an increasingly higher level.

As a husband, you should dwell upon the analogy Paul made that your love for your wife is as Christ loved His church. Since Christ is the spiritual head of the church, being a strong spiritual leader of your family is a vital ingredient in the recipe for a fulfilled Christian marriage relationship. The terms *submit* and *respect* in the Ephesians passage imply that your wife not only should yield to your authority but also should honor you as one who merits this position of authority. It is difficult, if not impossible, for a wife continually to honor and respect a husband who has not assumed the role of spiritual leader of the family. Filling the role of spiritual leader in your family is the single most important way to convey your love and commitment to your wife and also enable her to respect and submit to you. The love you continually show your wife is an investment which will yield a hundred-fold in the love and respect that comes back to you.

"Just as the church is subject to Christ, so let the wives be to their own husbands in everything. . . . and let the wife see that she respects her husband." The Greek word translated "subject" is derived from the same word meaning "to yield" in the sense of yielding to another's authority. This does not imply that one person should control another but that the wife should yield willingly to her husband as the spiritual authority in the marriage. This concerns the smooth running of a relationship. This passage does not suggest that women should subject themselves to all men; this advice is strictly for the submission of wives to their own husbands. It implies respect for the husband not because he is a man but because he is the husband.

This love-and-submission concept ties in with the concept of mutual esteem discussed earlier. A man is often endowed with a hungry ego which needs feeding, and a woman is often endowed with a fragile self-esteem which needs boosting. A man who loves his wife and a wife who respects her husband is a God-given formula for building up the self-esteem of both members of the marriage relationship. A weak self-esteem makes both loving and submitting much more difficult. See how mutually beneficial God's design is?

The final message in God's design for the marriage relationship in Ephesians 5 is found in the phrases: ". . . as to the Lord . . . as the church is subject to Christ . . . as Christ also loved the church." These are qualifying conditions in order that the concepts of love and submission will work. "As to the Lord" implies love and submission according to the will of God for His design of the Christian marriage. A woman is not subject to her husband in things that are not in accordance to the will of God. These phrases also imply that there are three relationships in a marital union: husband-wife, husband-Christ, wife-Christ. In order to expect Christ's blessing on the marriage relationship, both husband and wife must commit their relationship to Christ.

What happens to a marriage that is not founded on these principles? A marriage that is not Christ-centered leads to the temptation to seek alternative fulfillment and thus weaken the marriage. The humanist's subtle message that one must be fulfilled as an individual before one can be fulfilled as a mate sounds reasonable and certainly modern on the surface. In practice, however, this "me first" concept just does not work. All too often what really happens is that one or both members of a couple first seek fulfillment outside the marriage relationship—in employment, status, recognition, and so on—and thereafter seek from the marriage whatever fulfillment hasn't been found elsewhere. This is the reverse of what God intended. Married persons should not look toward their mates for total fulfillment, or they will certainly be disappointed. However, they should seek fulfillment from the marriage relationship over other relationships, and certainly sexual fulfillment must be limited to the marriage relationship.

The following practical tips for a fulfilled Christian marriage also tie marriage to successful parenting.

1. As a husband, you should make a special attempt to show specific acts of love toward your wife each day. Consider the thought, *What can I do today to show her how much I love her and to convey to her how happy I am that she is the mother of our children?* Think what you can do to help her be more fulfilled as a person (knowing she is fulfilled first by the love of God). An unloved and unfulfilled wife has a low self-image and cannot submit, just as an unrespected husband has a low self-image and cannot love.

Many husbands have these feelings of love toward their wives, but they do not convey them clearly or often enough. For example, a friend of mine is married to a woman who is a full-time mother and wife. He said to me, "My wife is such a good mother that when I leave for work in the morning I feel that my children are in the hands of a godly woman." I replied, "That is a beautiful thought; you should tell your wife you feel that way."

Throughout the day, give your wife constant messages of "I care; you are a special person to me"—a touch on the shoulder as you pass by, an offer to help, frequent small gifts of appreciation, and so on. Make sure what you do to convey your love is being received as a love message by her. Ask her to give you a list of some things that make her feel loved. Having her back rubbed could be the most loving thing she could think of, but you may not know that. Then give her your list.

2. As a wife, you should show respect for your husband. One of the most beautiful human manifestations of wifely respect is the way she looks at him when he is

talking. It is similar to how a mother looks into the eyes of her child when she is really tuned in to him. Mutual listening to each other and acknowledging your interest by your body language convey the message, "I am interested in what you are saying because I am interested in what you are feeling because I am interested in you."

Wives are often more transparent than husbands in their show of respect. Next time you are with a group of married couples, look around the room at how wives are relating to their husbands. Some wives will have respect written all over their faces. Expressions of detachment and disinterest are the most identifiable red flags of unfulfilled marriage relationships.

3. Correct minor irritations before they snowball into major barriers. There will always be acts of irritation whenever humans live in close contact with each other. If you detect mounting irritation, jump on it early but in a loving attitude of "I care enough about our relationship to confront you with this."

4. As a husband, you should beware of the "where's Dad" syndrome. The disease of noninvolvement is one of the most common infections of today's marriages. Involve yourself in the daily care of your child. Be sensitive to the times when your wife's maternal reserves are exhausted. Step in and say, "I'll take over; you do something just for yourself." One of the most common statements I hear when counseling a woman suffering from burnout in the mothering profession is, "Well, my husband is very busy, you know; he works long hours." A woman who is experiencing mother burnout is also susceptible to wife burnout.

5. As a father, you should be an effective spiritual leader in your family. This is one of the most important stabilizing factors you can give to your marriage relationship and to your children. Spiritual leadership is God's design for the family and is a way to earn your wife's respect.

6. Pray daily for your marriage relationship. I strongly advise you to pray for each other together at least once a day. Not only does this daily marriage prayer bring God's blessing upon your relationship, it conveys the feeling of "I am reaffirming my continued commitment to you, my wife (or husband), and to God."

7. Parents, regard your profession as the most important job in the world—raising your child for Christ.

Most of these suggestions are covered in greater detail throughout this book. If the reader detects that these suggestions are in favor of the husband's having prime responsibility for the fulfillment of the Christian marriage, you are right. Not only should the husband be the spiritual leader of the family, but he also should make the leading effort in striving for the fulfilled Christian marriage. Husbands and fathers, keep your radar system turned on to the signals from your family.

FATHERING: COMMITMENT TO BEING A SPIRITUAL LEADER

Fathering is tough, and Christian fathering is even tougher because competition is trying to take your child further and further away from God. Fathers, I am writing to you not as one who has his spiritual act together but as one who has made many mistakes in his own fathering profession, as one who has confused his priorities, and as one who is still struggling daily to be an effective spiritual leader in his own home. For those of you who are also struggling, the following suggestions may help you become effective spiritual leaders in your homes and help you win your children to Christ.

Because the stakes are high, a plan for spiritual leadership is necessary. The vital importance of planning hit me many years ago when I visited the NASA space center in Houston, Texas. In a large room was a huge chart showing the master plan for going to the moon. At one end of this chart was the nation's commitment to put a man on the moon. At the other end was the final goal, the landing of a man on the moon. In between the commitment and reaching the goal were thousands of obstacles to be overcome and problems to be solved. One by one these obstacles were checked off as the final goal was being reached. All during this process the government reaffirmed the commitment (and the financial backing) to get to the moon.

For some fathers, becoming effective spiritual leaders may seem as difficult as putting a man on the moon, and the components of the plan are similar: (1) make the commitment; (2) define your priorities; (3) define your goals; and (4) define the obstacles which keep you from reaching your goal.

Make the Commitment

The central focus of fatherhood is commitment. My main goal in this life is to return to my Father in heaven. The second goal in my life is to lead my children there also. You can make this commitment too. Fix this commitment in your heart; reaffirm this commitment when you get up and when you lie down. Attach this commitment to the dashboard of your car, to the door of your office; place it on your desk; seal it to the doorframe of your house. In today's busy world the father is often overcommitted and overinvested in the things of the world and undercommitted and underinvested in his ultimate goal and that of his children. Making the commitment is the first step toward becoming the spiritual leader in your home.

Define Your Priorities

A father gets a tremendous amount of advice from the Christian media on how to father or be a spiritual leader. He may wonder, *Do these preachers really know how tough it is out there in the real world? Do they understand my job pressures, paying the bills?* Let me reassure you at the outset, I know how tough it is; I have been there, and I am still struggling to be an effective spiritual leader. It isn't easy to spend time studying the Scriptures every day when you have barely enough time to get your job done; it isn't easy to "give thanks" in everything (1 Thess. 5:16) when you have just lost your job; it isn't easy to say, "Don't worry, the Lord will provide" (see Phil. 4:19) when your house mortgage is overdue. It's tough to lead your children to Christ when you're not sure where you stand. It's tough to be a Christian father. It's the toughest job you will ever have. It's the longest and most enduring race you will ever run, but the rewards for finishing the race are beyond all expectations (2 Tim. 4:7–8).

In order to make this commitment stick, it is necessary to define your priorities and continually reaffirm your position. The order which I believe God sets for us is (1) God, (2) family, (3) job, and (4) church. This is not a rigid chain of priorities, not by the order they are taken nor by the time invested in each one; they are interrelated. Each priority must be met to enable the next priority to be met. Being a God-centered person is necessary to being a God-centered father of your family. Meeting your job priority is easier if you are first right with God and with your family. However, it is unrealistic to play down the importance of your employment outside the home. Job satisfaction is important. If you aren't satisfied with your job and your ability to provide for your family, your general self-esteem is lowered. As your child's self-image affects his behavior, so does your self-image in your job affect your relationship with your family and ultimately with God (your mate needs to be mindful of this). A job should be primarily a means to an end, not an end in itself; it should be a means for providing for a family, a means for serving God, a means for ministering to the unfortunate.

What gets many fathers into priority trouble is devoting so much time and energy to their jobs that they are dominated by them and allow them to compete with God and their families. God will not bless that which competes with Him. "Blessed is the man Who walks not in the counsel of the ungodly, . . . But his delight is in the law of the LORD . . . And whatever he does shall prosper" (Ps. 1:1–3). "Seek first the kingdom of God and His righteousness, and all these things shall be added to you" (Matt. 6:33). "Abide in Me and I in you" (John 15:4).

Define Your Goals

In order to be an effective spiritual leader in your home, you must first have certain qualities. The principle of leadership is that no one can give what he does not have. These qualities are found in the goals that Christ gave us as committed believers.

1. Love the Lord and love your neighbor as yourself.
2. Fear God and keep His commandments.
3. Pray for wisdom to make the spiritual decisions which lead you and your family toward your ultimate goal.
4. Have a knowledge of Scripture and apply it in your life.
5. Live a Christ-centered life in relationship with God as your Father.

Fathers, take time to get your own spiritual house in order. Take periodic (at least once a year) inventories of where you are relative to where you were and where you would like to be. Your spiritual growth chart should be as up-to-date as your business growth chart. In achieving these goals, define and eliminate the obstacles to your growth and emphasize those things that encourage your spiritual growth.

Define Obstacles to Your Growth

In an increasingly materialistic world there are many obstacles to spiritual growth. These obstacles will be different for every father, but I will mention some of the major ones confronting most fathers today.

For many, debt is an obstacle to spiritual growth. Many people are financially overextended, especially in a system that offers the uncomfortable option of being in debt or paying more taxes. They have become the victims of financial counselors who roam the world enticing us to write off all they own. I wonder if some day, as we stand before the pearly gates in front of the ultimate Accountant, He might single us out with, "Mr. X, your life has been a series of write-offs. You wrote off your wife, you wrote off your children, you wrote off your friends at lunch and during recreation. I now must write you off."

Debt weighs especially heavy on those in the world of business. In my pediatric practice, I see how their children are affected by their money worries. Children often inherit a sense of financial pressure from the atmosphere at home.

Perhaps the greatest obstacle to spiritual growth for all Christians is materialism, a preoccupation with satisfying ourselves with the world's attractions. Not only do worldly matters compete with godly matters for a parent's time and energy, they are habit-forming. Fathers have been programmed toward entertainment, fulfillment, a break, and escape. They have become so used to the instant gratification of material things that spiritual matters do not sink in easily. This is a habit you must get out of your system in order to grow spiritually.

"Where your treasure is, there your heart will be also" (Matt. 6:21). It is interesting that this principle, which is emphasized most by Christ, is followed least by Christians. Why? Because it is difficult to reprogram a direction and a habit which has been ingrained in you since childhood. Because the practice of self-denial and of delayed gratification has been so difficult for me, I have realized that one of the main goals of spiritual leadership in my family is to train our children to practice them and to be filled by spiritual treasures from within rather than by material turn-ons from without.

Recent history has taught that many children in their teens have realized the superficiality of material fulfillment. To seek alternative turn-ons they have turned to cults. At the time in their lives when they were seeking a means of fulfillment, their parents did not provide them with viable answers, so they became involved in unreal alternatives. In the past twenty years, society has seen a generation of children without direction. These children refused to buy into their parents' systems, but they adopted alternative values and lifestyles that were just as dead-ended; their systems were no better. Children must be filled with something. It is up to Christian parents to fill them with truth.

Before making a purchase, go through the following checklist.

1. Do I need it more than I want it?
2. Will it directly or indirectly contribute to my spiritual growth and/or that of my children?
3. Can I afford it? Could the money be spent better elsewhere?
4. Will I worry about it?

I cannot overemphasize the concept of delayed gratification; saying no to an extra scoop of ice cream as a four-year-old is the forerunner of saying no as an adult to an act of infidelity that may dissolve a marriage. By role modeling the life of Christ you not only rid your own life of attachment to material items but you also remove one of the greatest obstacles to spiritual growth in your child and allow his perceptive mind to turn toward the things of God.

Practical Tips for Christian Fathering

Consider the spiritual leadership of your children as a business venture. The competition for the values and minds of your children is tough. The competition has more money and experience, and it is intensely motivated. The following practical "business tips" can help you beat the competition and win the hearts of your children over to Christ.

Be a role model. Role modeling is one of the prime determinants of your children's behaviors and values. Children see your values in your daily living. What is important to you is important to them. If God has blessed you with riches, please realize there is nothing intrinsically unchristian about wealth. The Bible tells of many men to whom God gave prosperity because they walked in His ways. It is the attitude toward wealth that can go wrong. It is no sin to be rich; it is a sin to act rich, to let your money control your actions.

Children are naturally attracted to big cars, fancy houses, and any expensive toys their fathers may have. The adage, "the only difference between men and boys is the price of their toys," does have some merit. Children astutely watch how their fathers value their own toys. Are you constantly talking about your toys, working on them, talking about business deals to pay for them, expressing how good they make you feel, and getting angry when your toys are broken or don't give you the instant gratification you expect from them? Do you spend most of the day getting turned on by the electronic stimulation the competition is constantly turning out? Do you fail to fit God into your busy schedule by not going to Sunday school and not having a ten-minute bedtime prayer? If your children see this role model, they learn one important lesson: toys are more important than God. "Where your treasure is, there your heart will be also" (Matt. 6:21)—and so will the hearts of your children.

God had the foresight to know that the competition against Him would be great. To meet this competition He gave parents a set of rules for a successful Christian child-rearing business. The Author of life Himself gave you His Word. If you follow His rules, He promises that you will win out over the competition which tries to seduce your children. God, your Father, shows you the importance of modeling. In addition to *telling* you how to live, He sent His beloved Son to *show* you how to live.

Begin early with small things.   The critical period for your children to be influenced by role modeling is when they are three to six years of age. At that time they view the world through the eyes of their parents. What is important to you is important to them. If they constantly hear that "Coke is the real thing," they will believe it; if they constantly hear that "God is the real thing," they will believe that.

By four to six years of age children should be able occasionally to delay their gratifications. Young children are very food-for-pleasure oriented; therefore, food is one of the easiest and most available tools for teaching delayed gratification to them. Perhaps one of the best ways to a child's soul is through his or her stomach. The young child should hear you occasionally say, "I surely would like to have . . . but I'm going to give this up for . . ." The young child needs to learn, "It makes me strong to say no now and then to myself." Your modeling of the concept of prayer and fasting is more important than your words. Also be prepared to substitute more of yourself for what he has given up.

One day I was talking to my seven-year-old son, Peter, about being strong, saying no, and giving up certain food pleasures when he was complaining about being refused a second helping of ice cream. He promptly reminded me that the night before I had become angry because my wife had neglected to purchase my favorite ice cream to go along with the pie she had made.

Teaching young children how to give up small things occasionally, such as an ice-cream cone, sets the pattern for saying no to more elaborate material things when they are older. If a child is going to make it as a Christian in today's world, he or she must learn to say no. This is the first step in becoming a responsible Christian. Fathers, let your children see you say no to yourself in small things so that later on they can say no in larger things.

Provide an alternative to materialism.   Too much materialism is not healthy for your child, but if he is told constantly what he can't have, he will rebel against your whole system and feel that "it's no fun to be a Christian." In Deuteronomy, chapters 6 and 11, God foresaw difficulty in this area. His advice was to saturate the child's environment with things of the Lord instead of things of the world. Fill your children with spiritual things when you are in control of what goes into them, lest they fill themselves with worldly things at a later age when they are beyond your control.

Teach your children to share their wealth.   If God has blessed you with an abundance of material wealth, you need not hide it under a basket. Share it in order to enrich the lives of the less fortunate. If you have been blessed with a summer home or winter home, share it with those who can barely afford a single home. If you have been blessed with a possession such as a large van, share it with church groups. Let your Father in heaven and your child on earth see where your heart is. They are the only persons who need to know about your charity. You won't even have to tell your child. He or she will see your actions. Encourage your children to serve the handicapped and invite handicapped children along with them to special occasions such as baseball games. You can teach sharing to your children in a multitude of ways, beginning with your own attitude of generosity to others in your family and to visitors.

Do not neglect prayer and Scripture reading.   You cannot be a good father without outside help. Prayer and study of Scripture are necessary. The following Scripture verses are particularly helpful to fathers who are struggling to be spiritual leaders in their families. Memorize these verses, meditate on them, and fix them in your hearts:

Matthew 18:6	Numbers 11:12
Luke 12:16–21	Deuteronomy 5:9–10; 6:4–9
2 Corinthians 12:14	1 Samuel 2:12–22
Ephesians 5:25, 33; 6:4	Proverbs 22:6
Colossians 3:20	Isaiah 46:3
Exodus 20:5	Jeremiah 17:7

In these references, God is talking directly to fathers. Throughout Scripture God tells you how to be model fathers to your children.

The most important goal in teaching Scripture to your child is your own attitude toward the Word of God. Your child is focusing on one big point, How important is the Bible to my dad? If you say it is important to you, then by the principle of modeling, the Bible becomes important to him or her.

Does your child see you reading Scripture frequently? Do you rely on Scripture to solve both major and minor problems when they arise? Can you quickly refer to the appropriate Scripture when your child gives you an "opener" and wants an answer not only from his dad but from God? When your children ask for your opinion or advice on a subject, think how much more meaningful it is if you can give them your own opinion and then quote an appropriate Scripture to back it up. This drives home to your young children the important point that their father's life is directed by God's Word.

It is important that your child sees you spending as much, if not more, time in God's Word as you do in the books relating to your interest or hobby. It is inexcusable for a Christian father to become competent in his job but illiterate in Scripture.

Pray daily with your child for two things: (1) for guidance and wisdom to role model spiritual things for your child and (2) for God to go deeper with your child than you can and fill your child with the Spirit by whom his or her behavior will be directed. Praying does not come easily, especially for new Christians. Don't fear that your words won't sound quite right. Just as your Father knows your heart and not your words, your child is more sensitive to your attitude and sincerity of prayer than your verbiage. Again, you are role modeling; your child sees that "prayer is important to Daddy, so I want to pray too."

Children need to learn the power of prayer. To illustrate this, let me share two situations that occurred in our family from which our children learned the power of prayer.

Sailing is our family hobby. One day my sons and I were sailing down New York River past the Statue of Liberty, which was a very moving and patriotic experience for us. We then sailed out toward the ocean through the busiest shipping channel in the world. A pea-soup fog set in, but I was not worried because I felt we were protected by our radar system. We were surrounded by so many ships entering the harbor that our radar screen looked like a video game. It was night and we were leaving the harbor and entering the ocean when our radar system stopped. I was scared. (A father is allowed to be scared but never out of control in front of his children.) My sons and I knelt down and prayed, and soon thereafter the radar system came on again and we continued safely through the fog. My sons learned the power of prayer in this situation, but more importantly they learned, by role modeling, that their father relies on prayer and believes in prayer power.

The next story illustrates the power of prayer in healing. Medicine is a humbling profession, especially in pediatrics. Often the pediatrician must say to the parents of an extremely ill child, "There is nothing more I can do; we must pray."

Some years ago, I cared for a three-year-old boy who nearly drowned in a swimming pool. He was resuscitated, brought to the hospital, and placed on life-support systems. I had to say to the parents, "We are doing everything humanly possible to save your child's life." After they asked what they could do, I said, "Pray."

Pray from morning till night. "Call for the elders of the church, and let them pray over him, anointing him with oil in the name of the Lord. And the prayer of faith will save the sick, and the Lord will raise him up" (James 5:14–15). By all medical standards this child had a very slim chance of surviving and an even slimmer chance of surviving without severe brain damage. Five days later the child awoke, and all life-support systems were gradually discontinued. When he left the hospital a week later, he seemed to be a normal child. One year later he showed absolutely no evidence of brain damage from this accident.

My children were involved with praying for the complete healing of this child. Since I involved them in daily prayer for the child's health, they learned the power of prayer and healing. As a father, I hope that this vivid illustration of God's answer to prayer will make a lifelong impression on my children, prompting them to go to their heavenly Father in times of need.

There are three times during the day when prayer is most meaningful to children: (1) in the morning as they begin the day, (2) at mealtimes when it becomes part of family communication, and (3) before bedtime, to thank God for the blessings of the day. The first words that come out of your mouth in the morning and the last words at night could contain a message from the Lord, "Have a good day in the Lord, Jim." As the spiritual leader, you can help your child begin and end the day with the Lord. This modeling carries over into your child's view of God: "If God is top priority in Dad's thoughts, He must be a very important person, and therefore He will be top priority in my thoughts."

Besides the special prayer times during the day, take advantage of teachable moments, or what I call "prayable situations." Perhaps during a drive you see an accident, and your son says, "Dad, those people must be hurt." Take the opportunity to turn the incident into a prayable situation: "Bobby, let's pray together and ask God to help those in the wreck."

When you pray together, the content and the attitude of your prayers have a greater influence upon your children than any other single model. Use prayer as a means of conveying to them how you want them to relate to you. You've often heard that your concepts of God are determined in some ways by the kind of relationship you have with your earthly father. In the same way, as your children hear how you pray to your heavenly Father, they will be learning how they ought to look toward you (and toward God). If your children hear you submit to and obey your Authority, they will pick up on how they should submit to their father, and their respect for authority in general will be raised to a higher level.

Give your child memories.   Remember Bob Hope's theme song called "Thanks for the Memories"? One of the most beautiful gifts you can give your children is to fill their receptive minds with vivid memories of their father in various roles—as a Christian, as a spiritual leader in the home, as a husband to their mother, as a fun friend, as a provider, and as someone who gave his children daily priority. Memories keep the model you set for your children constantly in their minds.

Fathers often underestimate how an apparently insignificant event such as a ball game or a stroll in the woods can make a vivid and lasting impression on a child. To illustrate this, ask a group of teenagers to recount some of the memorable moments they have had with their fathers. One time in our Sunday school class I asked a group of young fathers to recount some pleasant and some unpleasant childhood memories they had of their fathers. The responses indicated that unpleasant experiences were remembered more vividly and longer than pleasant experiences, but how their fathers walked with God was one of the most vivid good impressions. The next most vivid impression was the priority the son had in relation to his father's job. As one man shared with me, "In our house there was no doubt where I stood. My father's job came first, and I was a distant second."

Be a hero in your family.   Our children are being reared into a hero-worshiping society. Advertising agencies capitalize on this hero worship by employing movie stars and sports figures to advertise products. To a child, if these heroes eat a certain candy bar or wear a certain piece of clothing, then this must be the way to go. Television advertising is the epitome of role modeling to a child. To illustrate hero modeling, I asked a group of six-year-old boys to think about their favorite heroes and whom they would want to be like when they grew up. I received many answers, but not one child gave me the answer I was hoping for—"my father."

Fathers often wonder how much of their modeling and spiritual training sinks into their children. If someone were to ask your children who their favorite hero is or whom they most want to be like when they get older, and they each answered "my father," it would be the best testimony that you have done your job well.

Spend time with your child.   One of the greatest obstacles to effective fathering is having enough time for your child. Many demands on today's father rob him of parenting time. In answer to this dilemma, many writers have sold the concept of quality time: the amount of time you spend with your child is not as important as how you spend it. There is certainly an element of truth in the quality-time concept, but it is certainly not a substitute for quantity time.

48

Children are spontaneous in their actions, and their moods determine their receptivity to guidance. If a father is not around when something exciting or important happens, or if he tries to guide when a child is not in the mood to be guided, both the father and the child have missed the opportunity for a teachable moment that may not come around a second time.

Proverbs 20:11 states, "Even a child is known by his deeds." Fathers, study your children. Spend both quantity and quality time with them. There is no good substitute for simply being with your children. Be available, be approachable, be "on call" for them.

One of the best compliments my then four-year-old son, Peter, has ever given me was, "Dad, you're fun to be with." If you are a fun father who spends both quality and quantity time with your child, your job as a spiritual leader is given a real head start.

Establish special times.   It is often difficult for a busy father, especially if there is more than one child, to know where he stands with his child and where his child stands with God. To solve this problem in our own family, I have instituted the practice of "special time" with each one of my children at least once every week or two. I make a date with my child, and usually it's to take him or her out for breakfast on the way to school. Early morning is prime time for busy fathers and hungry children.

This special one-on-one relationship has the following benefits to father-child rapport. First, it conveys that you care enough to take time out of your busy schedule and give your child top priority as you begin your day. Second, you give that child focused attention. He or she does not have to compete with other children for your attention, nor must you compete for his or hers. Third, it gives you a time to take inventory in the following important areas.

1. How your child feels about himself or herself.
2. Where your child stands with God.
3. How your child is getting along with peers, parents, schoolwork, and whatever else he or she needs to share.
4. How special needs or problems are affecting him or her.
5. Where you stand in relation to your child. Are you getting through to him or her?

Keep the conversation meaningful but light. You want your child to look forward to these outings because he enjoys your company. He or she should not feel as if an oral report is necessary or that it is a time to be quizzed and drilled.

Avoid vague openers such as, "How's your self-image? How's your spiritual life?" Your first motive is for your child to enjoy communicating with you on topics that are important to him or her, and then you can gradually ease into topics that are important to you. Whenever I am spending this time with one of my teenage sons, the two most pressing items on my inventory are (1) how he feels about himself and (2) the degree of his commitment to God. One of the most frustrating situations for a father is the realization that teenagers are very private and usually will not betray their full feelings. Pressing a child to go deeper than he or she is comfortable with is doomed to failure.

Each time during your special time together try very simply to leave your child with the following messages.

1. I love you more deeply than you ever can imagine.
2. I am interested in how you feel and what you do.
3. I want to be involved in your life—to help, not to interfere. I am available for advice not because I am better than you but because I have lived longer and have profited by the experience of time.
4. And, finally, my most important wish for you, my child, is that you learn to love your God and walk in His ways.

You are not hitting your child with each of these heavy messages as though you were reciting the Ten Commandments to him. You are subtly discussing them in between bites of pancakes, an account of the last football game, and comments about a current steady romance. In answer to your concern about where he or she stands with God, you may get a simple but meaningful response, such as, "Dad, I simply couldn't live without Him."

Spiritual Leadership Benefits Your Marriage

Once you have become an effective spiritual leader in your home you will find that your family relationship operates on a much more meaningful level. Your Christian wife has more respect for you as the chairman of your own home than she would have for you as the chairman of your own corporation. One of the greatest gifts you can give your wife is to train your children in the way they should go. Men often fail to appreciate the incredibly deep desire mothers have for the well-being of their children. You as a father have this desire also, but in some way it seems to be deeper in your wife, perhaps because children seem more a part of herself.

If you are an effective spiritual leader in your home, the support you will receive from your wife will be beyond your greatest expectations. Why does it seem to work this way? Because this is God's order in the family. When the husband is the spiritual leader, both the wife and the children profit, and the entire family relationship operates on a higher level.

What's in it for you? How do fathers who are effective spiritual leaders in their families ultimately profit from this leadership? Fathers who have their spiritual houses in order earn respect from their children. Obedience is certainly their God-given right as parents; however, respect results in obedience from the heart.

Esteem for the person of the father, an admiration of his personal qualities, makes children want to obey their father. This is the level of obedience that you as an effective Christian father can achieve. This is a beautiful level of discipline to be on. If you have provided your children with the Christian model that Christ gave His disciples ("His children"), your children will follow your model because they want to, not because they have to. Achieving this respect will give you a tremendous lift in your self-esteem. As your self-esteem is boosted, you will become comfortable interacting with your children, and your entire father-child communication network will operate on a higher level.

What's in it for your children? Do children reared in a home where their father is an effective spiritual leader feel or act any differently? The answer is a resounding yes! Remember, your children may not give you instant gratification for your many years of input. The effects of spiritual training may come very slowly; you may not see the full fruits of your labor until your children are much older.

Children reared in a home in which their father is a strong Christian leader have direction. "Train up a child in the way he should go, / And when he is old he will not depart from it" (Prov. 22:6). They show direction in the three areas that I feel are the most important ones for fathers to model. These are called the "three Ms" of the goals we wish for our children: a Master, a mate, and a mission. How fathers love and serve their Master, how they love and serve their mates, and how they work toward their missions in life will leave lasting impressions on their children. Children who have had strong Christian fathers see them accomplish these goals and therefore learn these values from them.

Second, because these children have direction, their self-worth is increased.

They feel more valuable to themselves because they have purpose in life. I feel the number one problem facing today's troubled teenagers is a low self-worth and a lack of purpose and direction in life.

Third, these children have proper priorities. They are able to say no to those things of the world which compete for their relationship with God, and this is very difficult for most teenagers to do.

Fathers, if you were to stand before your Father in heaven today and be held accountable for rearing your children according to God's plan, what would your judgment be? Christian fathering is indeed a long-term investment.

CHAPTER 2

PREGNANCY TO DELIVERY

V ery early in their pregnancy, a Christian couple should ask the following questions.

1. What Christian support groups are available in our community?

2. What natural childbirth classes (preferably Christian) are available in our community?

3. Who will be the best obstetrician (or midwife) for our pregnancy and delivery?*

4. Who will be the best pediatrician or other primary health care provider for our baby?*

5. Where should we have our baby and what birthing alternatives are available in our city?

MAKING IMPORTANT CHOICES

Choosing a Christian Support Group

Some type of support group is helpful for first-time parents just as a good Bible study group is for the beginning Christian. Support groups consist of experienced parents who are prepared to help new parents.

By acting as an extended family, your support group will assist you in making basic decisions early in your pregnancy. It will also help you develop your own parenting philosophy while, at the same time, making you more aware of what

---

*It is unwise to compromise medical competence just to get a Christian doctor. Seek out a doctor who is both professionally competent and a Christian; if this combination is not available, select the best doctor. Select a prolife M.D. whenever possible.

resources are available in your community. Look into some of the following support groups early in your pregnancy.

Parenting classes within your local church. Some churches, especially very large congregations, offer Christian parenting classes, such as Apple Tree Family Ministries. (Address: P.O. Box 9883; Fresno, California 93794-0883.) These classes may be directed to the newly pregnant and first-time parents. If your church does not offer such classes, perhaps they can recommend some in your community.

La Leche League International (LLLI). The LLLI is perhaps the largest mothers' organization in the world. It was organized by a small group of mothers approximately thirty-five years ago for the purpose of promoting breastfeeding education at a time when the majority of mothers did not breastfeed. Although this group does not advertise itself as Christian, many principles held by LLLI are applicable to Christian parents. Monthly meetings are held in the home of a local La Leche League member. Each leader, besides having practical parenting experience, has special training in counseling new mothers about common concerns of breastfeeding and child care. She also enjoys access to a lending library, a board of medical consultants, and her own continuing education which she passes on to you. I would advise you to attend a series of league meetings. Although the LLLI motto is "Good mothering through breastfeeding," you will find that the league's policy is basically "good mothering" in all aspects of parenting. (Address: P.O. Box 1209, Franklin Park, Illinois 60131. Phone: 1-800-LA-LECHE)

Natural Childbirth Classes

I highly recommend that as a first-time pregnant couple you enroll in a natural childbirth class around the sixth month of pregnancy. If possible, find a Christian childbirth class that teaches biblical principles to alleviate the fear of childbirth. Most hospital-based childbirth classes teach couples what the hospital and the doctors consider important. A better choice would be a reliable private teacher or a consumer-based organization that will help you prepare for the birth you want. The following list names the more popular organizations that teach childbirth classes. They differ mainly in the techniques of relaxation and coping with the stress of childbirth. Christian childbirth classes often incorporate the best techniques from these organizations.

1. Apple Tree Family Ministries—a Christian organization

2. The American Society for Psychoprophylaxis in Obstetrics (ASPO)—also known as the Lamaze method

3. The American Academy of Husband-Coached Childbirth—the Bradley method

4. International Childbirth Education Association (ICEA)

5. Alternative Childbirth Educators (ACE)

Choosing Your Obstetrician

In perhaps no other medical specialty is the art of patient-doctor communication so important. The following suggestions will guide you in selecting your obstetrician.

As with all of your major decisions throughout your parenting career, pray for wisdom that God may guide you in choosing the right doctor for you. In my opinion, an obstetrician should be 100 percent pro life—many women find it impossible to be attended at birth by a doctor who also terminates life.

When making your first appointment, let the obstetrician know you are making the appointment solely to discuss the doctor's philosophy of childbirth and his or her attitudes toward your needs. It is quite advisable and customary to interview doctors before choosing the right one for your family. Both parents-to-be should attend this first appointment.

When you first meet your prospective obstetrician, take a written list of questions specific to your needs. Some sample questions you may wish to ask include: We have the following concerns about our pregnancy and birth (name your specific concerns); what help can you offer us? Remember, the more frank and open you are with your obstetrician, the more sensitive he or she can be to your individual needs. What childbirth education classes do you recommend? Which hospital do you advise, and what are the alternative birthing concepts within that hospital? What are your policies concerning father involvement, mother-baby separation at birth, and rooming-in (or any other practices important to you)? Will you pray with us in time of need?

Because of the increasing numbers of prepared and discerning parents, most obstetricians are becoming more flexible about offering alternative methods of birthing to meet the parents' requests. As you ask your obstetrician to be sensitive to your needs, please be sensitive to your doctor. The physician you are speaking with is a highly trained medical professional who has a sincere interest in the medical safety of your childbirth. For this reason you will probably receive an answer like this, "I respect your desires completely, but I must, for the best medical interest of yourself and your baby, reserve the right to intervene medically should the need arise. You will have to trust my judgment." A Christian obstetrician may add, "We must pray that God will give us both the wisdom to trust each other's judgment." Your doctor is asking of you the same respect and flexibility that you are asking of him or her.

Choosing Your Pediatrician

When selecting your pediatrician, follow basically the same guidelines for choosing your obstetrician; consider the doctor's competence, communication abilities, and his or her walk with God. It is just as important to have a face-to-face interview with the pediatrician during pregnancy as it is to interview the obstetrician. Otherwise, your first meeting with the pediatrician will take place in the hospital shortly after delivery when he or she makes the initial examination of your newborn. This initial patient-doctor communication is often compromised by the confusion or hubbub of a busy hospital ward, an extremely tired mother, or a hurried doctor. For these reasons it is strongly advisable for you to interview your prospective pediatrician during the latter months of your pregnancy. This prenatal visit will give the pediatrician an idea of what you really want and also will increase his or her respect for you as prospective parents.

Bring a written list of your most pressing questions and concerns. Attempt to keep the interview brief since most pediatricians do not charge for this prenatal visit. Respect the doctor's time.

Ask your prospective pediatrician his or her philosophy about the aspects of child rearing that are most important to you. Ask your pediatrician what his or her schedule for routine examinations is and how he or she will be involved in the care of your baby in the hospital. How do you reach the doctor in case of emergency?

Avoid negative openers. Nothing is more nonproductive than opening the interview with a list of "I don't wants"; for example, "I don't want my baby to have any bottles in the hospital." It is more productive to ask, "What is your policy about giving bottles to breastfeeding babies in the hospital?" Remember, your purpose for the interview is to determine if you and your prospective pediatrician are on the same wavelength. Negative openers close your mind to a possibility that you may, in fact, learn something by your doctor's response, something you may not have considered before your interview although you were certain your mind was completely made up. Persistently negative openers may set up a barrier for trusting future communication.

To help you get the most out of your prenatal visit with your pediatrician, look at this visit through the doctor's eyes. All during the interview he or she is filing away bits of information from which he can draw his conclusions about his future level of service to you. A sample thought process of an intuitive pediatrician would be: *These parents are certainly off to the right start. Parenting seems to be a top priority in their lives at this moment. They have taken time to interview me, and I can tell from their questions that choosing a pediatrician for their baby is also a high priority. These parents care, which makes me want to care. Therefore, I will make a special effort to be a good pediatrician for them.*

A caring pediatrician and intuitive parents are a winning combination that brings to your child a level of pediatric care that most parents and children want and deserve. Some parents feel confident enough in their parenting that they want a lesser level of involvement of the pediatrician in their family; he is on standby should a medical problem arise. Others parents, especially first-time parents, often want a highly involved pediatrician, a sort of Uncle Harry who becomes a trusted extra member of the family.

One of my most memorable new-patient visits was from a couple who said to me, "We'll pray for you; we always pray for our doctors." That simple statement said it all. From then on I knew what level my relationship was to be with that family.

Choosing Where to Deliver Your Baby

One of the most exciting, long-overdue changes in obstetrics is the many childbirth choices available for today's couples. These various options are termed *alternative birthing concepts* or the ABCs of modern obstetrical medicine. Where and how you deliver your baby are probably two of the most important decisions you will make during your pregnancy. These decisions should be made in much prayer and consultation.

Many variables go into making the right decisions: Is this your first baby? Are you anticipating any obstetrical complications? What can you afford? How far do you live from your hospital or birth attendant? How important to you are the setting and the environment of your childbirth experience? The following options are available for you to consider.

1. *A traditional method of delivery.*   I only mention this option to discourage it. Fortunately, gone are the days (or at least they should be) when birth was marketed

as a disease and a woman went to the hospital to be relieved by means of a medical and/or surgical procedure. Natural childbirth classes were not encouraged. A father was made to feel unclean and inept and was banished into the waiting room while the mother labored and delivered alone. As in any routine surgery, the mother's perineum was shaved. (Fortunately, studies have shown that this humiliating practice has no effect on lessening infection.) The lonely, laboring mother was required to remain on her back. (Laboring while lying on one's back is not only the position of maximal pain, but it is often the least beneficial position for the fetus because it lessens the blood flow to the uterus.) The mother was then medicated on an operating table and strapped into stirrups. After the birth, mother and baby were taken to separate rooms to "recover" from this operation of birth. A newborn baby was often kept in a bassinet, cared for by experts in the nursery, and brought to this mother only at convenient intervals. The father, meanwhile, viewed his baby through the glass windows of the nursery. The baby was fed a scientifically tested formula that was supposed to be as good as and certainly more convenient than what the Creator had designed. Fortunately, nearly all couples today have the wisdom to demand more from the birth event than what these antiquated practices provide.

2. *Birthing or LDR rooms.* Most hospitals now offer a childbirth option called "labor, delivery, recovery" or "birthing room." It is located within the usual obstetrical ward of a hospital and is sometimes referred to as ABC (alternative birth center). At first glance this room (or suite of rooms) looks like a normal bedroom and is designed to convey a homelike environment. Furnishings may include colorful curtains and bedspread, plants, rocking chair, stereo, kitchenette, Jacuzzi, and similar conveniences. The bed does not look like a delivery table but resembles most hospital beds (or even a homey queen-size brass bed) and is adjustable for the laboring mother. Some rooms have birthing chairs. All the medical and surgical equipment that may be needed is unobtrusively but efficiently near at hand.

The laboring couple is admitted to the birthing room. They labor together in this room, deliver in this room, and spend their postpartum course in this room. They are not transported from room to room as they would be in "traditional" births. A very important feature of the birthing room is that the baby can stay with the mother from birth to discharge from the hospital and is taken into the nursery only if the mother wishes or medical complications occur. The birthing room represents more than just a physical facility. It represents an attitude that birth is a normal process in life until proven otherwise.

An important factor for an expectant couple to consider in choosing a hospital is the level of newborn intensive care available should medical complications arise during or after birth. If a complication occurs around the time of birth, it is usually with the baby. Therefore, parents should base their choice of a hospital on the level of newborn care facilities as well as the facilities available for mother care.

3. *Birthing Centers.* Free-standing birthing centers are located and run separately from any hospital but are usually within minutes of a medical facility where the laboring mother can be transported if complications arise. Birth centers are staffed by certified nurse midwives (or by lay midwives in some states) and have medical supervision. Some are even owned and operated by physicians who rely on midwives to provide some or most of the prenatal and birth services. In this type of birth environment couples can find the homelike setting so important to them without the restrictions still encountered in hospital birthing rooms. A well-trained and experienced midwife is the ideal birthing attendant because her mindset is one that is dedicated to the concept that birth is a normal, healthy process for *at least* 90 percent of all women. She is also able to discern which women will need the services of an obstetrician and she is wise enough to screen her clientele carefully. Hospitals are beginning to recognize the value of midwives. This is good because I see that this is where the future of health care for expectant families lies. Many midwives are dedicated Christian women who see their profession as a ministry as God revealed in Scripture (Ex. 1:15-21).

4. *Home births.* The home-birth movement arose because the traditional system of maternal care failed to recognize an honest consumers' need. Increasing numbers of couples have reacted to the childbirth-is-a-disease-needing-treatment-by-an-operation attitude by taking the birth event back to where it was in biblical days, the home.

Because of the possibility of obstetrical complications, both the American Academy of Obstetrics and Gynecology and the American Academy of Pediatrics advise against giving birth in the home. The person who has the highest risk, the baby, has no voice in this decision. I am in deep sympathy with couples who wish to give birth at home. I can speak with some insight into this dilemma, since four of our seven births were at home. It is a beautiful human experience for parents and baby. As with all the options of childbirthing environments, prayer and consultation are needed before choosing to have a home birth. I do acknowledge that there are couples whom God will lead toward properly attended home births. Perhaps the answer to this dilemma is a homelike birthing environment in the hospital or birthing center.

In summary, use prayerful discernment in deciding where to birth your baby. The option of childbirthing environments that I would encourage most expectant couples to choose would be a hospital that has both a genuine alternative birthing center for low-risk obstetrical patients and expert newborn care facilities for unanticipated medical complications. The choice between "natural" or "technological" childbirth should not be an either-or decision. I thank God for the technological advances that have saved the lives of many mothers and babies, but I feel that modern maternal care should be a blend of parental intuition and medical science. The parents and the baby should not be deprived of either one.

CHRISTIAN CHILDBIRTH CLASSES

If you are properly and prayerfully prepared, your childbirth most often will be a good, natural experience. For Christian couples there is an added dimension of childbirth preparation with which they can equip themselves. God's promises for them in pregnancy and in childbirth are a tremendous source of strength and blessing, but a source that is often untapped. These scriptural promises will be explored in the following section.

Birth, marriage, and death are important events in a person's life. No Christian would dream of approaching them without the support of prayer, Scripture, and fellowship. Christian childbirth classes combine the benefits of physical and emotional training with thorough spiritual preparation.

Overcoming Fear

Overcoming fear is one of the oldest and most effective helps in childbirth preparation. Dr. Grantly Dick-Read did the pioneer research on the effects of fear on women in childbirth. His research was not easily accepted by his professional colleagues because, at that time, the scientific answer to fear was anesthesia. In the 1940s Dr. Dick-Read published *Childbirth Without Fear* (now in its fifth edition), and as a result, *natural childbirth* became a household term. He knew instinctively that childbirth was not intended by God to be a time of severe suffering, and he recognized the role that fear played in making it so. This truth is borne out beautifully in God's Word. Scriptures refer to childbirth as a joyful time (Gen. 21:6–7; Luke 1:58; and John 16:21).

Helen Wessel in her book, *Natural Childbirth and the Christian Family,* researched the original Hebrew meaning of certain terms relating to childbirth. She showed how modern translators have done childbearing women a disservice. For example, Genesis 3:16 reads, "To the woman he said, 'I will greatly increase your pains in childbearing; with pain you will give birth to children'" (NIV). The word *pains* in the first half of the verse is translated from the Hebrew root word *itstsabon*, meaning "sorrow" or "toil"; it is actually referring to the mental state rather than to a strictly physical state. God was telling Eve that as a consequence of her disobedience she would have to work hard and struggle mentally and physically giving birth to children that He could have freely and easily given her had she not broken communion with Him by sinning. Today, women must also live with the toil of labor and with a mental state of concern that all will go well with the new little lives they are bringing forth.

To show how unfair some modern biblical translations are in treating this area of childbirth pain, consider Genesis 3:17 where God said to Adam, "Cursed is the ground because of you; through painful toil you will eat of it all the days of your life" (NIV). The word *toil* is translated from the same Hebrew word *itstsabon*. Cultural programming has caused the word to be translated *pain* concerning Eve but *toil* concerning Adam. Basically, God was telling Adam and Eve that having sinned, they both would have to work hard to bring forth the fruit they desired. The so-called curse of Eve in which women are supposed to be penalized by pain and suffering during childbirth actually has no scriptural basis.

To illustrate how some modern translators have perpetuated this myth, notice the difference in translations of Genesis 3:16 between the 1978 New International Version and the original King James Version. The KJV reads, "I will greatly multiply thy *sorrow* and thy conception; in *sorrow* thou shalt bring forth children" (italics added). The NIV reads, "I will greatly increase your *pains* in childbearing; with *pain* you will give birth to children" (italics added).

As you can see, there is nothing about physical pain and suffering in the King James translation. The term *sorrow* probably refers to the whole of motherhood, not birth. For example, think of the sorrow Eve must have felt when Cain killed Abel. Many Christian childbirth educators do not accept that a woman must suffer pain in childbirth; they teach expectant women not to expect severe pain and suffering during their birthing experiences.

We must be aware that hard work in labor is not "suffering" in labor any more than hard work in farming the land is suffering. Many childbirth educators feel that a mother benefits from being able to experience the full sensation of her body in

61

labor. They feel that seeking to abolish all feeling denies the sensuality of birth. No one wants a mother to suffer during childbirth, but a mother may greatly regret a nonexperience. Some studies have suggested that the reality of seeing and feeling the entire birth experience has significant benefits for successful bonding in the newborn period and the mother's postpartum adjustments. However, a negative birth experience in which fear and pain predominate may also negatively affect a mother in postpartum adjustment.

Birth is hard work, as is running a hard race. The exertion is intense. At times during the race muscle pain is felt, similar to the "hurdler" pain that is felt during a highly competitive track meet. This is a productive, positive type of pain that drives the runner toward the finish line. It is far different from the pain of a traumatic sports injury that is negative and nonproductive.

Labor pain becomes suffering in one of two ways: either there is a high element of fear present, or there is a physical problem causing severe pain. Modern obstetrics is able to deal most effectively, and in a lifesaving way, with situations involving physical disease, malfunctions, or malpresentations. For example, a baby's head may not fit the space in which it has to maneuver for descent into the birth canal, no matter how hard and painfully the muscles work. In these situations a Cesarian birth or some other form of intervention becomes *truly* necessary and we can thank our heavenly Father for the advances in technology that allow these mothers and babies to be helped. In fact, some form of medical or surgical intervention is necessary in about 5 percent of all births. It is to the other 95 percent of births that fear can become the enemy and produce a much larger percentage of problems. "Failure to progress" is the largest category of reasons for Cesarean section.

Cesarean birth has become "epidemic" and now accounts for 25 percent of all births. Much attention is being given to reducing this percentage by professional committees and by lay organizations such as Cesarean Prevention Movement, Inc., P.O. Box 152, Syracuse, N.Y. 13210.

Vaginal birth after Cesarean (VBAC) is now an important option for women who have had a Cesarean birth previously. The adage "once a Cesarean always a Cesarean" is no longer accepted by even the most conservative obstetricians. At least 70 percent of all previous Cesarean births can be successful VBACs.

The natural birth process that God designed is one of the most awe-inspiring miracles witnessed. Only God could have figured out so intricately the way in which hormones, muscles, bony structures, and emotions interrelate in labor and birth. Even though God's design is so perfect, Satan can still rob women of the wonder and beauty of birth through deceitful fear. Fear and the resulting tension can lead to serious problems for mothers because they prevent labor from progressing, and for babies because they result in fetal distress. The use of drugs as the answer to the fear-tension-pain cycle is inadequate and unsafe. Instead, natural childbirth classes with a Christian emphasis are valuable as couples equip themselves to experience birth. Couples learn all they can about pregnancy, labor, and birth so that the fear of the unknown no longer can defeat them.

Fear works against the woman in the birth process. The birth muscles—the uterus and the birth passage—are designed to press forward and open the "baby door" gradually and smoothly so that there need be no suffering, only some really intense emotional and physical sensations. The idea is to coordinate the opening of the birth passage with the muscular contractions of the uterus so that the intense force does not become unbearably painful. If fear enters the process, tension results, and the muscles of the birth passage become rigid, causing terrible pain because the baby is pushed down against those hard, unyielding muscles.

Breaking the fear-tension-pain cycle at any one of several points greatly increases the ability to enjoy childbirth. By overcoming fear (especially the fear of the unknown), by learning why the physical sensations occur, by reducing the tension in muscle and mind produced by that fear, by using relaxation techniques, and by learning how to work *with* rather than against their bodies in labor, most women do not have to suffer or be drugged to give birth.

This is not to say that the birth process is painless, but natural childbirth classes teach you to interpret birth sensations for what they really are—part of the normal physiological process for which the female body was designed. Severe pain in childbirth is not normal but is a sign of an underlying problem, as severe pain is a sign that any normal body process is not operating properly. If that problem can be corrected (or avoided), intolerable pain can be reduced to the level of an acceptable sensation that you can tell feels right and is nothing to fear. If that problem cannot be corrected, then medical and surgical intervention is to be used appropriately and without condemnation.

What are some of the sources of fear? Where does this destructive emotion come from that takes over our minds and causes tension in our bodies? There are as many answers to these questions as there are women giving birth.

Fear of the unknown, based on horror stories passed down from generations that did experience birth as a dreadful and sometimes fatal event, is one kind of fear. Perhaps these fears are further validated by a woman's own past unprepared labor experiences. Fear also can be based on an ambivalent attitude about the pregnancy—unwanted pregnancy, economic insecurity, husband-wife problems, unsupportive or interfering relatives. A woman also can have fears that her baby will not be normal or that she will not be a good mother.

A woman may fear being in a hospital. Underlying her fear is that the main reason she has gone to the hospital to give birth is that she fears something may go wrong with her delivery. The hospital unconsciously reinforces this kind of fear. An intravenous procedure is used for fear of dehydration, "failure to progress," and the need of emergency medication. Electronic fetal monitoring is often used for fear that something may go wrong with the baby during labor; and the delivery room is set up like an operating room for fear that something may go wrong and an operation may be necessary. Those "in case of" practices by the doctor may be interpreted "for fear that" by the mother. A good childbirth class can help overcome many of the fears that the current medical system has perpetuated.

How a Christian Childbirth Class Functions

In a Christian childbirth class, couples learn all they can about pregnancy, labor, and birth so that fear is no longer an obstacle. The sensations of giving birth are less difficult when the couple understands what is happening and how they can cooperate with the process.

In addition to providing physical and emotional understanding, a Christian childbirth class finds and studies Scripture verses about fear. Meditation on these verses will show that faith is the antidote to the fear. Isaiah 41:10 is a great source of strength: "Fear not, for I am with you; be not dismayed, for I am your God. I will strengthen you, yes, I will help you, I will uphold you with My righteous right hand." Imagine being in labor cradled in the arms of your Father-Creator! As stated in 1 Peter 5:7, you can cast "all your care upon Him, for He cares for you." As you are held by Him in labor, hear Him saying your name, soothing away your fears with the promises of Isaiah 43:1: "Fear not, for I have redeemed you; I have called you by your name; You are Mine."

The message of 1 John 4:18 is definite: "There is no fear in love; but perfect love casts out fear." What greater expression of love is there than giving birth—giving love by bearing what was conceived in love—a new person with whom to share God's love? God wants us to overcome our fears and look to Him, as He said in John 14:27, "Peace I leave with you, My peace I give to you; not as the world gives do I give to you. Let not your heart be troubled, neither let it be afraid." The world makes childbirth a thing to be feared, but Jesus, the author of life, said, "Do not be afraid." First Timothy 2:15 says, "She will be saved in childbearing if they continue in faith, love, and holiness." And 2 Timothy 1:7 says that God did not give us a spirit of timidity (or fear); that spirit comes from Satan.

Fear in childbirth can result in a long line of undesirable effects, even to the point of affecting your total commitment as parents. Mothers who have negative birth experiences have high risks of postpartum adjustment problems. This is one of the main ways Satan defeats the strength and unity of the family.

Your family's birth event needs to be bathed in prayer and faith so that the evil one cannot get you off to a bad start. Faith predominates over fear so that even if you do find yourself confronted by a surgical or medical intervention, you will be able to turn it over to God and proceed in a spirit of faith, not fear. During childbirth preparation, you will learn how to overcome fear and tension together and how to work with the labor process. You will have the best labor support system available—the promises of God. You can look to Him as the Great Physician and rest secure in His care so that childbirth without fear can be a reality.

A Christian childbirth class is led by a qualified childbirth educator. Couples are part of a small, intimate support group that learns and prays together. The series of eight to ten classes starts in the sixth month of pregnancy and meets once a week for about two hours in the comfort of someone's home, if possible. One of the fathers opens each class with prayer, committing their special time together to learning God's plan for each couple in their own childbirth experience. A list of Scripture references provides a study of various topics, such as the ones already mentioned concerning fear and pain. For example, for the discussion of physical conditioning, refer to Proverbs 31:17; Exodus 1:19; 2 Chronicles 15:7. For nutrition, use 3 John 2 and 1 Corinthians 6:19–20. For labor and birth, read Psalm 22:9–10; Isaiah 66:7–9; Psalm 71:6. For relaxation, refer to Matthew 11:28–30 and Psalm 37:7. The possibilities of relating Scripture to childbirth are endless and creative. Verses can be copied on index cards to be used during difficult moments of the labor.

During the class, couples share experiences from their previous births. These can be a great encouragement and lesson for first-timers.

In addition to stressing Christian principles, the classes provide the same basic ingredients of any good childbirth class—exercises, relaxation, breathing, a physiology of pregnancy and birth, comfort measures, information on various medications and procedures, and specific instructions on how the couple can work together (supporting and working with the mother's body). Alternatives of childbirth methods are covered, such as birthing rooms, siblings at birth, bonding, and rooming-in. Nutrition is emphasized, and things to be avoided during pregnancy are discussed.

A good class usually provides a lending library and presents slides or films showing labor, birth, and the surrounding events. Breastfeeding information and discussions of life with a new baby are improtant. Postpartum adjustment can be a big shock physically and emotionally to first-time parents, so some discussion and sharing in this area are important.

My wife, Martha, taught childbirth preparation for seven years. As a pediatrician, I looked forward once a week to opening up our living room to the joyous instruction of expectant couples. A particular aspect of those Christian childbirth classes I enjoyed is what I call the "show-and-tell" night. A few weeks after everyone in the class has delivered, couples and their babies meet for a postnatal discussion class in which they share how beautifully God worked in the miracle of birth. It is also a night of prayer and praise—prayer for any of the new parents who were having postpartum adjustment problems and praise for the new lives God has given them. Eventually, these couples may decide to continue meeting as a support group for Bible study as they progress through the challenges of parenting. A Christian childbirth class is the ideal. If there are none nearby find the best natural childbirth class you can (not always the one taught at the hospital, where often what you learn is how to be a good patient). Supplement this class with the books recommended in the appendix. Start reading early to help find the "right" class. (*Childbirth without Fear, Natural Childbirth and the Christian Family,* and *Under the Apple Tree* are good resource books.)

Couples must take their childbirth class seriously, giving it top priority in their schedules. Getting thoroughly and competently prepared for the birth of a child reaps benefits out of all proportion to the time invested.

THE PREGNANT COUPLE

The term *couple* is used here because, although the mother alone physically carries the baby, both mother and father spiritually carry the baby and each other through pregnancy. As the baby is growing to maturity, the Christian couple also can ripen spiritually. The following suggestions will help you grow spiritually during your pregnancy.

Prayer and Pregnancy

A custom we have enjoyed as a pregnant couple is the nightly prayer ritual of laying our hands upon the pregnant womb. Our prayer would go something like this: "Father, we thank You for giving us the tiny life within this womb. We acknowledge You as the architect of our developing child. Watch over every dividing cell, every organ, every system as the child You are building nears completion. Into Your hands we commit our child." (Psalm 139:13–16 is a beautiful prayer to use during pregnancy.)

You might also extend this prayer ritual. In addition to praying for the health of your unborn child, pray daily for your own health and the health of your marriage. This daily prayer, beginning early in pregnancy, gets Christian parenthood off to the right start. By inviting God's protection, you are claiming the promises of God in 1 Timothy 2:15, "She will be saved in childbearing if they [husband and wife] continue in faith, love, and holiness, with self-control." Talking to your child in the womb and praying daily for him or her acknowledges that your fetus is already a

67

member of your family to be prayed for. Prayer during pregnancy sets the stage for the moment of birth when you truly can thank God for answering your prayers. Francis and Judith McNutt have written a unique book entitled *Praying for Your Unborn Child: How Parents' Prayer Can Make a Difference in the Health and Happiness of Their Children* (see bibliography for a more complete description).

This daily pregnancy prayer and the ritual of laying your hands on the womb may be the father's first act as the spiritual leader of the family and his first step toward a strong father involvement. In our family, this nightly ritual for our preborn baby became such a habit that after her birth I couldn't get to sleep without first laying my hands on our newborn's head and praying for her. I was already hooked! This attachment had begun *in utero.*

How Pregnancy Changes Your Marriage

The responsibility of a child can bring a higher level of maturity to your marriage relationship; pregnancy can add a finishing touch to your commitment. However, if your marriage is on shaky ground, you may be particularly vulnerable to the unstable emotions of pregnancy. A baby does not usually stabilize a marriage that is built on a weak foundation. This is why the principles covered in Chapter 1 are vitally important for Christian parenting before, or at least during, pregnancy.

In Chapter 1 mutual giving is established as the hallmark of a fulfilled Christian marriage. In parenting, this giving concept is taken one step further—you both give to a third person. In some respects, giving to your child is easier than giving to each other because a child is a biological extension of yourselves and is more dependent. In pregnancy, you continue the process of coming out of yourselves and accepting another person.

Throughout your pregnancy you are preparing yourselves for a very important aspect of parenting—having a high level of acceptance of whatever temperament your child is blessed with. When you are aware of and sensitive to each other's needs and how to respond to them during pregnancy, you are making a good preparation for parenting. In order to help you be mutually sensitive to each other's needs as a pregnant husband and wife, look now at the many physical, emotional, and spiritual changes which occur during pregnancy and discover how these changes all come together to help you mature into parenting Christians.

The First Trimester

Pregnancy is not just growing a baby; it is growing a relationship, and pregnancy adds a real change to the marriage relationship. The physical changes are obvious, but with each physical change there are accompanying emotional changes due to the effect of the hormones of pregnancy. For example, the hormone prolactin, which causes the mother's breasts to develop in order to nourish the baby, also may cause her to feel more maternal.

Husbands need to be aware that the hormones necessary for the development of the baby also are responsible for the unstable emotions experienced by their pregnant wives. Pregnancy may be considered a developmental stage, much like adolescence, and ambivalent feelings are normal. One minute a pregnant wife may feel like praising the Lord for enabling her to be pregnant, and the next minute she may have an identity crisis: "I am going to be somebody's mother, but what will happen to the 'me' I know now?" She may experience the positive feelings called the "pride of pregnancy," which is the proof of her fertility and a delight in nourishing another life within her own body. Or she may have negative feelings: fear of miscarriage, fear of becoming less attractive to her husband, ambivalence about leaving her present job, or worry about her capabilities as a mother. The more unpleasant the wife's symptoms of pregnancy (for example, morning sickness), the more these negative feelings may increase. The first trimester is a period of acceptance and adjustment for both of you, and most of your prayers should be directed toward these ends.

The Second Trimester

The second trimester is usually a quieter period. The fears of the first trimester and the discomfort of morning sickness and fatigue probably will have lessened. The highlight of this period is feeling your baby move (around sixteen weeks for the mother and twenty weeks for the father). Feeling this life together, mother's hand upon the father's hand and both parents' hands upon the baby, will trigger desire to pray for the life inside. At this point, the father feels there is really a baby in there! Feeling your baby move is often the high point of prayer and praise during your pregnancy.

Dependency feelings run high in the second trimester. The wife may feel an increased dependence on her husband as the protector and provider and often may express her own need to be "mothered" and loved, as he is instructed so beautifully in Ephesians 5:25–29. The husband also will depend upon his wife to nourish the child within her.

Pregnancy is the time for you to share positive and negative feelings about your present and future role changes. Weak communication and a lack of appreciation of the emotional and physical changes during pregnancy can mean the difference between regarding pregnancy as a richly rewarding experience and seeing it as the low point of your marriage.

If, by the beginning of the second trimester, your marriage communication is not on a spiritual level of prayer and praise to God for the life all three of you have created and if you are not mutually sensitive to each other's needs, then you should seek professional counsel. Anticipatory guidance, an effective counseling tool during pregnancy, can help you prepare for many of the reality changes of your pregnancy. Communication problems during pregnancy usually stem from one partner's not being aware of the ambivalent feelings within the other person or of how these feelings are responsible for his or her behavior. With prayer and consultation, pregnancy should be a high point of your communication since there certainly is a lot to talk about.

Marital disharmony contributes to a woman's vulnerability to anxiety and depression during pregnancy. Although some of these ambivalent feelings are normal, extreme depression and anxiety for Christian parents may signify a breakdown in the continuum of God's order for marriage and parenting. God ordained that a marriage have a firm foundation before a child is brought into the relationship. Perhaps much of the depression and anxiety during pregnancy arises from concern for what will happen when a child enters a home that is wobbly because the spiritual foundation is weak. The skills necessary for successful, natural childbirth require that a couple be spiritually in tune.

The Third Trimester

By the third trimester (often sooner, of course) the wife's pregnancy will be showing obviously, and like most women she will begin to experience tremendous pride in her fullness and in the special status that is given to pregnant women. Offers of help will come from all around. Some of the anxiety levels that were high during the first trimester and low during the second trimester will peak again in the third trimester in anticipation of the time of birth.

In spite of the radiant glow that many pregnant women show, at times they may not feel so radiant. In the third trimester, the wife needs constant reassurance from her husband that he loves her in this "state." Special attention to good grooming, taking care of herself (as in being nice to herself, not just "looking good" for others), will do wonders for her self-image at this stage.

The wife's sexual desires will go up and down throughout pregnancy because of the fluctuations of hormone levels and physical changes in her sexual organs.

Toward the end of pregnancy, her diminishing sexual interest will result from both a feeling of awkwardness as a sexual partner and a fear of inducing premature labor. This fear is unfounded if your pregnancy is normal. Pregnancy itself may fulfill sexual needs. Bear in mind that although hormonal changes may be a valid reason for diminished sexual desires, the husband's hormones do not change during pregnancy. Near term the wife may become increasingly aware of her husband's sexual needs and also of her inability to satisfy them. Inventiveness in sexual techniques may be useful at this time. *Making Love During Pregnancy,* by Elisabeth Bing and Libby Colman, is sensitively written and illustrated and especially helpful for first-time expectant couples. Cliff and Joyce Penner's book, *The Gift of Sex: A Christian Guide to Sexual Fulfillment* (Waco, TX: Word, 1981), is a wonderful book to encourage couples at any time during their marriages, especially when one or both of them may be struggling to understand and appreciate the gift of sex, including the spiritual aspects of this union God designed.

The Final Month

In the final month the couple's anticipation level will be high. Insomnia for the wife will be common due to her anticipation and to her inability to assume a comfortable sleeping position. Many women leave their jobs in the final month, although others continue to work until the last minute in order to reduce the anxiety of anticipation.

God has provided most women with a nesting instinct, a quiet time in the final month of pregnancy whereby a mother tunes in to the child inside her and feels that her unborn child is a person within the family. This should be a time of peace and quiet, a time to relax and slow down and begin mothering your unborn child. This is probably an early attachment stage so vital to the continuum of the mother-infant attachment after birth.

Part of the nesting instinct may be a sudden burst of energy to clean the house, prepare the nursery, and have everything just right for your baby. Be careful not to overdo it and wear yourself out. Laboring in an exhausted state is not an advantage.

A word about preparing your nursery. It is more important for a Christian couple to prepare their minds and souls for the coming of their baby than to prepare a room. A refreshing change in priorities that I have noticed throughout the past decade is that expectant couples seem less preoccupied with the properly appointed nursery. This fact came home to me following the birth of our fourth child. Shortly after her birth we opened our house as part of a tour of homes for a local church charity. I was amused to see the confusion in the eyes of the perceptive visitors when they exclaimed, "But where is her nursery?" Our newborn's "nursery" was right where we believe God intended it to be—in the bed and arms of her mother and father.

Feelings of an Unwanted Pregnancy

For a variety of personal reasons you may not want to be pregnant, but the wife misses her first period and the question of pregnancy arises. This circumstance is one of the most real opportunities you have as a Christian couple to put God's will before your own. Before you have a pregnancy test to confirm your suspicion, pray that you may joyfully accept God's will in the result of the test. Prepare your minds and hearts to accept joyfully what God has designed for you. It is more meaningful to begin this prayer before you know the results of the test because the immediate feeling you have when you know (either positive or negative) can have a snowballing effect on your attitude during your entire pregnancy and can even affect the self-esteem of the child as he or she grows. Accepting the will of your Creator over your own desires is perhaps the most difficult but the most maturing Christian struggle. Psalm 143 is a good opening prayer for you in this circumstance, especially verse 10: "Teach me to do Your will, for you are my God; Your Spirit is good. Lead me in the land of uprightness." Also, remember who is forming and knitting together this new life in the womb (see Psalm 139:4-8)!

FATHER'S FEELINGS DURING PREGNANCY

Whereas God has blessed the mother with the privilege of carrying, birthing, and nourishing a baby, as a Christian father, you still play a vital role in the pregnancy, birth, and care of your child. In the previous section the wife's feelings during pregnancy were discussed. They are more appreciated because they are more obvious. The father also will have adjustment problems during pregnancy and often will need as much or even more prayer and consultation than his wife.

One of the earliest feelings the father will have is a pride in his masculinity and his fertility. This can be a normal and healthy pride similar to that felt from any accomplishment. To keep this pride in Christian perspective, thank God for your pregnancy and acknowledge Him as the ultimate Creator of life.

As the reality of another mouth to feed sinks in, the fact of responsibility and the concept of the family may weigh heavily upon you. In addition to the dependency of the new life to be, your wife may show a high level of dependency on you throughout the pregnancy. These increased responsibilities may make you question your ability both to father the baby and "mother" the mother.

It is unfortunate that in a beautiful family event such as pregnancy, the subject of money has to be considered at all. However, economic worries are among the earliest concerns of the new father. Like many fathers, you may exaggerate this worry way out of proportion. You may worry about how you are going to educate your baby even before the birth.

Some men actually experience pregnancy-like symptoms during pregnancy and may show a subconscious desire to share their wife's physical condition. Other fathers do not envy pregnancy at all, and they regard this period as a necessary nuisance toward having a baby. Husbands, if this is your attitude, you may tend to focus on your baby's arrival, and subconsciously you may ignore the pregnancy and, therefore, the mother. This tendency often will be overruled by your wife's constant physical and emotional changes that serve as a reminder of the reality of the family pregnancy.

Toward the end of the pregnancy the husband may have ambivalent feelings about how the baby will affect his marital relationship. The following tips may help you handle these uneasy father feelings during pregnancy.

1. *Take stock of your situation.* As the fetus matures so will you. As your wife is growing your child, pregnancy may be a time for you to ripen spiritually and become a more mature man. Pregnancy can be inventory time in the fathering business: a time to sit back and define your priorities. It is a time to account for where you have been and where you are going. Specifically, take a hard look at how you are walking with God and how you are walking with your wife. Is your marital relationship God-centered? This is a prerequisite for God-centered parenting. Are you sensitive to your wife's needs during the family pregnancy? As described in Ephesians 5:25, one of the greatest ways you can prepare yourself for loving your child is to continue loving the mother. Does your current job assume priority over your marital relationship? It is important to put your marriage before your job at this stage so that later you can put your fathering before your job.

2. *Get involved in the pregnancy.* The earlier you are involved in the family pregnancy, the more involved you will be throughout the pregnancy and the years of child rearing to come. Involve yourself with the choices you and your wife will make early in your pregnancy: which doctor, which pediatrician, which birthing

environment, and so on. Accompany your wife on her visits to the obstetrician or midwife. Involvement increases knowledge of what is going on, and knowledge increases comfort and may therefore result in your shying away less from these many decisions.

3. *Attend Christian childbirth classes.*   Father involvement in the childbirth event is one of the major focuses in these classes. In many instances, I feel that the fathers actually benefit as much as or more than the mothers.

4. *Help prepare the nest.*   Assist your wife in the tasks of getting ready for the baby, such as going on shopping trips and preparing and decorating the nursery (if you have one). A word of advice: respect your wife's nesting instinct. If major changes in your lifestyle, such as moving to a new house or changing jobs, are necessary, do not make these changes in the last couple of months of pregnancy or too soon after birth.

5. *Pray daily that God will show you the wisdom to be a father* as He designed fatherhood and to be a husband according to His order for a husband. Read the following Scripture verses during your pregnancy to help you overcome your uneasy father feelings and to prepare you for being a Christian father: Ephesians 5:25; 6:4; Colossians 3:19, 21; Philippians 4:19. Successfully handling these father feelings and becoming a God-centered Christian father during pregnancy will lay the foundation for you to become an effective Christian father when your child arrives.

I pray that God will prepare your heart and soul for the arrival of the new life He has entrusted to your care and for whom He will hold you accountable. What a beautiful sensation you will have if you operate from this level of involvement with your wife and with your God during the time of pregnancy. The deep feeling of involvement will carry over into your commitment to your wife as her spouse and to your child as his or her father, and this commitment will be the foundation from which all future fathering will spring forth.

MOTHERING YOUR PREBORN CHILD

Nutrition during Pregnancy

An expectant mother must feed herself spiritually as well as feed herself and her baby nutritionally. Feeding the baby begins even before conception. Good prenatal nutrition, or the lack of it, can affect the development of the fetus profoundly.

What you eat is more important than how much you eat. The main nutritional requirements for all growing persons (in this case, mother and fetus) are proteins (at least seventy-five grams per day), calories (approximately five hundred extra), vitamins, and iron. Each day you should eat the equivalent of the following:

- two eggs;
- one or two servings of fish or lean beef or chicken (eight to ten ounces), and liver (one to two times a week);
- a large salad of fresh, leafy green vegetables;
- one quart or more of milk (whole or skim);
- one serving of cheese or yogurt (more if you aren't drinking milk);
- two to three slices of whole grain bread;
- one serving of whole grain cereal;
- one serving of yellow vegetables and one whole baked potato (three times a week); and
- at least one serving of citrus fruits or fruit juice.

Note: If you are allergic to dairy products, increase the protein in the meat group and supplement calcium correctly.

What is a normal weight gain during your pregnancy? This varies from woman to woman, but there are some general guidelines. At one time, when "not looking pregnant" was fashionable, strict limits were placed on weight gain. Providing you eat the right foods, such limits are not necessary. The usual, or normal, weight gain during pregnancy is about twenty-four to thirty pounds, and this is distributed as follows:

- Weight of baby—7½ pounds
- Weight of placenta—1½ pounds
- Weight of uterus—3½ pounds
- Weight of amniotic fluid—2½ pounds
- Weight of extra blood volume and fluids—8½ pounds or more
- Weight of breasts—1 pound

A general guide for weight gain during pregnancy is three pounds during the first trimester and about three to four pounds per month thereafter. If underweight to begin with, a woman may show a larger weight gain, adding catch-up pounds early in her pregnancy. This is the body's message that she needs more. Weight gain is an individual situation that should not be legislated by anything except good nutrition. If you are overweight, pregnancy is not the time to try to diet and come out closer to your ideal weight after you give birth. The above nutrition plan should be followed in order to nourish your preborn child properly.

It is unlikely for an expectant mother to put on too much weight by indulging in the foods suggested here. Most women gain excessive weight because they eat the wrong kinds of foods. Avoid junk food and excess salt. It is good to nibble on nutritious snacks between meals. Do not skip meals, and above all, *avoid crash diets* during pregnancy. Poor nutrition can cause low birth weight and premature babies. Your appetite and food consumption should parallel your pregnancy. During the last three months of pregnancy you may be consuming an extra five hundred nutritious calories a day without abnormal weight gain. You may be subject to certain cravings, many of which are high in carbohydrates and are not high in nutritious proteins. You do deserve to pamper yourself occasionally, but it is not wise to overindulge. If you feel well, eat mostly nutritious foods, and show no evidence of abnormal water retention, a restriction of your weight gain should not be necessary.

What to Avoid during Pregnancy

Certain chemicals called "teratogens" are known to cause defects in the fetus. Only a few drugs have absolutely proven to be teratogenic; however, knowledge of the subtle teratogenic effects of some drugs is incomplete. This dilemma is called the "threshold effect." This means that no one knows if a teratogen that harms the fetus extensively will harm it less in smaller doses. It is also possible that very low levels of teratogens may cause very subtle malformations that are difficult to identify. An example of a teratogen that has this threshold effect is alcohol. It is known that a lot of alcohol harms the fetus a lot, but it is not known whether a little alcohol harms the fetus a little.

1. *Drugs.* For this reason, you should pray and seek professional medical advice before taking a drug, even an over-the-counter drug. When you take a drug, your fetus also takes the drug. The drug is more likely to harm the fetus because he is a rapidly developing organism with limited capabilities to get rid of the drug.

An example of a harmful drug is marijuana. At this writing, marijuana has no *proven* detrimental effects on the fetus. It is known, however, that marijuana can damage brain cells and reproductive cells in experimental animals and probably also in humans. Common sense should dictate that it would be risky to smoke marijuana during pregnancy. Cocaine is a drug that has been proven to be definitely harmful to the preborn baby.

Sometimes a potentially harmful drug is taken during the first month of pregnancy before a woman knows she is pregnant. This is the time of highest risk to the fetus. Before you take even an over-the-counter medication for a suspected "flu," consider whether your symptoms could be due to pregnancy. It would be wise not to take any remedies, such as aspirin or nasal sprays, without first consulting your physician or being sure you are not pregnant. During pregnancy, unless directed so by your physician, refrain from taking any drugs (stimulants, depressants, and others) that alter your bodily functions to an unnatural state.

2. *Nicotine.* Do not smoke during pregnancy. Do *not* compromise. Nicotine decreases the blood supply to your placenta and therefore to your baby. Your smoking can cause your baby to be premature, to have diminished brain growth, and to be smaller than normal; this risk increases in proportion to the number of cigarettes you smoke each day.

3. *Alcohol.* "You shall conceive and bear a son. Now therefore, please be careful not to drink wine or similar drink" (Judg. 13:3–4). Recently, experts have recognized that alcohol is one of the most potentially harmful drugs during pregnancy. Excessive alcohol consumption during pregnancy can cause a large spectrum of abnormalities called the "fetal alcohol syndrome"—small baby, unusual facial features, and mental retardation. Nearly every organ may be potentially affected by alcohol in the fetal blood, and the greater the alcohol consumption, the greater the severity of the fetal malformations. How much alcohol can you drink without causing damage to your fetus? As has been established, the threshold effect of teratogens is not known. It is known that five or more drinks at one time or an average of two drinks per day throughout pregnancy can harm your fetus. The term *drink* is defined here as one ounce of alcohol (hard liquor, such as whiskey), one twelve-ounce glass of beer, or one eight-ounce glass of wine. Unfortunately, many heavy drinkers are also heavy smokers. This can be a disastrous combination for the fetus.

It is interesting how God designed the human body to care for itself by sending out warning signals. During pregnancy, many mothers have a natural distaste for cigarettes, alcohol, and caffeine. Because no one knows the exact threshold effect of alcohol, it seems wise not to drink any alcohol during pregnancy.

4. *Caffeine.* At this writing, it is uncertain whether caffeine is harmful to the human fetus. However, caffeine that has been given in very large doses to experimental animals may result in malformations in their fetuses. Until this caffeine question is settled, the Federal Food and Drug Administration advises pregnant women to limit their consumption of products containing caffeine as a precautionary measure. In order of highest caffeine content, these are coffee, cola, tea, and chocolate. Some over-the-counter pain and cold remedies also contain caffeine; their labels usually identify their content.

Prenatal Bonding

Throughout this book, the concept of harmony with your baby will continually be stressed as one of the most important aspects of God's design. This harmony begins during pregnancy. A new and exciting field of research is concerned with fetal awareness, which means that the emotional state of the mother during the last three months of pregnancy may affect the emotional development of the baby. It is an awesome responsibility to consider that the emotional state during pregnancy can influence the baby's personality.

Recent research has shown that when a pregnant mother becomes anxious or stressed, her stress hormones (adrenalin and cortisone) are increased. These increased hormones cross the placenta into the fetal circulatory system and may cause the baby to be agitated. The hypothesis is that an agitated baby is a disturbed baby. A mother and her preborn baby become a hormonal communication unit. When mother is upset, baby is upset. Constant exposure of the baby's developing brain to stress hormones may result in an overcharged nervous system, later resulting in an emotionally disturbed infant. This may account for the common statement made by parents of a hypersensitive baby, "He came wired that way."

You may create a peaceful womb experience by following these suggestions.

1. *Resolve stress promptly.* Most mothers experience some stress during pregnancy because of their normal ambivalent feelings and because of so many changes that happen so fast. How quickly and effectively you deal with this stress is the important issue. Researchers in fetal awareness believe that temporary stresses do not appear to have any lasting effects on the fetus. Chronic, unresolved conflicts and anxiety throughout most of the final months of pregnancy are most likely to disturb the baby. Keep in mind that you and your baby may share your emotions.

2. *Talk and sing to your baby.* Give your baby pleasant womb memories. Studies have shown that infants later recall the familiar voices that talked and sang to

them *in utero*. Newborns were better able to attend to their fathers' voices if they had talked to them before birth, and children were able to learn songs more easily that their mothers had sung to them in the womb.

3. *Play harmonious, calming music.*   Preborn babies are calmed by soothing music such as Vivaldi, Mozart, and classical guitar, but they are agitated by rock music. Professional musicians relate they could learn more easily the musical instruments their mothers played during pregnancy (see *The Secret Life of the Unborn Child,* by Thomas Verny and John Kelly, Summit Books, 1981).

4. *Encourage your husband's active involvement.*   How your husband feels about you and the baby during pregnancy is an important contributing factor to your emotional harmony. Studies have demonstrated that the fetus becomes very agitated during periods of husband-wife conflict.

5. *Pray for your baby as discussed previously.*   I can't help feeling that your baby inside you senses the commitment that awaits him after birth. The following suggested Scripture verses will help you encourage a peaceful womb environment and harmonize your emotions during particularly stressful times.

Isaiah 41:10	Psalm 127:3	1 John 4:18
John 14:27	Psalm 4:1	Proverbs 3:5
Isaiah 66:9	1 Peter 5:7	Proverbs 17:22
1 Timothy 2:15	Psalm 71:6	Psalm 139:13–16
Psalm 37:4–5	Philippians 4:6–7	
Psalm 22:9–10	Matthew 11:28–30	

How a baby in the womb also senses joyful emotions is beautifully illustrated in Luke 1:44. When Mary greeted Elizabeth, "the babe leaped in [her] womb for joy."

CHAPTER 3

THE BIRTH OF A CHRISTIAN FAMILY

BEGINNING LABOR

The long-anticipated event is near, and you are beginning labor. You are excited and well prepared. With strength from God you have developed the confidence that you will be able to cope with the work of labor and delivery. The childbirth classes you have taken prepared your mind and body to accept the child that God will give you, as well as the type of labor and delivery necessary to birth the child. Many couples prepare themselves for the ideal delivery, and when medical complications necessitate a departure from the "natural" way, they are disappointed. "I feel like a failure," one mother who needed a Cesarean section confided in me.

As your labor begins, pray a prayer of acceptance asking God to give you the strength to cope with whatever type of labor and delivery you are blessed with. Ask for the flexibility to accept your doctor's judgment should a medical complication occur that necessitates a departure from the type of delivery you are anticipating.

The length, severity, and characteristics of labor vary greatly from woman to woman and even from one labor to the next for the same woman. The following description of a labor and delivery is a compilation of several labor reports sent to Martha and me from couples who have taken our childbirth classes. It is meant to illustrate how couples rely on the strength of the Lord during this momentous event: "Behold, children are a heritage from the LORD, The fruit of the womb is His reward" (Ps. 127:3).

Anne wondered what it would be like. The instructor in the childbirth class had said there was no way to describe accurately the sensation of labor to a first-time mother because no two women experience exactly the same thing. Only after she had had a baby would she know fully what the term *labor* entails. Even then, each birth would be different, although her first probably would be the hardest.

Anne had sat wide-eyed through all the classes, gleaning all the information she could get from those who had been through it before. She felt as prepared as she had ever been for anything, and yet in a way she felt totally in the dark. No one had been able to tell her exactly what would happen, how she would react, or what her own experience of labor would be. This caused her to be anxious and fearful, but then she recalled God's Word on the subject: "Be anxious for nothing, but in everything by prayer and supplication, with thanksgiving, let your requests be made known to God" (Phil. 4:6). Giving control to God kept her from building up a lot of fear, and it strengthened her faith in God's ability to do His part. It also helped a lot with her relaxation training.

Anne's last visit to the doctor confirmed that all was well and that the baby really could come any time. Actually her due date had already passed, and she was grateful she hadn't let herself become impatient as the day came and went. She was getting rather uncomfortable with her bulkiness, but she knew that babies are born in God's own time and that He knew the exact hour and minute her little one would be ready. In a way it seemed incredible that the time had gone so quickly. It seemed such a short time ago that the nurse was telling her the pregnancy test was positive; she could still feel the joy that swept over her when she heard the news. And now her baby was nearly ready to be born.

Her baby? She didn't often slip into the singular possessive, because, of course, this was their baby, hers and Bob's. He was already a good father, going to child-birth class, helping her practice, indulging her needs, and best of all, praying for the baby. Just tonight as they had lain in bed praying together, Bob placed his hand on her bulging abdomen, right where they could feel the little feet kicking, and asked the Lord's continued blessing on their child. They watched the baby's movements, so clearly visible in the light from the bedside lamp, and Bob was amazed. They both laughed in agreement when Bob predicted, "That baby is ready."

Little did she know that she would sleep very little that night. She was kept awake by what she thought were Braxton Hicks contractions, which were somehow a bit different from those she had been feeling for months now. The tightenings of her uterus felt more like heavy menstrual cramps, front and back, but without the intensity or discomfort she had imagined she would have in labor. One reason they kept her awake was that she had to get up to go to the bathroom every hour because of the pressure on her bladder. Just as she would get settled and relaxed and would be able to ignore the cramping, it would be necessary to make another trip to the bathroom. This went on all night long, but still she rested and marveled at the goings-on in a pregnant woman's body. It occurred to her that all of this nocturnal activity was good training for when the little one would need her during the night, which would be a lot, if her friends with children were right.

At the 6:00 A.M. trip to the bathroom, Anne had a surprise in store. She found a "bloody show," the red-tinged mucous she had been told to watch for. It was a sign that all those Braxton Hicks (or real labor?) contractions were loosening things up in her cervix, the very early phase of eventually opening up wide enough to let the baby pass through. She knew that this show in itself didn't mean she was in labor, but if the periodic tightenings were to become more regular and pick up in intensity, then this would be it! She tried for some semblance of calm as she slipped back into the bedroom and stood next to Bob who was still sound asleep. She *had* to share this incredible news but in a way that would assure him she was really fine and that nothing was urgent. Her hand on Bob's shoulder produced a sleepy-eyed greeting that became wide-eyed as she spoke the words, "I think I could be in labor." Anne then shared with Bob the events of the night, and together they wondered what to do next. They prayed for guidance and for the Lord's blessing on what they were about to experience.

Anne decided to take a shower and then, throughout the next couple of hours, alternately walked and lay down, noticing that during the time she was up and about, the contractions were more regular. She was still not sure that she was experiencing labor. She thought, *Labor is supposed to hurt, isn't it? At least like cramps anyway?* And her contractions were painless.

Finally, after Anne had more bloody show, Bob suggested she call the doctor. The doctor advised them to come down to the hospital and be checked. On the way to the hospital, they talked to the Lord. Anne confessed her anxiety and fear of the unknown that lay ahead, and Bob quoted the scriptures they had prayed over together all through their pregnancy. As Anne heard God's Word from Bob's mouth, she repeated each word and absorbed it fully into her spirit. The knowledge that she was resting in the arms of God gave her the freedom to relax fully and do the deep-sleep breathing she had learned in class. Good thing, too, because all this activity of getting ready and traveling the distance to the hospital was producing more regular contractions. Anne handled them so well that, as Bob told her later, he thought it must be a false alarm.

ENTERING THE HOSPITAL

They arrived at the hospital at 9:00 A.M., and at the words, "Think we're in labor," the receptionist called for a wheelchair. As she and Bob sat waiting to be taken to the labor ward, Anne felt her excitement mounting even more. She was grateful that Bob could be with her and that he would be staying with her the whole time. On the last visit, their doctor had reassured them that hospitals now recognize that a mother responds a whole lot better when her husband is not only allowed but actually encouraged to stay alongside her, providing the support he has learned to give.

Anne felt a bit silly riding in the wheelchair because she certainly didn't consider herself an invalid, and it was not too comfortable to deal with a contraction as she was being pushed along the corridor and into the elevator. She decided that if she had another contraction in the wheelchair, she would ask the nurse to stop for a minute.

But then they were at the labor ward and were being taken to one of the birthing rooms. Anne walked around the pleasant room, admiring the pretty drapes and homey bedspread. She headed straight for the rocking chair and sat in it, thinking that in a matter of hours she would be sitting in it, rocking their newborn baby. Bob turned on the stereo so they could listen to the tapes they had chosen to bring along, the relaxing classical music and the soft inspirational singing that Anne loved so much. Bob was in a silly mood and soon had everyone laughing as he and Anne were introduced to their own nurse who would be with them through the labor and birth. This lighthearted mood was good for Anne, for "a merry heart does good, like medicine" (Prov. 17:22); the joking put her completely at ease, as she would have been if she had been at home.

The nurse helped Anne get settled comfortably and into a nightgown, and then checked her progress. Anne was 80 percent effaced and two centimeters dilated, so they could see that all those contractions, even though painless, were having their effect. Bob and Anne were left alone during the next couple of hours to rest and relax, and they both dozed a bit to make up for their early rising. Now that Anne was completely relaxing, she found the contractions to be less uncomfortable somehow, even though they were coming every five minutes and seemed to exert a lot more pressure.

84

By 11:30 A.M. Anne was 100 percent effaced and four centimeters dilated. This was wonderful news—it looked like all systems were "go." They had previously agreed with Anne's doctor that if she were not in active labor they would be able to go home till things got moving. As the morning passed into afternoon, the contractions got harder, but using deep-sleep breathing and relaxation, Anne was able to remain fairly comfortable. She was able to release her abdominal muscles rather than brace them against the contractions. Bob shared some of the Scripture verses from time to time that Anne had written on three-by-five-inch cards. Anne was especially pleased when she and Bob could pray together, keeping the Lord as involved with the labor as they were.

Anne spent a lot of time moving around the room and occasionally strolled down the hall to have a change of scenery. She felt the contractions were really a lot more comfortable when she was up and about or when she was sitting in the rocker. She remembered to use the bathroom every hour to keep her bladder empty so the baby would have lots of room to move down. This also kept the contractions more comfortable.

By 4:00 P.M. labor had become more intense. Anne felt a lot more serious about things, and Bob found that she stopped midsentence to respond to a contraction with deep breathing and relaxing. He also learned to stop joking around and to pay full attention to her, especially during a contraction, to be sure she kept her limbs, face, abdomen, and pelvis relaxed. So with all this help, even though labor was now very intense, it was still bearable. Bob stayed busy rubbing her back, giving her ice chips and sips of juice, wiping her forehead, and now and then sharing more Scripture verses with her. Sitting in the rocker or on the side of the bed was no longer comfortable, so she stuck to walking around. She occasionally lay down on the bed for a rest, using the side-lying position she had found so comfortable for sleeping in the last months of pregnancy.

The doctor came in to check Anne and said she was seven to eight centimeters dilated. This progress seemed slow, but they thanked God for His timing and for His love and care for them. Only a few minutes after the doctor left the room, Anne's water broke with a gush. The labor suddenly became much harder, more intense, and rather painful, especially in her lower back. Anne and Bob both realized this was because the bag of water was gone, and the cervix was now being wedged open by the hardness of their baby's head.

Anne began to get upset and frightened because she couldn't breathe slowly enough and because she had cried out once when the sensations seemed over-

85

whelming. Bob had been watching for these symptoms that they had learned might occur during transition. Anne was skeptical when he reminded her this phase would soon pass. Bob was really busy now, using counterpressure on her back and breathing slowly and loudly in order to help Anne pace her own rhythm.

Bob appreciated the nurse's presence, who had come in when Bob signaled that the water had broken. The nurse suggested a change in position. They helped Anne into a recliner-chair position by adjusting the bed and putting pillows under her knees to help her relax her legs. Anne was having such an overwhelming sensation of rectal pressure that she began to bear down with one especially strong contraction. So at 5:00 P.M. the nurse checked again and found that she had dilated to nine centimeters. What good news! All this hard stuff *was* the transition phase, and the cervix was nearly completely dilated. Anne was asked not to push until the rim of the cervix could disappear. She found it very hard to obey these instructions because she had such an overwhelming urge to push, so the nurse finally pushed the rim away manually during a contraction. "Now you can push," the nurse said, and Anne was ready.

As the nurse summoned the doctor, Bob helped Anne get upright into a squatting position, reminding her what was needed for proper pushing. When she felt the urge, she would take two full breaths, holding the third breath as she leaned forward into the push with her back rounded, head forward (chin on chest), knees wide apart, and pelvis tilted to curve around so that the birth passage would open to the fullest angle. As Anne bore down evenly, she let her breath out evenly and slowly and then took in another chestful of air. She continued pushing this way until the contraction was gone.

The nurse reminded Anne to relax the "baby door" muscles and reminded her that the strange sensations she had low in her pelvis and perineum were normal birthing sensations and nothing to fear. Anne found that when she followed her body's urge to push hard and long with each contraction, everything felt so good, so right. Even though she had been feeling extremely tired before the pushing started and had wondered how she would manage (she even asked the Lord to give her a little vacation, just skip one contraction), she found a second wind and her energy returned. She thought, *So this is what they meant when they called it labor!* Anne felt her body working harder than it ever had before, yet everything felt right. Even the burning sensation in her perineum didn't unnerve her because the doctor announced that he could see some dark hair about the size of a silver dollar—the baby's head! What a reward for all their labor!

Bob was sent to the bathroom to change into a scrub suit, and, to Anne, he seemed to take forever. She called him, "Bob, I need you . . . *now!*" Things seemed to be happening so fast, and Anne felt she could not control the situation alone. Bob hurried back to her side, scrub suit half on, mask and cap dangling untied. With Bob's help to hold onto her legs and the nurse's encouragement to reach down and feel her baby's head, Anne's pushing became effective again, and she worked with the powerful forces in her uterus, feeling the baby advance a bit with each contraction. She heard Bob encourage her with the words of Philippians 4:13: "I can do all things through Christ who strengthens me." She pushed well for two more contractions, resting gratefully in between. Halfway through the next contraction the doctor said, "Don't push . . . breathe." The doctor wanted her to "breathe the baby out" while he supported her perineum and did the maneuvers needed to avoid an episiotomy. This took a lot of concentration on Anne's part because of the incredible pressure. But Bob helped by reminding her to keep her perineal muscles relaxed. He also told her to keep her eyes open so she wouldn't miss the birth.

They watched in awe as the baby's head emerged. Then there was a bit of a rest, and the pressure eased somewhat. They saw their baby's face for the first time as the baby's head turned toward the side and then up as the doctor eased each shoulder free. Anne could not believe the flood of physical and emotional sensations she felt as the baby moved through her body. She actually could feel the baby's chest movements as the baby lingered half in and half out of her body. Anne had waited so long for this moment. She reached down and took hold of the tiny little body, while the doctor used a rubber bulb to suck out the mucous from the baby's mouth. Then she (with the doctor's help) drew him up onto her abdomen. The baby gave two short, strong cries as he deeply breathed in air for the first time. At the same time the doctor exclaimed, "Praise the Lord! You have a boy." Anne stroked his little back and cradled him close to her while the nurse covered him with a warm blanket. Then the baby was quiet, peaceful, and eager to look around, his eyes coming to rest and gazing right into the eyes of his mother.

"David, little David! Oh, Bob, God gave us a son! Thank You, Lord! Thank You!" Anne and Bob both broke forth with prayers of thanksgiving as they drank in the sight of their baby boy with hungry eyes. Anne looked at Bob and saw tears streaming down his face. They shared something at that moment that surprised them both, a surge of love warmer than ever before, and they felt closer to each other and closer to God. The next few hours were spent basking in feelings of closeness and warmth. Everything felt so right, as though it had been specially designed by the Creator for this time of opening up and including little David into their circle of love.

The doctor and nurse quietly finished up their tasks of making sure all was well and seeing to the comfort of the new family. No one interfered with the precious bonding process taking place—the birth of a family. A prayer came through Anne's mind over and over: "Thank You, God, for dealing so bountifully with Bob and me. Oh, heavenly Father, who gives only perfect gifts, You really outdid Yourself when You created David."

This birth description is unique. No birth will be exactly like it, and many will be quite different. This is part of God's creative world. Helen Wessel's first book, *Natural Childbirth and the Christian Family,* is an excellent source for learning more about this miraculous process.

WATER—AN EXCELLENT RELAXATION TOOL

Relaxation skills during labor do work to decrease or eliminate pain, but not all women are able to master the art of total body relaxation even during pregnancy. Once labor begins and escalates, the inability to relax takes its toll. Immersion in a warm tub (98 to 100 degrees, body temperature) deep enough to cover the mother's abdomen is a very simple, drug-free method of enabling a tense, laboring woman to fully relax so that her uterus can get on with the work of birth without the obstacle of tension and pain. The buoyancy of the water enables the mother to more easily support her body and relax during the contractions. As she relaxes, her stress hormones decrease and the natural birth-progressing hormones (oxytocin and endorphins) flow uninhibited.

During the labor with our seventh baby, Martha experienced excruciating suprapubic (low front) pain. After trying the all-fours position and other comfort measures without relief, she got into the tub. She was finally able to relax enough and the pain literally melted away. When the birth was imminent she got out of the water to deliver, and then we saw the reason for the unusual pain—the baby's hand came out wedged alongside his head, a compound presentation.

Birthing tubs are intended to be used to ease the pain and improve the progress of labor. Many women actually give birth in the water, and studies show lower rates of infection than in traditional births and no detrimental effects on the baby.

(For an in-depth discussion of the benefits, techniques, and safety of water-birthing, see the following reference: *Journal of Nurse-Midwifery,* Vol. 34, pp. 165–170, 1989).

THE FIRST HOUR AFTER BIRTH

Bonding at Birth

Bonding is a term used to describe the close physical and emotional attachment between you and your child at the time of birth. Bonding was designed by the Creator to enable you to get to know each other right away. During your pregnancy you began to form a bond with your baby. This bond was strengthened by the constant awareness of the life inside you. The physical and chemical changes occurring in your body reminded you of the presence of this being. After birth, this bond does not stop simply because your baby is no longer a physical part of you. Birth should not break this bond but should further cement it. Birth gives reality to the mother-infant bond. You now can see, feel, and talk to the little person whom before you knew only by the bulge, the movements, and the heartbeat you heard though medical instruments. Bonding allows you to transfer your life-giving love for your inside infant to the care-giving love for your outside infant. Inside, you gave your womb; outside, you give your milk, your eyes, your hands, your voice—your entire self. This continuum of mother-infant attachment should not be interrupted by trivial routines nor diluted by depressant medications.

The first hour after birth is a sensitive period. Unless a medical complication prevents it, your baby should be placed immediately onto your warm, soft abdomen and breasts instead of onto a hard, uncaring surface or into a plastic box. This immediate, postpartum period should be a private time of mutual touching. This initial family time should be spent touching, talking to, and suckling your baby. The first hour after birth is an important milestone for your entire parenting career. It is a special time in which mothers and fathers are very high from the excitement of the birth, and babies are in a state of quiet alertness, the state of awareness in which babies are most receptive to their care-giver. Neither you nor your newborn should be deprived of this special time.

How does this early bonding benefit you and your baby? Medical science is continually trying to prove what mothers have intuitively known and God designed from the beginning. Much of the research on mother-infant bonding was popular-

ized by Doctors Klaus and Kennell in their book, *Parent-Infant Bonding*. These researchers compared two groups of mothering styles: the early-contact group bonded with their babies immediately after birth, and the delayed-contact group were temporarily separated from their babies immediately after birth. They found that the following mothering abilities were greater in the early-contact group: (1) They were more successful at breastfeeding; (2) they talked with their infants more and used descriptive speech; (3) they spent more time in the face-to-face *(enface)* position of eye-to-eye contact; and (4) they touched and groomed their infants more.

These researchers postulated that there is a sensitive period lasting about one hour after birth when the baby is most sensitive and receptive to his care-giver. Mothers who bonded with their babies during this period were more confident in exercising their intuitive mothering; whereas, the mothers who were separated during this period were less confident. These researchers also found that fathers who were present at birth and who bonded with their babies during this sensitive period continued this involvement and were closer to their children.

What happens in a situation in which a medical complication, such as a Cesarean delivery, temporarily separates mother and baby after birth? What happens in cases of adoption? Is this parent-baby relationship permanently affected by a temporary separation, or can you make up for the time you were separated (delayed bonding)? Recent studies have questioned the conclusions that bonding or not bonding during the first hour after birth can have any lasting effects on either parent or child. This is an important point. Parents who are medically unable to bond with their baby immediately after birth should not feel guilty that their child has been permanently affected. Immediate bonding after birth is not like a glue that cements the parent-infant relationship forever. Many steps must be taken throughout infancy and childhood that lead to a strong parent-infant attachment. I feel that there is probably no scientific rationale for concluding that being deprived of this initial bonding can permanently affect the parent or child. I do feel, however, that bonding during this biologically sensitive period does give the entire parent-child relationship a head start. Regardless of whether Klaus and Kennell's studies are scientifically accepted or rejected, it is true that their pioneer work in parent-infant attachment has been a valuable impetus toward changing many hospital policies that have separated parents and newborns after birth.

Bonding Tips

The following suggestions are designed to get you off to the right start and help your bonding relationship be more meaningful.

1. *Be prepared.* A positive birthing experience usually encourages maternal bonding; whereas, a negative birthing experience in which fear and suffering predominate often lessens the desire for a mother to bond with her infant. Two important factors that contribute to a positive birthing experience and, therefore, indirectly promote a positive bonding experience are Christian childbirth classes and a supportive father during labor and delivery.

Pain-lessening drugs given to the mother during labor may decrease the mother's and the baby's receptiveness to the bonding experience. Mothers who have been well prepared for birth by a childbirth class do not require any (or require far fewer) drugs during labor. If for any reasons beyond your control you have had a negative birthing experience in which fear and suffering predominated or medical complications occurred, realize that your feelings of attachment to your baby may be temporarily lessened. This is a time for sincere prayer and consultation, asking God not to allow your feeling of disappointment in the birthing experience to lessen your attachment toward your baby. Pray for healing from this difficult experience.

2. *Breastfeed your baby right after delivery.* Some babies have a strong desire to suckle the breast immediately after birth, and others are content simply to lick the nipple. Medical research clearly demonstrates that babies should be put to the breast immediately after birth. Sucking and licking the nipple release the hormone oxytocin into your bloodstream. The oxytocin increases the contraction of your uterus and lessens the complication of postpartum bleeding. This early suckling also stimulates the release of the hormone prolactin, the milk-producing hormone, which also enhances your mothering abilities after birth. I like to call prolactin the "mothering hormone."

3. *Touch your baby.* Ideally, immediately after birth your baby should be skin to skin on you, his or her chest to your abdomen, with your arms around him or her and a blanket over your arms. The skin is the largest organ of the human body— your newborn will enjoy the stimulation he or she receives from this skin-to-skin contact. Gently stroke your baby, touching his or her whole body. It is moving to see a new mother stroke her baby's entire body with a gentle caress of her fingertips and to see the father place an entire hand on his baby's head as if symbolizing his commitment to protect the life he has fathered.

4. *Look at your baby.* Place your face in the *enface* position so that your eyes and your baby's eyes meet on the same vertical plane. Your newborn can see you at best within the distance of twelve inches. Because they are in a state of quiet alertness after birth, many infants will open their eyes more during the first hour after birth than they will several hours after birth when they are usually in a state of deep sleep. The feedback you will receive by staring into your infant's eyes may trigger a rush of beautiful mothering feelings. Cradling your baby in your arms while breastfeeding lends itself to the *enface* relationship. Request the nurses to delay the eye ointment (given to prevent eye infection) until after the bonding period since this ointment may lessen your baby's ability to open his or her eyes.

5. *Talk to your newborn.* Mothers naturally speak to their newborn babies in high-pitched, mothering voices. Your newborn's ears are already attuned to your speech, and you may notice that your baby moves rhythmically in response to your voice.

6. *Have some private time.* If no medical problems occur, a perceptive hospital staff will leave mother, father, and baby alone for a while after birth. This should be

a time of peace and privacy, the birth of a family. It is a time when all three of you should embrace each other. It is a time to acknowledge God's presence in the birthing room (if you haven't already) and to pray a prayer of thanksgiving for the life that He has given you.

Rooming-in

Rooming-in is the natural extension of the bonding period. After birth, both you and your baby will fall into a much-deserved sleep. After the baby's initial hour of alertness, he probably will reward you with two or three hours of deep sleep. For most mothers, the ecstasy of the birth event is eventually overruled by the tiredness of their bodies, and mothers also can enjoy their much-needed, long sleep.

The next attachment decision is, Who will be your baby's primary care-giver in the hospital, you or the nursery staff? Like so many other options that have diluted the parenting profession, there are several options of newborn care, some of which unfortunately may interfere with mother-infant attachment in the hospital. One option of newborn care, which I strongly discourage, is giving the baby's primary care to the nursery staff who bring the baby to the mother on a predetermined schedule or at their convenience. In my opinion, this option should be reserved only for sick mothers or sick babies. Not only does it deprive the mother of caring for the life she nourished for so long, but it is not conducive to early mother-infant attachment. This scheduled newborn care puts the mother in the role of secondary care-giver, a role not at all in accordance with God's design. Hospitals should not consider mothering as a drug for the baby that is to be dispensed in concentrated doses at prescribed times.

A second option, and one many mothers elect, is that of modified rooming-in. In this option the newborn spends most of the day with the mother but spends the night in the nursery and is brought out as needed for night feedings. In theory this modified type of rooming-in seems attractive, and the mother apparently gets the best of both worlds. Actually, this situation often becomes confusing to both mother and baby, and the baby may wind up spending a lot of time in the nursery.

The third option, and the one I strongly encourage, is full rooming-in. In my opinion, healthy mothers and healthy babies should stay together from birth to the time of discharge from the hospital. The nursery should be reserved for sick babies or babies of sick mothers. Full rooming-in will allow you to exercise immediately your intuitive mothering at a time when the hormones in your body are pro- grammed to help you begin your mothering profession. Studies have shown that infants who room in with their mothers cry less and more readily organize their sleep-wake cycles. As a former director of a university hospital newborn nursery I noticed that the mother and baby who fully room in together enjoy the following benefits.

1. The mother has fewer breastfeeding problems. Her milk is established sooner and her infant is more satisfied.

2. The newborn has less jaundice, probably because he or she gets more milk.

3. The mother actually seems to get more rest since she experiences less separation anxiety, and the newborn will sleep most of the time anyway.

4. Babies in a large nursery are soothed by tape recordings of a human heartbeat. Rather than being soothed electronically, the baby who is fully rooming in with his mother can be soothed by the real thing.

5. The newborn seems more content because he interacts with only one caregiver, his own mother. The rooming-in mother is much more competent and intuitive in the care of her newborn once they get home.

6. Research has shown that the rooming-in mother has a lower incidence of postpartum depression.

Rooming-in truly does allow the best of both worlds. It encourages you to exercise fully your intuitive mothering according to your desires and the needs of your baby rather than the impersonal nursery clock. This arrangement also affords you the luxury of having the attending medical personnel in the roles of advisor and consultant should the need arise. In my opinion, the ideal newborn care arrangement for most mothers and babies is for the mother to assume the role of primary and nearly complete care-giver and for the attending personnel to assume the roles of advisor and helper. Rooming-in is the natural extension in the continuum of attachment—mother's womb to mother's room.

ROUTINE HOSPITAL PROCEDURES

Apgar Scoring

Within the first five minutes after birth, your newborn will be given a score called the Apgar score, which is a measure of the general health of newborn babies developed by Dr. Virginia Apgar over thirty-five years ago. The Apgar scoring is performed at one and five minutes after birth, and your newborn is given from zero to two points for each of the following parameters: color, breathing efforts, heart rate, muscle tone, and general reflexes. An infant who receives a score of ten has received two points for each of these parameters, indicating that each system was functioning at its maximum; whereas, a score toward the lower end of the scale (four or five) indicates that some of these systems were not functioning at their maximum within the first five minutes after birth.

Since it is often customary to tell the parents the Apgar score, let me explain its real meaning in order to alleviate any anxiety you may have. Infants who are pink all over, cry lustily, breathe rapidly, have good heart rates, and show strong muscle movements are usually given scores of ten. Most of the time, normal, healthy newborns do not achieve scores of ten. It is quite normal for the hands and feet of a newly born baby to be somewhat blue because it takes a few minutes for the newborn's circulatory system to become adjusted to his postnatal environment.

It is a misconception that it is healthy for a newborn to cry lustily after birth. Some newborns are born in a state of quiet alertness. This is a normal state of peace and contentment for which the newborn would lose two points on the Apgar score. A baby who scores ten is not necessarily more healthy than a baby who scores seven or eight. The Apgar score is only valid if done by a trained medical person whose only responsibility in the delivery suite is to calculate that score. The score number given to the parents after birth has little or no predictive value as to the health of the baby. A lower score should not be a source of anxiety to the parents. It only serves to alert the attending medical personnel to observe the baby more closely over the next few hours in case circulatory or respiratory problems occur.

Injections and Medications

Immediately after birth your newborn will be given an injection of vitamin K because most newborns are deficient in this vitamin that enhances normal blood clotting. It is also a law in most states that your baby be given some medication in both eyes in order to prevent any infection of the cornea that may have been picked up during passage through the vaginal canal. Silver nitrate was the solution most commonly used, but this solution may temporarily irritate the eyes. It is now replaced by a milder but equally effective ointment such as erythromycin.

Although these procedures are necessary to ensure the health of your newborn, it is not necessary that they be administered immediately after birth. Parents who wish to have the special time of bonding and thanksgiving prayers after birth can request the attending medical personnel to delay these routine procedures until after you have finished.

PKU Testing

Phenylketonuria (PKU) is an extremely rare metabolic disorder occurring in approximately one out of fifteen thousand infants. If diagnosed shortly after birth, it can be treated with a special diet. If left untreated, it can result in brain damage. The PKU test, required by law in most states, is usually done just prior to discharge from the hospital, and it is conducted on a few drops of your baby's blood. Because of the rarity of this disease, sometimes too much anxiety is produced in the parents by this simple test. I became aware of this when new parents came into my office one day concerned that their baby had missed the "mental retardation test" because they had left the hospital too early. This misunderstanding illustrates the importance of properly explaining hospital procedures to parents.

Thyroid Testing

Your baby's blood is also analyzed for sufficient thyroid hormones. Congenital hypothyroidism (low thyroid at birth) occurs in about one out of five thousand infants and may cause retardation if untreated. The earlier this disease can be detected and treated, the more effective is the treatment.

Jaundice

Jaundice is listed under the category of routine hospital procedures and tests because almost all newborns develop some degree of jaundice, and parents often are anxious over what in reality is a variant of a normal physiologic process. Jaundice is the yellow color in a baby's skin caused by a buildup in the blood of a yellow pigment called bilirubin. The body normally produces some bilirubin from the breakdown of worn-out red blood cells. This bilirubin is usually disposed of through our livers and intestines and does not reach high enough levels in the blood to cause yellow deposits in the skin. If too many blood cells are broken up too fast, or if the liver is unable to get rid of the excess bilirubin fast enough, this excess bilirubin is deposited into the skin, giving the yellow color.

Newborns are susceptible to two types of jaundice: (1) normal and (2) abnormal. I use the term *normal jaundice* (also called "physiologic jaundice") because almost all babies have some degree of jaundice. This is due to a series of immaturities within the newborn baby, temporary immaturity of the liver and intestinal mechanisms to dispose of the bilirubin. Within the first few weeks, your baby's systems mature enough to dispose of the bilirubin, and the jaundice subsides. Your pediatrician will tell you whether your baby's jaundice is normal or whether it is due to some abnormality. Because this normal type of newborn jaundice causes much anxiety in the new mother and is often overtreated, the following is a detailed explanation to alleviate this unnecessary anxiety. Ways also are given in which you can often lessen the level of jaundice in your newborn.

The first concept to understand is that in many cases jaundice is a reflection of the fact that God's design for mother-infant togetherness has been tampered with. As a director of a university hospital newborn nursery, I have noticed that babies who are allowed to room in with their mothers and are breastfed on demand have much less jaundice than those who do not room in and feed frequently. Recent studies have confirmed my observation by showing that the more frequently mothers are allowed to breastfeed babies in the hospital, the lower the bilirubin in their babies. The medical reason for this curious observation is that milk helps wash out the excess bilirubin in the intestines, and infants who do not receive enough milk have fewer calories, which is another cause of jaundice.

Unfortunately, mothers often are advised to stop breastfeeding because the breast milk is assumed to cause the jaundice. A very rare type of this disease called "breast-milk jaundice" is why this treatment is advised. For an unknown reason, the breast milk of some mothers causes prolonged jaundice in a newborn baby. This only occurs in about 1 percent of breastfeeding babies; therefore, it is rarely necessary to stop breastfeeding temporarily when your baby is jaundiced.

There is also an abnormal type of jaundice in which the bilirubin levels may go high enough to cause brain damage in the sick newborn or premature baby. The cause of this type of jaundice is usually blood group incompatibility (such as the Rh factor difference in mother and baby) or an infection. If your baby has jaundice, your doctor will inform you if you should be concerned.

One of the most common modes of treatment of high jaundice is called "phototherapy." Your baby is placed under a bilirubin light that dissolves the bilirubin in the skin, allowing it to be disposed of more adequately through the kidneys.

Regardless of the cause of your baby's jaundice, there is seldom a reason to separate you and your baby. One of the best ways that you can prevent or lessen your baby's jaundice is by keeping your baby with you in the hospital and breast-feeding frequently. Since the jaundice may increase once your baby gets home, your doctor may require that baby be taken back to the hospital for a follow-up blood test to check the bilirubin level. If it is too high, a home phototherapy light may be required. This explanation is pertinent only for full-term, healthy babies. Premature babies or sick babies at birth follow different rules for the treatment of jaundice, and your doctor will advise you if this is the case. Whatever the cause of your baby's jaundice, it is necessary that both the bilirubin level of the baby and the anxiety level of the parent be appropriately diagnosed and treated.

CIRCUMCISION

Up until recent years circumcision was considered a routine procedure for newborn males, but parents are beginning to ask if circumcision is really necessary for their babies. In the following discussion, I will present some information and considerations by which parents can make an informed choice regarding circumcision.

Biblical Basis for Circumcision

Genesis 17:10–12, 14 are the master verses dealing with circumcision in the Old Testament:

This is My covenant which you shall keep, between Me and you and your descendants after you: Every male child among you shall be circumcised; and you shall be circumcised in the flesh of your foreskins, and it shall be a sign of the covenant between Me and you. He who is eight days old among you shall be circumcised, every male child in your generations. . . . And the uncircumcised male child, who is not circumcised in the flesh of his foreskin, that person shall be cut off from his people; he has broken My covenant.

It is clear from this verse that, according to Mosaic law in the Old Testament, God commanded all males to be circumcised.

However, in the New Testament, many verses state that circumcision is not necessary: "Circumcision is nothing and uncircumcision is nothing. . . . Let each one remain in the same calling in which he was called" (1 Cor. 7:19–20); "Circumcision is that of the heart" (Rom. 2:29; see also Gal. 5:6; 6:15). As evidenced in Acts 15, there was much controversy about circumcision among the early Christians. The Pharisees believed that the Mosaic law should be followed and that a Christian could not be saved unless he was circumcised (Acts 15:1, 5). Paul, however, taught that it was not necessary for salvation (1 Cor. 7:18; Gal. 5:2). It seems that the Mosaic law was followed concerning Jesus' circumcision: "On the eighth day, when it was time to circumcise him, he was named Jesus" (Luke 2:21 NIV).

The religious necessity for circumcision was even more controversial in New Testament times than the medical necessity of circumcision is today. There is enough evidence in the New Testament for anyone to conclude that circumcision is not necessary for salvation. Scripture says nothing about circumcision being important for body hygiene. Circumcision for the Hebrews was a *blood rite,* a sacrifice symbolic of the blood covenant God made with Abraham. It was never intended to be a health or hygienic measure. For Christians this covenant is made obsolete by the new covenant of Jesus' blood sacrifice on the cross. (For more information on Christianity and circumcision contact: Peaceful Beginnings, 13020 Homestead Court, Anchorage, Alaska 99516; phone: 907-345-4813.)

Is Circumcision Necessary?

The American Academy of Pediatrics has taken the stand that routine circumcision is an unnecessary procedure. Some parents still ask their pediatricians to help them make a decision regarding circumcision. The following questions and answers are intended to help you make this decision.

1. *How is the circumcision performed?*   The baby is placed on a restraining board, and his hands and feet are secured by straps. The tight adhesions between the foreskin and the penis are separated with a metal instrument. The foreskin is held in place by metal clamps while a cut is made into the foreskin to about one-third of its length. A metal bell is placed over the head of the penis, and the foreskin is pulled up over the bell and cut circumferentially. About one-third of the skin of the penis (called the foreskin) is removed.

2. *Is circumcision safe? Does it hurt?*   Circumcision is usually a very safe surgical procedure, and there are rarely any complications. However, as with any surgical procedure, there are occasional problems such as bleeding, infection, or injury to the penis. Yes, it does hurt. If the skin is clamped and cut, of course it hurts. A newborn baby has painful sensations in the skin of his penis, and it is unrealistic to convince yourself that this procedure does not hurt. God has endowed babies with a mechanism by which they can withdraw from pain. Many babies will initially scream and then withdraw into a deep sleep toward the end of the operation.

3. *Can the baby have an anesthesia to lessen the pain?*   Yes. A *local anesthesia* can be used. Ask your doctor about this. Although many physicians do not use local anesthesia, painless circumcision should be a birthright. If your doctor is not aware of this technique, he or she can find a description of the procedure in the *Journal of Pediatrics,* vol. 92 (1978), page 998.

4. *Does circumcision make hygiene easier?*   The glands in the foreskin secrete a fluid called "smegma." In the adolescent and adult male these secretions may accumulate beneath the foreskin but are easily cleansed during bathing.

What happens if the foreskin is left intact? Leaving the foreskin intact protects the glans from excoriation and infection from diaper rash. At birth it is impossible to make a judgment about how tight the foreskin will remain since almost all boys have tight foreskins for the first few months. But by one year of age in about 50 percent of boys, the foreskin loosens from the head of the penis and retracts completely. By three years of age, 90 percent of uncircumcised boys have fully retractable foreskins. Once the foreskin retracts easily, it becomes a normal part of masculine hygiene to pull back the foreskin and cleanse beneath it during a bath. While it is true that infection from the secretions beneath the foreskin is more often a problem in uncircumcised males, simple hygiene can prevent this problem.

5. *If the foreskin does not retract naturally, will he need a circumcision later on?* Circumcision is *very rarely* necessary for medical reasons, but when the foreskin does not retract, it becomes tight and infected and obstructs the flow of urine. This condition, called "phimosis," requires circumcision. However, if circumcision for phimosis is necessary later in childhood or adulthood, an anesthesia is given, and the boy is involved in the decision process.

6. *If he isn't circumcised, won't he feel different from his friends?*   Parents cannot predict how their son will feel if he is circumcised or intact. Children generally have a wider acceptance of individual differences than adults do. It is difficult to predict whether the majority of boys will be circumcised or intact in the future. The number of circumcised boys has been steadily declining in recent years as more parents begin to question routine circumcision.

7. *My husband is circumcised. Shouldn't my son be the same as his father?* Some fathers have strong feelings that if they are circumcised, their sons should be, and these feelings should be explored. However, many fathers change their minds once they are fully informed.

8. *We have a son who is already circumcised. Should brothers in the same family be the same?*   Many parents feel that sameness is very important among the males of the family since little boys do in fact compare the styles of their penises. Your problem will most likely not be in explaining to your intact child why he is intact but rather in explaining to your circumcised why he was circumcised.

9. *Do circumcised boys experience any particular problems?*   The foreskin

100

acts as a protective covering of the sensitive head of the penis. Removal of the protective foreskin allows the head of the penis to come in contact with ammonia in the diapers. Sometimes this irritation causes circumcised babies to develop painful sores on the tip of the penis that may obstruct the flow of urine.

10. *Does circumcision prevent any disease?*   Circumcision does not prevent cancer of the penis. Cancer of the penis is a very rare disease anyway, and it occurs more frequently in males who do not practice proper hygiene. Circumcision does not prevent cervical cancer. Cancer of the cervix is not more common in the sexual partners of intact males who practice proper hygiene. Circumcision also does not prevent venereal disease.

11. *Does circumcision make sex better?*   The head of the penis is very sensitive, and this sensitivity may lessen if the protective foreskin has been cut off. Some men who have been circumcised as adults and who compare their sexual experiences before and after have claimed that their penises were more sexually sensitive before the foreskins were removed. Because of this consideration, a custom developed many years ago to do a partial circumcision in which only a small part of the foreskin was removed, thus allowing the foreskin to cover about half of the head of the penis. In my opinion, partial circumcision should not be done because the part of the foreskin still covering the head of the penis may become tighter and the circumcision may have to be repeated later on. This also defeats the purpose of the circumcision because foreskin care is still necessary and adhesions form between the partial foreskin and the head of the penis. In many ritual circumcisions a very generous amount of foreskin is removed. In my experience, more problems arise from circumcisions in which not enough foreskin has been removed than in circumcisions that have removed too much.

12. *When should the circumcision be performed?*   Genesis 17:12 states, "He who is eight days old among you shall be circumcised." The probable reason for this was that the newborn baby's blood clots faster by the eighth day. Today, it is medically unnecessary to wait until the eighth day, but for those babies who do not receive an injection of vitamin K shortly after birth, it may be wise to wait until the eighth day for circumcision. Usually circumcision is done in the hospital within the first couple of days after birth at the convenience of all concerned. Up until recent years it was often the custom to do the circumcision immediately after delivery. Because of the increasing regard for the feelings of the newly born baby and the emphasis on the bonding period after birth this practice fortunately is being gradually disregarded. Circumcision shortly after birth is also incompatible with the

trend toward gentling the newborn baby and making every attempt to smooth the transition from intrauterine to extrauterine life.

In the previous discussion, I have presented to you my opinion that routine circumcision is neither biblically nor medically indicated. Your individual family custom and desires should be respected. If you are having difficulty deciding whether to circumcise your baby or leave his penis intact, pray to God for wisdom to make this decision. I advise you to consider circumcision with the same prayer and care you would give any other elective surgical procedure for your child.

If you choose to leave your baby's foreskin intact, follow these suggestions on its care. I call this the "uncare" of the foreskin. In most babies the foreskin is tightly adhered to the underlying head of the penis during the first year. The foreskin gradually loosens itself, but it may not fully retract until the second or third year. *Leave the foreskin alone* until it begins to retract easily, which is usually between six months and three years. The age at which the foreskin begins to retract varies considerably from baby to baby. Respect this difference and *do not retract* the foreskin since this may prematurely break the seal between the foreskin and the head of the penis, allowing secretions to accumulate beneath the foreskin. As the foreskin naturally retracts, gently clean out the secretions that may have accumulated between the foreskin and the glans of the penis. This should be done as part of the child's normal bath routine. Usually by three years of age, when most foreskins are fully retracted, a child can easily be taught to clean beneath his foreskin as part of his normal bath routine.

CHAPTER 4

POSTPARTUM PARENTING

THE MOTHER'S ADJUSTMENT PERIOD

Bringing home the new baby cements the reality that you are now a family. The euphoria of giving birth begins to wear off, and you as a couple will probably experience some degree of difficulty adjusting to the postpartum period. In the following discussion you will be helped to understand why these feelings occur. With the help of the Lord and her husband, the new mother can cope with these feelings.

Postpartum Changes

"If birth is so wonderful and my baby is a precious gift from God, why do I feel so sad (awful, depressed, upset)?" First of all, mothers, appreciate that you are not alone in your feelings. About 50 percent of all women giving birth in North American hospitals experience some degree of after-baby blues. One hundred thousand women are treated in outpatient clinics for varying degrees of postpartum difficulties and about four thousand women per year are hospitalized with severe psychiatric disturbances within six months after giving birth.

The difference between the "baby blues" and postpartum depression is a matter of timing and degree. Most women experience some degree of temporary baby blues within a week or two after giving birth. These emotional changes are due in part to the fact that often in human adjustment, a low follows a high. From six to eight weeks after birth, actual postpartum depression may occur, manifested by the following signs and symptoms:

- Fatigue
- Episodes of crying, anxiety, and fear
- Confused thoughts and difficulty in concentrating
- Insomnia (even if baby is asleep)
- Periods of nervousness and tension
- Loss of appetite
- Feelings of failure and panic
- Fear of going crazy
- Worry about physical appearance and unattractiveness, with diminishing desire to groom yourself
- Negative feelings toward husband
- Irritation by trivial things—tendency to "make mountains out of mole hills"
- Heart palpitations
- Shaky feelings

In addition, a woman may experience doubt and frustration—doubt about her mothering abilities and frustration at her apparent lack of success. These feelings may lead to despair, which may result in occasional negative feelings toward her baby, which in turn are followed by sensations of guilt for having had these seemingly terrible feelings. Mothers, remember that it is not abnormal (or unchristian) to have these feelings, but it is unhealthy to let them get out of hand. Ventilate these feelings to a trusted person, preferably your husband, and also to your physician.

WHAT CAUSES POSTPARTUM DEPRESSION?

Most postpartum difficulties are caused by too many changes too fast, and depression is the woman's body signal that she has exceeded her physical and psychological capabilities to adapt to these changes. Everyone's capacity to adjust to combined stresses is different. She should not consider this a weakness in herself but realize instead that she has reached a certain stress level exceeding her ability to cope. The usual stresses contributing to postpartum depression are both physical and emotional.

Physical and Chemical Changes

In the postpartum period the woman's body chemistry is going through tremendous fluctuations from the pregnant to the nonpregnant to the lactating states. Her hormones are particularly affected. Changing body chemistry often brings with it changing moods and feelings, and her sleep cycles also have undergone a tremendous change. The mother and father have had to adjust their sleep needs to the cycle of their baby. The sleep-when-your-baby-sleeps advice is indeed necessary for adjusting to the new baby's sleep patterns (or lack of patterns), but this sudden adjustment is not easy for many parents.

Actually, I feel that downright exhaustion either causes or contributes to a slow recovery after giving birth. This is particularly true if, for reasons beyond her control, the mother has experienced a traumatic birth (Cesarean section or prolonged and difficult labor in which fear and pain predominated). A difficult physical recovery from birth may be compounded by disappointment that the ideal birth did not occur and expectations were shattered.

Emotional Changes

With the birth of their first children, many women experience status changes. This is particularly true of a very young mother or of a woman who has had an exciting career outside the home from which she received much status and affirmation. A new mother may feel her identity is blurred: "I'm Johnny's mother, and I'm Bob's wife, but what happened to me as a person?" These are normal feelings that any person would have when his or her self-esteem is threatened. Perhaps at no other time in a married couple's life are there as many changes so fast as in the immediate postpartum period: change in lifestyle, role changes for husband and wife, disrupted routines, disrupted sleep patterns, changing economic status, and on and on. Whether most of these changes are for the better or for the worse, the reality is that a lot of the changes bring unusual feelings, which in turn bring the need to cope.

PREVENTING OR LESSENING POSTPARTUM DEPRESSION

Know specific risk factors

During pregnancy and delivery a woman can identify certain factors that may increase her risk of having postpartum depression.

1. A previous history of depression or difficulty coping with combined stresses;
2. Exchanging a high-status career for motherhood, with ambivalent feelings about this status change;
3. An unwanted pregnancy and ambivalent feelings of how a child will fit into the current lifestyle;
4. Marital discord and unrealistic expectations that a child may solve marital problems;
5. A negative birth experience in which fear and pain predominate;
6. An ill or premature baby; and
7. Any situation that separates mother and baby and interferes with a close mother-infant attachment shortly after birth.

If you have any of these risk factors, pray and seek counsel during pregnancy and in the early postpartum period.

Make adequate preparation

A woman should prepare her heart and body for the coming of her baby by following the suggestions discussed in Chapter 2. During this preparation period she can form relationships with various parenting groups, such as the La Leche League International, that may serve as a positive support group after delivery. Since this type of depression is shared by thousands of other women, women can find comfort from other mothers in these support groups.

Be flexible. When a woman enters the hospital, she should ask God to give her the strength to accept the labor and birth she has even as she plans for the "ideal" delivery. There will always be something about the birth experience that she will want to change "next time."

106

Ask for rooming-in.   Unless a medical complication prevents it, continue the rooming-in started in the hospital (Chap. 3). Mother-infant detachment is one of the contributing factors to postpartum depression. Avoid extreme fatigue at all costs. Although tiredness is a realistic expectation of the parenting profession, new parents can do some things to lessen it, such as obtaining help at home from friends, relatives, or hired help if that is economically feasible. This is a time for Christian friends to rally around the new parents, help with the housework, prepare the meals, and simply "mother" the new mother. In my experience much postpartum fatigue is due less to the many needs of the baby and more to the efforts of the new mother to be all things to all people (see the section, "The Father's Postpartum Role," in this chapter).

A new mother must learn how to delegate responsibilities. The housework, cooking, and dishes can be done by someone else, but no one can mother your baby as you can. One new mother with a large family shared with me, "I simply sit in my rocking chair, dressed in my nightgown, nursing my baby and directing traffic." If the baby has older siblings of "working age" (more than four years old), some of the simpler household chores can be delegated to them. Make them feel that they can help Mommy and their new little brother or sister.

The expectant mother should get as much rest as she can in the final months of pregnancy. The final month of pregnancy should be a time of peace and quiet, allowing her to tune in to her unborn child and rest her mind and body for the coming birth. A mother who enters labor tired is likely to be more tired after birth.

Consider yourself.   New mothers need to take a few hours out each week to do something for themselves. They may protest, "But my baby needs me all day long." Yes, a new baby does need his or her mother, but she needs herself also. Meeting her own needs is not being selfish or unchristian. It is realizing that only giving is going to wear thin after a while. If she feels good about herself as a person, she will be more effective as a mother, and her child ultimately will profit.

The special time a mother saves for herself should be spent on a relaxing activity, some physical exercise, a hobby, or just a peaceful walk in the park. This special time is analogous to a doctor's going off call. A doctor who never signs out to a trusted colleague and goes off call will soon experience burnout and become less effective as a doctor. In reality, a nursing mother can never go off call completely; but she can sign out occasionally to a trusted mother-substitute during brief periods when her baby has fewer needs. (I admit this is more easily said than done.) Fathers make the best mother-substitutes and they are handy—they come home from work every day. That's the time to take a soak in a bubble bath (together if baby is asleep!). At the very least, mothers, don't often "waste" the baby's naptimes on housework. A good book (for those who love reading) can be read in snatches, even while breastfeeding (if you can tear your eyes away from your baby's face). This is also a good time to pray.

Keep yourself attractive.　　If a woman looks good, she most likely will feel good. Give proper attention to good grooming even if you have to force yourself to take a weekly trip to the beauty parlor, if that is what you did before baby. Or get a manicure or a new haircut or buy a new lipstick. Join forces with a close friend who can be trusted to see ways you can stay beautiful.

Have a balanced diet.　　Your doctor may advise you to continue your prenatal vitamins. Avoid junk food because it may cause blood-sugar swings and contribute to postpartum blues. If you are nursing, you will need the same nutritious calories and balanced diet that you needed during pregnancy. Postpartum weight loss should occur mainly by increased exercise and not by crash diets. Dietary deficiencies may contribute to postpartum depression, especially combined with the stresses of pregnancy, giving birth, and new-parent fatigue. A consultation with a nutritionist who is experienced in postpartum problems may be necessary. Ask your doctor or midwife for a referral. A nutritional consultant can be helpful for any new mother. Ask at your hospital about having an appointment before you leave the hospital, or arrange for it when the baby is several weeks old and you feel like getting out.

Avoid too many visitors.　　In the first few weeks after coming home, limit visitors. "Thou shalt not entertain" is one of the commandments for a new mother. Remember, "help" (even if it's your mother) is to *help you* and is not to be entertained. The helping person should know you are going to care for the baby most of the time; she is there to care for the household duties and other routine matters. Clarify this ahead of time to avoid hurt feelings. Make a written list if it is hard for you to tell this person what things need to be done. Being all things to all people is what gets a new mother overly tired.

Avoid isolation.　　Seek out friends and visitors when you want them. Surround yourself with positive people. Avoid negative advisors who may try to pressure you into a mothering style that does not feel right to you. Mothering in a way that basically goes against your God-given intuition (the unique blueprint for mothering your own child) is a setup for postpartum depression. The human, emotional organism is not equipped to operate constantly outside God's basic design. Any advice that does not feel right to you and is not working should be dropped.

Exercise.   Force yourself to get at least a half-hour of sustained exercise each day even if it is simply walking in the park with your baby in a front carrier. Physical exercise is absolutely mandatory for a new mother. Tiny babies are very portable. Nothing in the mother-infant contract says you must stay home all the time. Home to a tiny baby is where his or her parents are.

Involve your husband.   Be specific in telling your husband what you need (laundry or dishes done, a housekeeper, help with the other children, and so on). Remember, your husband is undergoing some postpartum adjustment difficulties of his own. Quite honestly, many men are slow to sense exactly what new mothers need, so you simply may have to make your needs known in a nice way but also loud and clear! Your husband may perceive a situation as tiny and insignificant and therefore ignore it, but to you it is a major need. Tell him.

Avoid drugs.   In my experience, drugs are not the answer to postpartum depression. Unless your depression requires hospitalization, try to avoid drugs altogether.

THE FATHER'S POSTPARTUM ROLE

Fathers, your wife needs mothering too. Be tuned in and sensitive to her physical and emotional needs. If your wife is having a problem with a status change, help her feel she has stepped up the ladder of personal worth and not down. Constantly express genuine love and support, "You are doing the most important job in the world, mothering our child."

Beware of the many physical and emotional changes going on within your wife. This is a time of sincere, high-level communication in which you sympathize with her feelings: "You must feel very tired. I understand. How can I help?" Also realize that your wife may be somewhat reluctant to ask for your help since she may feel this is a sign of maternal weakness. She may be trying to act like supermother: the perfect wife, the perfect mother, the perfect hostess, the perfect housekeeper, the perfect everything.

Everything drains on the new mother. The responsibility falls to the father to be sure the mother is not totally drained. Even in the economically poor cultures in the world a new mother is given a *doula* (from the Greek word meaning "servant").

A *doula* is a person who can take over the household chores and free the new mother to be a mother. Anyone can be a *doula* to the new mother, even the father. If your friends ask, "Is there anything you need?" answer, "Yes, please bring over supper tonight."

Be sensitive to signs.   Be sensitive to the early signs of depression: insomnia, loss of appetite, unfounded nagging, lessening attention to grooming, not wanting to get out of the house. If these red flags appear, take steps immediately. Seek prayer and professional counsel before these early warning signs progress into a full-blown depression and you wind up being both mother and father while your wife is recovering in the hospital.

Respect the nesting instinct.   During the final month of pregnancy and for the first few months after birth, the mother needs a stable nest. Avoid making major changes near the time of childbirth. This is not the time to change jobs or move into a new house or move across the country. Remember, the nesting instinct is very strong in a new mother.

Control visitors.   Be sure that well-meaning friends and relatives help instead of hinder the new mother. An overextended visit in the first few weeks can be very draining, especially when baby has been up a lot at night. The new mother needs time to rest or sleep rather than entertain yet another visitor. If someone comes at a bad time, say so.

Care for older children.   Take charge of most of the physical maintenance of the older children. This frees your wife to concentrate on their emotional needs, which often go up when a new baby arrives; they also want mother's prime time.

Show love.   Convey your love for your wife. You may say, "Of course I love my wife." But do you show it? Because of the previously mentioned reasons, your wife will have problems with her self-esteem during the postpartum adjustment period. One of the greatest gifts you can give your child is to show love to his or her mother.

Seek prayer and counsel.   The principles of Christian natural childbirth should lower the risks of postpartum depression since you have begun relying on the Lord for strength even during your pregnancy. The following Scripture passages are selected readings for depressed mothers who rely on the Lord for their strength:

Psalm 46:1	Psalm 9:9–10	Ephesians 4:23–24
Psalm 42:5	Psalm 107:28–29	1 Chronicles 28:20
Jeremiah 29:11	1 Peter 5:7	Psalm 34:18

Nehemiah 8:10   Psalm 27:5   Isaiah 41:10
Isaiah 26:3   2 Timothy 1:7
John 14:27   Psalm 34:4

TEN COMMANDMENTS FOR THE POSTPARTUM MOTHER

1. Thou shalt not give up thy baby to strange care-givers.
2. Thou shalt not cook, clean house, do laundry, or entertain.
3. Thou shalt be given a *doula*.
4. Thou shalt remain clothed in thy nightgown and sit in thy rocking chair.
5. Thou shalt honor thy husband with his share of household chores.
6. Thou shalt take long walks in green pastures, eat good food, and drink much water.
7. Thou shalt not have before you strange and unhelpful visitors.
8. Thou shalt groom thy hair and adorn thy body with attractive robes.
9. Thou shalt be allowed to sleep when baby sleeps.
10. Look to the Lord, and He will give you strength: thou shalt not have prophets of bad baby advice before you.

CHAPTER 5

DEVELOPING A PARENTING STYLE THAT WORKS

In the first few weeks of your parenting career you will be bombarded with a barrage of conflicting advice on how to care for your baby. All of your well-meaning friends and relatives are going to offer you their personal how-tos of baby care. Caring for your baby is known as "developing a parenting style." I like to think of a parenting style as a relationship that develops naturally with your baby. From this relationship the how-tos automatically unfold. My dear parents, bear in mind that because you love your baby so much you will be vulnerable to any advice that may claim to make you a better parent or your baby a better child. In this section you will find suggestions on how to evaluate baby-care advice.

My opinion is that God loves us so much that He gives each parent a special intuition to know how to care for and to enjoy his or her child. Implied in this divine design is the law of supply and demand: as long as a parenting style is practiced that allows this intuition to develop, God will supply as much intuition as the child's needs demand. Some parents feel less confident than others, and some children have higher needs than others. I strongly believe that each parent's intuition for child care will match his or her child's needs—but only if the parent allows this relationship to grow according to God's design.

The purpose of this chapter is to help new parents develop a parenting style that is in accordance with God's design. The term *Christian parenting style* means a series of relationships between you and your child that will give you a greater chance of achieving the three primary goals of Christian parenting: (1) knowing your child, (2) helping your child feel right, and (3) leading your child to Christ.

A flurry of books and articles on parenting styles has surfaced in the past twenty years. Titles such as *Choices of Parenting Styles* and *Options for the Busy Parent* convey that new parents can choose a system of child care that fits most conveniently into their own lifestyles. According to these parenting options, parents should identify what lifestyle makes them happiest and then conform their children to it "because children are resilient." I do not feel this style of convenience parenting is in accordance with God's design. Be mindful of the Father's advice, "Train up a child in the way he should go . . ." (Prov. 22:6), meaning the way God has ordained for this child. Seek to determine God's way for your baby. Then help your child grow up in that way even though it may not be the most convenient way.

Another parenting style that is commonly recommended is what I call "restraint parenting." The catch phrases of restraint parenting are: "Don't be so quick to pick up your baby every time he cries"; "Don't let your baby manipulate you"; "What? You're still nursing? You're making him too dependent"; "Don't let your baby sleep with you; she may get into the habit"; "You're going to spoil her"; "You've got to get away from that kid." These common admonitions from trusted advisors to vulnerable new parents only detach parents and babies. Restraint parenting keeps you from knowing your child, keeps your child from feeling right, and ultimately keeps you from fully enjoying your child. Detachment or restraint parenting is not in accordance with God's design.

ATTACHMENT PARENTING

The style of parenting I sincerely believe is God's design for the father-mother-child relationship is a style I call "attachment parenting." My dear Christian parents, my feelings about conveying this style of parenting to you are so strong that I have spent more hours in prayerful thought on this topic than on any other topic in this book. Attachment parenting is not just my own theory. It is a parenting style I have derived from (1) parenting our own seven children, (2) observing and recording my patients' parenting styles throughout the past twenty years, and (3) becoming involved in parenting organizations whose principles I respect. I have a deep personal conviction that this is the way God wants His children parented. It works!

When discussing attachment, I refer mostly to the mother, not because I feel the father has a minor role in parenting, but because I feel God prefers greater maternal involvement in the first few months of a child's life. However, let me say to fathers that mother-infant attachment is difficult to achieve unless the father is the spiritual leader in a supportive environment. Most of the problems in the parent-child relationship are not a fault in the design or the Designer; they are a result of a total breakdown of the support system that allows a mother to follow God's design.

What is attachment? Mother-infant attachment is a special bond of closeness between mother and baby. This is a unique relationship designed by the Creator to enable the young of the species to reach their fullest potential. I feel that God placed within each mother a type of programming we call "mother's intuition." Some mothers naturally have a more developed intuition; others have to work at developing it, but it is there!

When your child is born, he or she comes complete with a unique set of characteristics we call "temperament." This child also is born with specific needs that, if met, will help modify this temperament and benefit the child's total personality. Some children have higher needs than others. Some children have different sensitive periods for different needs. No two children come wired the same way.

It logically follows that God would not give a certain mother a child whose needs she cannot meet. This is in keeping with what I believe the concept of the Creator to be. God's matching program is perfect; God's law of supply and demand will work, but only if parents develop a parenting style that allows God's design for the parent-child relationship to develop. If parents care for their children according to the divine design, they have a greater chance of claiming the promise, "Train up a child in the way he should go, And when he is old he will not depart from it" (Prov. 22:6).

Attachment means that mother and baby are in harmony with each other. Baby gives a cue; mother, because she is open to baby's cues, responds. Baby likes the response and is further motivated to give more cues (because he or she learns he or she will get a predictable response), and the mother-baby pair enjoys each other. They get used to each other. As one attached mother told me, "I'm absolutely addicted to her." Once this happens, the mother's responses become more spontaneous and the how-tos naturally flow. How do you know when you get that attached feeling? When your baby gives you a cue and you respond, if you have a feeling of rightness about your response, and if you are continually sensitive to your baby, you are there. The attachment style of parenting helps you build up your sensitivity.

Why is attachment parenting preferable to restraint parenting? Compare these two styles and the effects they have on parent-child relationships.

Attachment Parenting Advice	Restraint Parenting Advice
"Be open to your baby's cues."	"Don't let your baby run your life."
"Take your baby with you."	"You've got to get away from that kid."
"Throw away the clock and the calendar."	"Get that baby on a schedule."
"Respond promptly to cries."	"Let your baby cry it out."
"Travel as a unit."	"You and your husband need to get away."
"Sleep wherever you all sleep best."	"Don't let your baby sleep in your bed; she'll get used to it."
"Let your baby sleep when he is tired."	"Put him down at 7:00, and let him cry; he'll learn to sleep."
"Wean when both of you are ready."	"What, you're still nursing?"
"Let her decide when she is ready to be independent."	"You're making her dependent."
"Allow discipline to flow naturally from harmony with your baby."	"You're spoiling him; he'll never mind."
"Let authority flow from trust."	"She's controlling you."

Attachment Parenting Results	Restraint Parenting Results
You develop trust and confidence in your parenting intuition.	You do not trust your instincts, and you rely on outside advice.
You know your child better.	You and your baby have a strained relationship.
You develop realistic expectations.	You compare your baby to other babies.
You adjust more easily to your new lifestyle.	You suffer burnout more easily.
You enjoy your baby more.	You seek alternative fulfillment.
You find discipline to be easy.	You find discipline to be strained.
You find spiritual training to be rewarding.	You find spiritual training to be stilted.
You are more discerning of advice.	You are vulnerable to unwise advice.
You keep pace with your child.	You play catch-up parenting.

Attachment Parenting Results for Your Child	*Restraint Parenting Results for Your Child*
Your child trusts care-givers.	Your child doesn't learn trust.
Your child forms attachments easily.	Your child resists new relationships.
Your child feels right, acts right.	Your child is anxious and dissatisfied.
Your child becomes loving and giving.	Your child becomes withdrawn and restrained.
Your child separates from you easily because he or she was attached to you early.	Your child separates from you with difficulty.
Your child has a good model for his or her own parenting.	Your child is confused about his or her role as a parent.

An objection to attachment parenting is, "I'm not going to let this tiny baby dominate me; I'll get her on *my* schedule rather than listen to her needs." Being open to your baby's cues does not mean that you are losing control. Being open simply provides the conditions for fully developing your God-given intuition. Openness implies trust in three relationships: (1) you trust your baby to give you the cues to tell you what he needs; (2) you trust yourself and your ability to respond to your baby's cues appropriately; and (3) you trust that God's design for a mother-baby communication network will work if allowed to operate as designed. When your baby cries in the middle of the night (for the third time) and you respond, don't feel you are "giving in"; you are simply giving.

It is important for you to realize that God would not have designed a system of child care that does not work. If you are a mother who says, "I don't feel I have any intuition," respond consistently to your baby without restraint and you will find your shaky intuition maturing. Try to see parenting as a stimulus-response relationship. For example, your baby cries, you pick him up; your baby is restless at night, you sleep with him; your baby enjoys nursing, you don't wean him before his or her time. By freely exercising this stimulus-response relationship, you become more confident in the appropriateness of your response.

What if you are confident in your intuition but are blessed with a very demanding baby (see Chap. 9, "The Fussy Baby")? Again, the law of supply and demand works. Your intuitive response and your perseverance level increase in proportion to your baby's needs. You stay in harmony, in sync, with each other. However, if you succumb to outside pressure not to be open to your baby, you soon restrain your responses, trust yourself less, and eventually lose harmony with your baby. Restraint parenting leads to a strained parent-child relationship. In subsequent chapters, important attachment principles will be addressed that help the mother-baby relationship develop according to God's design.

Because of the great variability in family situations, you may not be able to practice all of the disciplines of attachment parenting all the time. However, the more these parenting styles are practiced, the greater your chances are of truly enjoying your child.

THE JOYS OF ATTACHMENT PARENTING

A Harmonious Relationship

What attachment parenting does for you may be summed up in one word, *harmony*. A harmonious relationship allows you and your baby to be more in sync with each other, to become sensitive to each other. You, too, will become addicted to your baby.

A "Hormoneous" Relationship

Attachment parenting also permits you to have a sustained chemical change in your body. Breastfeeding stimulates the hormone prolactin (the milk-producing hormone). This hormone can give you the added boost you need during trying times. I suspect this hormone may be part of the divine design of mother's intuition.

By now, you may be feeling that this attachment style of parenting is all giving, giving, giving. To a certain extent, this is true. Parents are givers and babies are takers; that is how God designed them. Baby's turn to give will come later, and better takers make better givers. But because of this "hormoneous" relationship, baby still can give something back to mother—more prolactin. This mutual giving is a beautiful example of the divine design: mothering stimulates more mothering.

There are nearly two thousand references to "giving" in the Bible. Isn't that what Christianity is all about? Parenting according to God's design helps both parents and children grow to be giving persons.

WHAT CAN YOUR CHILD EXPECT?

Children who experience attachment parenting exude a feeling of rightness, the basis for a strong self-esteem. If your child feels right about himself, he will be a source of great joy to you. Attachment parenting can give you a better opportunity to enjoy your child.

Attachment parenting also can give your child an appropriate model to follow when he or she becomes a parent. Remember, you are parenting someone else's future husband or wife, father or mother. How your child was parented will influence how he or she parents. The lack of definite models is what causes confusion in many young parents today.

Attachment parenting's real payoff is in caring for what I call the "high-need child." This child goes by many names—the fussy baby, the demanding baby, the strong-willed child—but I prefer the term *high-need child* because it more accurately describes the level of parenting this temperament requires.

God's law of supply and demand works especially well for the high-need child. Attachment parenting increases your parenting energies as your child's needs increase, and you stay in harmony with each other. Restraint parenting may cause you to go out of sync with your baby so that you do not enjoy this special child.

Practicing attachment parenting does not guarantee that your child will not later depart from your teachings. It simply increases the chances that your child will turn out to be a blessing to you. There are three reasons why you cannot claim full credit or blame for your child's future: (1) every child comes wired with a unique temperament; (2) throughout life, your child will be continually bombarded with outside temptations and alternative lifestyles; and (3) God has given your child a free will. Comparing child-rearing with planting a seed may help you understand this concept. Certain styles of care give a seed a better chance of bearing good fruit. However, each seed is unique, and the fruit it bears will be vulnerable to the forces of nature. Your child is subject to forces beyond your control including his or her free will. You can understand why the most well-attached child may bend a bit.

Because God knew children would have erring, human parents, I feel He builds into each child an ability to adjust to a wide range of parenting styles. Most children have a wider acceptance of parenting styles than parents have of their behavior. However, the closer your style of parenting is to God's design, the less your children will tap into their reserves of resilience. As a result, certain undesirable behaviors of childhood that I call "diseases of detachment" are less common (anger, tantrums, depression, withdrawal, distancing).

Attachment parenting lays the foundation for discipline and spiritual training within the first two years of your child's life. Because you know your child better, you are able to assess his or her behavior more accurately and can respond to it more appropriately. Because your child feels right, he or she is more likely to act right. Such an attitude in your child makes punishment seldom necessary, and when necessary, it is administered more appropriately. Because of the attachment you have, both you and your child trust each other. Trust is the basis of authority, and authority makes the final goal of parenting, spiritual training, more effective.

FATHER FEELINGS AND MOTHER-INFANT ATTACHMENT

Occasionally, fathers share these feelings with me: "She's too attached"; "All she does is nurse"; "I feel left out"; "We need to get away alone." These are real feelings from real fathers who sincerely love their children, but feel displaced by them. If you are a father who is feeling displaced, let me assure you that your father feelings and your wife's attachment are very usual and very normal. Perhaps an understanding of God's design for mother-infant attachment and the changes that happen in your wife after birth may help you understand her apparent preference for your baby.

Before she gives birth, a woman's sexual hormones dominate her maternal hormones. After she gives birth, the reverse is true. The maternal hormones increase and stay at high levels for at least six months, during which time a woman's maternal urges may appear to take priority over her sexual urges. This shift of hormones may be part of the divine design to ensure that His young get mothered. A new mother also may feel drained by the incessant demands of her baby, so that by evening she has no sexual inclinations. Mothers commonly describe this feeling as being "all touched out."

A new mother is programmed to be attached to her baby physically, chemically, and emotionally. This does not mean that the father is being displaced by his baby but that some of the energies previously directed toward him are now being directed toward his infant. In time, these energies will be redirected toward the father. Let me share with you an investment tip I have learned in my practice and in my own family: if you are a caring, involved, and supportive husband during this early attachment period, these energies will return to you at a higher level.

I call the early attachment period a "season" of the marriage, a season to parent. If the harvest of this season is tended with care, the season to be sexual will again return.

THE OVERATTACHMENT SYNDROME

Be sensitive to the needs of your husband. God designed the family to function as a father-mother-child unit, not as a mother-child unit separate from the father. If you do not have a stable, fulfilled Christian marriage, the father-mother-child relationship ultimately will suffer.

You should not have to choose between your marriage and your child. If both relationships are kept in perspective, both will operate on a higher level. A child should not divide a marriage; a child should be a catalyst to bring husband and wife closer together, if their marriage is God-centered.

The following is a common story about what I call the "overattachment syndrome." Mary and Tom had a reasonably good marriage, but their relationship still needed a lot of maturing and it was not well-founded on Christ. After their baby arrived, Mary tried very hard to be a good mother. Tom was somewhat uncomfortable about handling babies, but he loved his little daughter very much. Mary sensed Tom's uneasy father feelings and was afraid to trust him to comfort the baby when she cried for fear he might upset the baby more. Tom felt more and more left out, and gradually they drifted down separate paths, Mary into her mothering and Tom into his work.

As Mary became more attached to the baby, Tom became more attached to his job and eventually made a few "attachments" of his own. Finally, Mary found herself in her pediatrician's office wondering why her marriage was disintegrating. "But I tried to be such a good mother," she said. "My baby needed me. I thought Tom was a big boy and could take care of himself." This common scenario occurs when there is fundamental breakdown in God's order for the family.

Watch out for "red flags" in your attachment relationship: Is the stress causing a division in your marriage? Are you spending less and less time with each other? Is Dad working more and enjoying fathering less? If these red flags are occurring, bring prayer and consultation into your relationship before the diseases of detachment take hold.

Pray daily for your child, for your marriage, and for your parenting relationship. If you bring Christ into your marriage and your parenting relationships, you have a head start toward the attachment mothering and the involved fathering that I sincerely believe are God's order for the Christian family.

A PERSONAL EXPERIENCE

I chose the most attached mother in my practice and asked her to tell what mother-infant attachment has meant to her. The following is what she wrote.

Before birth, a mother and infant are totally attached to each other. Within minutes, birth makes a drastic change in their physical attachment, but in every other way the attachment changes only gradually over a period of years. In some ways, such as emotionally and intellectually, the attachment actually increases. In other ways—functionally and biologically—the attachment takes new forms and gradually lessens.

Immediately after birth the baby and the mother need to remain physically together. Although the physical link between them is severed, the necessity for closeness is intense. The baby needs to be surrounded by familiarity, to be warmed and suckled. The mother needs to be assured that the tiny kicks she had become accustomed to from inside are still there, and that the pregnancy she has "lost" is very surely "found" in the squirming little baby placed on her abdomen. She needs to envelop with her arms and drink in with her eyes and ears the feel, sight, sound, and smell of her newly born child. She needs to marvel at the miracle God has wrought in the depths of her body.

In the first days after birth, the attachment shows itself in new ways. The slightest whimper, the subtlest change in breathing rhythm, or the least shifting of the little body brings the mother to immediate attention. She very quickly responds by drawing her baby close to her, and she feels a rightness flood over her body and mind.

She begins to sleep with "one eye open" in case her baby needs her. If her baby is in a separate room for the night, she sleeps fitfully. She wakes often to listen for his or her cries and often goes in only to find the baby sleeping quietly.

As she performs her daily routine, she keeps her baby near her. If by some chance she discovers her baby has been crying, she is full of remorse that she was not there the instant the baby needed her. The discomfort this brings to her increases her vigilance and her determination that it not happen again. As she settles down to soothe her baby by holding, stroking, crooning, or nursing, a warm feeling of rightness melts away the pain and dismay in a flood of maternal emotions.

As the weeks pass, a pattern of attachment develops that is custom-made for the mother and her baby; it is a secret code known and trusted only by the two of them. The father knows and understands this attachment only in part by watching it unfold before him. He develops an attachment of his own to the baby, but it doesn't seem to ease the feeling he has sometimes of being left out of the inner circle around mother and baby. How good it is when he feels secure enough not to interfere with their closeness and not to feel threatened by it.

The father eventually becomes intrigued with the fine tuning he sees between his wife and their baby. "How did you know?" he'll ask, incredulous that such a subtle clue from the baby (indiscernible to himself) could be so completely and accurately understood by the baby's mother. The mother herself is amazed by her sixth sense about what the baby needs. He doesn't have to cry to let her know he wants to nurse or be picked up or shifted to a change of scene. The baby has a language of gestures, glances, and tiny noises that communicates his needs. The mother and baby are so close, so attached, that the baby seldom cries. The mother has learned to read her baby.

The attachment brings daily discoveries to the mother about herself and about her baby. She finds that if her baby takes an unusually long nap, she begins to yearn for her baby to wake up. She tingles with excitement when she finally notices him or her stirring awake; she has missed her baby and it is good to be reunited.

She makes another discovery in the church nursery debating with herself whether or not to leave the baby for the first time. She watches other babies being handed over to the nursery workers and put into their assigned slots—one in a swing, one in a crib, one in an infant seat. She pictures herself handing her baby over and considers what instructions she will give. But it doesn't feel right. She watches for a while longer and feels a growing conviction that she should keep her baby with her. As she leaves the nursery with her baby still in her arms, she is relieved the separation hasn't happened.

Another day she discovers that the baby has a finely developed sense of attachment in terms of measuring acceptable distances. As long as she is within touching distance or within seeing or hearing distance, the baby feels OK. Depending on the baby's need at a particular moment, he or she can tolerate lesser or greater amounts of distance between himself or herself, and his or her mother. Her constant availability enables the baby to develop a trusting nature.

As the baby gets older, the mother feels less urgency in responding to her baby's expressions of need. She feels OK about hurrying through a task, calling "Momma's coming," rather than dropping her work instantly to tend to him or her. Their attachment is now strong enough to handle a slight delay: the mother knows just how long the baby is able to wait before he or she will push the panic button. And these panics rarely occur now that she has learned so much about her baby and about herself as a mother.

A major milestone has been reached, and there will be many others. The attachment that started out to be so total and so intense has changed and will change even more, but there will be one constant thread throughout: the mother and child have a bond that will last a lifetime; it will serve the divine order for both their lives. The mother will have nurtured and the baby will in his or her turn nurture. Their attachment has given birth to human love for generations to come and has guaranteed the fulfillment of God's design for His children.

FROM ONENESS TO SEPARATENESS

Timely separation is a very important concept. A child must be filled with a sense of oneness with the mother before he or she can develop separateness. A baby must first learn attachment before he or she can handle detachment. A baby must first have a strong identity with his or her mother before he or she can evolve into his or her own self-identity. The age at which babies go from oneness to separateness varies tremendously from baby to baby.

Going from oneness to separateness according to God's design enhances child development. When a baby is securely attached at one stage of development, he more easily progresses to the next stage of development. Eventually the natural desire for independence stimulates the baby to begin to detach gradually from the mother. *It is important that the baby detach from the mother, not the mother from the baby.* For example, a toddler who is just learning to walk cruises farther and farther from his or her mother but periodically turns toward home base to check in. He or she feels secure detaching because his or her mother is there. However, if mother leaves during this separation-sensitive stage, the toddler might become less secure in exploring because home base is gone. Dependence actually fosters independence as long as it happens according to divine design.

Realizing that healthy attachment makes separation easier is good protection against those who insist attachment parenting makes your baby too dependent. Exactly the opposite is true. The baby who is the product of attachment parenting is actually less dependent later. Over the past ten years, research has confirmed what mothers have intuitively known—that early attachment fosters later independence. (I have summarized these scientific studies in my book *Growing Together*, published by La Leche League International, Franklin Pack, Illinois, 1987.) The concept of oneness to separateness has long been appreciated in secular books on child care. Unfortunately, it has not been understood among writers of Christian child-care books.

When Can I Leave My Baby?

If your attachment parenting has been practiced according to divine design, you will not want to leave your baby. You will probably experience some withdrawal symptoms the first time you leave your baby. For example, I see new mothers peering through the window the first time they leave their babies in the church nursery. They are not being possessive, which means keeping a child from doing what he needs to do because of some personal need. They are simply being attached. If you are a new mother and you feel a continual urge to get away from your baby, I advise you to pray and seek counsel because very often this desire implies some departure from God's design. You should enjoy being with your baby so much that, although an occasional outing may seem necessary, you really have difficulty being away from him or her.

How often and at what age a mother leaves her baby depends on many variables, including her need to get away. You may honestly feel you need occasional relief. If you feel a need to be refilled by some outside interest, follow your desire; an empty mother is no good to anyone, especially her baby. Oftentimes your restlessness will not be the need to get away from your baby, but the need for a change of scenery. Consider taking your baby along. You may feel you're not the stay-at-home type. "Home" to a tiny baby is where his mother is; take your baby out. God's design is for mother and baby to be tied together, not tied down. The divine design is a bond, not a bondage. When planning a time to be apart from your baby, the following questions need to be considered.

How separation-sensitive is your baby?   Some babies separate more easily than others because of their individual temperaments.

What is your baby's need level?   High-need babies separate with difficulty; they are designed that way.

125

Who is the substitute care-giver?   When you leave your baby, be sure to give explicit instructions on how you want your baby mothered in your absence. For example, tell the care-giver, "When she cries, I want you to pick her up immediately and comfort her." If possible, try to leave your baby during his or her prime time, which is the mornings for most babies. Try not to leave your baby during fussy times when he or she needs your nurturing.

CHAPTER 6

THE DILEMMA OF THE WORKING MOTHER

One day on a TV show, my wife Martha and I were discussing my first book, *Creative Parenting*, with the host. I was asked my views on the working mother. As I was struggling to muster up some inoffensive answer, Martha put a touch of reality in the show by proclaiming, "If I hadn't been a working mother while my husband was a student, he wouldn't be here today as a physician and author even to answer this question." Women have a way of getting right to the point when commenting on the subjects that are written about by men but experienced only by women. This was, however, in our early years as parents and, even though Martha worked part-time only enough to pay the rent, we now realize we could have made better choices.

The issue is not the working mother. Mothers have always "worked" and worked very hard. The issue is working at a job outside the home. Like so many issues in parenting, difficult problems do not have easy solutions.

CHOICES

Many sincere, caring, and devout Christian mothers are faced with the dilemma of having both to mother and to work outside the home. For this reason, I wrote this section with much prayer and consultation so that my comments would offer understanding support and advice, not judgment.

Many of you have already made the choice between returning to work and staying at home, but if you are having difficulty with this important decision, here are some important considerations that, if supported by prayer and counsel, will help you.

How Does Being a Full-time Mother Affect the Child?

It has been stated previously that a strong mother-infant attachment is God's design so the young can reach their fullest potential. The development of this attachment is an ongoing maturing process that begins with the mother's strong biological commitment to her baby. Just being close to each other allows her God-given instinct, or mother's intuition, to develop to its fullest potential and gives her baby the environment of love and security to help him or her develop to his or her fullest potential.

The harmonious relationship.   Being constantly in touch and in tune with her baby allows both mother and infant to be in harmony with each other. Mother, your baby has a need and gives you a cue. You pick up on this cue and appropriately respond to the need. When this happens, your baby is motivated to continue giving cues because he trusts your consistent and appropriate response. You become more comfortable with your responses because you see the feedback and appreciation from your baby. The end result of the harmonious relationship is that you accomplish two of your three parenting goals: (1) you know your child and (2) your child feels right. This feeling of mutual rightness within mother and child results in your child's acting right; a child who feels right and acts right is more of a joy to parent. The mother who senses this positive feedback from her baby feels right mothering, and the entire mother-child relationship is elevated to a higher level. A strong mother-infant attachment is especially important for the high-need child (see Chapter 9) and has far-reaching effects on later childhood (see Chapter 16 on disciplining).

The "hormoneous" relationship.   In Chapter 3, the hormone prolactin, the milk-producing hormone, was postulated to be the chemical basis for mother's intuition. Just being close to your baby is a powerful stimulus for prolactin secretion, which further stimulates the mothering instinct, and the cycle goes on. What a beautiful design! Science is finally proving God's design that both mother and child benefit from being close to each other.

These concepts of a harmonious and a "hormoneous" relationship are particularly meaningful for the new mother who previously had a high recognition job and worried about whether she would be able to be fulfilled by full-time mothering. Let me advise this mother to practice as early as possible all the disciplines in the attachment style of parenting. More often than not I notice that mothers who really practice these disciplines from the time of the child's birth usually elect not to return to work. One mother who found this attachment feeling shared with me: "Because I really liked my job, I had planned to return to work when my baby was three months old. Now, I can't return to work; I'm addicted to her. I never knew there could be so much joy in being a mother. My friends can't understand how I can stay home all day with my baby, but I love it." The term *addiction* is a good one for this feeling of attachment when this relationship is allowed to develop according to God's design.

What Are the Effects of Mother-Infant Separation?

Essentially, both mother and baby are deprived of the benefits of mother-baby attachment. An important part of the mother-infant attachment design, which a mother deciding to return to work should evaluate, is that in order for a baby to grow and develop to his or her fullest potential, the baby must first learn a consistent attachment. He must learn this before he or she can comfortably handle separation. Child development experts believe that a child should separate from the mother on his or her own terms in order to explore his world, but the mother should not separate from the baby. Separation from the baby during the sensitive period from six to eighteen months may deprive the baby of the person who gives him or her the security to attempt independent tasks. As a result, the baby may regress in his or her developmental skills.

To what degree this level of attachment is weakened depends on (1) the need level of the baby, (2) how separation-sensitive the baby is, (3) the substitute caregiver's ability to respond appropriately to the baby's needs, (4) how much you are away from your baby, and (5) to a lesser degree, what the mother does when she is with her baby. I feel the main effect of prolonged mother-infant separation is that the baby may become confused and insecure.

Early in the mother-infant communication process the baby learns to expect a certain response to certain cues. He or she learns that his or her needs will be consistently and appropriately met and that his or her cues will be consistently understood; this is called "imprinting," or attaching one's self to one's primary care-giver. Substitute care-givers, no matter how caring, how loving, and how Christian, do not have this God-given biological attachment to your baby. They do not enjoy the previously mentioned harmonious and "hormoneous" relationship. When an infant's cues are not consistently and appropriately met, he or she stops cuing. His trust in his or her care-giving environment is weakened.

The feedback a baby receives for a developmental accomplishment is one of the most stimulating factors toward his or her development. For example, the way a mother responds to a child's primitive attempt to communicate verbally is a powerful stimulator toward a child's speech development. An infant who does not receive his or her anticipated reward becomes less motivated.

How about Quality Time?

Quality time is an example of New Age thinking (everyone going for his or her own potential) and has been capitalized upon by the child-care industry. This concept has become popular because it alleviates the guilt a mother sometimes feels when she returns to a full-time job outside the home while her baby is very young.

Actually, the idea of quality time developed in reference to fathers working long hours, often far away from home. They had little time to be with their children, but it was considered "quality time." This rationale has now been taken up by working mothers. The child who now receives quality time from both parents is squeezed in between their busy careers at their convenience.

This quality-time concept ignores some basic truths: children are spontaneous; their learning is often mood dependent; and they have unanticipated needs. Although God made children resilient and adaptable, their needs cannot be scheduled. One of the fallacies of child care is the feeling that parents always have to be stimulating or giving input to their children. The parent as a constant giver is only part of the parenting role. Many times the major role is simply being available and approachable when teachable moments occur.

This quality-time concept allows many couples to justify their lifestyles. Why is only the parent-child unit blessed with quality time? Why can't school teachers dismiss their students after only one hour of quality-time teaching instead of a full day of quantity time? Why not say to your boss, "I am only going to work an hour today, but it will be quality time"? This new math for parents says one hour of quality time equals seven hours of quantity time.

130

In some situations, such as that of a single working mother, quality time is really the best that can be accomplished. One sincere, caring Christian mother shared with me: "I have to work all day; so quality time is all I can afford. I give up a lot of time I would ordinarily spend on entertainment to be with my child, so that when I'm not working I'm fully devoted to my child. Besides quality time, I probably give him more quantity time than many nonworking mothers who spend a lot of time each day pursuing their own forms of entertainment." This mother is truly doing the best she can do.

Is There an Answer?

Beware of the cycle of nonattachment, which is a subtle problem that creeps into the lives of some mothers and babies. A mother who has a priority outside the home or who lacks confidence in her mothering abilities may have difficulty really getting into mothering and forming a close mother-infant attachment. Although this mother sincerely loves her child, she has ambivalent feelings about attachment mothering and resorts to an increasing use of substitute care-givers. Since the mother is not confident in responding to the baby's cues, she does not do so appropriately. As a result of this loss of appropriate feedback from his or her mother, the infant does not reward her with his or her own feedback of appreciation that would, in turn, stimulate her mothering. Mother and baby gradually drift further apart, the mother into her career outside the home and the baby into dependence on the substitute care-giver. Periodic attempts to get back into mothering are uncomfortable and therefore unsuccessful because the continuum of mother-infant attachment has been interrupted at a very early stage. The cycle of nonattachment is a particular problem when there is a mismatch of temperaments between mother and baby.

Often there are no easily identifiable effects of detachment on the older child. However, studies have shown that daughters of career-outside-the-home mothers do tend to place more emphasis on nonmothering careers, and the cycle continues into the next generation. God's design for infant attachment continues to be weakened.

"I want to work for my own fulfillment."

"I want to use my education."

"If I stayed home all day, I would go stir crazy."

"I am a better mother if I am away from my child for a while and also am fulfilled outside the home."

These are real feelings from real Christian mothers who truly love their children. Again, understanding the dilemma of today's women is more important than being judgmental. It helps to remember that developing a harmonious mother-infant attachment is the main issue, not whether a mother has to stay at home. While full-time mothering definitely gives this harmony a more stable foundation, there is more to be considered.

To understand better the dilemma of the working mother, review what has happened historically to the changing roles of women. In past generations, even in biblical times, women worked at home. Proverbs 31:10–31 is a beautiful description of the working mother at home. However—and this is an important consideration—the father also usually worked at home. The family business operated out of the home or farm. Parenting and working were integrated. With the coming of industrialization and urbanization, men began leaving the home to work. Men became more educated and prepared to join the work force, and women were culturally prepared for motherhood at home. In the first half of the twentieth century two world wars took women out of their homes into the industrial world to do traditionally "male" jobs. Next, the educational system equally prepared boys and girls to "become something," and for women, this "something" was not motherhood.

Today's women are given many more options, many more career choices. If you ask a class of high school girls what they are going to be, seldom will you get the response of "I'm going to be a homemaker" or "wife and mother." Although no one actually has said it, the subtle message is that full-time mothering is less fulfilling and has a lower status than a job outside the home. Women have begun leaving home just as men did in previous generations. Day care is the parent. "Get out and work; get fulfilled" is the message which fits in nicely with the secular ideas that gained prominence in the sixties. Total fulfillment at all cost, fulfillment from without and not from within, has become the goal of the times.

As a result of this philosophy, many women have come to feel more fulfilled by careers outside the home than by motherhood. I have counseled many women who believe they wouldn't feel right if they stayed home full time and cared for their children. They would do so resentfully; their children would sense the underlying tensions; and both they and their children would lose. But, by pursuing a part-time career outside the home or, *best of all, inside the home,* a mother can have her self-image—not selfish image as some people would say—elevated; she feels better as a person and therefore feels better as a mother. Both mother and children profit. I support the mother who has come to this decision after much prayer and deliberation.

If you have these ambivalent feelings concerning the dual-career dilemma, the following suggestions may help you to resolve them. (1) During your pregnancy, pray, asking God for the wisdom to see His career plans for you. Be open to His direction. (2) Give full-time mothering a chance. Don't enter your mothering career with expectations that you won't be fulfilled. If you do, you won't. (3) Practice the mothering styles noted earlier in this book. You may be surprised at how fulfilling mothering can be when God's design for mother-infant attachment is followed. If, after prayer and counsel and at least several months of mothering experience, your decision is to return to your career, then do so considering the next three sections.

Mother Has to Work

There is a story about a fundamentalist who said to a working mother, "You should be home taking care of your child." The mother replied, "We have no home; that's why I'm working." Actually *having* a home and *owning* a home are separate issues. Unfortunately the American dream of owning a home is beyond the reach of many young couples with young children, and a second income may *seem* the answer. Mothers, before you decide to return to work while your child is an infant, consider these points.

Evaluate your priorities.   No material possessions are more valuable to your infant than you yourself. Consider whether you can afford not to give your child your full-time self.

What is your worth in dollars and cents to stay at home?   Consider exactly what you will have left over by the time you deduct from your paycheck the costs of clothing, food, transportation, child care, increased taxes, and medical bills (children in day-care centers get more infections). You may be surprised at how little you have left over by the time you deduct these expenses.

Plan ahead.   Economize and save as much money as you can during the early years of your marriage and during pregnancy, letting the savings from your second income help your family while you are a full-time mother. Saving enough for at least the first three years is wise if possible. Many couples become accustomed to a standard of living that depends on two incomes. Early in your marriage, consider living on one income and saving the other lest you become trapped in the two-income standard of living after the baby arrives.

Consider borrowing the extra income you need until your child is approximately three years old and you can return to work. I don't generally encourage debt, but when it is used to allow a parent to nurture a baby, in my opinion, debt is justified. A common example is when Dad is a student. Our first child, James, was born while I was a "poor intern." Martha juggled mothering and working part-time. We didn't consider alternatives. We could have used her inheritance. Or we could have lowered our standard of living considerably and then borrowed the rest short-term. It is easier to repay money than reparent children. One of the best investments you can make in your child's future is to give him or her the commitment of yourself, at least for the first couple of years and longer if economically possible. Grandparents are often a willing source if they realize that this is probably one of the most valuable investments they can make in their grandchild's future. To illustrate this case, let me share a situation from my own practice. A friend of mine is an investment counselor, and he is always trying to get me into some sound investments. Shortly after the birth of his first grandchild, his daughter mentioned to me that she was planning to return to work within a couple of months because they had become used to a second income and they felt they still needed it. After convincing her of the wisdom of staying home with her child for at least two years and borrowing the extra income, I decided to present this "investment" to her father. I presented the situation to him by saying, "John, I'm calling you about an opportunity for perhaps the best long-term investment you have ever made. Come on down to the office and let's talk about it." After talking to him about his daughter's situation, John agreed that helping care for his grandchild was, indeed, a good investment.

WORKING AT HOME

Having a home business may be a realistic answer to the second-income dilemma. Mothers, this works best when you take time to find the type of work you want to do. Doing work that you dislike will wear thin after a while. Some examples of home businesses are caring for children, typing, selling by phone, bookkeeping, sewing, doing arts and crafts, giving piano lessons, and being a sales distributor—jobs in which much of the work is done at home and in which you can take your baby along when you make your calls. Some professional women bring their businesses into their homes and turn their spare rooms into offices. You may be surprised at the variety of work you can do during your baby's times of lower need. I know a mother who is an editor and works on her own portable home computer that is tied into the main office. This mother "goes to the office" without leaving her nest. Another mother has a business of delivering fresh cut flowers that she arranges to homes and offices—her clients love the service and love seeing her baby every week. In her book, *The Heart Has Its Own Reasons,* Mary Ann Cahill explores endless possibilities for families who are committed to keeping Mother (or at times, Father) available in the home to nurture the children (see Bibliography).

WORKING OUTSIDE THE HOME

If having a home business is not possible for you, you may want to consider some other alternatives.

Part-time work.   Part-time work has been the greatest change in the working world in the past decade. There is an ever-expanding market for part-time workers because, according to industrial studies, part-time workers offer employers increased efficiency but require fewer financial obligations and fringe benefits. Part-time work is often more attractive to the woman who *wants* to work than it is to the woman who has to work.

A client of mine who switched from full-time to part-time work said, "Full-time work was too much for my baby; full-time at home was too much for me."

Flex-time work.   Flex-time is part-time work with flexible hours. Flex-time allows the mother to adjust her hours to be at home when her child is sick or has a special need.

Shared jobs.   This type of work arrangement requires the cooperation of two people, each sharing the work of one full-time job. Both parents may share the responsibilities of one job, or two mothers may agree to "cover" for each other when their children have special needs: "I'll work for you if your child is sick, and you'll work for me if my child is sick."

Let's suppose an anxious mother comes to me and says, "I have prayed about this decision and have sought counseling. I have decided that for my personhood and our own family situation, it's best for me to return to my previous career, even though my baby is only three months old. But I want to be a good mother also. I need help." What do I tell her?

I take the Christian approach of offering constructive advice and exploring alternatives instead of imposing destructive guilt. In such cases, I assure mothers that since continuing the attachment relationship is most important, breastfeeding is a positive way to do this.

135

Efficiency Tips for the Working Mother

If you must work outside the home, the following tips will help you continue your good mothering and indirectly benefit your career.

Plan ahead.   Organization is the key to efficient working and mothering. Working outside the home does not allow you much time for cooking and housekeeping. Sit down with your husband and plan menus and chore-sharing so your quality time with your child is not diluted by hours spent on household duties.

You can breastfeed and work.   Many mothers would consider breastfeeding and working incompatible. On the contrary, I especially encourage a working mother to breastfeed because this gives her a special tie to her baby and alleviates some of the disappointment of having to leave the baby to go to work.

Some suggestions for breastfeeding while working include:

1. Encourage a long breastfeeding before you go to work, when you return home, and when you put the baby to sleep, depending upon your working hours. Be available and open to other shorter nursings "on demand" throughout the time you are together. Be prepared for some night nursing.

2. Avoid engorgement. When your breasts feel full, manually or with a pump express your milk to avoid uncomfortable engorgement and a possible breast infection. Store it in a refrigerator or a cooler for the next day's use. You can store your breast milk in an ordinary refrigerator-type freezer for two weeks and in a deep freeze (zero degrees Fahrenheit) for many months. You have a right to request time out from work or a somewhat extended coffee break to pump your milk at least once while at work. Twice is better in terms of having a better milk supply.

3. If you do not work far from home, have your baby-sitter bring your baby to you a couple of times during the day for breastfeeding, or go home at lunch time for a nursing.

4. Some major corporations have day-care centers in the building so that mother and baby can be within nursing distance of each other. You have a right to this time off to express milk or breastfeed. A doctor's prescription can be obtained if necessary; in cases where the employer has objected, the courts have upheld the mother's right to breastfeed her baby while on the job.

5. Expect your baby to nurse several times during the night and more frequently on weekends when you resume full-time mothering. This is a realistic expectation, but you will be understandably tired.

6. Advise your baby-sitter of your expected time of arrival at home, and advise

him or her not to feed your baby during the last hour before that time. In this way your baby will eagerly take your breast as soon as you arrive. The first hour after you arrive home should be a special time of closeness and breastfeeding, a time to be reunited with your infant without any interference from telephones or pressing household chores. Take the phone off the hook, put your feet up, turn some music on, and settle down to nurse your baby. This is also a well-deserved time to unwind from a hard day's work.

FATHER FEELINGS AND WORKING MOTHERS

Fathers, be sensitive to the dilemma facing many of today's mothers. Job satisfaction is equally important to them. It can be difficult for a woman to give up using her hard-earned college degree to stay at home and be a full-time mother. This change of status is especially difficult for the woman who has had an exciting career outside the home before settling into her career inside the home.

It's not easy for a woman to be thought of constantly in reference to somebody else, as somebody's wife or as somebody's mother. What about the woman as a person in relation to herself alone? She isn't really a "self alone" anymore, and neither is her husband. The two became one flesh when they married. They both gave up some of their individual personhood to the relationship.

As a sensitive, caring husband, you should be mindful of these feelings that your wife will probably have at some time during her early adjustment to mothering. Give her positive reinforcement. Convey your consistent love for her as a person, a wife, and a mother. Constantly give her the message that she is doing the most important job in the world: raising another person for Christ.

A good example of what not to do is portrayed in the movie *Kramer vs. Kramer*. Prior to having a child, both Mr. and Mrs. Kramer had exciting professional careers. After the birth of their first child, as many professional women do, Mrs. Kramer decided to stay home and devote herself to professional mothering. As Mrs. Kramer became more deeply involved in mothering, Mr. Kramer became less and less involved as a father and more involved in his career. Instead of meeting his wife's emotional needs when he was home, he spent most of his time talking about how exciting his career was. Needless to say, Mrs. Kramer became less and less fulfilled as a person, gave up mothering (and the marriage) entirely, and returned to her career outside the home. Only after Mr. Kramer took over the parenting responsibilities did he realize the daily challenges facing a full-time mother. He learned the real value of the term *homemaker*. This is a classic example of what happens when a husband fails to perform his supporting role in God's design for the family.

If the mother works outside the home, the father works more inside the home. Shared child care is a realistic fact of life especially if the mother has a job outside the home. The mother also needs some "down time." Nothing in God's order of the family or in the biological makeup of men says men cannot do housework. If the traditional role of the woman is changed somewhat, the traditional role of the man must also change to meet the needs of the entire family.

Father, pitch in and do your share of housework. Help meet your child's daily needs. Actually, one of the fringe benefits of the working mother has been to bring many fathers back into their homes to get them hooked into fathering and into knowing their children better. Father-involvement and shared child care are especially important if your wife continues breastfeeding while working, and I encourage you to encourage her to do just that.

CHOOSING A BABY SITTER

One of today's great paradoxes is that at the very time when God's design for mother-infant attachment is becoming more and more realized, the demand for substitute care-giving is increasing. You may be greatly disappointed when you search the marketplace for quality substitute mothering and find that the demand is far greater than the supply. Also, substitute care-giving is just that—a substitute, not a replacement for the mother. The following suggestions discuss different options in child care and how to choose a substitute mother.

Baby Sitters Are Substitute Mothers

I don't like the term *baby sitter*. It's too static and unfeeling. Try to find a mother substitute who practices the child-care style you value. Ask leading questions such as, "What do you do when an infant cries?" If you are uncertain about his or her child-care philosophy, say exactly how you want your child mothered in your absence. Be specific: "When he cries, he should be picked up. He should be mothered to sleep. He should be carried around and be in your arms a lot. He should not be left unattended in front of a television set."

Parents, remember, no substitute care-giver has a biological attachment to your child. Don't expect anyone else to have a built-in radar system that intuitively responds to your baby's cues as you do. For this reason you must give your substitute care-giver detailed instruction on how to recognize your baby's cues and how to respond to them. Emphasize the importance of feedback stimulation that is so vital to infant development. When your baby exercises a newly acquired developmental skill, impress upon your care-giver the importance of acknowledging your baby's accomplishments. If no one responds to a developmental skill, a child may be less motivated to exercise that skill. Mothers, spend time together with your baby and the care-giver so he or she can see your mothering modeled.

Use the Same Care-Giver

A child who has various baby sitters will have difficulty forming a love attachment to them. As I have mentioned repeatedly, the ability to form love attachments is one of the major developmental goals of early childhood. Children who are deprived of this consistency may show certain "diseases of nonattachment" that are reflected in aggressive and impulsive or withdrawn behaviors. As your baby learns to talk be prepared for him to call both you and his care-giver "Mama."

Options in Child Care

Toddlers are often more comfortable being cared for in their own homes where they are secure. A one-to-one care-giver-to-child relationship is usually the best for the infant under one year. A rule of thumb is that one care-giver can adequately care for the number of children equal to the number of years, for example, one care-giver per one one-year-old, two two-year-olds, three three-year-olds. The problem with this rule of thumb is that children's needs do not really lessen as they get older, they only change.

If a one-to-one relationship is not economically feasible, try to find a friend with children of a similar age who will care for your child in his or her own home. You also may try the shared child-care arrangement in which a group of three or four working mothers with similar values jointly hire a sitter to come to one of their homes.

Parent cooperative child care is another alternative. Four or five working mothers with similar values arrange to care for each other's children one day a week. Cared for in a home environment, these children are often of similar ages. This arrangement usually requires that you be licensed by the proper authorities if you care for more than one family's children. Some mothers have opened their homes to care for children as a means of supplementing the family's income; some godly mothers even feel that this is their ministry to children. In most cases, home care is preferable to commercial day-care centers.

Tips on Selecting a Day-Care Center

If a day-care center is the only economically feasible option for your family situation, visit the prospective center and look for the following conditions: (1) What is the ratio of care-givers to children? One care-giver to four infants is the maximum you should accept. (2) Examine the credentials of the staff. Determine if they have special training in cognitive development and have realistic expectations of children at various stages. (3) Are they nurturers? Are they genuinely sensitive to a baby's needs? What do they do when a baby cries? Do they understand the difference between chastisement and punishment (see Chap. 16)? (4) Examine the facilities and the equipment. Are they clean, safe, and designed appropriately for the age and the stage of each child's development?

Parents should look for specific qualities in an infant care-giver. When visiting the facility, watch the prospective care-giver in action and examine his or her nurturing qualities. Does he or she look at, touch, and talk to the child with the message of, "I care, I am interested in you as a person with needs, I am sensitive to you"? Does he or she have a working knowledge of the usual developmental milestones and the realistic expectations of children at various stages? Is he or she resilient and able to adapt to the ever-changing moods of some toddlers? Does he or she have a spontaneous sense of humor? This is a real must for coping with toddlers. Watch how he or she handles a child who has gotten out of control. Is he or she kind but firm? Most importantly, observe how his or her Christian values carry over into his or her child caring. Parents should take their children along to the interview and see how their children relate to the care-giver and vice versa. Children are often the best critics of their own care, but unfortunately they often have no voice in that choice. If a child has a certain sparkle in his or her eyes as he or she relates to the care-giver, parents you can be sure that there are meaningful waves of communication going between the care-giver and the child. Unfortunately day-care workers have a very high rate of turnover, so the likelihood of having a consistent care-giver is minimal. For this reason alone, day-care centers are inadequate for the child under three.

I am truly sympathetic with mothers who are faced with the dilemma of a dual career. I assure you that we have struggled with this in our own home and have concluded that difficult problems do not have easy solutions. The ideal cannot always be achieved in today's society, but with prayer and support from your Christian community you can try to come close to that ideal.

CHAPTER 7

NIGHTTIME PARENTING

"Lord, please give me one full night's sleep" is a common plea of an exhausted new parent. How to cope with night waking is probably one of the most common problems new parents face. This problem is frustrating for both parents and doctors. It's frustrating for the doctor who has no answer for how to get *all* children to sleep every night. It's frustrating for the parents who plead, "I've tried everything, and nothing works." Difficult problems do not have quick and easy answers, but there are some suggestions to help parents have realistic expectations of how babies sleep (or don't sleep) and to help both you and your baby get enough sleep.

BABIES' SLEEP PATTERNS

Just as there are wide variations in babies' personalities, there are wide variations in babies' sleep patterns. It is important for you to approach parenting with no expectations, no preconceived images of what a baby should be like, especially about how he should sleep. One tired mother shared with me: "Before our baby came, I thought that all newborn babies did was eat and sleep. All my baby did was eat."

Early in their parenting career, preferably before the birth of their baby, I advise parents to pray an acceptance prayer frequently asking God to guide them in accepting whatever temperament their baby is blessed with and to give them the energy to parent according to the needs of their child. Some parents are blessed

143

with easy sleepers (we have never had one, but I hear about them); other parents are blessed with frequent wakers. In both cases, the parents are blessed to have their child as he is.

You also need to be open to adjusting your parenting style to your baby's needs. If you approach your nighttime parenting with the same style of openness previously discussed in regard to daytime parenting, you and your baby will eventually sleep well and, more importantly, will feel right about it. If you approach your nighttime parenting determined to make your baby fit into a sleep pattern you feel he or she ought to have, you will experience many frustrating and sleepless nights.

Have Realistic Expectations of How Babies Sleep (or Don't Sleep)

Babies' sleep patterns differ from those of adults. Babies don't sleep through the night; they get their days and nights mixed up. They awaken frequently for feedings. One of the first facts of parenting life that new parents should know is that babies do what they do because God designed them that way.

When people fall asleep, they progress through many stages of sleep, from a very light sleep to a very deep sleep. To simplify the explanation, sleep can be divided into two stages: (1) light sleep and (2) deep sleep. Most adults spend the greatest percentage of their sleep time in deep sleep while babies spend most of their sleep time in light sleep.

If you watch your baby sleeping, you can identify easily which state of sleep he or she is in. In a state of light sleep, which is the more active sleep, babies appear to sleep although they are squirming, their breathing movements are somewhat irregular, and sometimes their eyes are only partially closed. If you lifted their eyelids, you would notice that their eyeballs were often moving. In fact, this state of light or active sleep is called "REM," or rapid eye movement sleep. When babies are in a state of deep sleep, their body is much quieter, and they are not easily aroused.

Since your baby is most easily awakened during this period of light sleep, one of the goals of parenting your baby to sleep is to minimize the arousal stimuli during that time. The first few months the average baby sleeps fourteen to eighteen hours per day, but that is not true for every baby. The sleep pattern of tiny babies resembles their feeding patterns—small, frequent feedings and short, frequent naps.

In their first three months, babies' sleeping states are poorly organized because, at that age, the concept of day and night has little meaning to them. A realistic expectation of nighttime parenting is for parents to organize their lifestyles and sleep styles around their baby's. The mother is advised to sleep during the day when the baby sleeps. In the first months, it is much more realistic, especially for the mother, to "sleep like a baby" than to expect the baby to sleep like an adult. As your baby gets older and his or her developing brain becomes capable of inhibiting arousal stimuli, the relative percentage of his deep sleep increases, usually reaching adult levels within two years.

Infants Go to Sleep Differently

Not only are infants' sleep patterns different from those of adults, but their way of going to sleep differs. Adults can "crash" rather quickly. Adults can go directly from the awake state into the state of deep sleep without passing through the initial period of REM or light sleep. Infants cannot do this. They enter sleep through an initial period of light sleep (lasting about twenty or thirty minutes), then enter a period of transitional sleep, and then drift into deep or non-REM sleep. If an arousal stimulus occurs during the initial light sleep, a baby will awaken easily because he never reached the deep-sleep phase. This pattern accounts for the difficult-to-settle baby about whom mothers often state, "He has to be fully asleep before he can be put down."

As babies mature, they begin to go directly to the state of deep sleep. They settle more quickly; they can be put down to go to sleep. This difference in sleep entry explains why infants need to be parented to sleep, not just put to bed to fall asleep on their own. They need to be nursed or rocked to sleep and gentled through this initial phase of light sleep. One of the arts of nighttime parenting is learning how to induce sleep in your baby by gentling him through the REM.

Why Your Baby Doesn't Sleep through the Night

Throughout the night people experience peaks and valleys of light and deep sleep, or sleep cycles. The adult sleep cycle is about twice as long as an infant's (ninety minutes compared to forty-five to fifty minutes). The vulnerable period for night waking is during the transition from deep sleep into light sleep. Since babies have more of these transitions because their sleep cycles are shorter, they are more likely to wake up frequently during the night. One of the ways to minimize night waking, as shall be covered later, is to gentle your infant during these vulnerable periods.

Babies settle more easily as they get older. *Settling* means getting off to sleep easily and staying asleep through the night. The age at which babies settle and their number of hours of straight, uninterrupted sleep vary tremendously from baby to baby. In sleep studies, settling is defined as sleeping from midnight to 5:00 A.M. Expecting a baby under one year of age to sleep through the night from 8:00 P.M. to 8:00 A.M. is unrealistic.

If you are blessed with a somnolent baby, consider this a luxury. As your infant gets older, he or she undergoes what is called "sleep maturity" when the percentage of light sleep decreases and deep sleep increases, and the vulnerable periods of night waking lessen. Some studies show that about 70 percent of babies settle by three months and 90 percent by one year. Ten percent of babies never sleep uninterruptedly during the first two years. Even those babies who settle well may continue to have periodic night waking.

Toward the end of the first year, as your baby's brain becomes more capable of blocking arousal stimuli, both you and your baby will probably enjoy a brief period of an uninterrupted night's sleep. However, just as you feel your baby has kicked the night-waking habit, he or she may begin waking up again. Some children will go to sleep easily and stay asleep; some go to sleep with difficulty but stay asleep; some go to sleep easily but do not stay asleep; and some children want neither to go to sleep nor stay asleep. Fears, separation anxieties, disturbing dreams, and nightmares are the main stimuli for night waking of children from one to three years.

Why Some Infants Are Not Easy Sleepers

Parents, be assured that the maturity of your baby's sleep pattern is not a reflection of your parenting. A baby's sleep pattern often reflects his basic temperament. This may come as a surprise to some parents, but even-tempered babies enjoy a larger percentage of deep sleep. Children who exhibit very active temperaments during the day usually have a higher degree of restlessness and squirming activity during sleep. These high-need babies seem to carry their waking personalities into their sleep, having shorter periods of deep sleep and more frequent night waking. On the surface this would seem to be a mismatch of temperaments and sleep patterns. You would think that the more active babies would need more sleep (at least their parents do). I believe the reason for this paradox is that high-need babies do not have a well-developed stimulus barrier during the day or night.

Night waking may be of divine design.　　The longer I practice pediatrics and the more children my wife and I have, the more I learn to respect the fact that babies do what they do because they are designed that way. Babies do not awaken to annoy or to exhaust the parents on purpose. I feel that God may have designed frequent night waking for young babies for two reasons: (1) survival benefits and (2) developmental benefits.

Night waking may be a survival benefit.   In the first few months, the infant's needs are highest, but his or her ability to communicate these needs is lowest. Suppose your baby had your sleep patterns and enjoyed more deep sleep than light sleep so that he or she was not easily aroused. If he or she became hungry and needed food, he or she might not awaken; if he or she got cold and needed warmth, he or she might not awaken; if his or her nose were plugged and his or her breathing compromised, he or she might not awaken. I feel that a baby's sleep patterns are part of the divine design for the survival of the young of the species in order that the infant may be allowed a state of awareness in which to communicate his or her survival needs.

Night waking may have developmental benefits.   Some prominent sleep researchers theorize that the predominance of light sleep during the first year is important for development of the baby's brain. During the state of light sleep, the brain continues to operate; whereas, during the state of deep sleep the higher brain centers shut off, and the baby operates on the lower brain centers. The theory is that during the stage of most rapid brain growth (the first year), the brain needs to continue functioning during sleep in order to continue developing. As brain development gradually slows down, the infant has less light sleep and more deep sleep. (I have summarized the pertinent scientific studies relating to children's sleep in my book *Nighttime Parenting*, 1987, published by New American Library, New York.)

If tired parents have faith that God has indeed designed babies according to some nighttime plan that has both survival and developmental benefits, they may better accept their nighttime parenting. One day in the office I was consoling a tired mother by offering her the explanation of why frequent night waking may be in accordance with God's design for development of her infant's brain. She responded, "In that case, he's going to be very smart."

Although frequent night waking may be according to God's design for some babies, I also feel that persistent fatigue in both babies and parents may not be. For this reason, I feel that part of the divine plan for nighttime parenting is that parents have the ability to help the baby organize his or her sleep patterns. I firmly believe that God would not have designed a baby with a sleep pattern too difficult for the parents to cope with. Tired parents and tired babies simply do not enjoy the relationship God has intended. For this reason, the following sections offer tips on how to help your baby organize his or her sleep patterns and how to widen your acceptance level and survive your baby's nighttime needs.

Sharing Sleep

One of the earliest decisions for nighttime parenting, and one that is very important to helping your baby organize his or her sleep pattern, concerns where your baby should sleep. Quite honestly, I feel that whatever sleeping arrangement gets all three of you the most sleep and leaves all three of you feeling right is the right sleeping arrangement for your individual family. What works for one family may not work for another.

Sharing sleep is an arrangement whereby you welcome your baby into your bed early in infancy and allow him or her to remain until he or she can sleep alone comfortably. Many Christian parents are confused about the conflicting opinions on this subject. They ask, "Is it all right for our baby to sleep with us?"

This section will present reasons why it is good to sleep with your baby and why it may in fact be according to God's design. My opinion, one that I have formed after much prayer and experience, both personal and professional, is that God intended the young of each species to sleep in close contact with the mother until the baby can comfortably sleep independently. I have advocated the concept of sharing sleep in my pediatric practice for the last twelve years, and we have practiced this arrangement in our own family. It is beautiful! It works! Perhaps this sleeping arrangement does not work for all families at all times, but in my experience it works for most families most of the time, provided it is done with the attitude that God has intended. The baby's sleeping close to or with the parents is a part of the natural continuum from mother's womb to mother's breasts to parents' bed, and weaning from all three places of security should occur only when mother and baby are ready.

The concept of sharing sleep is more an attitude than a decision about where your baby sleeps. It is an attitude of acceptance and mutual trust whereby an infant trusts his or her parents as a continually available support resource during the night just as the infant trusts them during the day. It is an attitude of trust for the parents, too, in that they trust what feels right in parenting their child rather than accept the cultural norms of the country or yield to the dictates of peer pressure. It is often difficult for new parents to listen to and accept the cues of their child about what type of care he or she needs. This is usually because of the many unfounded cultural taboos that have hampered intuitive child rearing and because of the unreasonable fear that they don't want their child to manipulate them.

148

Be open to accepting whatever sleeping arrangement works for your family. If all three of you sleep better with your baby in your bed and you all feel right about it, this arrangement is best for your family. This sleeping arrangement is sometimes called "the family bed." I prefer to call it "sharing sleep" because that implies more than sharing just a *place* to sleep; it also means that parents and babies share sleep cycles and attitudes about sleep.

Help Baby Organize His Sleep Patterns

The previous section established that babies have a vulnerable period for waking up as they pass from deep sleep into light sleep. Since they have these sleep-cycle changes every hour, babies are vulnerable to waking up as often as once every hour. Sleeping with a familiar, predictable person helps baby settle through this vulnerable period and resettle into the next stage of sleep before he or she is able to awaken fully.

In the first year, babies do not have object permanency. When something is out of sight, it is out of mind. Most babies under a year old do not have the ability to conceive mother as existing somewhere else. When babies awaken alone, their aloneness may keep them from resettling into the next stage of sleep without awakening with a stressful cry.

When adults awaken from sleep, they wake in various states of confusion, but they usually can drift into the next state of sleep without becoming fully awake because they know where they are. The security of knowing where they are is often provided by a familiar somebody next to them. For a baby, waking up to a familiar attachment person often smooths the transition from one state of sleep to the next and may keep him or her from waking fully or at least help him or her resettle into the next state of sleep without a great deal of separation anxiety.

When I wake in the morning and gaze upon the contented face of our "sleeping beauty," I can tell when she is passing through this vulnerable period because she often reaches out and touches one of us. When she reaches her anticipated target, a smile appears, and an "I'm OK" expression radiates from her face. Her eyes remain closed, and she often does not fully awaken. This advantage of nighttime parenting can only be realized by being open to your child at night.

Mothers Sleep Better

Parents, you may be surprised to discover that not only does baby sleep better when sharing sleep, but you do too. The reason for this may be summarized by one word—*harmony*. Just as it is important to achieve harmony with your child during the day, sleeping with your baby at night allows this harmony to continue so that baby and mother get their sleep cycles in sync with each other.

When this harmony is achieved, babies awaken their mothers during their mutual light-sleep cycles and sleep during their mutual deep-sleep cycles. Mothers are awakened less often from a state of deep sleep, which is what leads to the feeling of not getting enough sleep. Being awakened from deep sleep by a hungry, crying baby is what makes the concept of nighttime parenting unattractive and leads to exhausted mothers, fathers, and babies.

A "Hormoneous" Relationship Develops

In Chapter 3 you read that the hormone prolactin is possibly the mothering hormone and the chemical basis of God's design for the term *mother's intuition*. Three situations make prolactin increase in your body: (1) sleeping, (2) breastfeeding, and (3) touching or simply being with your baby. Sleeping with your baby allows all three of these situations to occur throughout the night. When your baby shares sleep with you, he touches you and nurses from you, which stimulates the release of more prolactin.

It is noteworthy that it is not nighttime that stimulates prolactin but the act of sleeping itself. This is why mothers are encouraged to take frequent naps and sleep with their babies during the day also.

Mothers who share sleep with their babies and have mastered this nighttime harmony often tell me that as time goes on they seem to need less sleep and feel more rested despite their babies' waking and nursing frequently during the night. Their acceptance and tolerance of nighttime mothering seem to broaden. Could this also be in God's design? Is it possible that the increased prolactin (which I also call the "perseverance hormone") could be responsible for the increase in tolerance in nighttime mothering?

There are probably many beneficial effects of sharing sleep that are in the divine design that is not known about yet. Some researchers have even suggested that mothers' and babies' sleep and dream cycles and brain wave patterns are in unison when they sleep and nurse together. Science is just beginning to confirm what God has designed and intuitive mothers have known all along—that something good happens when babies and mothers share sleep.

Breastfeeding Is Easier

When baby and mother are in close proximity they can meet each other's needs often without either one's becoming fully awake. A mother who had achieved this nighttime nursing harmony with her baby shared the following story with me: "About thirty seconds before my baby wakes for a feeding, my sleep seems to lighten and I almost wake up. [She is entering her phase of light sleep.] By being able to anticipate his feeding, I usually can start breastfeeding him just as he begins to squirm and reach for the nipple. Getting to him immediately keeps him from fully waking up, and then he drifts back into a deep sleep right after nursing."

What happens is that the baby probably nurses through the vulnerable period of awakening and then re-enters the state of deep sleep. If mother and baby had not been near each other, the baby would probably have had to wake up crying to signify his need. By the time the mother reached the baby in another room, both mother and baby would have been wide awake and would have had difficulty settling back to sleep.

"My baby wants to nurse all night" is a common concern of nighttime mothering. This occasional "marathoning" also may be in accordance with God's design. Babies have periodic growth spurts during which they need extra nighttime nutrition. It is interesting that one of the oldest medical treatments for the slow weight-gaining baby is the simple advice, "Take your baby to bed and nurse."

May Be Advantageous in Child Spacing

In my experience, natural family planning in which breastfeeding is used as a contraceptive seldom works unless mothers and babies share sleep. (For a complete discussion on natural family planning see Chap. 13.) If you believe in a divine design for child spacing, it follows that the concept of sharing sleep also may be part of God's design.

May Prevent SIDS

The current theory is that Sudden Infant Death Syndrome (SIDS) may be a basic disorder of sleep in some infants. Researchers feel that SIDS may be due to the inability of some infants to breathe automatically during the state of deep sleep or to arouse from sleep and trigger a self-start mechanism in response to a breathing problem. My hypothesis is that nursing and sharing sleep may prevent SIDS in certain high-risk infants. I have presented this hypothesis at scientific meetings in order to stimulate research in this area. Sharing sleep and nursing increases mutual sensitivity between mother and baby. This arrangement also increases the amount of REM (Rapid Eye Movement) sleep which acts as a protective state against breathing failure. During shared sleep mother acts as a respiratory pacemaker to remind baby to breathe. (For further reading on this very sensitive topic, the reader is referred to my book *Nighttime Parenting*.)

DISPELLING MYTHS

In the following section some of the popular myths concerning sleeping with your baby will be explained and hopefully dispelled.

Myth One. "Doctor, won't she become dependent and never want to sleep alone?" Answer: yes and no. Yes, your baby will seem dependent temporarily and will not want to leave your bed. This is natural. When you are close to someone you love and you feel right about it, why give up a good thing? It's a question of trust, not dependency. Your infant trusts that you will listen to his other cues, and you trust your ability to respond appropriately to these cues.

No, your baby will not grow up to be more dependent. Your baby will eventually sleep alone; however, the age at which a child goes from oneness to separateness varies from child to child. What is important is that you allow your child to go from oneness to separateness on the terms that feel right for both of you, not according to some preconceived time chart determined by peer pressure or child care advisors. In my experience, children who are given free access to sharing sleep actually become more secure and independent because they reach their stage of separateness when they are ready and are not hurried into separate quarters too soon.

Another consideration is that it is not the parents' responsibility to make a child independent. Parents should create an environment of security that allows the child's independence to develop naturally, rather than grudgingly.

Myth Two. "Won't we have sexual disturbances?" Nonsense! Absolutely not! This may be the bed where he was conceived. How can love between two parents adversely affect the product of their love? As a father of seven who has practiced the concept of sharing sleep, I do not think our babies have "come between us" that much.

Usually parents have the wisdom to be discreet about how much affection they show each other in front of their child at any age. A child should not come between husband and wife. The concept of the family bed and the family bedroom requires some ingenuity toward having a private place for husband and wife to be together.

152

The master bedroom is not the only place for lovemaking to occur. Couples who have successfully enjoyed the concept of the family bed have humorously related to me that every room in the house is a potential love chamber. This attitude probably leads to more variety in the couple's sexual relations. Also it is usually not difficult, if you and your husband wish to be alone, to request kindly but firmly that your child leave your bedroom "because Mommy and Daddy want to be alone for a while." I feel it is healthy for a child to get two messages concerning the master bedroom: (1) the door is open to me if I have a strong need to be with my parents, and (2) there are private times when Mommy and Daddy want to be alone that are nonnegotiable. Again, it is the attitude within the bedroom that counts to the child, not the actual timing of physical relations.

Myth Three.   "I might roll over on my baby and smother him." This is one of the oldest myths and does indeed disturb some parents; therefore, I will attempt to alleviate your fears with a thorough explanation of the subject. The biblical verse that has contributed to this myth is 1 Kings 3:19, "And this woman's son died in the night, because she lay on him." This could have been a case of sudden infant death syndrome. In early days the concept of SIDS was not fully understood and was erroneously interpreted as smothering.

Where there have been reports of babies being overlaid there has been an unusual element such as a drugged or drunk parent or too many persons squeezed into too small a space. If the account in First Kings was actually an overlaying, remember these mothers were prostitutes so conditions were far from ideal and may have involved drunkenness or crowding (1 Kings 3:16).

Safety tip! Besides one or both parents being under the influence of drugs or alcohol and overcrowding, another precaution must be mentioned. When lying on a waterbed face down, an infant may be unable to lift his head clear of the depression that forms, or he may get his head wedged between the waterbed mattress and the bed frame. The firmer "waveless" type would be much safer or use a special covering to firm up the surface.

Mothers I have interviewed on the subject have shared with me that because infants and mothers are so physically and mentally aware of each other's presence when they sleep together, both of them would awaken immediately if overlaying did somehow occur. One mother told me that if her infant were struggling to breathe or had any signs of imminent SIDS, she would want to be by her infant's side. If her infant died by her side, she would feel that she had done everything possible to save her baby. If her infant died in another room, she would always have had the feeling she was not there when her baby needed her and that she might have been able to save his or her life.

Fathers sometimes worry about the possibility of flopping an arm over on baby or being less sensitive to baby's presence. I feel the best arrangement is for baby to be between mother and a guardrail. (See illustration on page 156.)

I make the following statements without offering any scientific documentation to support them; they stem from my pediatrician's intuition regarding sharing sleep. I feel that when a baby and a mother sleep close to each other they have a form of communication even when they are sleeping. Any disturbance in this communication network will be perceived by the mother, and she will awaken to correct the interference in these waves of communication. Experts who study SIDS no longer list overlaying as one of the causes of SIDS.

Myth Four.   "Isn't this an unusual custom? What will people say?" Just the opposite is true. In most cultures from biblical times to present times (1 Kings 3:20; Luke 11:7), babies have slept with their mothers. Even in Western cultures mothers have been following this practice for years but were afraid to tell their doctors and their in-laws about it. If you want to get a feel for how prevalent this custom really is, walk into a meeting of young mothers and confide to one of them, "My baby is sleeping with me. What do you think about this arrangement?" Your confidante will probably look around to make sure nobody else is listening and then whisper back, "My baby is, too, but don't tell anybody."

These mothers are doing what their maternal instinct tells them is right, but because of erroneous cultural taboos they are made to feel that this concept may be morally wrong. Infants' sleeping with their mothers is not a recent fad but an attempt to return to traditional values that time and maternal instinct have proven to be right. Early medical books recommended the family bed. For example, a child care book written in 1840, *Management of Infancy* by A. Combe (New York: Fowlers and Wells), stated that "there can scarcely be a doubt that at least during the first four weeks and during winter and early spring a child will thrive better if allowed to sleep beside its mother's side and be cherished by her warmth than if placed in a separate bed." An East African tribal chief once said, "At night when there was no sun to warm me, my mother's arms and her body took its place."

I predict that the family bed will be practiced more and more until it becomes the usual custom in Western culture. This sleeping arrangement will mature in popularity as will many of the more traditional and time-proven concepts of child care. It is interesting that breastfeeding was unusual in the 1950s in the Western culture. Now many of these "unusual" customs are coming back because, in reality, they never left the intuitive hearts of mothers.

Myth Five. "But my doctor told me not to let our baby sleep in our bed." Parents shouldn't ask their doctors about sleep sharing, and doctors shouldn't give definite yes or no answers. This doctor's response is a carryover from the "dependency pediatrics" of the fifties and sixties when a mother's intuition had been so culturally programmed out that a new mother felt more comfortable taking her doctor's advice than following her own God-given instinct. The doctor was put on the spot to come up with a rather dogmatic answer on a subject for which he had no training. Most doctors elected to join the camp of "separate sleepers" because the detachment and separation philosophy was popular at that time and there was some security in numbers.

There are some aspects of child care on which your doctor does not need to give you advice. Where your baby sleeps and whether or not you should let your baby cry in a particular situation can be answered only by you. When it comes to maternal-infant attachment (see Chap. 5), you should follow your intuition above the advice of anyone else since the other person has no biological attachment to your infant.

Take heart. Some doctors now realize they will have to spend less time correcting sleep problems in children at a later age if they counsel parents on how to prevent sleep problems in their children at an early age. Fortunately, female doctors and the wives of male doctors are influencing the medical profession to promote God-given maternal instincts concerning sleeping arrangements.

FATHER FEELINGS ABOUT SHARING SLEEP

"I want my baby to sleep next to me, but my husband refuses." It is vital to God's order for the family that both husband and wife agree on where the baby sleeps. If this is a problem in your family, let me offer the following advice. Many husbands fall prey to the previously discussed myths. Read this chapter together; listen to the cassette tape "Surviving Your Baby's Sleep Patterns" (for publication information, see the end of this chapter). Pray together asking God to guide you on the best sleeping arrangements for your family. Discuss the advantages of sharing sleep. If God's design for the family is followed, your child should never be allowed to divide you as a couple. This statement may not sit well with some parenting organizations, but I have given this concept of God's order for the family considerable thought and prayer. I have seen disastrous consequences to the whole family result from the "overattachment syndrome" (see Chap. 5).

Father, if you have ambivalent feelings about your baby's sleeping in your bed, I urge you to trust your wife's instinct. This is one instance in which mother knows best. Having the baby sleep between parents concerns some fathers. If this bothers you, let me suggest the sleeping arrangement shown in the illustration below; baby can sleep between mother and a guardrail if you prefer.

Actually, once reluctant fathers get used to sleep sharing, most of them learn to enjoy it. It is an occasion for wonderful closeness that many fathers initially accept and later enjoy. If you consider how little time you spend being physically close to your baby during the day, then nighttime fathering may be a boost to your father-infant relationship. Again, whatever sleeping arrangement gets all three the most quality sleep is the right sleeping arrangement for your family. King-size beds are a wise investment for all new families and are actually cheaper than buying a lot of unnecessary baby furniture that your baby will probably not use or outgrow quickly.

Be prepared for a few humorous situations such as the one we experienced when our baby daughter got her directions mixed up and rolled over to nurse from me instead of Martha. You might also enjoy the experience one father related to me. When he awakes because of some worry, instead of letting his worry keep him from

going back to sleep, he looks over and sees the face of his child sleeping soundly within the security of those who love him. The sight of a peaceful child usually will dispel any worry of the world since it keeps his priorities in perspective.

ARE THERE ANY DISADVANTAGES TO THE FAMILY BED?

Occasionally parents complain that they cannot sleep well with their baby in their bed. There are several explanations for this.

When parents have not welcomed their baby into their bed early enough, neither parents nor baby is used to the arrangement. Most squirmers can be taught to respect other sleeping family members' space by being picked up and put into another room or sleeping location. They soon get the idea that squirming is an unacceptable nocturnal habit.

Parents may try the family bed reluctantly. They may accept their baby into their bed out of desperation: "I'll try any arrangement so we can get some sleep, but I really don't like this idea." A baby senses when he is an unwelcome guest in the family bed. These negative vibrations turn a positive experience into a negative one that seldom works.

Occasionally, a Christian mother who sincerely loves her children will share with me, "I've been with my children all day long; I simply do not want my baby in my bed. This is my special time with my husband alone." This feeling should be respected, and I fully sympathize with this mother's wish.

Most children wean themselves from the family bed by two to three years of age and into their own rooms by three to four years of age. Thereafter they sleep comfortably and independently, returning to the comfort of the parents' bed only during particularly stressful times. Weaning from the parents' bed usually requires intermediate steps, such as a mattress next to your bed for a while or the alternative arrangement of sleeping with an older sibling.

I am absolutely certain that there are no psychosexual disturbances that are caused by sleep sharing. In my opinion, this is God's design for sleeping for most families, but you must be comfortable with it to work for you. If you are having sleep problems within your family, ask God for guidance concerning the right sleeping arrangement.

COMMON SLEEP PROBLEMS

At the beginning of this chapter I mentioned that children have different sleep cycles from those of adults. They are aroused from sleep more easily and have more difficulty resettling. Nighttime is scary for little people who are used to being with or seeing somebody. The following are the most common reasons for children awakening:

1. Physical discomfort—teething, hunger, wet diaper, stuffy nose, ear infection, pin worms, uncomfortable sleeping position, gas pains and stomachaches, allergies, kidney infection.
2. Noises—a squeaky crib, environmental noises (barking dog, cars, weather).
3. Emotional disturbances—nightmares, dreams, fears, or separation anxieties.

Some common sleep problems occur at various ages. These usually fall into one of two classes: (1) child not going to sleep, and (2) child not staying asleep. Remember, difficult problems do not have easy solutions. Sleep problems are among the most individual problems in pediatrics. The following proposed solutions may or may not fit your individual baby.

Situation One.   "My baby is six weeks old. She used to awaken only once or twice and then resettle after nursing. Now she awakens every two hours for a feeding, and I have difficulty resettling her. I'm exhausted." Perhaps your baby is going through a growth spurt and needs to marathon nurse. Redefining your daytime priorities is necessary during this temporary marathoning in order for you to catnap during the day and recharge your nocturnal parenting battery at night. Marathon nursing is one instance when it would be wise to welcome your baby into your bed and enjoy nursing there. This relationship will give her more milk during this growth spurt and should interrupt your sleep less.

Situation Two.   "My baby is six months old and waking more often and resettling less well, yet he doesn't seem hungry." At about six months of age, babies are awakened by physical discomforts such as teething, stuffy nose, and the collection of profuse saliva in the back of the throat that usually accompanies teething. Babies begin teething pain between four to six months, and if this pain occurs during the

158

light phase of sleep, they may awaken. The increased mucous produced during teething may lodge in your baby's throat and awaken him. Hunger is also a possibility, but hungry babies usually settle well once fed. The mother should try a long nursing before she goes to bed and then make sure the baby really feeds when he wakes up at night, rather than having a series of wakings in which he sucks just long enough to lull himself back to sleep but does not deal with his hunger. You may have to actually sit up in bed and pick the baby up so he will actively feed long enough to get a full tummy.

Six-month-old babies often do not resettle easily for two reasons. First, they are intensely interested in their environment and want to look around. For this reason, try to keep the lights off and use quiet, soothing words. Second, not seeing the mother he feels and touches all day long may also keep baby from resettling. Remember that your six- to nine-month-old baby might be suffering separation anxiety because he lacks object permanency, a capacity your baby will develop toward the end of his second year.

Situation Three.   "My baby is one and a half years old and awakens happily at 4:00 A.M. ready to get up and play, but I am not." The baby needs some repatterning similar to the baby who won't go to bed. It is unrealistic to put some babies down at 6:00 to 7:00 P.M. and expect them to sleep until 7:00 A.M. Repattern your baby's sleep by delaying her nap until later in the afternoon, keeping her up later in the evening, and mothering or fathering her to bed later. Many mothers confess, "She's not ready for bed at 7:00, but I'm ready for her to go to bed." Realistically, I feel children who are put to bed early miss some meaningful evening time with their fathers.

If repatterning is necessary, the eighteen-month-old to two-year-old child is verbal enough to understand that nighttime is not playtime. Give your child a loving hug, tell her firmly that Mommy and Daddy are going back to bed, and you expect her to do the same. The baby who wakes up for playtime but does not seem to be afraid can be made to understand your policy regarding playtime and sleeptime. You may offer to lie down with your child or let her lie on a mattress next to your bed, or you can convey in some other way that this is not playtime.

Some parents feel they should not have to negotiate or use creative ways to get their children to sleep. They feel it is in their power as authority figures to say when and where the child sleeps. I continually affirm the necessity for a strong authority role for parents, but authority does not mean your mind is closed to what your child is telling you.

Wise authority stems from two-way communication in which you are in charge and reserve the right to make the final decision, but you are still open to listen to your child's cues. Your child should sense your openness. Many parents get hung up by the term *manipulation* and feel that if a child does not sleep at preassigned hours in a preassigned place, then any other alternative the child wishes is manipulation. This is simply not true. I'm horrified by advice that says if a child won't stay in her crib, put a net over her crib so she can't get out. If a child is continuously standing up in her crib, rattling her cage, or climbing out, the message is clear—she doesn't want to sleep in her crib. The parent can insist that she will sleep in the crib, but this leads to unending nighttime struggles in which nobody wins. The wise parent may listen to what the child is actually saying and give the child other alternatives of sleeping arrangements. In my opinion, this is not manipulation. This is communication; this is trust. It is trusting your child that she really should have a say about where she feels right sleeping; it is trusting yourself that you are confidently and appropriately responding to your child's cues.

Situation Four. "My two-year-old is awakening more and more frequently and generally will not stay in his crib. Sometimes when I get up in the morning I find him asleep outside our bedroom door. He's becoming increasingly more difficult to resettle in the middle of the night unless I stay with him." This child is exhibiting separation anxiety and probably has nightmares. By two years of age most infants have achieved object permanency and can understand that mother is in another room. Yet, the child who falls asleep outside the parents' door obviously wants to sleep in the parents' room. Is it too humiliating to parents to listen to their children? Welcome your child into your bedroom, and if his sleeping with you is not an option with which you feel right, give your child a mattress or a sleeping bag next to your bed. At this point you can tell him firmly that if he wishes to sleep in the family bedroom, you expect him to sleep quietly until the morning and not disturb you. Tell him, "If you wake up, you know we're right here and you can go back to sleep."

Most of the time, in return for sleeping in the family bedroom, your two-year-old will keep quiet so he can continue this sleeping arrangement. Being allowed into the family bed or the family bedroom is a real boost to the child's self-esteem. You are conveying to your child the message that he is as important to you during the night as he is during the day.

Situation Five. "My two-year-old just doesn't know when to give up. I know she's tired by her droopy eyelids and her yawning, but she fights going to bed."

160

Some children do not want to put away the excitement of the daytime world. In this case, you should know best, and oftentimes a child is waiting for someone in authority to override her lack of wisdom. Have a quiet hour before a realistic bedtime; instead of energetic activities, try wind-down activities such as reading a soothing story and rocking in a rocking chair. Bedtime rituals are good. A warm bath, a story, and a good-night lullaby make a winning combination to help heavy eyelids overcome busy minds. Fathers should assume the major role in the bedtime ritual.

Situation Six. "It takes my husband too long to put our two-year-old to bed. We have a large family, and we run out of time." This is a common ploy of young children in a large family. Sometimes the only time a child gets one-on-one attention from Dad is at bedtime, and he is going to play this special time for all he can get. Parents need to accept this as a normal attachment phase, and be thankful that their children want to be with them. Do the best you can. One of the realistic expectations of fathering a large family is that he can't give enough time to all his children all the time. I feel that your children and your God will understand this dilemma.

Situation Seven. "My three-year-old is afraid to go to bed alone and wakes frequently with scary nightmares." Children from two to three years of age have vivid imaginations and often distort reality in their dreams; a dog may look like a dinosaur in a dream. Attempt to find out what the scary thing is. It may be something your child saw on TV that day. Make a game out of the situation by saying, "Daddy went into your room and chased out the dragon." This may work well, but I am a little leery of always fighting fantasy with fantasy. Some children may see through this or may think there really are dragons in their rooms. Game playing to alleviate fears and chase out scary animals at least conveys to your child your sympathy and your availability to help. Often children need a parent's continued presence for the "dragon" to be gone.

Situation Eight. "My six-month-old baby wants to nurse at night." The case of the frequent night nurser is one of the most common and most exhausting occupational hazards of nocturnal parenting. Because I'm reluctant to offer advice that might deprive some babies of a basic need, I will attempt to explain why some infants nurse at night and why you should *not* discourage it. I feel that it is God's design for some infants to nurse more at night, and I do not wish to be listed in the Lord's "Book of False Prophets" for bad baby advice, for which some day I may be held accountable.

Babies want or need to breastfeed during the night because they are easily distracted during daytime nursing. Between two and three months many babies become interested in the sensual world around them. They suck a little and look a little, constantly interrupting their feeding because something more interesting comes along. During the day there is often more competition for the baby's and the mother's interest. However, at night the baby has the mother all to himself so that there are fewer distractions for both of them. These nocturnal nuisances are especially common in busy households or in those with breastfeeding mothers who work outside the home during the day. Remember, babies are perfect parasites, and I feel God designed them that way.

Babies learn at a very early age how to get what they need. Some child psychologists would consider night nursing a manipulative behavior, a way of getting what a baby wants—not what he or she needs. In my opinion, most babies nurse at night from need rather than habit.

Situation Nine. "My five-month-old daughter cannot sleep longer than an hour at night, even though she sleeps in our bed. When she wakes she screams or fights and insists on staying awake. Then when she goes back to sleep she tosses and turns. And she can't nap unless I lie down with her the whole time."

Allergies (environmental or dietary) can greatly disturb sleep. The baby may be showing no other signs of allergy, or the fitful sleep may also be accompanied by rashes, colic (or history of colic), fussiness, chronic ear infections, and/or persistent runny nose and puffy, reddened eyes. The profile of this type of night waking includes fitful tossing and turning, crying out, waking every sixty to ninety minutes, crib rocking or head bumping. Often this baby cannot nap for longer than twenty minutes and the mother is exhausted.

Cow's milk proteins in the mother's diet (or directly in the baby's diet if on formula or eating dairy products) is often the culprit. Bovine beta-lactoglobulin has been shown to enter human milk, causing a sensitive baby to have sleep problems. Other protein foods, such as wheat, corn or other grains, certain nuts, shellfish, or egg whites may also be implicated. If she is breastfeeding, the mother must eliminate the offending food from her diet and also from her baby's diet. Start with cow's milk and all cow's milk products (even reading labels to detect whey or casein). Improvement is usually seen within one or two days, although often the symptoms will reappear temporarily around the fifth or sixth day. The food should be eliminated for at least three to four weeks. There may be several offending foods that

162

need to be eliminated simultaneously and then gradually reintroduced on a rotation basis.

Testing for food allergy can be very uncertain and most of the determination will be on a trial and error basis. Consulting a nutritionist or food allergist may be necessary if the mother becomes confused or feels she needs help pinpointing the problem foods. (*Tracking Down Hidden Food Allergies,* by William Crook, M.D., is a helpful book.) She may also need a calcium supplement to be sure she gets the required daily food allowance (RDA) of 1500 mg. for a lactating woman. Environmental irritants such as smoke, feather pillows, molds, mildew, certain laundry products, polyester sleepware, and even some bedroom furniture made with particleboard can be responsible.

Situation Ten. "I have a two-month-old baby whose colic is not getting better and who spits up a lot after feedings. The worst part, though, is the way she wakes with painful cries at night. She seems OK as soon as I nurse her, and she goes back to sleep well, but then the whole thing starts all over again. We have tried everything, and there is no relief."

A newly recognized cause of night waking is the Pediatric Regurgitation Syndrome. The acidic stomach juices are regurgitating up into the esophagus causing a painful, burning sensation. This syndrome usually includes frequent spitting up and a baby who cries a lot and awakens frequently. Breastfeeding upon night waking relieves the pain momentarily. Occasionally, babies with this syndrome do not actually spit up so that the regurgitation is not observed, and the diagnosis may be missed. Special abdominal X-rays confirm the diagnosis, and treatment is with medications.

Let me share a humorous story that happened when one of our children was enjoying one of her many middle-of-the-night meals. I am a very light sleeper and am easily awakened by unusual sounds. Our rather large Labrador retriever has a habit of drinking out of her water bowl on the back porch with an exceptionally loud slurp. One night this sound occurred, and I jumped out of bed determined to put an end to our dog's nighttime thirst quenching. My wife was quick to inform me that it was not our dog I heard but our baby who was nursing vigorously because she had been particularly distracted from nursing that day. I feel that God has given us all a sense of humor in order that we may survive parenting and our children may survive their parents.

A SUMMARY OF BEDTIME SUGGESTIONS

1. *Consider the concept of sharing sleep.* Sleeping with or close to the parents will prevent or alleviate most sleeping problems in children.

2. *Have a quiet time before going to bed, a time of winding down.*

3. *Parent your child to sleep; don't just put your child to sleep.* A breast (or bottle) and a rocking chair make a winning combination for the tiny infant. Mothers, lie down in bed with your infant, allowing him to fall asleep in your arms and at your breasts. Some babies have to be rocked to sleep before being put down; others like to be put down awake and then mothered or fathered to sleep in your bed and your arms (you may fall asleep before your child does). Encourage the child's favorite bedtime ritual if it is a wind-down not a wind-up activity.

4. *Engage in "back to the womb" activities.*
   a. Give your baby a before-bedtime bath and a soothing massage.
   b. Make sure your baby is covered suitably. Some babies settle better in less coverings that allow them more freedom of movement, but others settle better when they are securely swaddled.
   c. Lie down with your baby and snuggle, cradling your baby in your arms. My wife calls this ritual "nestle nursing." This continuum from a warm bath to warm arms to warm breasts to a warm bed will usually induce sleep.
   d. Use a moving bed such as a cradle or a rocking bed. Rocking in general, whether in your arms or in a cradle, should be about seventy beats per minute, which is the rhythm of the heartbeat your baby has grown accustomed to.
   e. Immediately after putting your baby down to sleep, to avoid protests of succumbing to sleep, lay your hands on your baby's back or head and rhythmically pat his or her back or bottom. Very gradually lessen the pressure of the pats as you notice your baby drift off to sleep.
   f. Adjust baby's sleeping positions. In their first few weeks, tiny infants sleep best on their side. Place a rolled up towel in the crevice between baby's back and the mattress. When baby begins to roll over, putting him to sleep on his stomach is usually the best position.
   g. Play soothing tape recordings of running water or ocean sounds, classical music, a metronome or a clock.

h. Provide a warm fuzzy. Falling asleep on Dad's chest is a warm fuzzy. Tiny babies enjoy this sleeping arrangement when they are small enough not to wiggle off easily, usually during their first two months. A lambskin mat is also a warm fuzzy that babies can get used to and that will condition them to sleep wherever the mat is placed.

5. *Soundproof the sleeping area.* Oil all the squeaks in the crib and put rubber coasters under the crib posts or a rug under the crib.

6. *Run a humidifier in the bedroom,* especially during the dry winter months of central heating.

7. *Be sure all systems are clear*—clear nose, dry diaper, full tummy.

8. *Pray soothing and reassuring prayers* that convey to the child that Jesus will watch over him or her during the night. Sensing the presence of God watching over him or her is comforting to the child who feels that nighttime is a scary, lonely time. Avoid the common scary prayer of "If I die, I pray the Lord my soul to keep." No child should be put to bed with the suggestion that he or she might not wake up.

For more detailed suggestions on getting your baby to sleep, see the reference list at the end of this chapter.

The psychological rationale for allowing babies to cry themselves to sleep is reinforcement: negative behavior if reinforced will continue and if not reinforced will not continue. It sounds nice if parents think that crying is negative behavior, but in many cases this is not true. Crying is baby's language to communicate a need. If a baby's language is responded to during the day but not during the night, the baby may be confused and may experience a feeling of "not rightness" that goes against the goals of parenting mentioned throughout this book. But, you say, "Doctor, this waking up could be a habit, not a need." Yes, I agree. Habits are negotiable; needs are not. If your baby's cries are reaching increasing intensity and your inner parenting voice says this is a need you must satisfy, then listen to yourself first and not a book or an advisor. If your baby's individual cries wind down shortly after they begin and your inner parenting sensor is not heavily signaled, then this is probably a habit. Habits are easily broken; needs are not. But the difference is often difficult to discern. (See Chap. 8 for further discussion of why babies cry.)

THE EXHAUSTED-MOTHER SYNDROME

You may gather from this discussion that I favor nighttime parenting. I do. It's part of the investment in your child's trust relationship with his care-giver and his emerging sense of feeling right and of self-esteem. However, mothers may reach a point where their maternal reserves run out and negative feelings toward their child set in. When giving of herself at night compromises her effectiveness as a mother during the day, the entire mother-child relationship suffers a net loss. Her marriage may be strained, too. If you are a mother who has reached this point, your need for sleep takes priority over your child's needs for nocturnal parenting. This is a difficult decision. Sometimes I step out on a limb and advise a tired, exhausted mother that for the benefit of the entire family, her need to sleep must come first. I also preface my advice by stating: "This is a problem in which you are not going to like any of the solutions, but you must try something in order to recharge your mothering reserves."

Survival Tips

Shift work.   For a couple of nights the father gets up with the baby, rocks the baby, walks with the baby, gives a bottle if bottle fed, and if nothing else works, takes the baby for a car ride. Meanwhile, the mother sleeps (or tries to). If she is breastfeeding and the baby is not settled after feeding, and hunger is not the obvious cause, then the father should rock, walk, or burp the baby while the mother goes back to sleep. Certainly if the mother has a job outside the home during the day, both parents should share these nocturnal interruptions.

Sedatives.   This solution is unpopular, but it is certainly worth a try when you have reached the end of your rope. Sedatives, if used for only a few nights, will not harm your baby or be addicting (long-range usage is addicting and sedative-induced sleep is usually not the highest quality sleep). Ask your doctor for a sedative for your baby to be used for two or three nights in order to reset his sleep cycles and allow you to recharge your battery. You may need to try several different sedatives in varying dosages before you find one that works. Again, I recommend this only after you have tried everything else and have reached the honest decision that your need for sleep takes precedence over your baby's need for nocturnal parenting.

Letters from Tired Parents

Because sleep problems are one of the greatest occupational hazards of early parenting, I want to share some letters from mothers who have written to me concerning various sleeping arrangements for various family situations. I hope you are able to identify with some of these mothers and profit from their advice.

Dear Dr. Sears,

After the birth of my first baby I went through an experience that I was in no way prepared for: postpartum depression. The tension and stress I felt from suddenly becoming a new mother caused me to actually be scared of my baby at times. Compounding my tensions was the thought that since I'd be returning to work soon I felt like I would be "abandoning" my baby. All of these doubts and uncertainties were manifested in a bout of insomnia that stretched for four days.

I'd lay my baby in her crib at night, then go to my room and just pray that I would get some sleep before she woke up for her next feeding. This was a bad mistake. While I tried to force myself to relax I was aware of every turn, gurgle, and sigh that she was making in the next room. [Mother and baby were not in harmony.]

By the time I called my pediatrician I was desperate for help. He suggested that I bring her into bed with me at night. I tried it, and although I was slightly nervous at first, afraid I would roll onto her, I quickly found that I was able to sleep and relax when she was next to me. I also think that having a family bed has brought us closer together as mother and daughter. [They are now in harmony.] Spending the night together, holding her and then breastfeeding her when she wakes up has made me feel less uncomfortable about leaving her with a sitter during the day. Besides, like my husband says, what better way to start a day than to wake up with your lover and your child next to you.

Dear Dr. Sears,

There were many reasons why we decided to have our baby sleep with us. Although there were some problems, we have been able to overcome them. My husband was afraid that he would roll over on her, but he never did. Friends told me that the romance would go out of our marriage if we had a baby sleep with us. If anything, I think it has made us more loving. We know she is safe and she has us there if she needs us.

167

We did run out of room as she got older. That problem was solved by attaching a one-sided crib to our bed. We removed one side of a crib and adjusted the mattress to the level of our mattress. Now she loves to go to her "bed" and get tucked in. She can still see us and crawl to us if she needs to. Having her with us has made nursing a breeze.

She almost never cries at night or, for that matter, during the day. She and her father are very close. Occasionally she still will fall asleep on his stomach. All in all, having her with us has been great. We feel good knowing she is secure and not lonely. More importantly, she knows we are there for her if she needs us. We will miss her when she goes to her own bed.

The following letter illustrates how a couple incorporated their nighttime parenting into their general style of attachment parenting.

Dear Dr. Sears,

After meeting our six-month-old son, his grandfather was impressed that John seemed so secure and well-adjusted. This was an encouragement that our parenting principles are on the right track.

Our pregnancy was entirely positive, with my husband participating in every way possible. Childbirth classes were taken seriously . . . homework included. A number of people had "prepared" us for the "terrible" experience labor was to be; consequently we were happily surprised to have a very positive birth. As a couple, those hours during labor and birth brought us the closest we had ever been, and I felt I was literally watching the two of us become a family.

Our baby roomed-in with me in the hospital, creating a special three-day private family time for us. The first weeks of parenting did not bring the tension between us that we had been warned about. This baby was someone we both had planned for and wanted very much, and we were ready to pour ourselves into the little life.

Totally breastfeeding and nursing our son on demand encouraged us to try the family bed; a big plus is not getting out of a warm bed several times a night to feed the baby, and we have fine-tuned our nursing techniques so that now neither Mom nor baby fully wakes for a feeding.

My husband was to be the barometer in this relationship. Wanting to respect his feelings, we decided that if he thought it was not working out, we would get a crib. We don't have one yet. All three of us enjoy the closeness, and we rest secure knowing John is OK—warm, right next to us, and easy to find in the dark. In anticipation of a large family, we are making plans for a larger bed. John rarely wakes up crying in the morning. He is content and happy, a nice way to start each day.

On particularly demanding days, I appreciate nursing, knowing that if John were bottle fed, I would tend to bottle propping. This way I must sit down and spend some time touching and holding him. I cannot compromise my responsibilities.

We travel together almost everywhere. As a twosome my husband and I were very devoted, and bringing our son with us now is the natural extension of our loyalty. We find we like to be together and have not as yet wished for the proverbial weekend away.

My husband and I feel very positive about the way we parent, and we work hard at being a couple as well. Unfortunately, people's opinions and comments do matter. We dislike hiding the fact that we sleep together or nurse on demand in order to avoid judgment. We view all the advice given us as unfortunate and negative. It does not sit well with us; we do not see any error in our ways, and we do not run out to engage a baby-sitter. Deep inside we "know" to continue as before, but closer to the surface I panic. (Are women affected more by others' opinions than men?)

When someone suggests that "we must let our baby know where he stands" and "make certain he is not running our lives," it leads to self-doubt. Until it is brought to my attention, it doesn't even occur to me that I may be taken advantage of. If I don't feel right about leaving him in certain situations and he doesn't like to be left, are we both wrong? If I leave him at someone else's recommendation and we're both miserable, who benefits?

Ultimately, I know that the wisdom that we parents need must come from the Lord. Though people may err in offering damaging advice, I, too, err in putting so much stake in their words. Perhaps God allows this to teach me to trust Him, and to underscore the importance of having His Word dwell richly in my heart. As I continue to grow in Him, my confidence will be increasingly in Him, and when questions arise regarding parenting, I'll know who to ask.

This chapter has barely skimmed the surface of what is a very difficult problem in parenting. For this reason, the following references are recommended to parents who are struggling to develop a style of nighttime parenting:

Surviving Your Baby's Sleep Patterns by William Sears, M.D. (Ventura, California: Vision House, 1984). This hour-and-a-half cassette tape contains many testimonies from tired parents in my practice who have also used the power of prayer to make it through the night. This tape is available from Vision House, 2300 Knoll Drive, Ventura, California 93003.

The Family Bed by Thevenin Tine. This two-hundred-page book presents the author's experience and study of the advantages of sleeping with your baby. It is available from the author at P.O. Box 16004, Minneapolis, Minnesota, 55416.

Nighttime Parenting—How to Get Your Baby and Child to Sleep by William Sears, M.D. (New York: New American Library, 1987).

CHAPTER 8

HOW TO RESPOND TO YOUR BABY'S CRIES

"**S**hould I let my baby cry?" is one of the most common questions new parents ask. More wrong advice is given by the Christian community about this question than about any other aspect of parenting. To illustrate the confusion, let me share the responses to a questionnaire I recently sent to a group of Christian parents.

The questionnaire pertained to parenting styles. One of the questions was, "What advice do friends and relatives give you about what to do when your baby wakes up crying in the middle of the night?" Most of the parents answered that they received restraint parenting advice: "Let him cry it out"; "She must learn to be independent"; "Don't pick her up, or you might spoil her"; "You are creating a habit if you come every time he cries."

In response to the question, "How do you feel about the 'let your baby cry' type of advice?" I received the following answers: "I can't let her cry when I know that I have the means to comfort her"; "It goes against my instinct"; "It just doesn't feel right to me"; "It would drive me nuts if I let him cry"; "I feel so guilty if I let her cry."

The difference between what parents hear and what they intuitively feel illustrates that there is a lot of confusion about how to respond to a crying baby. In this chapter, I will present what I feel is God's design for this special type of communication.

A BABY'S CRY IS A BABY'S LANGUAGE

A mother once said to me, "If only my baby could talk, I would know what she wants." I responded, "Your baby can talk, you just have to learn how to listen." Throughout the Old Testament are more than one hundred references to how people communicate with God through crying. Psalm 72:12, for example, says, "He will deliver the needy when he cries." In these biblical passages crying conveys need and a trust that crying will be heard.

The crying communication between a mother and her baby is very similar to the cries throughout Scripture. A baby has genuine needs. When he calls out to someone whom he trusts, he confidently expects an appropriate response. This section will show you how to develop this communication network so that an appropriate response to your baby's cry benefits both you and your baby.

Develop a Sensitivity to Your Baby's Cries

In their first few months, babies cry a lot because they need a lot. Their needs are high, but their ability to communicate them is low. When they are three to four months old, babies are attempting to adjust to their new environments. During this adjustment period, they are very sensitive; some are more sensitive than others. Babies who have difficulty adjusting to their new environments are called "fussy babies," "colicky babies," or, as I like to call them, "high-need babies." Sensitivity characterizes these babies. They signal their normal biological needs and their sensitivities by crying. The key to modifying their behavior is for their parents and other care-givers to develop their own sensitivities.

Every new mother has a built-in receiver to her baby's cries. The more she allows herself to respond spontaneously and promptly to her baby's cries, the more sensitive she becomes to her baby. And the more sensitive she becomes, the more intuitively she responds. When a mother says to me, "I can't stand to let her cry," she is showing that she has built up her sensitivity.

Becoming a sensitive parent is an indication that you are becoming a sensitive Christian. Part of your development as a Christian is to become sensitive to others' needs. If someone is in need and is hurting, your inner sensitivity drives you to respond to that person's need. The compassion of Jesus is a recurring theme in Scripture.

The physiological changes that occur in a new mother's body when she hears her baby cry further illustrate that it is God's design for her to respond promptly to her baby's cries. In response to her own baby's cries, the blood flow to a mother's breasts increases, often accompanied by the urge to nurse. This is a biological clue that God designed a mother to pick up her baby (and usually nurse him) when he cries.

How a mother and baby develop their crying communication network is a forerunner to building another important aspect of their relationship: trust. Their trust is interrelated: the baby trusts his mother to respond to his cries; the mother trusts her baby to communicate his needs; and she learns to trust her ability to meet his needs.

How to Trust Your Response to Your Baby's Cries

The more you exercise a skill, the more skillful you become; the more promptly and appropriately you respond to your baby's cries, the more confident you become in your ability to comfort your baby. When a mother picks up and nurses her crying baby, she will observe the peaceful feeling her prompt response gives her baby. This immediate gratification of her consoling efforts creates a feeling of rightness within her. This further increases her confidence and trust in herself.

To reassure parents of high-need babies it must be stated that some babies are not as easily consoled as others, not because of their parents' abilities but because of their own sensitive temperaments. If a baby does not stop crying when she is picked up and consoled, a new parent's confidence is absolutely shaken. Some very sensitive babies cry a couple of hours each day of their first few months, no matter how experienced their care-givers are. If you have been blessed with a baby whose cries are not easily consoled, God will give you the strength and ability to console your sensitive baby, providing you do not interfere with His design. The conditions of this design are that you continually remain open to your baby and promptly respond to his cries. Eventually you will be able to supply the comforting measures necessary to meet your baby's demands.

Parents who persevere through prayer eventually can comfort their babies. One mother of a high-need baby shared with me, "When he becomes unglued, I now feel I can help him pull himself back together. It has been a long, tough struggle, but I feel I am finally beginning to cash in on all my efforts." This mother is saying that she trusts herself because she has let herself be open to the conditions that allowed her trust to develop.

173

What Can Your Baby Expect?

Because the mother and father are learning to trust their parenting abilities, the baby is learning trust also. Trust is a prime determinant for developing harmony in the parent-child relationship. The more you trust your infant's signals, the more he learns to trust them. By your believing that your baby cries because he has a need, not because he is manipulating you, your infant trusts that you trust his cues. The more you respond to his cues, the more he trusts his developing ability to signal his needs. This trust is the forerunner of his developing self-esteem.

Put yourself in your baby's place. When his cries are answered, he probably feels, "I trust that my cries will be consistently, predictably, and appropriately responded to; therefore, I am a special person. When I cry, someone listens. Therefore, my message must be getting through."

HOW TO RESPOND TO YOUR BABY'S CRIES

From the day she is born, regard your baby's crying as communication, not as a habit to be broken. This starts your parent-baby communication network off on the right "ear." Be open to your baby; take a risk. With time, your ability to interpret your baby's cries will get easier and easier because you have allowed yourself the openness to let this communication network develop the way God designed it to work.

You may take a little longer to interpret your baby's cries, and your baby may take a little longer to respond to your comforting measures, but you two will get together as long as you do not do anything to interfere with God's design for the natural development of this special communication network. When your baby cries, respond spontaneously, intuitively, and freely to the first little blip that comes in on your radar system.

If you feel the urge to analyze your response to your baby's cry in a given situation, analyze your response after and not before you respond. If you wait until you have figured it out, you take this beautiful communication network out of the realm of an intuitive art and put it into a science, and the science of "cryology" simply does not exist. A baby's cry is her own unique language. No two people talk the same, no two babies cry the same. No two mother-baby units are wired the same.

The After-Cry Feeling

After you have responded intuitively to your baby's cries, examine your feelings. If you feel right, then you made the right decision and responded appropriately. If you have not responded appropriately, you will not feel right. The feeling of rightness or nonrightness after you respond to your baby's cries is part of a crying-consciousness that goes into your maturity as a parent.

To understand this concept, consider your crying-consciousness to be similar to an inner computer in which a certain stimulus, your baby's cry, is matched with a certain response, your quickness and appropriateness of response to his cry. Picture yourself with several response buttons that are labeled (1) red alert, respond immediately; (2) hold off a bit; and (3) sit tight, grin and bear it. When you press the response button that matches your baby's crying signal, your feeling of rightness is like an "OK" light that comes on in your computer. If the stimulus-response network is not in harmony with your baby, a feeling of unrightness is the result and a sort of "guilt" light comes on. This accounts for feeling guilty when you let your baby cry. It is a healthy guilt that means you have developed an inner sensitivity, a crying-consciousness that has told you your response was not appropriate and needs to be refined.

I feel that God puts this crying-consciousness into a mother for the survival of the baby and the development of the mother. It is the unwillingness to listen to this crying-consciousness that gets new parents in trouble.

How you respond to your baby's cries in the middle of the night is an example of this crying-consciousness. Suppose your baby awakens from a very deep sleep. This usually means that the stimulus that is waking him is very strong. As a result, he cries a piercing "I need immediate attention" kind of cry. Your "red alert" or jump-up-and-respond light goes on; you settle your baby, and everybody feels right about it.

Another type of middle-of-the-night cry is the settling cry a baby makes when he is in transition from one state of sleep to another or when he is adjusting his sleeping position. This cry is usually of low intensity and is neither unsettling to your baby nor alarming to you. The cry lasts a few minutes and quickly diminishes. This type of crying stimulus usually matches well with your "hold off" button, and your baby often settles himself back to sleep without any outside help. Because your stimulus-response network was in harmony, your "OK" light goes on and a feeling of rightness results.

If, however, your baby emits a persistent, high-intensity cry and you press the "grin and bear it" button, you will be left with a feeling of unrightness and your "guilt" light will go on. If this happens, listen and learn from the feeling of unrightness that results, and the next time a similar cry appears, push the right button.

If you continue to push the wrong button, insensitivity results. When it comes to responding appropriately to your baby's cries, no third-party advisor can push the right button for you. Your baby's crying circuitry is wired into your computer, nobody else's.

Repeating this stimulus-response-right-feeling cycle further develops your inner sensitivity and crying-consciousness as you both mature in your relationship.

The Ultimate in Harmony

One intuitive mother who had developed a very sensitive crying-consciousness said to me, "Isn't it a shame that a baby always has to cry to get what he needs." The ultimate design for harmony between you and your baby is for you to be so tuned in to your baby's cues that he does not necessarily have to cry to get attention. The more you follow the attachment style of parenting, the more often you will reach this sensitivity.

Parents who always have their radar systems tuned in toward their babies often can sense when they are hungry just by the looks on their faces or by how they act. Attachment parents are also always on the lookout for stress indicators and often will respond before their older babies start crying. For example, when our baby, Erin, looks up at me with raised arms, she is signaling, "Daddy, pick me up." If I pick her up, no cry results. If I miss her opening cue, next follows a cry. I have never had a particularly high tolerance for a baby's cries. In our home, we have found it much more pleasant to create an atmosphere in which our babies usually do not have to cry to get what they need.

A behaviorist may object that if you pick up a baby every time she lifts her arms to you, you are spoiling the baby. Let me offer an alternative viewpoint. If you respond to your baby's signals before your baby has to cry, you are reinforcing those signals instead; whereas, if you let your baby cry, you are teaching him or her that babies who are left to cry learn to cry harder; babies who are responded to promptly learn to cry better.

Restraint parenting is common, especially in Christian circles. I want to address this issue point by point for the benefit of those who advise new parents to allow their children to cry.

THE PRINCIPLES OF RESTRAINT PARENTING

Leaving babies to cry is a carry-over from the fifties and sixties. Parents in this generation worried that their children would run their lives or manipulate them. Schedules, formulas, and checklists were in vogue. Parents wanted quick and easy answers to difficult child-rearing problems.

This mode of parenting accounts for one of the most popular and, unfortunately, still prevalent pieces of advice concerning the child who wakes up during the night: "Let your baby cry for three nights and on the fourth night he will sleep." Not only does this advice usually not work, but quick-result parenting is an unrealistic expectation.

"You Might Spoil Him"

Spoiling is one of those words that has crept into baby books over the years but never should have. Spoiling implies something has not been attended to properly; it was left alone, put on a shelf and left to rot. Actually, restraint parenting is more apt to spoil children than attachment parenting.

Spoiling originated with restraint parenting, which teaches that if you respond to your child's cries when he is an infant, you will create a whiny child who cries when he doesn't get his way. Several studies have confirmed that infants whose cries are promptly responded to actually cry less when they are older.

"You Must Discipline Your Baby"

Discipline is another goal of the "let your baby cry" advice. This idea is also a carry-over from the sixties when discipline was confused with control. If you responded promptly to your baby, your baby was controlling you, and you were losing your authority.

Many Christian parents were drawn to this concept of control. Books on how to discipline children flooded the Christian book market, and if someone wanted to be guaranteed a large audience to a talk on parenting, the speaker would always put *discipline* in the title. Parents cried (especially those who practiced restraint parenting), "I don't know how to discipline my child." What they really were saying was, "I don't *know* my child." They had restrained themselves from listening to their babies' cries, had failed to communicate with them, and were unable to establish discipline.

177

"It's Good for a Baby's Lungs"

Another bit of erroneous advice is that crying is good for a baby's lungs. To my knowledge, crying has no beneficial effect on a baby's lungs. In fact, some babies often turn blue when crying hard, and older children may hold their breath and faint while crying uncontrollably.

NEGATIVE EFFECTS OF RESTRAINT ADVICE

Restraint advice goes against a mother's instinct. A mother is not designed to let her baby cry, and a baby is not designed to be left to cry. When God's design for this crying-consciousness is not followed, disharmony results in the mother-baby relationship. Mothers, have faith in your God-given instinct. If any advice runs counter to your inner feeling of rightness about a certain piece of advice, don't follow it.

There may be in every person an instinct to respond to a crying baby. Even two-year-olds instinctively respond to the cries of their newborn siblings. For example, a mother brought her twenty-two-month-old daughter and her one-month-old baby for a well-baby exam. As soon as the newborn baby began to cry, the older child pleaded, "Quick, Mommy, pick baby up." The mother then said to me, "She always feels this way. I can't get to her baby sister fast enough."

Restraint Advice Is Presumptuous

When a mother has been advised to let her baby cry, other people are presuming that they know why her baby is crying. But they don't. They are presuming that the baby is crying to manipulate or to annoy and that he really does not need to cry. This is unfair and untrue. Others are presuming that nothing is really wrong with the baby, but they do not have the facts to warrant such a conclusion. They are also presuming that the mother would be better off if she let the baby cry, which is also untrue. Finally, they are presuming to know better than the mother knows why the baby is crying. This is not true, since they probably have no biological attachment to that baby and are not near him at 3:00 A.M. when he cries. Outsiders have neither a harmonious nor a "hormoneous" relationship with that baby. In essence, they do not qualify as baby advisors. This kind of advice is unfair to the baby, unconstructive to the mother, and basically unchristian. "Be kind to one another" (Eph. 4:32).

I do not wish to offend the new parents' friends or relatives who may be reading this section. I am sure you mean well and sincerely care about the well-being of both mother and baby, but I wish you to consider the effects of your advice before offering it. Keep in mind that the new parents, especially the mother, are vulnerable to any child-care advice because they love their child so deeply. Their love is coupled with natural concern that they do not do anything harmful to their baby. Even though allowing their baby to cry goes against their inner wisdom, they may feel unsettled and think, *We will not be good parents if we don't follow this advice* or *Our child may be affected harmfully if we don't let our baby cry.*

The "let your baby cry" advice is probably the most counterproductive advice in child rearing. It creates within the mother a dilemma and a confusion between what she hears and what she feels. The writers and preachers who continue to teach restraint parenting should reassess whether or not their doctrine is in accordance with God's design.

Restraint Advice Desensitizes the New Parent

I sympathize with parents who fall prey to restraint advice. One day I was sitting in our backyard reading a psychology book on reinforcement of behavior (which indeed is a valid concept as long as one uses discernment in deciding what is reinforcement of negative behavior and what is restraining a response to normal behavior). While I was reading this book, I was generally in a restraining mood toward any child's behavior because this was the topic of the book. Our little one-year-old, Erin, cruised by on her bike and tumbled off into the soft grass. She certainly did not appear to be hurt, but she started whimpering a bit. Her whimper steadily increased to an all-out cry. During the development of this crying syndrome, I was heavily involved in the mental gymnastics of *Is she crying because of habit or need? Will I be reinforcing negative behavior? Will she be manipulating me?* As I was thinking these ridiculous thoughts, Erin looked over at me as only an infant can do, with a look on her face that said, "Dad, cut the psychology. Follow your instincts and come over here and pick me up." I eventually did, and we both felt right. Perhaps Erin was telling me to quit doing so much reading and start doing more intuitive fathering.

Restraint Parenting Encourages Mistrust

If you trust that your child is crying because she has a need, your child learns to trust her ability to give cues and to trust that her cues will be appropriately and consistently responded to. When you use a nonresponding (or nonresponsible) ap-

179

proach, you are using the principles of nonreinforcement: if you do not reinforce the behavior, the behavior soon stops. This is a popular psychological principle that is valid if it is controlled.

Sometimes this principle of reinforcement becomes too behavioristic and bothers me for two reasons: (1) it assumes the baby's crying is negative behavior, which is a false assumption, and (2) this approach may have a damaging effect on the baby's emerging self-esteem. If a baby's action elicits a positive reaction, he is further motivated to develop better communication skills with his responder, meaning that he is motivated to communicate with his care-giver in a noncrying way.

Occasionally a parent will report, "But it works . . . he stopped crying." I have questioned several hundred parents about how they respond to crying, and for the majority, the restraint approach does not work. Let's analyze the possible effects of this restraint on the babies for whom this approach works.

By not responding to your baby when he cries in the night, you are not really teaching your baby to sleep; you are teaching him that his inner form of communication is ineffective. He may fall back to sleep, but he has to withdraw from the disappointment of not being listened to. By not giving in to your baby, you are teaching your baby to give up. I have my doubts about the wisdom of this approach.

Parents who have restrained themselves from responding to their babies' cries often report that when they later pick up their babies, they feel the infants withdraw from them. They sense a feeling of "baby anger." What the babies are exhibiting and the parents are feeling is basically a sense of disharmony, that God's design for parent-infant response was ignored.

RESPONDING AS A ROLE MODEL

Responding to your crying baby models a parenting style for your older children. How they see you parent a new baby has a great effect on their own future parenting styles. The importance of modeling became evident to us one day when Martha and I were in the kitchen and we heard our nine-month-old daughter, Erin, crying from our bedroom. As we started toward the bedroom, we heard her crying stop. When we reached the bedroom, we saw a beautiful sight: our sixteen-year-old son, Jim, a big, athletic boy, was lying down next to Erin, gentling and consoling her. Why was Jim doing this? Because he had learned from us that when a baby cries, someone listens.

180

CHAPTER 9

THE FUSSY BABY ALIAS THE HIGH-NEED CHILD

God has "blessed" some parents with a particularly difficult baby who is known by various titles, such as "fussy," "demanding," or "exhausting." As these babies grow older they acquire additional labels, such as "hyperactive" or "strong-willed." I prefer to call this kind of baby "the high-need child." This is not only a kinder term, but it more accurately describes what these children are like and the level of parenting they need. Since understanding increases acceptance, it is important to understand why high-need babies fuss and why you react the way you do. Also included in this section are some survival tips to exhausted parents.

Do not be too quick to judge from your baby's temperament the person he or she later will become. Many difficult babies turn out to be even-tempered children. There is a wide range of temperaments among babies. This section is to be read as a general guide; some of this advice may apply to you and some may not.

PROFILE OF A HIGH-NEED BABY

I have pulled from my gallery of high-need babies the following personality traits that mothers have shared with me about their babies.

"He is supersensitive."   High-need babies are keenly aware of changes in their

environments. Most babies are endowed with stimulus barriers that allow them to filter out disturbing stimuli and receive pleasant experiences selectively. This process is called "adaptability." Sensitive babies have more permeable stimulus barriers. They startle easily during the day and settle with difficulty at night. These babies appeal to their parents to provide the security and stimulus barriers they cannot provide for themselves.

"I just can't put him down; he wants to be held all the time." These babies crave physical contact and are not known for their self-soothing abilities. New parents often have unrealistic expectations that their babies will lie quietly in their cribs and play attentively with dangling mobiles, gazing passively at interested onlookers. This is certainly not the play profile of the high-need baby. These babies are most content in their parents' arms and at their mothers' breasts.

"He is so intense." Fussy babies spend a lot of energy on their behavior. They feel things more intensely and express their feelings more forcefully. They cry with gusto and are quick to protest if their needs are not met.

"He wants to nurse all the time." The term *feeding schedule* is not in these babies' vocabulary. They need prolonged periods of non-nutritive sucking and do not wean easily.

"He is hypertonic and uncuddly." While most babies mold easily into the arms of care-givers, some high-need babies arch their backs and stiffen their arms and legs in protest at any attempt to cuddle them.

"He awakens frequently." A tired mother lamented, "Why do high-need babies need more of everything but sleep?" These babies carry their general sensitivity into their naptime and nighttime. They seem to be constantly alert as if they have been endowed with internal lights that are always turned on and not easily turned off. Parents often describe their special babies as "tiring but bright." This brightness is usually what keeps high-need babies awake.

"He is unpredictable." Unpredictability is another behavior trait of these special babies. High-need babies are inconsistently appeased. What works one day often does not work the next. One exhausted father exclaimed, "Just as I think I have the game won, she just keeps upping the ante."

"He is demanding." High-need babies are certainly demanding. They convey a sense of urgency to their signals. "Red alerts" dominate their crying vocabulary. They have no respect for delayed gratification and do not readily accept alterna-

182

tives. They are quick to protest if their needs are not met or if their cues have been misread. Their incessant demands account for a common complaint from their parents: "I feel drained."

This profile of the high-need baby may appear to be predominantly negative, but it is only part of the natural history of parenting these special babies. I advise professional counseling for all parents of high-need babies. Those who have had professional counseling and who practice the attachment style of parenting gradually begin to see their babies in a different light and use more positive descriptions such as "challenging," "interesting," and "bright." Parents of high-need babies need to realize that the same exhausting qualities that first seem to be liabilities are likely to become assets for their children. The intense baby may become the creative child; the sensitive infant, the compassionate child; and the little taker may become the big "giver."

THE NEED-LEVEL CONCEPT

A high-need baby can bring out the best and the worst in a parent. I believe that part of the divine design for the parent-child relationship is what I call the "need-level concept," a concept designed to bring out the best in both parent and child.

Every child comes wired with a certain temperament that is determined primarily by genetics and is influenced somewhat by the womb environment. The child also needs a certain level of care proportional to his temperament in order that he fit well into his environment. Some babies need a higher level of care than others. In order to signal the level of care he needs, a baby has the ability to give cues to signal his needs. Part of the divine design is that babies with higher needs give stronger cues. High-need babies come wired with the ability to extract from their care-giving environments the necessary comforting measures to satisfy their needs. For example, a baby who needs to be carried all the time will cry if he is not carried enough. This is how he merits the label "demanding."

Parents should view the term *demanding* as a positive character trait that has developmental benefits for their baby. If a baby were endowed with high needs yet lacked the corresponding ability to signal her needs, her developmental potential would be threatened and her emerging self-esteem would be in jeopardy. I feel high-need babies are naturally demanding in order to extract a level of care needed to reach their maximum potential.

How does a parent measure up to the incessant demands from the high-need baby? Another part of the need-level concept is that the needs a baby signals bring out the nurturing responses of his parents. As babies come wired with certain temperaments, mothers also are endowed with certain nurturing responses. For some mothers, nurturing develops proportionately to their babies' needs. For others, nurturing is not so automatic and needs maturing. I do not believe God would give parents a baby with greater needs than they can meet. This would not fit with the concept of Creator; God's matching program is perfect. Keep in mind God's law of supply and demand: God will supply you with the level of energy you need to meet your baby's demands providing you seek His help in practicing the style of parenting that allows this to happen.

SURVIVAL TIPS FOR PARENTING THE FUSSY BABY

The following survival tips are designed to help you comfort your baby and yourselves.

Don't Feel Guilty

Many new mothers think, *What am I doing wrong?* or *I'm not a good mother,* when their babies are fussy. However, the "goodness" of their babies is not a measure of their effectiveness as mothers. Babies fuss because of their own temperaments, not because of their mothers' abilities.

Your fussy baby can shake your confidence as a new mother and absolutely destroy many of the rewarding aspects of parenting. The less confident you become, the less you are able to comfort your baby's needs and the more inconsolable he becomes. This cycle often results in escape mothering, an unfortunate break in the continuum of parenting. This tendency to want to escape when the going gets tough is often a normal reaction to relieve your guilt and preserve your sanity.

Remember, your responsibility is not to make your baby stop crying—your responsibility is to comfort him to the best of your ability, seeking any means that may help until things get better. Your baby may still cry but you are responding and you are not leaving him to cry alone. Your baby needs you to be strong and to be there for him. He doesn't need you to hush him just because his crying is aggravating or upsetting you.

Try to pinpoint whether his crying makes you feel desperate or helpless or panicked, and try to discover why you may be feeling this way. Your anguish of heart may be rooted in very early pain you experienced when you were left to cry it out as a baby. Take a deep breath, pray, and ask the Lord to heal that. Then, carry on comforting.

My heart goes out to mothers who hang tough in the compassionate care of their fussy babies. Their reward will be great both on earth and in heaven.

Learn to Accept Your Blessing

Parents of fussy babies need to develop a high level of acceptance. In counseling parents of fussy babies I often start with, "You have been blessed with . . ." Quite frankly, by the time many parents come in for counseling they feel anything but blessed and would be happy if God would take their little "blessing" back.

I tell them, "You have been blessed with a baby of high-need levels. God has blessed you with a special child, and He will help you become special parents." In many instances, our Creator has matched the temperaments of mothers and babies so that a fussy baby may have a mother with a high level of acceptance. Occasionally a family may have a fussy baby and a mother with a low level of acceptance. This high-risk situation needs much prayer and consultation.

The law of supply and demand. I have faith in the divine design that God would not bless you with a baby who demands more than you are able to give. Your level of giving will increase if you fulfill the conditions that allow God's design to work, such as the attachment style of parenting covered earlier.

Fussiness is often in the eyes of the beholder. I often refer new parents who feel they have a fussy baby to parents who have coped successfully with a fussy child. After meeting with these parents, the new parents often exclaim, "Praise the Lord, we don't have a fussy baby after all." Parental expectations of what babies are like are often not realistic. When parents understand more about the differences in temperament among babies, they can accept better this aspect of parenting.

Parents of fussy babies often feel a bit disappointed that they have been so blessed. They want to enjoy their babies but often don't. Their babies also want to feel right but don't. As a result, everyone is disappointed. Parents can resort to prayer, support, and counseling to help them adjust, but babies have no recourse but their parents.

Don't compare babies. A Christian mother of a high-need baby confided her feeling to me by saying, "Why can't I handle my baby? Other mothers seem more in control of their babies. They can leave them and get other things done; I can't." I advised this mother not to compare her baby with other babies. The other mothers may not share her views toward attachment parenting. High-need babies are not "better" or "worse" than other babies—just *different*. Besides, many people tend to exaggerate the goodness of their babies. Comparing babies contributes nothing to your relationship with your baby and may lead to frustration and burnout. It is common to have both easy and high-need babies in the same family. Our first three babies were relatively easy, our fourth was high-need. We had to "throw out the books" and start fresh—in fact, this baby inspired me to write a book on the subject—*The Fussy Baby*.

Don't Let Your Baby Cry

One of the most common dilemmas of parents, especially parents of fussy babies, is whether or not to let their babies cry. This problem is thoroughly explained in Chapter 8, but the following will remind you of a few points.

Young babies do not cry to annoy, to manipulate, or to take advantage of their parents. They cry because they have needs. To ignore their cries is to ignore their needs.

A fussy baby is endowed with a high-need level and a low stimulus barrier. Trust in his environment is one of the prime determinants of his eventual personality. An infant who does not receive a predictable response to his signals soon learns not to trust his signals and sometimes not to trust his care-givers. He eventually becomes less motivated to cry and will stop, but at what expense to his self-esteem? In this situation, a high-need baby completely resigns himself to a lower level of care.

Yes, babies are adaptable and resilient. Praise the Lord for having made them so; otherwise neither babies nor parents would survive child rearing. Yet babies whose cries fall upon deaf ears turn their outward anxieties inward and may experience behavior problems later on. Because they experience nonresponse as anger-producing (whereas response is experienced as love), they become angry babies and even angrier children.

Gentle Your Fussy Baby

Most fussy babies are calmed by two actions: motion and physical contact. One of the earliest forms of behavior modifications is called the "principle of competing behavior." By gentling your fussy baby you treat your baby's tense behavior with your gentle behavior. To comfort the fussy baby is to determine what type of motion and physical contact she likes and needs and how much you can give of yourself without exhausting your parental reserves.

You should experiment to find out what comforts your baby the most. Most babies prefer bare skin-to-skin contact. Some babies need almost constant stroking and patting, and they enjoy being left undressed. Other babies enjoy the security of being swaddled and held firmly. Experiment with which position she likes to be held: bent over your shoulder; up on your chest; flat over your knee; directly in front of you with one hand on her back and the other hand on her bottom so that she stares directly into your eyes while you sing to her and move rhythmically; or draped (stomach down) over your arm, her diaper nestled snugly in the bend of your arm.

After a while you will develop your own type of "colic carry." A winning combination for our family was for me to hold our baby firmly, chest against chest, with her head turned to one side and nestled under my chin, while I swayed rhythmically from side to side.

The combination of skin-to-skin contact, the baby's ear over your heart, your breathing movements, and your total body rhythm often will soothe a fussy baby. A mechanical baby swing can be useful, but be careful not to overuse it and let it become a parent substitute.

During the first few months of comforting your fussy baby, you may log many miles of walking, rocking, floor pacing, dancing, pram pushing, and so on. When all else fails, place your baby in a car seat and take a ride. This usually works. Baby carriers are ideal for calming a fussy baby, especially the sling-type carrier in which you can hold your baby facing forward and bent at the hips which helps relax his tense abdomen. Within a few exhausting weeks or months, your baby will have told you what mode of transportation he likes best. Another "soother" is a sound and rhythm that mimics mother's heartbeat, something he was accustomed to *in utero*, such as a metronome set at seventy-five beats per minute, a record of a heartbeat, or the ticktock of a clock.

Relax

A fussy baby can shatter the nerves of even the most shatterproof mother. Relax by whatever method works. Being held in tense arms may upset a baby who is already sensitive to tense vibrations. This is called "tense mother–tense baby syndrome." Here are some relaxation tips.

1. *Take a warm bath* with your baby. Recline in the bathtub and fill the tub to just below breast level. Let your baby partially float while he is nursing; this ritual may soothe you both.

2. *Get outdoor exercise.*   A relaxing walk in the park with your baby in a front carrier can be a daily ritual for a tense mother and fussy baby.

3. *Breastfeeding will usually soothe a fussy baby,* but sometimes even that doesn't work. If your baby refuses your breast and does not stop fussing, your baby may be signaling that he wants to lie down with you in bed and nurse tummy to tummy snuggled in your arms and breasts. In our family this has been a successful technique.

4. *Nap when your baby naps.*   Sometimes when your baby sleeps, take the phone off the hook and have a private relaxing time doing something just for yourself. Spending time in the reading of God's Word is a real lift. All give and no take wears thin after awhile, even for the most caring and giving Christian parent.

Plan Ahead

Scheduling is usually a bad word in baby care, but as many parents of fussy babies will tell you, the end sometimes justifies the means. Most babies have their best and their worst times of day, although being inconsistently appeased (what works one day does not work the next) is one of the hallmarks of a fussy baby. Most babies have some pattern of daily fussiness. Plan ahead by using your baby's good time for fun activities and attention to your other children, to yourself, and to your spouse. Some mothers use these times to prepare the evening meal ahead of time. Most babies have their main fussy periods from 4:00 to 8:00 P.M. If you've accomplished most of your daily duties by this time, you can settle down during the fussy period and devote most of your energy to comforting your baby.

Lean on Your Support Groups

You may reach a point in caring for your fussy baby when you need more support than advice. Surround yourself with supportive people and avoid the advice of the "let your baby cry" and "you're getting too attached" philosophers. In order to get the most out of your support group you must honestly state your feelings. Parenting is a guilt-producing profession. Nearly all parents at some time have the feeling of "I am not doing a good job." If you have a low acceptance level of your baby's crying and have reached the end of your rope, say so.

Many sincere and caring mothers have had momentary thoughts of "I hate my baby," "I feel like I am being had." If you confide these normal feelings to other parents who have survived fussy babies, you will probably receive the following comments: "It's OK to have these feelings," "You are not being taken advantage of," "You are not spoiling him," "You are doing the most important job in the world—raising a human being."

Join a Christian Support Group

A mother in my practice started a morning Bible study for mothers of high-need babies. Their support group was based on the theory that if they remained in harmony with God, they would remain in harmony with their children. Their study sometimes included the following verses, which I call "cope verses":

2 Chronicles 15:7	Isaiah 40:31	Philippians 4:13
Proverbs 3:5	John 14:27	1 Thessalonians 5:18
Proverbs 31:17	Philippians 4:6–7	1 Peter 5:7

THE FUSSY FAMILY

Having a fussy baby can become a problem for the whole family. Because you have been blessed with a high-need baby, you probably will expend so much energy comforting your baby that you have little energy left for the needs of your spouse or other children. It is difficult to be a loving spouse or parent when you are emotionally and physically drained by the end of each day.

This next statement is not going to sit well with many mothers: most Christian writers agree that God's order of priorities is God, marriage, children, job, and church. It is difficult for many devoted mothers to put their marriage relationship before their children, especially when they seem to have so many needs.

With prayer and consultation this should not be an either/or decision. Parenting a fussy baby is a family affair. Both parents must work together to convey love and comfort to their baby and to each other. The fussy baby demands shared parenting. If a mother finds she has no time left for her husband, she should look closely at what other things (besides the baby) take her time and then make some changes. Time with husband is more important than housework. It is easy for parents of a fussy baby to experience burnout early in their parenting profession and in their marriage. Wife, keep a few channels of your communication network open for your husband. Husband, be sensitive to your wife. The single best support system for a fussy baby is a healthy Christian marriage.

A CHECKLIST FOR POSSIBLE CAUSES OF YOUR BABY'S FUSSINESS

Although most babies fuss primarily because of their own temperaments and not because of any physical problems, occasionally pain-producing illnesses or disturbing stimuli in a baby's environment account for their fussiness. Discovering these takes a lot of detective work by the baby's parents and a physical examination by his pediatrician. Some of the more common causes of pain or discomfort in young babies are listed here.

1. *Does your baby have a medical problem*—ear infection, throat infection, eye irritation, constipation, hernia, an allergy, irritating rash, or gastroesophageal reflux (also called pediatric regurgitation syndrome, see p. 241 for description)?

2. *What about the mother's diet?*　If your doctor finds your baby to be healthy and there is no apparent pressure or pain-producing illness that could account for his fussiness, he may be intolerant to a substance in your milk. Suspect a digestive problem when your baby's fussiness is the colicky type. The following items in your diet could cause your baby's fussiness (in order of frequency): (a) milk and milk products; (b) caffeine-containing substances taken in excess—coffee, tea, colas, and chocolate, and some medicines; (c) gas-producing raw vegetables—broccoli, cabbage, onions, green peppers, and beans; (d) citrus fruits or juice; (e) eggs; (f) medicines; and (g) decongestants, cold remedies, and prenatal vitamins containing iron. *Anything* in your diet could be causing trouble. Consider wheat, corn, oats, nuts, shellfish, tomatoes. Keep a record of what you are eating to help track down the offending foods. If you suspect any of these offenders, eliminate the suspected allergens for a period of at least three weeks. Sometimes it is a combination of several.

3. *What about the baby's diet?*　She may be allergic to dairy products or formula; consult your doctor about a less allergy-causing formula. Vitamins or fluoride may cause reactions in some children.

4. *Check for environmental irritants,* such as cigarette smoke, perfumes, hairsprays, cleaning products that give off a strong odor, or recurring noises.

190

5. *Is your baby hungry?*   (See Chap. 10 for suggestions about baby's getting enough to eat.)

6. *Is your environment too busy?*   Birth is a social event that often brings a long line of well-wishers into the home of tired parents and a baby who may not be ready to be a socialite. Some babies fuss because of overstimulation: too many sitters, loud noises on TV, overly excited older siblings. Surprisingly, some babies actually enjoy a busy environment and settle better when there is a lot of noise.

HOW TO AVOID HAVING A FUSSY BABY

How can you prevent your baby from becoming a fussy baby? Try these simple preventive measures near the time of birth to ease your baby's adjustment to his new world.

1. Get in harmony with your baby *in utero*. Some researchers in the field of fetal awareness suspect that a mother's emotions during pregnancy can affect the baby's personality. Read Chapter 2 for a discussion of how you can create a pleasant womb environment. Continue this harmony into your birthing environment.

2. Consider if the hospital newborn-care policies that separate mothers and babies in the Western culture may contribute to the fussy baby problem. Contrast these policies with those of other cultures where the baby is born into the arms and breast of her mother, is carried close to her chest while she is working, is fed on demand, and sleeps skin-to-skin with her until she shows signs of comfortable independence. Researchers who have studied this type of immersion mothering in other cultures have noted that these babies fuss far less and seem much more content than babies in Western cultures. Smoothing the transition from the intra-uterine to postnatal environment helps lessen what is called "missing the womb."

3. Practice the principles of attachment parenting mentioned in Chapters 3 and 4 (bonding at birth, rooming-in at the hospital, breastfeeding on demand, and im-mersion mothering postpartum). These practices give your baby a smooth welcome into his world. Although I am not sure that the parents have less fussy babies, I have observed that parents who practice the principles of getting the right start are able to respond intuitively to their baby's cues and cope more effectively with a fussy baby.

ADVANTAGES TO HAVING A FUSSY BABY

Are there any advantages to parenting a fussy baby? Your first impulse may be to answer, "Absolutely none. This isn't any blessing!" There are certain fringe benefits enjoyed by parents who have sought proper counsel and prayed their way through the first six months of raising a fussy baby.

Their most impressive benefit is that they know their child. Their radar systems have been so intensely tuned in to their child that they intuitively sense their baby's needs and respond to them.

Because they have been blessed with a baby with high-need levels, their acceptance and intuition (by constant usage) have matured to a higher level.

Because these parents know their child and have learned to anticipate their baby's behavior, they are better able to discipline their child when he or she is two and three years old. They always seem to be ahead of their child. Parenting a fussy baby is similar to parenting a child with a physical handicap or a painful illness. It brings out the best in intuitive parenting.

A fussy baby can actually bring a couple closer to God and closer to each other through prayer and consultation. Parents who have relied upon Scripture as their cope book learn a vital lesson that raises their entire parenting career to a spiritual level. They have asked God into their homes early in life.

These children are above average from the time of their birth. They need above-average parenting at home and above-average teaching in school. They will tax the ingenuity of teachers just as they do their parents. Give them above-average input, and you will be rewarded by children who are probably very intelligent and creative and who will bring joy to you and service to God.

WORDS OF COMFORT

"If my baby is fussy, is this an indication of what he will be like when he gets older? Will he be a hyperactive child?" The eventual behavior patterns of fussy babies vary from child to child. Some babies will fuss for their first six months and then settle down to become smooth and quiet children. Other babies who start out being a handful in early infancy often will remain a handful throughout childhood.

One day after counseling mothers of fussy babies, tired mothers, and mothers who were barely coping, I thought, *God must surely be reserving a special place for mothers.* I began to imagine what God says to mothers, and I wish to share these thoughts with you.

And God said to the mother . . .

When you were so tired that you thought you could not cope with your fussy baby another minute, I watched you; I was with you and you coped.

When you questioned My matching program for mothers and children, when you asked, "Lord, why have You given me such a difficult child when my friends have such easy babies?" I said, "Trust in Me with all your heart and lean not on your own understanding. I will not give you a cross you cannot bear."

When you prayed, thanking Me for a gifted child, I replied, "To whom much has been given much is expected."

When you felt the need to escape, you asked for help and I strengthened you.

When you were angry at your child's defiance, when you nearly lost control, you consulted Me and I guided your hand.

When you chastened your child instead of going too quickly to the rod, I saw your perseverance and this incident did not go unrecorded.

When you listened to your baby's nighttime needs, you pleaded, "Lord, I'm exhausted; if only I could get one full night's sleep I could go on." I heard your plea. I was awake with you. I gave you strength and you went on.

When you doubted your worth as a person, I listened. You and your child are precious in My sight. I reminded you that you are doing the most important job in the world, raising My child whom I have given you on short-term loan to nurture and return to Me. You have trained your child in the way he should go, and he has gone the way he should go. Come into My kingdom for I have reserved a special place for you.

HOW TO AVOID MOTHER BURNOUT

"I feel trapped"; "I can't cope, but I have to"; "I can't handle this any longer"; "I'm not enjoying motherhood"; "God, I feel so guilty." These are quotes from Christian mothers who have shared their mothering difficulties and feel they are burning out.

What Is Burnout?

Burnout is a syndrome of signs and symptoms very much like those discussed in the section on postpartum depression (see Chap. 4). It is due to a total exhaustion of a mother's reserves and an increasing lack of fulfillment in the mothering profession. Burnout also stems from a chronic disenchantment, a feeling that motherhood is not all it is cracked up to be. In fact, some mothers think they are cracking up just being mothers. Throughout Scripture, children are presented as being a joy to parents, not a burden. Burnout implies that there has been some fundamental breakdown in God's design for the joy in the parent-child relationship.

What Causes Mother Burnout?

I think the most common cause of mother burnout is the *aloneness* that plagues today's mothers. Never before in history have mothers been required or expected to do so much for so many with so little support. Today's society is caught up in the supermom myth. Shortly after giving birth, the new mother is expected to resume her previous roles as impeccable housekeeper, loving and giving wife, gourmet cook, gracious hostess, and contributor to the family income. Few mothers today are allowed the luxury in the first few weeks after birth of following God's design— mothering as a first priority and all else following when time and energy permit. Today's women often enter motherhood with confusing role models, inadequate prenatal preparation, unrealistic expectations of what babies are like, and no coping skills to handle the babies they get.

How Can You Avoid Burnout?

Since one of my ministries is to advocate attachment parenting, I also have an interest in what happens when God's design is not followed. Throughout this book I mention the law of supply and demand as being part of God's plan. By that I mean

194

that God will supply to both mother and father the energy to meet the demands of their child as long as the conditions are met that allow God's design for attachment parenting to operate. In my experience, when I look into cases of mother burnout, I can usually pinpoint one or more steps in the attachment style of parenting in which God's design was not followed; usually too many demands are placed on the mother that divert her energy away from her baby, or the mother is not allowed to operate in a supportive environment that allows her intuitive mothering to flourish.

Besides dispelling the supermom myth, I would like to correct the assumption that the baby is to blame for mother burnout. It is true that a high-need baby places a strain on the mother. However, if each situation is examined carefully, some interfering influence is detectable that has thrown off God's law of supply and demand, and the mother is not supplied with the energy she needs to cope with her high-need baby.

Mothers who have experienced burnout shouldn't feel guilty or feel they are not good mothers. In fact burnout is more likely to occur in highly motivated mothers. Mothers who strive to be perfect mothers or who want to fill all the roles are most likely to burn out. Also mothers who are attracted to this attachment parenting are candidates for burnout. A person first has to be on fire in order to be burned out.

The following checklist may help mothers avoid burnout. Mothers, can you identify any risk factors you may have that predispose you to mother burnout?

1. Do you have a history of difficulty coping with combined stresses? (This is discussed in the section on risk factors for postpartum depression, Chap. 4.)
2. During your pregnancy, did you have ambivalent feelings about how your child would interfere with your current lifestyle?
3. Were you involved in a high-recognition career before you became a mother?
4. Did you have poor mothering role models from your own mother?
5. Did you make adequate prenatal preparation, or did you have unrealistic expectations about how easy it is to care for babies?
6. Did you have labor and delivery in which fear and pain predominated, a generally negative birthing experience that was not what you expected?
7. Did you not have a bonding relationship shortly after birth?
8. Is yours a high-need baby?

9. Is there a mismatch of temperaments? You have a high-need baby, but you have a low level of acceptance.

10. Did you have marital disharmony, and did you hope that a baby might solve your marital problems?

11. Does your baby have an uninvolved father?

12. Are you highly motivated and compulsive? Do you strive to be the perfect mother?

13. Are you an overcommitted mother with too many outside priorities?

14. Have there been too many changes too fast, such as moving, extensive remodeling, or redecorating, to upset your nesting instinct?

15. Is there a medical illness in mother, father, or baby?

16. Do you have financial pressures?

17. Are you becoming confused by conflicting parenting advice?

18. Have you had too many babies too soon, that is, less than two years apart?

Mother burnout is usually the result of a combination of several of these factors, which, put together, have a cumulative effect.

Recognize Early Warning Signs of Burnout

When I see a mother who has several risk factors, I place a red star at the top of her baby's chart, signifying a red alert that this mother is subject to burning out unless preventive medicine is administered. I urge pastors, friends, relatives, and health care professionals to be on the lookout for these red flags. Some early warning signs of impending burnout include:

1. *"I don't enjoy my child."*   Not enjoying your child means that you are not in harmony with your child.

2. *"I'm not a good mother."*   Realize that because you love your child so deeply, these feelings of shaky confidence are normal. The more you love and care for another person, the more vulnerable you are to your own feelings of inadequacy. What is not normal is the persistence of these feelings to the point that you do not enjoy your mothering and you begin to search for alternative forms of self-fulfillment.

3. *"I don't feel right with God."*   Many mothers have shared with me that they have the most difficulty being in harmony with their children when they're not in harmony with God.

4. *"I can't sleep."*   If you're not in harmony with your baby at night, you have a greater chance of being burned out during the day. (See Chap. 7 for suggestions on achieving nighttime harmony.)

SURVIVAL TIPS FOR THE BURNED-OUT MOTHER

Have Realistic Expectations

Realistically prepare yourself during your pregnancy. Become involved in support groups that help you develop realistic expectations of what babies are like. Many parents do not realize that a new baby absolutely will dominate their lives and completely change their previously predictable and organized schedules. A common complaint I hear when tired couples come for their babies' two-week checkup is "Nobody prepared me for this."

Encourage Father Involvement

I have never seen a case of mother burnout in a home in which the father "mothered" the mother and created an atmosphere in the home that allowed God's design of attachment parenting to flourish. In most homes suffering from mother burnout, the mothers did not recognize the signs of burnout and did not call for help, and the fathers were insensitive to their wives' impending trouble.

Father, be sensitive to these early warning signs and risk factors. Don't wait for your wife to tell you she is burning out, since wives do not usually confide these ambivalent feelings to their husbands, perhaps because they do not want to shatter their perfect-mother image. As one exhausted mother complained to me, "I'd have to pass out in front of my husband before he would realize how tired I really am."

Burnout is common in homes in which there is what I call the "misattachment syndrome." In this situation, the parents are usually blessed with a high-need child. Mother immerses herself into meeting the needs of this demanding child and tries her best to mother according to God's design. Father, on the other hand, because he feels a bit shaky handling a fussy baby and also feels his wife is becoming too attached, often withdraws and retreats to interests away from home that he can control more easily.

A high-need child, a burning-out mother, and a withdrawing father make up the highest potential for a total family burnout. It has the highest potential for a marriage burnout. When mother becomes overly attached to her baby, father may form outside attachments of his own, and the whole family eventually may become detached because God's design for this support system was not followed.

Father, be sensitive to your wife's burnout signs and give her the message, "I'll take over, you do something just for yourself." One of my favorite stories illustrates this point. One day a noninvolved father sent his burning-out wife into my office for some counseling, which gave the subtle message, "It must be her fault we have a demanding kid she can't handle." Since it was the father who sent the mother in, I thought it was my professional duty to prescribe the medicine that got right to the heart of the problem. I gave the mother a prescription and said, "Now, be sure your husband fills this prescription for you." The prescription read, "Administer one dose of a caring husband and involved father three times a day and before bedtime until symptoms subside."

How does the father benefit from becoming more involved? A burned-out mother soon becomes a burned-out wife, and the entire marriage relationship suffers. Quite honestly, by supporting your wife according to God's design in the early months of mothering, you will reap rewards beyond your greatest expectations. The mother-father roles are not as well-defined in today's society as they have been in the past. Because of the breakdown of the extended family, today's mothers feel alone. The father needs to make up for this aloneness and become the mother's most reliable support system.

Mother, tell your husband what you need. A mother often is unwilling to release her child or to be assertive asking her husband to take over some of their child's care. But this harmony and mutual sensitivity are vitally important for the Christian family to survive in today's society. I advise you to sit down periodically and write an "I need help" list. Tell your husband exactly where and how you need help. A sensitive husband also can relieve the pressure on his wife by saying that he doesn't expect the house to look as it did before the child's arrival.

Practice Attachment Parenting, Not Restraint Parenting

Attachment parenting, if given the time and the commitment to develop, helps you develop harmony with your baby, increases your perseverance level, helps you know and have more realistic expectations of your baby's behavior, and generally helps you enjoy your baby more. Enjoying your baby is stressed because it seems to have a snowballing effect on your acceptance level and your self-confidence. Restraint parenting, on the other hand, ultimately leads to chronic disenchantment with the whole parenting role.

A common error in advice to mothers facing burnout is encouraging restraint parenting. It may work for some mother-child relationships, but in my experience, it is a short-term gain for a long-term loss. It is usually not separation from the child that the mother needs; it is a complete overhaul of her support system to minimize the competing influences that drain her energy. She also needs to consider other factors that may boost her self-esteem.

Know Your Tolerance Levels

Just as there is wide variation in temperaments of babies, there is wide variation in the tolerance levels of mothers. Some mothers seem to have high-acceptance levels that allow them to mother a dozen kids and function like human gymnasiums all day long. Other mothers have lower acceptance levels and have more difficulty coping with the constant demands of too many children too soon, especially in the toddler age group. As one mother of a newborn and a two-year-old put it, "I feel like I'm still pregnant with our two-year-old."

If you already have a high-need baby and are having difficulty coping, you would be wise to consider spacing your children at least three years apart. Many mothers let themselves operate on their energy reserves too long before seeking help. If you find your tolerance level is nearing its saturation point, seek counseling now. A Christian counselor can help you and your husband have realistic expectations of your God-given acceptance level. Then you can make some necessary changes in the family situation that you can tolerate more realistically.

A graphic example of this acceptance-level problem was conveyed to me by a mother of a high-need child. She was frustrated by apparently not measuring up to all that was expected of her: "My life is a circle revolving around my child. But I need a square with some edges left just for me." During my years as a pediatrician, I have been impressed by the way so many mothers can cope with so many combined stresses for so long.

Define Priorities

The earlier you realize you cannot be all things to all people and still have enough energy left for yourself and your baby, the less risk you have of burning out. Sometimes it's necessary to sit down, make a list of all the daily activities draining your energy, and put them in the order of priority. This is a good time for a family council during which a mother defines realistically what she has to do and what she is able to do, and the father and older children define daily chores they can do. Then the family prays together for God's perspective and guidance in accomplishing this.

Mothers of high-need children often say, "But I get nothing done." You *are* getting something done, something important. You just don't receive the gratification of seeing instant results. For example, an exhausted mother of a high-need child recently shared with me that her most competing energy drain was her compulsive housekeeping habits. But one day she looked at the floor and exclaimed, "That floor doesn't have feeling. No one's life is going to be affected if that floor is not scrubbed every day. My baby is a baby for a very short time, and she has feelings." A wise mother determines just what *needs* to be done.

Save Some Energy for Yourself

Some mothers may feel honestly they cannot be satisfied by one role. Babies are takers and mothers are givers, but there will come times when mothers feel all given out. It is often necessary for a caring third party, preferably the father, to step into this mother-infant relationship and encourage the mother to take better care of herself so she can take better care of the baby. If a mother is allowed to burn out and continues to practice martyr-mothering against her will, eventually the whole family will burn out and nobody will win.

CHAPTER 10

FEEDING YOUR INFANT

In her baby's first year, the mother will spend more time feeding her infant than she will doing any other parenting task. Feeding your baby according to God's design helps you enjoy this relationship more. This chapter deals with what type of milk to feed your baby, when to administer solid food, and what kinds of foods to avoid.

MOTHER'S MILK

Let me make a very important point at the outset. In my opinion, unless a medical problem prevents it, every baby should be fed his mother's milk as often and as long as the baby wishes and the mother is able. Parents have heard confusing advice about what milk to feed their babies. They have been told that mother's milk is best but that scientifically produced milk is as good. This just isn't true. I sincerely feel that one of the most important gifts you can give your baby is your breast milk. The following pages will present my defense for feeding human milk to human babies.

Breast Milk Is God's Design for Each Species

God designed a total nutrient that is unique to each species. It is the oldest living recipe formulated especially for survival. This nutrient is called "milk." Just as the human mother has the complete capability of nourishing her baby for nine months *in utero*, she also is capable of completely nourishing her infant for at least nine months after birth. Each species has the capacity to feed its young until they triple their birth weight, which humans reach by the age of nine to twelve months.

The milk for each species is suitable for its particular environment. Seal milk is high in fat because seals need high body fat to adapt to their cold environment. The milk of cows and of other range mammals is high in minerals and protein because rapid bone and muscle growth is necessary for their mobility and survival—the calf is up and running within hours after birth. And human milk is high in protein, fat, sugar, and minerals to promote growth in the brain, the survival organ of our species. Only recently have scientists recognized this singular function of human milk, and I feel it is the tip of the iceberg of information left to discover.

Breast Milk Is a Dynamic, Changing, Living Tissue

Breast milk changes as your infant changes. Formula is static; it does not change. An example of this dynamic process is the change in your milk's fat content. Fat accounts for a large percentage of your milk's calories. The hungrier your baby is, the higher the fat content of your milk is. If your baby is only thirsty, he will suckle in such a way that he receives the thinner "skim milk." Your milk has a higher fat content in the morning, and your baby is usually hungrier in the morning. Your milk gradually becomes lower in fat as your baby gets older because he will need fewer calories per pound of body weight as he grows.

Your milk also changes to protect your baby against germs. He needs a supply of germ-fighting elements in his blood called "immunoglobulins." The immunoglobulins, which are unique to each species, protect your baby from the germs in his environment to which he is most susceptible. Shortly after birth your infant begins making his own immunoglobulins, but they do not reach sufficient levels to protect him until he is about six months old. To make up for this deficiency, God has designed the mother to give her baby her immunoglobulins until he is able to make his own, through her blood while he is in the womb and through her milk after he is born.

The very first milk your baby receives shortly after birth is called "colostrum," which is very high in immunoglobulins. Since your newborn baby is particularly vulnerable to germs, God has designed your milk to be most protective when your baby needs it most. Your colostrum may be considered your baby's first immunization.

202

Long ago, mother's milk also was known as "white blood," because it contains the same living white cells that blood contains. The white blood cells in your milk keep germs from entering your baby's intestines and fight germs that enter the blood. The white cells also produce a special protein called "immunoglobulin A," which coats your baby's intestines, preventing the passage of harmful germs from his intestines into his blood.

The Chemistry of Breast Milk

Certain chemical nutrients are found in all milk: fat, protein, carbohydrates, minerals, iron, and vitamins. The relative percentages of these nutrients vary in each species' milk according to that species' individual needs.

1. *Fats.* You have read previously how the fat content of your milk changes to meet your baby's changing requirements. Your milk also contains enzymes that help the fat to be digested completely. Because formula does not contain these enzymes, the fat in formula or cow's milk is not totally digested and some passes into the stools, accounting for the unpleasant odor of the stools of formula-fed infants. The lower fat content and the difference in sugars and bacteria in the stools of a breast-fed baby account for the sweeter smell. When I smell the stool of a formula-fed infant, I think that the lower end of the intestines has simply rejected part of what went in at the upper end, and the parents' negative reaction to messy diaper changes certainly will not go unnoticed by the egocentric infant.

The cholesterol issue is an example of how scientists have become confused in their efforts to "humanize" the milk that the Creator designed for cows. We know that adults who have high cholesterol in their blood and diets are more prone to heart and blood vessel diseases; therefore, scientists decided to make baby formulas low in cholesterol on the theory that it would prevent heart disease. However, breast milk is much higher in cholesterol than cow's milk or scientifically produced formulas. Common sense dictates that the milk designed and adapted for the survival of a species would not contain a nutrient that could harm it.

Scientists have studied what happens when some newborn rats are fed diets low in cholesterol and some are fed diets high in cholesterol. The results showed that God was right after all: the newborn rats fed high-cholesterol diets actually had lower amounts of cholesterol in their blood when they reached adulthood; whereas, the newborn rats fed low-cholesterol diets actually had higher blood cholesterol as older rats. Formula manufacturers are still uncertain what to make of these studies.

2. *Protein.* Since cows grow four times faster than humans, the amount of the protein casein in cow's milk is four times that of human milk. The curd produced from a mother's milk is smaller and more digestible than that of cow's milk or formula, which is why mothers have observed that the formula-fed baby remains "full" longer than the breast-fed baby. Researchers are also just beginning to isolate the amino acid taurine in human milk which stimulates brain growth.

3. *Carbohydrates.* The predominant sugar in breast milk is lactose. Researchers have noted that mammals with larger brains have a larger percentage of lactose in their milk. Human milk contains more lactose than cow's milk; that is why it tastes sweeter. To make the sweetness similar to mother's milk, cane sugar is added to some formulas, but all sugars are not the same. Cane sugar is digested more rapidly than lactose, and it is known that some older children have mood swings when they eat cane sugar. Perhaps the infant also has blood sugar swings from eating cane sugar in formula.

Lactose also favors the development of certain beneficial bacteria in your baby's intestines. This is known as the "ecology of the gut." It is interesting that God has designed certain bacteria that can live in your baby's intestines provided they have the ideal chemical conditions. These bacteria ward off other bacteria that cause diarrhea. The combination of the artificial, acid-forming sugars and the excess fat in the stools of formula-fed babies often accounts for the "acid burn" diaper rash that is common among them. I sincerely feel God did not design babies' bottoms to look as uncomfortable as they often do.

4. *Minerals.* Cow's milk is high in calcium and phosphorous because cows have a much higher rate of bone growth than humans. These excess mineral salts add an extra load to your infant's immature kidneys. Maybe God foresaw that mothers would not stick to the recipe He designed for their young; therefore, He made kidneys much larger than necessary to rid the body of its excesses. Your milk is lower in mineral salts and therefore is easier on your newborn's kidneys.

5. *Iron.* Your baby needs iron to make new red blood cells as she grows. As your baby was developing *in utero,* she received a lot of iron from your blood through the placenta. She uses up these iron stores within her first six months; therefore, she needs extra iron. The iron in your breast milk is different from any other kind of iron. Babies who are fed breast milk very rarely become anemic; whereas, babies fed cow's milk or formula without iron often will become anemic between one and two years of age.

204

The same amount of iron in formula and in breast milk has entirely different effects on a baby. Your baby can absorb only 10 percent of the iron in formula or cow's milk compared to 50 percent of the iron in breast milk. The reason for this difference is that God has provided in your milk a special protein called "lactoferin" that attaches to the iron in your milk. It helps your baby's intestines absorb the iron, thus protecting your baby against anemia; whereas, the excess iron in formula is excreted in the stools. This accounts for the green color of a formula-fed baby's stool. A baby's stools neither look right nor smell right when her intestines are called upon to handle milk they were not designed to handle. Excess iron in the intestines allows harmful bacteria (that can cause severe diarrhea) to thrive in your baby's intestines.

6. *Vitamins.*   Breast milk contains all the essential vitamins your baby needs so that vitamin supplements are not necessary in breast-fed infants.

The Advantages of Breastfeeding

Breastfeeding helps mothers know their child better. They learn to determine when their child is full by watching for signs of contentment rather than counting ounces of formula. The mother and her nursing baby have a greater potential for being in harmony with each other, and they establish a trust in their mother-baby dialogue.

Mothers, you become a giving person, and you enjoy this giving because you notice the peace and joy breastfeeding gives you and your baby. Isaiah 66:11–13 beautifully illustrates this feeling of rightness:

> *That you may feed and be satisfied*
> *With the consolation of her bosom,*
> *That you may drink deeply and be delighted*
> *With the abundance of her glory (u 11).*

Mothers who practice unrestricted breastfeeding have higher prolactin levels in their blood. The discovery that a nursing baby causes a chemical change within the mother is another example of how science is finally catching up with what God designed and with what intuitive mothers have known all along: something good happens to mothers and babies when they spend more time together.

Mothers often will describe breastfeeding as a loving event with their babies. Here is how my wife Martha describes this very special relationship.

God's design for breastfeeding goes beyond physical and emotional benefits. It is His way of bringing each new child into a love relationship with Himself.

We have been teaching our baby to love. When she hears the word, she responds by placing her head against the person holding her. To her, *love* means warmth, holding, closeness, gentleness, and a crooning "ah-h-h." This didn't just happen overnight. She has been learning this little by little since day one.

Psalm 22:9 says, "But You are He who took Me out of the womb; You made Me trust when I was on My mother's breasts." Breastfeeding continues the nurturing begun by God in the womb, and it begins the trust relationship that is so vital for the love relationship to develop. A breastfeeding mother is giving herself totally, and the baby gets the message. That message eventually will translate into the concept of love from God: the mother teaches the baby first to trust, then to be loved, then to show love to others, and finally to understand what it means to love God our Father and to be loved by Him. Our baby won't understand all of this for a long time, but even at age sixteen months when she looks at a picture of Jesus and we say, "Jesus loves you," she smiles. When we say, "Erin loves Jesus," she puts her head down on the book and snuggles. To this growing child, the concept of love will not be abstract, and the concept of love from and for God will be real. It all begins with the kind of love God teaches us about in the Bible. First Corinthians 13:4–7 says,

> *Love suffers long and is kind; love does not envy; love does not parade itself, is not puffed up; does not behave rudely, does not seek its own, is not provoked, thinks no evil; does not rejoice in iniquity, but rejoices in the truth; bears all things, believes all things, hopes all things, endures all things.*

John 3:16 says that "God so loved the world that He gave His only begotten Son"—He *gave* Himself. And John 15:13 says, "Greater love has no one than this, than to lay down one's life for his friends." A daily willingness to lay down your life for your baby means *giving of yourself*. John 15:12 says, "This is My commandment, that you love one another as I have loved you."

God designed us to do this as mothers. He gave us breasts to enable us to nourish our babies with *ourselves*. The breasts that our babies suckle are our own flesh. As we give ourselves, our Creator reinforces that love is basic and vital to our babies.

TIPS FOR SUCCESSFUL BREASTFEEDING

Why are some breastfeeding relationships more successful than others? Throughout the past ten years I have kept records of the most successful breastfeeding relationships in my practice and the reasons for their success. The following features were common among them.

1. Involvement in natural childbirth classes and La Leche League meetings
2. A positive birthing experience
3. Rooming-in and demand-feeding after birth
4. Correct latch-on, proper positioning, and sucking techniques soon after birth
5. No supplemental bottles unless medically necessary
6. Unscheduled demand-feedings
7. Sleep-sharing
8. A supportive husband
9. A strong mother-infant attachment
10. Prayer and consultation during the breastfeeding relationship

Preparation and Education

The most supportive and knowledgeable mother's group about breastfeeding is the La Leche League International (see Chap. 2). Mothers are strongly advised to attend their series of meetings midway through pregnancy and to purchase their book, *The Womanly Art of Breastfeeding*. The mother may wish to continue attending the monthly league meetings for continued advice and support after her infant's birth. In my opinion, this is the best support group for all-around sound mothering advice.

Be confident. Breastfeeding is a natural biological relationship that God has designed for the mother to nourish her baby. Breastfeeding often is described as a confidence game, and prayer is the best confidence-builder.

Getting the Right Start

The following suggestions will help you as a new mother learn how to breast-feed your baby most comfortably.

1. *Begin early.*   Unless a medical complication prevents it, begin breastfeeding immediately after birth.

2. *Forget the clock.*   Only your baby will know how long and how often he or she should nurse. Ignore the commonly given advice of "begin one minute and gradually increase the time each day so you won't get sore." In the first few days, every baby has a different suck. Some begin sucking enthusiastically immediately after birth; others snooze and lick for the first day. It is not how *long* a baby sucks but *how* he sucks that can cause sore nipples.

3. *Position yourself.*   If you are able, sitting up in bed is your easiest position for nursing. Pillows are a real must. Place them behind your back, head, and on your lap for your baby, and under the arm that will support your baby. Get comfortable before beginning to nurse. You may be more comfortable lying on your side, especially if you have had a Cesarean section.

4. *Position your baby.*   Undress your baby to promote skin-to-skin contact. Nestle him in your arm so that his head rests in the bend of your elbow, his back along your forearm, and his buttocks in your hand. His head should be straight, not arched backward or turned in relation to the rest of his body. Your baby should not have to turn his head and strain to reach your nipple (turn your head to the side or up to the ceiling and try to swallow!). Turn his entire body so he is facing you tummy to tummy. His head and body should face your breast directly, as if an imaginary line were drawn from the center of your breast to the center of your nipple to the center of her mouth. To further this close contact, tuck your baby's lower arm alongside his body in the soft pocket of your midriff so that it is out of the way.

5. *Support your breast.*   Cup your breast with the other hand, supporting your breast from underneath with only your thumb on top. Be sure your hand stays way back, clear of the areola. It is important to continue holding your breast throughout the feeding until baby is old enough and strong enough to manage the weight of your breast himself. Manually express a few drops of milk to moisten the nipple.

6. *Use correct latch-on.*   Incorrect latch-on is the most frequent cause of an unrewarding breastfeeding relationship. Using your nipple as a teaser, gently tickle your baby's lips with your milk-moistened nipple, encouraging him to open his

Tickle your baby's lips with your nipple until his mouth opens wide.

Then pull him close, keeping his head and body aligned with yours.

mouth widely (babies' mouths often open like little birds' beaks—very wide—and then quickly close). The moment your baby opens his mouth widely, direct your nipple into his mouth (be sure to place it above his tongue), and *quickly* draw him *very close* to you with the arm that is holding him. (If you don't do it quickly enough the little mouth will close and you'll have to start over.) Don't lean forward, pushing your breast toward your baby. Pull him toward you. Most new mothers do not pull their babies close enough.

Attempt to get a large part of your areola into his mouth. The key to correct latch-on is for your baby to suck on the areola, the dark area of your breast surrounding your nipple. Under the areola are the milk sinuses that should be squeezed for proper milk release. Pull your baby so close that the tip of his nose touches your breast. Don't be afraid of blocking his nose, since he can breathe quite well from the sides of his nose even if the tip is compressed. If his nose does seem to be blocked, use your thumb to press gently on your breast to uncover his nose or pull his feet in closer to change the angle.

If your baby is latching on correctly, you should not feel painful pressure on your nipple. If you are feeling that the baby is sucking mostly on your nipple, push down on his lower jaw and lip to open his mouth wider. You should notice an instant relief from the pain. If your baby does not cooperate, break the suction and start again. Some babies do not detach themselves readily. You need to break the seal by sliding your finger into the corner of baby's mouth and between his gums. If you just pull baby off you may damage your nipple. Because improper latch-on will cause sore nipples, it is important that he learn the right way. Most babies learn to suck as a natural instinct, but some babies have to be taught to latch on properly. If you have sore nipples that are getting worse, seek help from a La Leche League leader or a lactation consultant.

Sucking Styles

After a few weeks you will notice that your baby exhibits two kinds of sucking: comfort sucking, a weaker suck primarily with the lips in which your baby gets the foremilk; and nutritive sucking, a more vigorous sucking with the whole jaw. You will notice the muscles of his face working so hard that even his ears wiggle during intense nutritive sucking. This kind of more productive sucking rewards the baby with the higher-calorie hindmilk (the creamy milk which comes later in the feeding after the milk ejection reflex has been activated by the strong nutritive sucking). The visible contractions of your baby's jaw muscles and the audible swallow sounds (little gulping noises from his throat after every one to three sucking efforts) are reliable indications that your baby has good sucking techniques and that he is getting milk.

Improper Nursing Posture: *Baby's head and body are at different angles. Mother is leaning into baby instead of pulling baby close to her.*

Alternative Nursing Positions

If you have had a Cesarean section, it may be easier for you to nurse your baby lying down. Turn on your side and ask the nurse to position some pillows between your back and the bed rail, another pillow between your knees, and try an extra pillow under your head. Some mothers also want pillows supporting their abdomens. Ask the nurse to place your baby on her side facing you and nestled in your arm, and slide your baby up or down until her mouth lines up with your nipple area. Pick up and support your breast as mentioned previously, then tickle her mouth open with your nipple. When her mouth opens widely, pull your baby toward you, inserting your nipple and areola into her mouth.

211

The Clutch Hold:
If you have had surgery, rest your baby on a pillow beside you and support her neck with your hand.

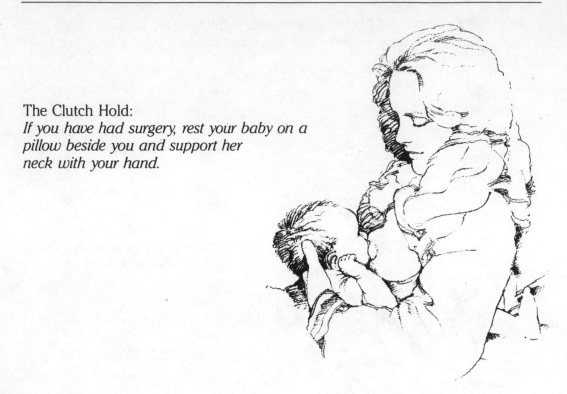

Another alternative nursing arrangement for a mother who is unable to stand the pressure of her baby on her incision after a Cesarean, or for a baby who has difficulty latching on, is the "football hold" or clutch hold (see figure). While sitting up, place a pillow under your arm and your baby on the pillow. Cup the back of his neck in your hand and let his legs rest against the pillow supporting your back. Follow the same procedure for proper latch-on as mentioned above. This clutch hold works particularly well for babies who squirm, arch their backs, and frequently detach themselves from the breast.

Some babies latch on to the breast and suck properly within the first day or so; other babies are slow starters and suck a little and snooze a little. These babies need to have a little prodding and need skin-to-skin contact in their mother's arms. With constant encouragement, the sleepy baby gradually will suck longer and more enthusiastically.

212

How to Care for Your Nipples

Teaching your baby to latch on correctly to your areola and your nipple is the best preventive medicine for sore nipples. If your baby's mouth is open wide enough and if he is drawn close enough to your breast, his jaws will be compressing the areola rather than your nipple. There is no need for special cleansing of your breast either before or after nursing. The little bumps on your areola around your nipple are glands that secrete a cleansing and lubricating oil to protect the nipples and keep them clean. Daily bathing or showering is all that is necessary to keep your breasts and nipples clean. Avoid using soap on your nipples since it may encourage dryness and cracking. After nursing, let your nipples dry thoroughly before you put your bra flap up.

The best massage mediums for sore or sensitive nipples are your own breast-milk or a drop or two of vitamin E oil from a capsule massaged completely into the skin two to three times a day after feeding. It is not necessary to wash this oil off before the next nursing. Massaging stimulates circulation which encourages healing. Be sure the cup of your nursing bra is not too small or too tight. Tight clothing will compress your breasts and encourage plugged ducts and infection. Cotton bras allow air to reach the sore nipples, and you may need to use a breast cup or shell to keep the nipple free of any clothing. Call La Leche League for help.

COMMON BREASTFEEDING QUESTIONS

"When Will My Milk Come In?"

The milk mothers produce immediately after birth is colostrum. Your true milk will appear gradually or quickly some time between the second and the fifth day after your baby's birth, depending on whether this is your first baby, the fatigue level of your birthing experience, how well your baby learns to latch on to your breast, and how frequently and how effectively your baby sucks.

"How Do My Breasts Make Milk?"

Your milk is produced in tiny milk glands throughout your breast. The milk drains into tiny channels that merge into reservoirs beneath your areola called "milk sinuses." Milk empties from these sinuses through approximately twenty openings in your nipple. When your baby sucks, the nerve endings in your nipple

213

stimulate the pituitary gland in your brain, which secretes prolactin. The prolactin stimulates your milk glands to produce more milk. The first milk your baby receives at each feeding is foremilk, which is thin because of its low fat content.

As your baby continues sucking, the nerve endings stimulate the pituitary gland to secrete another hormone called "oxytocin." This hormone causes the tissue around your milk glands to contract like a rubber band and squeeze a larger supply of milk from the milk glands into the sinuses. This latter milk, or hindmilk, is much higher in fat and slightly higher in protein and, therefore, has greater nutritional value. The hindmilk is the primary nutrient for your infant's growth. Most mothers have a tingling sensation in their breasts as the hindmilk is released from the milk glands into the milk sinuses. This is called the "let-down reflex" or "milk-ejection reflex." A successful milk-ejection reflex is a main key to successful breastfeeding.

"What Happens If I Have Too Much Milk?"

When your milk first appears, your breasts may feel very full because of the presence of milk and because of the swelling of your breast glands. This feeling is called "engorgement." Engorgement is your body's signal to get the milk out. Do not let this engorgement become increasingly painful because continued engorgement can lead to a breast infection. Standing in a hot shower, placing hot towels on your breasts, and encouraging your baby to suck frequently and effectively are the best ways to prevent continued engorgement.

If a breast infection (mastitis) occurs, above all, *don't stop nursing!* Your best prevention and treatment of breast infection is emptying your breasts. Immersing your engorged breasts in comfortably hot water for ten minutes can facilitate emptying. Use cold compresses to alleviate your pain. Use hot compresses and express your milk manually to soften your areola so baby can latch on more easily. If your breasts are rock hard, so that you can't get the milk to flow you will need to use continuous ice packs until the swelling has subsided enough to allow the milk to get out. If high fever, chills, fatigue, and increasing soreness and redness of your breasts occur, then you may need antibiotics. Call your doctor if you have these symptoms. Your baby still can breastfeed while you are taking antibiotics. Engorgement in the later weeks is often due to an upset in the baby's or the family's routine—too many visitors, missed feedings, excessive use of supplemental formulas—that throws the "timer" out of balance. Continued mother-infant attachment and demand-feeding in which you keep the harmony in tune are the best ways to prevent this uncomfortable engorgement.

"Should My Baby Be on a Feeding Schedule?"

Early in your breastfeeding relationship you will realize that the term *schedule* has absolutely no meaning in breastfeeding a baby. The only schedule your baby will have, and should have, is his own. Remember, breastfeeding is more than a mathematical exercise. One nursing mother put it this way, "I don't count the number of feedings any more than I count the number of kisses."

One of the most beautiful and natural biological negotiations is a mother and a suckling baby working together to get their own biological clocks synchronized and the law of supply and demand working comfortably. Listen to your baby's cues and don't clock-watch.

Breastfeeding cannot be scheduled easily because babies digest breast milk more rapidly than formula; therefore, breast-fed babies feel hungry more often and need to be fed more often. Also, babies have growth spurts during which they need more food for more growth. Babies enjoy periods of non-nutritive sucking in which they are more interested in the feel they get than in the food they get. Sometimes babies are only thirsty and suck a little to obtain some of the watery foremilk. Most babies breastfeed every two to three hours around the clock for the first few months. This is one of the many realistic expectations you should have about parenting.

"What If I Don't Have Enough Milk—or Any Milk?"

Most delays in milk production are the result of an interference in mother's and baby's timers. Giving supplemental bottles, not rooming-in, and scheduled feedings are the common causes of delayed lactation. As I am making my hospital rounds and a new mother tearfully expresses that her milk has not come in, I usually approach the well-meaning nurses and ask, "OK, confess. Who has been slipping this baby a bottle?"

Many times, nurses who do not wish to hear a baby cry will feed the baby a supplemental formula in the nursery. The formula temporarily satisfies the baby's hunger so that by the time he comes to his mother he is not hungry enough and does not suck enthusiastically. As a result the mother's milk production is not stimulated. If your milk is not appearing, keep your baby close to you for as many hours of the day as possible. Take your baby to bed with you and nurse lying down, having skin-to-skin contact with each other. Look at, caress, massage, and groom your baby while you are nursing to stimulate the milk-producing hormones.

Insufficient milk production during the first month may also mean that you are taking on too many outside responsibilities. Reorganize your commitments and priorities and get back into full-time mothering. Pray daily, asking God to give you the commitment and the milk sufficient to mother your baby in the way He has designed. Also, rid your house of negative advisors who drop defeating hints such as, "I couldn't breastfeed my baby either"; "She seems hungry all the time"; "Are you sure she's getting enough milk?" You don't need discouragement when you are trying to build up your confidence as a new mother. Surround yourself with supportive people and go to a La Leche League meeting.

"How Long Should My Baby Nurse?"

The duration of nursing varies from baby to baby because babies' sucking techniques and nutritional requirements vary. Your baby probably will nurse about ten minutes on one breast and five minutes or longer on the other breast. If your baby is an enthusiastic nurser, she will get most of her milk in the first three minutes of nursing. During that time you will have experienced a milk-ejection reflex. The remainder of the time is important for meeting her sucking needs. Less enthusiastic babies require a longer time to get sufficient milk. Also, you may experience a series of small milk-ejection reflexes throughout the feeding rather than one large one. Some babies, especially sleepy babies and small or premature babies, do better with the technique of switch nursing. (See "Why Isn't My Baby Gaining Weight?" page 218.)

"Does My Baby Need an Extra Bottle?"

The breast-fed baby usually needs neither a supplemental bottle of formula nor a bottle of water. Formula-fed babies need extra water to wash out all the formula's extra salts that they do not need.

"Why Does My Baby Want to Nurse All the Time?"

In their first few months babies have "frequency days" when all they want to do is nurse. I call this "marathon nursing." This supply-and-demand principle of breastfeeding is working in response to their sudden growth spurts. Some babies may also be going through periods of high-need levels. However, you may soon become exhausted as you try to fulfill your persistently hungry baby's needs. Try the following survival tips.

Be sure your baby is getting mostly milk at each feeding and not a lot of air.

Attempt to get more of your hindmilk into your baby to satisfy him longer. (See "Why Isn't My Baby Gaining Weight?" page 218.)

Avoid the "filler food" fallacy. You may be advised to give your baby cereal before bedtime or between nursings or have someone give him a bottle while you catch up on sleep. This is not good advice for your two- or three-month-old baby, and it seldom works anyway. Usually your baby wants and needs more milk, not filler food. Supplemental bottles, if used too frequently, may actually diminish your milk supply and lead to premature weaning. A suddenly increased demand to nurse is often misinterpreted as a need for solid foods, which is not likely to be the case until your baby is four to six months old. Your baby is simply signaling that he needs more milk to meet his sudden growth spurt. By accommodating your baby's demand for more frequent breastfeeding, your supply will increase to meet his demand after a few days; and your supply-and-demand relationship will be reestablished at a higher level of milk production.

Catnap when your baby sleeps. This requires delaying or delegating many of the seemingly pressing household chores. If you are blessed with a baby who nurses frequently, you may think, *I don't get anything done.* But you are getting something done. You are doing the most important job in the world—mothering a human being.

If your baby is a lazy nurser, try the following ideas. (1) Take your baby to bed with you and allow her to nurse a little and sleep a little. (2) Undress your baby to promote skin-to-skin contact. (3) Sit up in bed at a forty-five-degree angle and nurse if your baby is one of those exhausting babies who awaken as soon as they are put down. You both may sleep in this semi-upright position. (4) Try the burp-and-switch technique, which tends to keep sleepy babies awake long enough to nurse.

"How Do I Know My Baby Is Getting Enough Milk?"

After the first month or two you will know intuitively that your baby is getting enough milk. He will feel and look heavier. In the first few weeks it is not as easy to tell that your baby is getting enough milk, especially if you are a first-time mother. Here are some signs that your baby is getting enough milk in the first few weeks. (1) Your baby will have wet diapers often—at least six or eight wet cloth diapers (four to five wet disposables) and two or more bowel movements per day. (2) Your breasts may feel full before feedings, less full after feedings, and leak between feedings. (3) If you feel your baby sucking vigorously, hear him swallowing, feel your milk-ejection reflex, and then see your baby drift contentedly into never-never land, chances are he has gotten enough milk.

"Why Isn't My Baby Gaining Weight?"

The medical term for poor weight gain is *failure to thrive.* This section is about only the breast-fed baby who does not have any underlying illness that may cause him or her not to grow. In the first few weeks, most breast-fed babies who are not gaining weight properly are getting enough milk but not enough calories. Their mothers worry because their babies nurse regularly but look undernourished. This may be because they are getting only the low-calorie foremilk but not the high-calorie, creamy hindmilk they need to put on weight. These babies are active and require at least six to eight fresh diapers a day; however, they do not have enough body fat which makes their skin appear to fit loosely over their scrawny-looking muscles. This condition is usually caused by one of two problems: faulty sucking techniques or an inadequate milk-ejection reflex.

Usually, if a breast-fed baby fails to thrive, the basic principles for breastfeeding were not carried out successfully. The following suggestions are aimed at increasing the fat content of your milk and improving the efficiency of your baby's sucking.

1. *Improve your diet.*

2. *Get some rest.*   This may require reorganizing the household chores and responsibilities that compete with your nursing relationship.

3. *Spend a lot of time in touch with your baby:* skin-to-skin contact, eye-to-eye contact, grooming, caressing, and sleeping together. The more you are together, the more likely your baby is to suckle, which stimulates your prolactin.

4. *Increase the frequency of feedings* to at least one feeding every two to three hours, and wake your baby during the day if she sleeps longer than three hours. Take your baby to bed with you and nurse during the night. Your sleeping baby often will nurse very well when nestled in bed with you away from the competition of a busy world.

5. *Try switch nursing.*   In the traditional method of nursing, you encourage your baby to nurse as long as he wishes on one breast (usually about ten minutes) and to complete his feeding on the second breast, reversing the process on the next feeding. Switch nursing, also called the "burp-and-switch technique," operates as follows. Let your baby nurse on the first breast until the intensity of his suck and his swallow diminishes and his eyes start to close. Remove him from this breast and

burp him well; then, switch to the next breast until his sucking diminishes again and burp him a second time. Repeat the entire process. This burp-and-switch technique encourages a creamier, high-calorie hindmilk to come into your breast at each feeding. The technique is particularly effective for the sleepy baby, or what I call the "slurper-snoozer" or the "poopy sucker." Several times during nursing the milk-ejection reflex brings hindmilk into the second breast so that by the time the baby nurses on the second breast he is rewarded with high-calorie milk. This observation perhaps accounts for the old saying, "Babies grow best on the second breast."

6. *Try techniques of double nursing* which operate on the same principle of increasing the volume and fat content of the milk. After you nurse your baby and she seems to be content, carry her around in the upright position instead of immediately putting her down to sleep. Burp her well, and about ten minutes later, breast-feed her a second time, putting her down to rest with a fuller tummy. Your baby may regurgitate this larger volume of milk if put down immediately after feeding. In this case either put her in an infant seat, if she will be content, or carry her in a sling-type carrier for twenty to thirty minutes after feeding to allow her stomach to empty.

7. *Correct inefficient sucking techniques.*   Most infants instinctively know how to suck properly, but some infants have to be trained. Two bad habits that newborn nursers tend to develop are flutter sucking, which is sucking in short spurts with little or no cheek and jaw action, and nipple chewing.

Efficient sucking requires a baby to draw the areola well into his mouth and compress the milk sinuses under the areola with his lips and jaws. His tongue should compress the milk sinuses against the roof of his mouth and effectively "milk" the milk out of the sinuses, into the nipple, and into his mouth. Some babies do not get enough of the milk sinuses into their mouths or do not effectively compress the sinuses or do not coordinate their tongue actions and swallowing actions. As a result these babies get only the foremilk and do not empty the breasts well at each feeding, and consequently do not grow well. Review the positioning techniques for proper sucking as described earlier in this chapter. Also be sure that your breasts are not too full. An engorged breast is difficult to nurse from since your baby is only able to suck on a nub of your nipple and not on soft and compressible areola. If your breasts are too full, manually express some breast milk prior to each feeding in order to soften your areola; also use the milk-moistened nipple as a teaser.

219

8. *Avoid supplemental formulas* if your baby is not gaining weight properly, unless your doctor advises you otherwise. Introducing bottles too early (within the first two weeks) may cause nipple confusion, further interferes with your breastfeeding relationship, and may wean your baby before her time. Premature babies and babies who fail to thrive as a consequence of faulty sucking may need supplemental formulas until their own sucking mechanisms mature. If your baby needs a supplemental formula, it is best to feed it to her by way of a supplemental nutrition system (SNS), which is a small container that contains formula and hangs round your neck. A tiny spaghetti-like plastic tubing runs from the container onto your nipple. As your baby sucks milk from your breast, he also gets formula from the tubing. Having his mouth full of formula trains your baby to suck more vigorously on your breast thereby encouraging him to get more of your own milk. This system, which can be located through your local La Leche League, can be discontinued gradually as your lactation and your baby's sucking techniques improve.

9. *Try prayer and consultation.*   If your baby is not thriving on your milk, ask God to bless this special relationship. In my experience, babies do not fail to thrive on breast milk because their mothers are not producing good milk, but because some breastfeeding technique needs to be corrected. Most major cities have lactation specialists, such as the La Leche League, who can give you the proper support and advice you need.

All too often, a mother is advised to put her baby on a bottle because he is not growing on her milk. This advice is popular because it gets everybody off the hook, and no one has to work hard at finding the real reason a baby is not growing. Obtain proper consultation from a lactation specialist before succumbing to this advice.

"We're Adopting a Baby—Can I Breastfeed?"

This may come as a surprise to you, but yes, you can. This is accomplished with the use of an SNS. While your baby is receiving formula from the SNS, he also is sucking from your breast. Over a period of several weeks, you gradually will begin to lactate, and the baby will receive nourishment from you as well as the formula. Although an adopting mother seldom can produce enough milk for total nourishment of her baby, the continued sucking causes an increase in her prolactin levels.

NURSING NUISANCES

The Distracted Nurser

Between four and six months of age, babies become so interested in their surroundings that they suck a little and look a little. This nuisance makes nursing seem to last forever, and constant latching on and pulling off may become unpleasant for your nipples. If this curious nuisance develops, use the technique of closet nursing. Take your baby into a quiet, dark, and uninteresting room to nurse him when he is susceptible to too much visual stimulation.

The Nursing Strike

Another nursing nuisance that occurs between six and twelve months of age is the nursing strike; your baby may lose interest in nursing for a few days. This strike can come at any time. Don't immediately interpret this strike as the time for weaning. This lack of interest in breastfeeding can be the result of any number of occurrences. Your baby may have a cold or may be teething; he may be reacting to a change in his routine, his environment, or his milk supply; or he may be reacting to a physical or emotional change in you. During this temporary strike, give your baby extra love and security, pump your breasts frequently to keep your milk flowing, and spend a lot of time physically close together.

Relax, quit watching the clock, avoid bottles and pacifiers. I advise you again to take your baby to bed with you and offer your breast to him while lying down. Many babies will go off strike when they nurse in bed, especially if they are very sleepy. It sometimes helps to walk around as you breastfeed. A last resort may be to nurse your baby while he is sleeping. These nursing strikes seldom last for more than a few days, but plan to spend all your time with your baby as you win him back to the happy relationship you had before the strike.

The Sleepy Baby

Breastfeeding the sleepy baby is one of the most frustrating nursing nuisances for new mothers. During their first few weeks, some babies like to suck a little and sleep a little and apparently fall asleep before they get enough milk. This problem is common in small infants and premature babies. One of the baby's last mechanisms to mature is the feeding mechanism, so if she is three weeks premature, she

221

actually may require three weeks before she can suck vigorously like a mature baby.

Try the following suggestions for breastfeeding your sleepy baby.

1. Review the positioning techniques described earlier. Be sure to tickle the sleepy baby's mouth open wide enough for her to get enough of your areola into her mouth. Sleepy babies are also prone to flutter sucking.

2. Undress your baby and yourself to increase the skin-to-skin contact during nursing.

3. Manually express some of your milk before feeding; this will soften your breast and allow your little snoozer to get more of your areola into her mouth and thus get more milk.

4. During the feeding, as your baby's sucking intensity and swallowing diminish, gently prod her by tickling her cheeks and pulling her lower jaw down to help her keep her mouth open wide.

5. Sleepy babies tire easily at the breast and do not adjust well to the usual technique of feeding ten or fifteen minutes on each breast. Sleepy babies feed better with the burp-and-switch technique of breastfeeding.

6. Pray for perseverance. Sleepy babies are a real nuisance to nurse but the nuisance usually lasts only a week or two. Pray for perseverance in your breastfeeding relationship until your baby's sucking mechanism becomes more mature.

The Biter

When your baby is four to six months old and is feeling pressure in his gums from the early phase of teething, your nipple will become a handy teething object. Toothless gums chomping down on your tender breast can be disturbing enough, but cutting teeth justify a complaint—it hurts! Your surprised reaction to the pain—"OUCH!"—is sometimes enough to startle your baby loose, although he may instead clamp down even harder. Just don't overdo the startle effect or you might cause a nursing strike. You can quickly and smoothly disengage your baby's vise-like grip by pushing down on his lower jaw with your thumb. An alternative technique is to pull your baby quickly into your breast very close as soon as you sense he is clamping down. This "reverse psychology" requires him to let go if he wants to breathe. Being removed from your breast and hearing various sounds of disapproval will train your baby out of this pastime. You probably will find that he does this toward the end of a feeding or when he is not really hungry but just fussy from teething discomfort. Substitute a less sensitive object if he is desperate to have his gums eased.

FEEDING THE HIGH-NEED NEWBORN

Some new babies are a complete shock to their mothers. No mother can be prepared fully for the changes a new baby is going to bring into her life. Only as she experiences life with the new baby does she begin to realize what's in store for her as a first-time mom (or as a practiced mom who is having her first high-need baby). A friend calls to congratulate her on her new blessing and she replies, "You won't believe how much this little one needs. I can't put him down, as soon as I do he's awake and cries as though I've never fed him." This kind of baby needs to be nursed constantly and held constantly. One exhausted mother had a little energy left for humor and told me, "It's one constant holdathon."

After about three days at home with your high-need newborn, you might think, *I need some sleep; I can't keep this up; I'm going crazy; I'm desperate, exhausted, and look like death warmed over.* You may not know if the problem is within you (your breast, your milk, your mind) or within your baby (his sucking technique or his ability to concentrate long enough to suck enough milk). All you will want to do is give your baby a bottle, fill him up one time so he will sleep three hours (you thought all new babies did that) so you can sleep without hearing him cry five minutes after you put him down. One mother shared with me, "I can't even put him down long enough to go to the bathroom." Let's look at your options at this point.

Supplement with a Bottle of Formula?

The usual advice is "Just give the baby a full tummy once so you can get caught up on your sleep, recharge your batteries, and carry on." This seems to work, and the baby sleeps for two to three hours at a stretch, or maybe more. The problem with this option is that it is a short-term gain with a risk for a long-term loss. It does nothing to help the next day or the next, and actually it can hurt your milk supply because the supply-and-demand mechanism has been tampered with. All you may find out with this option is what you already knew—formula stays in the baby's tummy longer than breast milk. The fact that your baby slept longer with formula does not mean that you did not have enough breast milk. All it means is that you're not giving her a whole day of leisurely sucking. Your baby needs that sucking more than most babies and that is why she wakes up so quickly when the sucking and the warm arms disappear. Consider a very important fact: you are aiming for a long-term breastfeeding relationship. Getting your baby hooked on too many bottles too soon jeopardizes your entire breastfeeding relationship. In my experience, giving supplemental bottles to babies younger than six weeks of age often leads to premature weaning. Many nursing mothers need six weeks of total breastfeeding before their milk supplies are stable enough to withstand an occasional supplemental bottle.

Stop Breastfeeding?

You can stop breastfeeding, which is probably what will happen anyway if you keep giving the baby a bottle just to fill him up. He soon will prefer sucking from a rubber nipple and will want to suck less and less on your nipple. As a result, you sacrifice the supply-and-demand relationship which is working for you, at least on a marginal basis.

Do you really *want* to breastfeed? Remember, breastfeeding is 95 percent attitude. Why do you want to breastfeed? Is it because all your friends are breastfeeding and will think you are a bad mother or a failure as a woman if you don't? Or because your husband thinks it is the only way your baby is going to be raised? If your answer is honestly one of these reasons, you won't be happy breastfeeding and neither will your baby. You must be happy for him to be happy, especially since you are getting such a shaky start, which may in fact be due to your own inner unwillingness to breastfeed. You have to *want* to breastfeed, first for your baby's best, and secondly for your own self-fulfillment.

If you decide to bottle-feed your baby, you should be supported in your decision. But realize that switching to the bottle does not guarantee that your high-need baby will automatically become easier to handle. He may sleep more regularly for a day or two or a week or two; but if his basic temperament is that of a high-need baby, he still will be temperamental, and you may wonder if your baby would have benefited from all the early holding and nursing you could have given him had you stuck it out.

Stick with Breastfeeding!

This may not be the option your body or mind (what is left of it) wants to consider, but in your spirit you may say, "Yes, I want to stick with breastfeeding."

You may have to spend some time in prayer and counsel before wholeheartedly reaching this decision because it is a choice that definitely affects your spirit. You'll need help and lots of it; first, from your heavenly Father and, second, from someone who has overcome the same obstacles you are facing. Call the La Leche League and ask to be put in touch with a leader in your area who has nursed a baby like yours. She will tell you what helped her, and if she did it, you can do it. Remember, nursing is something you can do if you want to do it for the right reasons. If you don't, it is not worth the physical, emotional, and spiritual energy you'll have to invest and which you simply may not have.

So you choose to stick it out and you are back to square one. You can't put your baby down because he wakes and cries five minutes after you do, but you can't get him to stay awake long enough to suck hard enough to be really full. All you do is hold him and nurse him without getting rest or sleep. Try the following survival tips.

Hold a family council with your husband, relatives, and friends who have come to help. Make the following message loud and clear: "We have been blessed with a high-need baby. I need some help. I no longer can cope without your help." You may even read them the Ten Commandments for the Postpartum Mother as listed in Chapter 4. You need someone to hold your baby for you when you manage to get her to nod off to sleep. Your baby needs to be held by someone, but not necessarily always by you. Your husband, a relative, or a friend can relieve you one by one until you get yourself into a system of sleeping when your baby sleeps. High-need babies do cry a lot, but they should not be left to cry *alone*.

Try to learn the knack of nursing in bed so you can doze off when your baby does. You will spend a lot of time in bed in the first few weeks postpartum; so, have a comfortable gown and a robe to wear. One mother of a high-need baby shared with me, "I didn't get dressed in day clothes for three weeks after I came home from the hospital to avoid the temptation to put the baby down and spend that precious time doing housework."

Have a good, nutritious lunch prepared by your husband or a friend waiting in the refrigerator along with snacks to nibble on and liquids to drink throughout the day. Put them on a tray you can eat and drink from while lounging in bed. Take some good books to bed with you that may help you relax or help you get to sleep more easily. Do some needlework, or letter writing, or whatever you enjoy. Your Bible also should be handy for some quiet time with your Lord. The Psalms are a good source of relaxation and meditation for the postpartum mother.

You don't have to stay in bed like an invalid. You can go for a walk outdoors if you find that some physical exercise is relaxing and untiring. Be up and about in your home if you can resist the temptation to get some work done. The reason to stay in bed until the crisis has passed (and it will) is that when you are in bed you are physically resting even if you are not sleeping. You'll be surprised how little catnaps do add up. If you are the type who hates to be in bed "doing nothing," and you are tense and miserable, then get some help learning to relax. Review your childbirth relaxation techniques; have your husband rub your back or give you a massage; and meditate on scriptures such as Psalm 37:4–5, 7a; Proverbs 16:9; Jeremiah 6:16; Philippians 4:6–7; 1 Peter 5:7. Allow yourself the luxury of doing nothing. Pamper yourself. Be good to yourself: put aside all responsibilities except for you and your baby. This is your maternity leave; take it. The housework can be done by someone else, or it can be done next month. Caring for yourself and your baby is your only focus at this time. You actually must put yourself first, maybe for the first time in your life, because your baby depends on you to stay calm, rested, and happy in spirit.

One helpful idea that can give you confidence is to keep a log of the exact times that you and your new baby are sleeping in each twenty-four-hour period. You may be surprised that your baby really is getting enough sleep; remember, what's enough for one baby is only half enough for another baby. You also may be surprised that you are getting as much sleep as you do.

CHAPTER 11

WEANING, SOLID FOODS, AND OTHER DIETARY CONCERNS

I do not recommend early weaning for infants. I firmly believe that the custom of early weaning in Western society is not in accordance with God's design for mother-infant attachment. Weaning an infant before his time is an unfortunate break in the nurturing continuum. Women of the Western world are accustomed to considering breastfeeding in terms of months. When a mother asks me how long she should nurse her baby, I respond, "There is no set number of *years* you should nurse your baby."

There are many "weanings" throughout a child's life—weaning from the womb, from the breast, from home to school, and from authority at home. The pace at which children go from oneness to separateness should be respected in all of these weaning milestones. To hurry a child through any of these relationships may show disrespect for the child's dignity as a little person with big needs. La Leche League's term for nursing toddlers, *little nursing persons,* certainly demonstrates this respect.

THE BIBLICAL APPROACH TO WEANING

Weaning took place very late among the Israelites, at least by today's standards. Hebrew mothers often suckled their children for three years. Weaning was a festive occasion, not a feeling of loss or detachment: "Abraham made a great feast on the same day that Isaac was weaned" (Gen. 21:8). The peace and contentment a child should have by the time he is weaned is stated beautifully in Psalm 131:2.

> *Surely I have calmed and quieted my soul,*
> *Like a weaned child with his mother;*
> *Like a weaned child is my soul within me.*

A beautiful commentary on the meaning of this psalm is given in Lang's *Commentary on the Holy Scriptures*.

As the weaned child no longer cries, frets, and longs for the breast, but lies still and is content because it is with its mother; so my soul is weaned from all discontented thoughts, from all fretful desires for earthly good, waiting in stillness upon God, finding its satisfaction in His presence, resting peacefully in His arms.

The term *weaning* takes on a new connotation in 1 Kings 11:20: "Then the sister of Tahpenes bore him Genubath his son, whom Tahpenes weaned in Pharaoh's house." *Weaned* is used here to mean educating or bringing up the child. The NIV translation is "whom Tahpenes brought up."

The biblical story of Hannah and her son Samuel is an early account of mother-infant attachment and priority mothering:

And the man Elkanah and all his house went up to offer the LORD the yearly sacrifice and his vow. But Hannah did not go up, for she said to her husband, "I will not go up until the child is weaned; then I will take him, that he may appear before the LORD and remain there forever." And Elkanah her husband said to her, "Do what seems best to you; wait until you have weaned him. . . ." So the woman stayed and nursed her son until she had weaned him (1 Sam. 1:21-23).

Verse 24 describes the sacrifice Hannah offered when Samuel was dedicated to the Lord.

I regard Hannah's weaning Samuel as an example of God's design for weaning a child from his mother to his God. Bible commentators feel that Samuel's weaning occurred when he was three years of age. "Do what seems best to you" is a clear indication that Elkanah supported Hannah's God-given intuition.

Mothers, meditate on these scriptural passages, asking God to instill in you their meaning and the way in which they may be applied to your own mother-child relationship. I wish to share with you my own understanding of these passages. The Hebrew word for *weaned* in the above passages is *gamal,* which means "to ripen." The term implies a state of readiness. Weaning should not mean a loss or a detachment from a relationship but rather a state in which a child feels so full and so right that he is ready to take on other relationships. Weaning implies a smooth continuum from the security and instruction from his mother to the security and instruction from God. Weaning before his time of spiritual readiness may leave a child unfulfilled and just not feeling right. Perhaps a child who is weaned before his time from any childhood relationship and is hurried into other relationships may rebel both inwardly and outwardly and show what I call "diseases of unreadiness." My pediatrician's intuition tells me what are considered normal behaviors of infancy and childhood, such as aggression, tantrum-like behavior, and severe mood swings (all forms of baby-anger), may in fact be diseases of premature weaning.

Breastfeeding is for both nutritional and emotional nourishment. I would advise you to breastfeed your infant for nutrition at least *one year.* Many infants who are weaned before their time experience medical illnesses shortly after weaning such as ear infections, diarrhea, and allergies. Breastfeed past the first year for emotional nourishment. A nursing toddler is a beautiful sight. I enjoy hearing the little "nursing conversations" from a two-and-a-half-year-old during breastfeeding, such as, "all done—close the door." In the second year, breastfeeding functions more as a securing lift, a pick-me-up during times of stress, and a time mother and baby can relax and have their special dialogue. One of my two-year-old patients was in the office for a checkup. When she had finished nursing, she looked up at her mother and said, "Mommy's Moo. No caffeine, no sugar."

You may ask, "But, doctor, won't prolonged nursing make my baby too dependent on me?" The answer is an unreserved no! Most mothers who have nursed for several years have found their children actually to be more secure and more independent. Certainly in our own family this has been the case. Our four-year-old daughter, Hayden, enjoyed nursing until just after her fourth birthday and then willingly exclaimed, "I don't like it anymore." Martha was then pregnant with our daughter Erin, which accounts for the change in taste. Hayden then said, "I'll wait till the baby comes then the good milk will be back." Five months later she just wasn't interested anymore. Again, the age at which a baby evolves from oneness to separateness should be respected for each individual mother-infant couple.

THE DOS AND DON'TS OF WEANING

A basic principle of child care to remember is that as your child grows older, her needs do not lessen, they only change. *The American Heritage Dictionary* defines *weaning:* "to withhold mother's milk and substitute other nourishment." There are two phases in weaning: detachment and substitution. As a baby is detached from the nutritional nourishment of mother's milk and solid food is substituted for it, other forms of emotional nourishment also should be substituted for the emotional detachment from mother's breast.

There are some definite dos and don'ts for mothers in weaning.

1. *Don't wean by leaving your child abruptly.*   Except in unavoidable tragic situations, weaning by desertion is definitely to be avoided. Detachment from a mother's breast and detachment from the mother herself may be a combined stress that is too much for the baby to handle.

2. *Practice the "don't offer, don't refuse" technique* advocated by the La Leche League. Your baby probably will start to skip one feeding time a day because he is busy with other pursuits. After several weeks of skipping this nursing, you may find he will be equally willing to miss another feeding. As the weeks and months pass, he may be nursing only when he needs to fall asleep for naps and bedtime. Be prepared to allow him to retreat a bit (or a lot) during times of stress such as illness, new developmental stages, changes in environment, and so on. You may be willing, even eager, to continue this "put me to sleep" nursing for quite a while longer. If there is a definite reason, however, that *you* need to encourage an end to this, be careful to consider your baby's needs too. There is no shortcut in this process—you are still committed to filling your little one's needs, one way or another. If you must discontinue the bedtime nursing, try substituting stories and a cuddle, but you may have to cuddle in positions other than the familiar nursing position. Let your husband take over at these times if possible, and spend more one-on-one time together throughout the day to reassure your child of your availability and commitment. (See the Bibliography for good books on nursing your toddler.)

3. *Don't set up an arbitrary date at which you are going to wean.*   As in many aspects of child rearing, the clock and the calendar have no place in the breastfeeding relationship. You probably will feel different about your goal as the preordained time approaches.

4. *An important part of the weaning process is substituting alternative nourishment for mother's milk.*   This transitional time is a good opportunity for the father to become involved in weaning.

If you are having ambivalent feelings about continued breastfeeding, pray to God for the wisdom to know when and how to wean your child and for the perseverance toward infant-led weaning. The weaning period should be a time of contentment for both mother and infant and of changes toward other relationships, not a time of detachment and loss.

FORMULA FEEDING

Although I believe that breastfeeding with infant-led weaning is God's design for infant nutrition, the commercially prepared infant formulas are relatively safe and effective as an alternative source of nutrition for most infants. But because formula is a static nutrient and breast milk is a dynamically changing nutrient, formula is *only a distant second best*. Formulas are prepared using cow's milk or certain legumes, such as soybean, as a protein base. Vitamins, minerals, and chemically processed portions of various nutrients are added to "humanize" the infant formula.

Commercial formulas are available in three forms: powdered formula with directions on adding water, concentrated liquid formula that should be mixed half and half with water, and ready-to-feed formulas that can be poured directly into a bottle. Your doctor will help you choose which formula is best for your baby. A word of caution: *never mix the formula in greater strength than the directions advise.* Always add the specified amount of water. Adding too little water makes the formula too concentrated for your baby's immature kidneys and intestines to handle and may make him sick. Babies usually like their formula slightly warmed, like breast milk. Iron-fortified formulas should be used unless your doctor advises otherwise.

"How Much Formula Should I Feed My Baby?"

The amount of formula your infant will drink will depend upon his weight and his appetite. Use the following rule of thumb for your baby's first six months: *two to two-and-a-half ounces of formula per pound per day.* For example, if your baby weighs ten pounds, he may take twenty to twenty-five ounces of formula per day.

This amount may change from day to day. After six months, the daily volume of formula probably will remain the same or gradually diminish as your baby's volume of solid food increases.

Demand-feeding also applies to formula-fed babies. In demand-feeding an infant is fed every time her or his little tummy desires. In scheduled feeding, a baby is fed every three to four hours at preassigned times according to mother's convenience and baby's appetite. A third alternative is the semi-demand schedule in which your baby has one or two preassigned feedings and is fed on demand between them.

Formula-fed babies can be put on a schedule more easily since formula is digested more slowly. Demand-feeding caters to your infant's satisfaction; scheduled feeding is for your convenience and your own individual family situation. Most formula-feeding mothers elect the compromise of a semi-demand type of schedule. During the first few weeks they wake their babies for feedings during the day, if they sleep more than four to five hours, to discourage the exhausting feeding pattern of a day sleeper and night feeder. Frequent feedings during the day and bottles at 7:00 P.M. and at 11:00 P.M. seem to be the most comfortable feeding schedule for most parents.

Feeding time should be a time of special closeness. As in breastfeeding, talk to your baby; look at him and caress him during your bottle-feeding. You may partially undress yourself and your baby and hold him in close, skin-to-skin contact on your breast even though you are bottle-feeding. Remember, not only the kind of milk your infant gets is important but also how he gets it. Above all, resist the temptation to prop the bottle for your baby to drink alone. Not only is this practice unsafe, it is not nurturing.

"What about Vitamin and Fluoride Supplements?"

Commercial infant formulas contain all the vitamins necessary for your infant, but remember that in order for your baby to receive the daily recommended amount of vitamins, she has to take the entire can of formula. Many babies do not consume an entire can of formula every day until they are a few months old; so, vitamin supplements may be recommended by their pediatricians. In later infancy and childhood many children have erratic diets, eating well one day and poorly the next. Your pediatrician will recommend vitamins according to your child's individual needs. Fluoride supplements may or may not be prescribed by your physician depending upon how much fluoride is in your drinking water and upon how much water your child drinks.

232

Breast-fed babies do not need vitamin supplements. If your nutrition is adequate, your milk contains all the necessary vitamins and nutrients your infant will need for her first six to nine months.

Iron is necessary to make new red blood cells and to replenish the used-up iron that came from your blood *in utero*. Formula-fed infants should receive iron-fortified formulas from birth on, or at least from four months on. Parents may feel occasionally that the added iron causes gastrointestinal upsets in their infants, although controlled studies comparing iron-fortified formulas and formulas without iron showed no difference in the number of intestinal problems. If the iron-fortified formula does not agree with your baby, iron-rich foods, meat and iron-fortified cereal, may be offered to your baby at the age of five or six months, according to your pediatrician's suggestion. Iron-fortified formula often gives a baby's stools a green color, but this has no significance. Breast-fed infants rarely need iron supplements, at least not during their first six to twelve months.

"How Long Should My Baby Be on Formula?"

Keep your baby on formula for at least one year. If you are breastfeeding and choose to wean your infant within a year, wean to formula and not to cow's milk. Each species' milk is its ideal food (human milk for humans); it is not the ideal food when it crosses species (cow's milk for humans). Babies fed cow's milk before they are one year of age often have intestinal disturbances such as allergies and anemia, low iron in the blood. Since most formulas are basically cow's milk that has been modified for babies, formula gives babies the nutritional advantages of cow's milk without the problems of drinking it straight.

Generally, I advise mothers to keep their babies on formula until they lose the taste for it. If your pediatrician feels your baby is gaining too much weight on the usual formula (twenty calories per ounce), he or she may suggest you feed him a lower-calorie formula. Low-calorie formula is an attempted imitation of human milk, which naturally decreases in calories as your infant grows older because he needs fewer calories per pound of body weight. Switching from formula to cow's milk is often done for psychological rather than nutritional reasons, since this switch may be considered an index of the baby's "growing up." Thinking of your baby's formula as actual "milk" may help you overcome this temptation.

After deciding to switch from formula to cow's milk, you must decide what kind of cow's milk to feed your baby. Milk differs in fat content and, therefore, calorie content. Pediatricians advise against the use of skim milk before a baby is two years old since this lower-calorie milk deprives the infant of the valuable energy

233

source and essential fatty acids and because it contains more salt and protein than a baby's immature kidneys can handle. If your baby is overweight on whole milk, 2 percent milk is a safe alternative. If your baby is not overweight and is not a compulsive milk drinker, then use whole milk.

INTRODUCING SOLID FOODS—WHEN, WHAT, AND HOW MUCH?

Solid food is for the mature (see Heb. 5:14). Most infants under six months of age do not need solid food. However, your baby may show signs after he is four months old that indicate he is willing and ready to take solid foods.

Your baby's interval between milk feedings gets shorter and shorter, and your intuition tells you he is less satisfied even after three or four days of increased nursing. Solids are usually given to breast-fed infants later because breastfeeding mothers respond to a growth spurt by increasing the frequency of feedings for several days until the supply equals the new demand level. Bottle-feeding mothers are more likely to want to begin solids than increase the number of formula feedings since they are more in the habit of counting bottles than breastfeeding mothers are in counting nursings. The nutritional needs of most infants can be met fully by breastfeeding or by an iron-fortified formula alone for nine months.

Your baby's need to chew and bite becomes obvious when he starts to teethe, which is usually around six months. Her tongue and mouth muscles are ready for the new skill of taking in solid food and swallowing it. She watches you eat with great interest, and since the best way to explore any unknown is to grab it and put it in her mouth, that's what she tries to do with the food she sees you eating. When you find yourself competing with your baby for your own dinner, the time is right to let her discover this new way of eating. If she is in a highchair or on your lap, simply offer her a tiny taste on the tip of your finger. She will grab your finger and eagerly suck on it to experience this new material. If you use a spoon, fill just the very tip of it, because she will grab the spoon (be prepared for a mess). Your baby may get a pleased and excited expression on her face, or she may frown and let the offered food slide right back out. Most babies like ripe, mashed bananas or yellow vegetables, like squash or sweet potatoes, or rice cereal mixed with a little breast milk or water. Mashed bananas or small amounts of rice cereal are good test foods for solid feedings because they are most like milk in taste and texture.

Babies have naturally built-in protective mechanisms that push unpleasant objects out with their tongues. They have to outgrow this tongue-thrust reflex before they are ready for solid foods. If your baby eagerly and easily swallows her first dose, then she has demonstrated her readiness. If the banana comes back at you rather quickly or if your baby demonstrates difficulty in swallowing or a lack of desire, then she is not ready.

Introducing solid food is much easier when your baby has the maturity to handle the eating process: reaching out and touching food, sitting up with support, and "mouthing" the food. Babies usually show these signs of readiness by six months.

Infant feeders (or nipples with extra large holes) that allow babies to suck baby food through a nipple are not acceptable. Babies should learn to use different muscle actions for solid foods than suck-swallow. A baby who is too young to use the correct eating muscles is too young to be given solid food. If it is the mess you are worried about, here is a hint for less messy feeding times: put baby in a high chair facing you and gently hold his hands in your nondominant hand while you feed him with your other hand. Older babies should be allowed to feed themselves as much as possible with their hands. The goal here is not how much food you can shovel in but how well baby learns to explore and enjoy his food.

Feed solid food after your baby's bottle. Milk should be your baby's primary nutrition during the first nine months since it is the most complete source of balanced nutrition. Solid foods should complement the milk feedings, not interfere with them. The interval between the bottle and the solid food is a matter of your convenience.

Since infants have no concept of breakfast, lunch, and dinner food, it really makes no difference whether they get fruit for breakfast or for dinner. Morning is usually the best time to offer solid foods to formula-fed infants because it is usually the time of day when mothers have the most time to prepare their infants' food. Breast-fed infants should be offered solids when their milk supply is lowest, usually toward the end of the day. Begin with a small amount of solid food (possibly a quarter teaspoon) since your initial goal is to introduce your baby gradually to a variety of foods, not to fill him up. The following suggestions on when and what kind of solid foods to introduce are only general guidelines and should be modified to fit your baby's specific needs and desires.

Fruits

Fruits are about 96 percent carbohydrates and, therefore, are not a good source of balanced nutrition. Avocadoes are an exception in that they contain a good percentage of polyunsaturated fat (the healthy kind) which makes this fruit a good early food for babies. One of the main benefits of fruits is that they mix well with other foods and can be used to increase the acceptance of more nutritious but less palatable foods. For example, your baby may take cereal more readily if it is covered with bananas. First introduce the fruits that are less allergenic and that have less citric acid, such as bananas, pears, and apples. Bananas are a good first food. Ripe, mashed bananas are accepted by most babies because they are sweet, have a smooth consistency, and closely resemble milk. I do not usually recommend strawberries, since many babies have an allergic reaction to them.

Juice

I do not recommend offering infants less than a year old large volumes of fruit juice. Undiluted fruit juice is almost as high in calories as milk but is much less nutritious, and juice is less advantageous than the fruit itself because the pulp has been removed. Because juice is less filling than milk, infants often take lots of juice without feeling full. The consumption of large quantities of juice is a subtle cause of childhood obesity in some infants. For these reasons, I recommend diluting juice with an equal quantity of water, especially for the compulsive juice drinker. To avoid juice-bottle caries (dental cavities resulting from giving a baby a bottle of fruit juice at naptime), dentists recommend that feeding a baby juice be delayed until he can drink from a cup.

Cereal

Cereal, like bananas, is one of the first solid foods a baby readily accepts because its consistency is closer to milk than that of many other solid foods. Cereal is often used as a filler to lengthen a baby's intervals between bottles or to encourage him to sleep through the night. This filler-food concept usually does not work, and it may contribute to obesity if overused. A baby is more comfortable when fed small amounts of solid foods frequently. (Feeding involves more than just physical nourishment and nutrition; both the parent and child should enjoy this feeding relationship.) If you are an exhausted mother who is not enjoying the feeding relationship because you have to feed your baby too often, especially at night, then using cereal for filler certainly should not be discouraged. Begin with rice or barley cereal, which are the least allergenic. Avoid mixed cereals until your baby has experienced each cereal made with those grains and has proved to not be allergic to them. Begin with a teaspoon of rice cereal and mix it with formula or breast milk to the desired and acceptable consistency. Adding fruits such as bananas or pears to the cereal may overcome its blandness and increase your baby's acceptance of it. Never force-feed your baby since this introduces a negative experience into his early eating habits. When a baby is satisfied he will turn his head away or refuse the foods.

Meats

Meat is an excellent source of iron and protein. Meats and iron-fortified cereals are the prime sources of iron for infants who do not receive vitamin-fortified formulas. Avoid purchasing meat dinners or meat mixtures. The protein and iron content of these mixtures is lower than that of plain meat since these mixtures are very high in starch. Liver and beef are the meats that are highest in iron, but they may not be accepted as easily by your infant as lamb, poultry, and veal.

Vegetables

Vegetables are a good source of carbohydrates and protein. The yellow vegetables, such as squash and carrots, are usually accepted better by young infants because of their taste and consistency. In theory, vegetables should be introduced before fruits since they are a much better source of balanced nutrition than fruits; however, because of fruits' sweetness, infants usually accept them better than vegetables.

Egg Yolks

Egg yolks are a good source of protein and fat. Although egg yolks are rich in iron, the kind of iron contained in them may not be absorbed easily by human intestines. A baby may be given an egg yolk any time after she is six months old, and one egg yolk every other day is sufficient. Delay feeding her egg whites until she is a year old since egg whites tend to be more allergenic than yolks. If your baby is generally allergic or if you have a strong family history of allergies, delay introducing either yolks or whites until she is at least one year of age.

Dairy Products

It is wise to avoid cow's milk as a beverage until your infant is at least one year of age because younger infants often do not tolerate cow's milk sugars or are allergic to cow's milk proteins. Some yogurts and cheeses, however, are tolerated better than milk because the allergenic products have been modified in the culturing process. Yogurt and cheese give all the nutritional benefits of milk without the potential problems and may be introduced into your infant's diet when he is about nine months old.

GIVE YOUR INFANT A BALANCED DIET

Giving your infant proper nutrition involves two basic requirements: the right amount of calories and the proper distribution of calories. Nutritionists have determined the proper distribution of calories by analyzing God's perfect nutrient—breast milk. The calories your infant consumes should be distributed in the following proportions: 30 to 45 percent fats, 35 to 50 percent carbohydrates, and 7 to 15 percent proteins. Your infant uses these calories for the following needs: 50 percent for his basic metabolism (the number of calories he needs simply to keep his body going), 30 percent for the energy he expends during activity, and 20 percent for continued growth. The percentage of calories he needs for growth is greatest during his first few months, 30 percent, and gradually decreases to 5 to 10 percent by one year of age. For this reason, the sooner nutritional deficiency occurs, the more it affects your infant's growth.

Breast milk and formula contain the appropriate proportions of carbohydrates, fats, and proteins. By one year of age, most infants receive about 50 percent of their nutrients from solid food. Between their first six months and a year, most infants need twenty-five to thirty-two ounces of formula per day, depending on the amount of solid food they are eating.

Your goal is to balance the proportions of carbohydrates, fats, and proteins in your infant's solid feedings as you have in her milk. A one-year-old baby who consumes about twenty ounces of formula a day and a large amount of fruits and fruit juices but refuses other food has a nutritional deficiency since the calories she receives are almost all carbohydrates, no fats, and no proteins. Another infant consumes about forty ounces of formula per day but simply refuses solid foods. If he is receiving the proper iron-fortified formula, then probably no nutritional deficiency exists. This baby has chosen to retain milk as his prime source of nutrition and has a balanced diet. A baby who consumes a variety of solid foods (four ounces of meat, vegetables, fruits, cereals, and egg yolk) and only takes eight to ten ounces of milk a day also has a balanced diet but has chosen a feeding pattern based predominantly on solid foods. As long as your baby is receiving a proper supply and distribution of nutrients, the source is not important.

Adding solid foods to baby's diet will change the character of his bowel movements. The stool of breast-fed babies will lose the almost pleasant "ripe buttermilk" odor (one reason breastfeeding mothers hesitate to start solids). Some babies will get runny stools; other babies will get firmer stools. If your baby becomes constipated, see "Common Intestinal Problems" in Chapter 12.

HOW TO PREPARE YOUR OWN BABY FOOD

I am sympathetic to baby food industries that are trying to achieve the economically impossible by keeping quality up and costs down. They have tried to use additives to keep food from spoiling and make it more palatable, but parental pressure has prompted them to eliminate monosodium glutamate, sugar, salt, and other chemicals from baby food. This constant adding to and subtracting from baby food according to fluctuating pressures often leaves parents very confused when they read labels. The current labels emphasize more what foods do not contain than what they do contain.

A steady diet of convenience foods has no place in infant nutrition. Making your own baby food from fresh, lean meat and fresh, seasonal vegetables and fruit is nutritionally superior to commercially processed baby foods. The following tips can enable you to prepare your own baby food at home.

- You will need a blender, ice cube trays with individual one-ounce cube sections, small freezer bags, and a pinch of creativity. Puree the fresh foods (vegetables should be cooked by steaming rather than boiling to preserve the many nutrients) through the baby food grinder or blender and pour them into the ice cube tray; then freeze the entire tray full of cube-size baby food. After freezing, remove the cubes and store them in plastic bags. Each time a feeding is needed, simply thaw one of these frozen cubes by placing it in a dish in a pan of hot water and you will have instant, nutritious baby food.

- Liver is a very good source of iron that, when blended with cottage cheese, makes a creamy pâté that is very nutritious.

- Teething biscuits and nutritious cookies and crackers can be prepared from whole-grain recipes found in a number of cookbooks on the market. Wheat products should be delayed until at least one year of age.

- Your infant can drink the same fruit juice as the rest of the family, but

239

dilute the juice about half and half. It is never necessary to add sugar, salt, or any artificial preservatives to any baby food made at home. Lemon juice is often recommended as a natural preservative.

At about nine months, finger foods become fun; and self-feeding is good for baby's fine motor development, even though he may make a humorous mess. The following ideas for finger foods are both appealing and safe: pieces of peeled fruit, cheese cubes, cooked carrot "wheels," tiny broccoli "trees," rice cakes, bits of cooked hamburger, flakes of tuna or cooked white fish (remove any tiny bones), or chicken legs with a little meat still attached (take the sliver bone off).

FEEDING YOUR TODDLER—THE PICKY EATER

"My baby won't eat" is a common complaint about the one- to two-year-old, and periodic disinterest in foods earns the toddler the title of "picky eater." The normal eating behavior of your busy toddler has gone something like this. During his first year you grew accustomed to feeding him a lot because he grew a lot. However, his growth rate is not nearly as rapid during his second year; so, he eats less.

Feeding a toddler is a combination of basic nutrition and creative marketing. Here is a feeding tip more in keeping with the realistic expectations of toddler behavior: prepare a toddler nibble tray with nutritious bits of food—raisins, cheese cubes, whole wheat bread sticks or strips of toast, orange wedges, apple slices with peanut butter, slices of meat, broccoli trees, hard-boiled egg wedges, and so on. Place this well-displayed "rainbow lunch" on your toddler's table, a table from which he can eat at his own pace. You will notice that your toddler will cruise by the tray and nibble at least ten times a day as he makes his rounds around the house.

Sitting down at the table can be primarily a time for communication, and as your child grows older, it can be a time for cleaning his plate. The concept of nibbling between meals may not agree with some parents who are used to mealtime discipline and three square meals a day. However, there is a good medical reason for this suggestion: your child will have blood-sugar swings when he is hungry. This is why most children's behavior deteriorates in late morning and mid-afternoon or just before the next meal. The practice of nibbling consistently all day long prevents these blood-sugar swings and therefore may be beneficial for your toddler's behavior. Patternless eating is normal for your toddler. He may "eat well" one day and "eat nothing" the next. If you average out his intake throughout the week, you will be surprised how balanced his diet is. Be sure to provide the four basic food groups in your toddler's snack tray: (1) dairy products, (2) meat and poultry, (3) fruits and vegetables, and (4) cereals and grains. Feeding a busy toddler brings out the best in creative mothering.

FEEDING PROBLEMS

Spitting Up, Regurgitation

All babies spit up, but some babies spit up more than others. At what point does spitting up go from being just a nuisance to being something medically wrong? If your baby is gaining weight normally and looks happy and healthy, then spitting up is more a temporary nuisance than a prolonged medical problem. If your baby does not look well and is not thriving normally, then you should consult your doctor for further advice on why your baby is spitting up. Spitting up is usually caused by swallowing excessive air or food, by an allergy, or by a gastroesophageal reflux. Some babies spit up several times a day, and the volume of regurgitated milk always seems more than it really is. To lessen your baby's degree of regurgitation try the following suggestions.

1. Lessen air intake by properly burping your baby.
2. Offer a smaller volume of food more frequently, and burp your baby well during breastfeeding or halfway through a bottle.
3. Keep your baby in the upright position as long as you can after each feeding (at least twenty to thirty minutes). This technique is especially helpful for very young babies. In some tiny babies, the esophagus joins the stomach at less of an angle so that when the stomach contracts, milk is pushed back up into the esophagus and out the baby's mouth. As your baby gets older, this angle becomes greater and most of this reflux subsides. Keeping your baby in the upright position after feedings allows gravity to hold the food down in the stomach and intestines, thus minimizing reflux. At night, you may be able to feed your baby in the lying down position without any trouble. But reflux is a major cause of night waking so it would be helpful to prop your baby upright against

your body after the feeding to be sure he burps well and to give gravity time to settle the milk.

4. Keep your baby's nasal passages clear. A stuffy nose causes baby to breathe through his mouth, and mouth breathing aggravates air swallowing.

Spitting up usually subsides by six to eight months, at which time your baby is sitting up after feedings and gravity is keeping the food down. Thereafter, jostling or crawling after feedings may cause your baby to spit up temporarily.

The Colicky Baby

Colic is one of the most severe discomforts a baby can suffer during his first few months. His parents will need a lot of prayer and counsel to survive this period and will need a lot of parental intuition to comfort their unhappy baby. The typical colicky baby cries from an intense physical discomfort, draws his legs onto a tense, gas-filled abdomen, and clenches his fists as if he were angry about his uncontrollable pain. His parents feel equally helpless about alleviating his misery.

Colic has many causes, but this explanation is limited to the four most common causes: (1) excessive swallowing and retention of air, (2) milk allergy, (3) the pain-tension cycles in a hyper-excitable baby, (4) gastroesophageal reflux.

Swallowing and retaining a lot of air is the most common cause of colic. Babies who suck ravenously swallow enormous amounts of air, thus calling upon parents to continue the ancient custom of "burping," "bubbling," or "winding" the baby. I have enjoyed watching the nurses on the pediatric wards at some hospitals where there is at least one "burping specialist" whose feeding expertise is equated with the ability to get the most milk in and the most wind out. If the air a baby swallows settles on top of the milk in her stomach, the air can be burped up and out and usually causes no discomfort to the baby. However, when this air settles beneath the milk in the stomach two problems can result: regurgitation (spitting up) and pain or colic. When the stomach—which is distended by both milk and air—contracts, the milk goes up and the air goes down. The swallowed air winds its way through the intestines, stretching them and producing pain. The crying infant instinctively draws up her legs to relax her abdomen and pass the air through her rectum to relieve her discomfort. If the milk is regurgitated, it may carry some stomach acids that cause a burning feeling in the baby's esophagus; this may be another source of the pain.

Swallowing and trapping air also causes a common feeding problem, the persistently hungry baby. The swallowed air gives the baby a false sense of fullness in his stomach. The "full" baby falls asleep without taking much milk and seems satisfied, but as soon as the air passes, he wakes again, hungry for his next meal of milk and air.

There are several ways to comfort your colicky baby. Minimize the air he swallows by burping early in his feedings and more often, especially if your baby is a ravenous drinker or "gulper." Try to eliminate the air swallowing before it becomes trapped in the stomach. If your baby is always ravenous he could benefit from more frequent feedings so that he does not have the starved, anxious look, driven to suck too vigorously and gulp a lot of air. If he waits too long between feedings, try waking him sooner, not waiting till he's screaming to take a cue that he's hungry. If you are bottle-feeding, be sure the nipple's hole is large enough for milk to pass through it freely. If the holes are too small, your baby will have to suck more vigorously to obtain milk and consequently will swallow more air. Milk should drip out at a rate of at least one drop per second from a full bottle held upside down and not shaken. If the hole seems too small, take a small sewing needle and insert it eye-end into a cork and heat the needle on a stove burner until it is red hot. Poke a hole in the nipple large enough to see through. Collapsible plastic bags that fit into a bottle holder also may lessen air intake.

Colic does occur in breast-fed babies, but not as often. The human nipple has many holes that allow milk to flow according to the vigor of the baby's suck. These nipple holes also have a valve-like action that stops the spurt of milk when the baby stops sucking. If the mother's breast is quite full at the start of a feeding, her milk-ejection reflex will cause milk to spray out forcefully even if her baby stops sucking, causing him to swallow air. It may help for the mother to express some milk before starting to nurse, or let the gush of milk spend itself in a towel.

Some babies do not burp easily, and some babies need to burp more frequently than others. If your baby does not spit up persistently or suffer from significant colic, then your burping techniques are certainly adequate for your individual baby. If your baby does not burp well and your instinct tells you there is a trapped bubble of air in her tummy, try shifting her positions—lay her over your lap on her stomach or on her right side to burp her. This allows the trapped bubble of air to rise to the top of her stomach. After a few minutes, hold her sitting upright, leaning forward against your hand, and pat her back firmly to allow her to burp. A stubborn bubble often comes up after you've changed your baby's diaper and lifted her to your shoulder again.

If your baby continues to swallow air, feed him in a more upright position, which allows gravity to hold the heavier milk down and let the lighter air rise to the top of his stomach where it can be burped out more easily. Also burp your baby in an upright position. Place a "bubble cloth" over your shoulder and hold your baby against it, firmly patting and stroking his back, or walk around and rock him rhythmically. Avoid jostling your baby too much, which may aggravate the colic.

Develop your own individual "colic" carry. Parents who have survived and comforted their colicky babies have learned what position works most of the time to ease the colic. Massaging your baby's abdomen also can help move the gas through her intestines so it can pass out the rectum. Start by warming her tummy with a warm washcloth or warm heating pad (be careful not to overdo this heat on very tender skin). Then use your flattened hand to stroke in the direction of the large intestine, up, over, and down. As you do this, you may feel a pocket of gas. Your baby must be relaxed for this to be very effective.

One way to get a screaming, rigid baby to stop crying and relax long enough to eliminate his gas is a bit unusual, but it may be just the thing that works for you. Tape record your baby's cry (about two minutes' worth) and play it back, being sure he can hear it above his uproar. When he hears it, he will stop to listen and may relax long enough to be massaged or to pass some gas on his own.

Milk allergy may be the cause of your infant's colic, even if you are breastfeeding. You may have an allergen in your milk because of the cow's milk in your diet. Temporarily remove dairy products from your diet to see if this makes a difference in your infant's colic. (Refer to section on breastfeeding for more details.) If you choose to remain off dairy products, consult your doctor to be sure you are getting the proper substitute nutrition. If you are formula-feeding, change to a less allergenic formula and seek advice from your physician.

What appears to be colic in some babies actually may be their temperaments, and their fussiness results in a total family problem. These babies are more appropriately termed *high-need babies*. See Chapter 9 for an in-depth discussion of the high-need baby. Many of the survival tips listed for parenting a high-need child are also appropriate for the colicky baby. Gastroesophageal reflux, the regurgitation of stomach acids into the esophagus, may irritate the esophagus causing a heartburn-like pain and therefore irritability in the baby being labeled colicky. If your baby wakes in pain at night, then suspect a medical cause such as reflux. Ordinary colic usually does not affect a baby consistently during sleep. If you suspect this condition, consult your doctor. Spitting up does not always occur with reflux, so the diagnosis may require testing.

There is an old saying in pediatrics concerning many of the problems of young childhood: "It soon will pass." This is very true of colic. Most babies' colic disappears when they are between three and six months old. By that time, they are sitting upright and their intestines are more mature. Their parents have learned to cope with the colic and to gentle their fussy babies, and the babies have achieved a better feeling of rightness. If your baby has persistent colic, don't forget to pray to God, asking Him to relieve the pain in His little child.

Cow's Milk Allergy

Cow's milk allergy is one of the most commonly overlooked causes of illness in young infants. Because of the high incidence of milk allergy in babies younger than a year and because drinking large volumes of cow's milk may cause anemia, the American Academy of Pediatrics recommends that infants not be given cow's milk before they are one year old.

Why is cow's milk so allergenic? The protein in cow's milk is suited for the intestines of a cow. Exposing human intestines to this protein may cause the gastrointestinal tract to bleed in small amounts, which results in anemia, vomiting, diarrhea, abdominal pain, lower intestinal gas, and bloating. These allergenic proteins also may be absorbed into your child's bloodstream, causing the systemic symptoms of allergies: an eczema-like rash, runny nose, or wheezing. Also, repeated colds and ear infections may be caused or aggravated by milk allergies.

Sometimes the intestines of older children cannot digest the sugar (lactose) in cow's milk. This results in a condition called "lactose intolerance" in which undigested lactose accumulates in the large intestines and forms gas, causing a bloated feeling, abdominal pain, and diarrhea. Because many mammals become lactose intolerant after they are weaned, it is possible that lactose intolerance is a normal process of maturity and that some children who are weaned from human milk to cow's milk really do outgrow their need for milk.

If your child is allergic to cow's milk, breastfeed him as long as you can. The longer your infant is breastfed, the less likely he is to develop a cow's milk allergy in later childhood. If your family has a long history of allergies, I strongly advise you to withhold dairy products for at least one to two years.

There is no good nutritional reason for discontinuing formula as long as your infant likes it. Consult your doctor before deciding to use a less allergenic formula that is not based on cow's milk. Allergic reactions to cow's milk protein usually disappear by two to three years of age in most children. The lactose intolerance may, however, persist throughout childhood and even adulthood.

245

A child who will not drink her milk may in fact be allergic to milk. If you suspect your child is allergic to milk, withhold milk and dairy products from her diet for at least three to four weeks to see if her symptoms disappear. Then challenge her again with milk to see if the symptoms reappear. Repeat the process. If your child has improved on the milk-free diet in two successive trials, then she probably is allergic to cow's milk.

If your child cannot tolerate milk, you do not need to worry that she will not get enough calcium. There is some calcium in most foods, especially whole grains and vegetables. Since dairy products are still the prime source of calcium for most children, try feeding your child yogurts and some cheeses because the allergens often are changed in the processing. Like formula, yogurt has all the nutritional benefits of milk without the problems of lactose intolerance. Yogurt is made by adding a bacterial culture to milk; the culture ferments the milk and breaks down the lactose into simple sugars which are absorbed more easily.

Food Allergy

Food allergies ("food intolerance" may be more medically correct) often are called the "great masqueraders" because they mask a variety of symptoms in children that often go undetected. The most common symptoms of food allergies are eczema-like rashes (especially on the face), puffy eyelids, chronic diarrhea, and a persistently stuffy nose. Sometimes the symptoms of food allergies may be very subtle: a pale, tired, or droopy child; a child with headaches, abdominal pain, or muscle aches; or a child with recurrent colds and ear infections; night waking may be the only symptom in some children.

The most common food allergens in order of their prevalence are milk and dairy products, chocolate, eggs, cane sugar, citrus fruits, nuts, wheat products, corn, berries, and food colorings and additives. If you suspect your child is allergic to any of these foods, you may have to do a bit of detective work. Eliminate the suspected food allergens one by one from your child's diet until the most obvious symptoms disappear. Then include them in his diet a second time to see if the symptoms reappear. If you strongly suspect your child has a food allergy, consult your doctor for a proper way to use an elimination diet. If you have a strong family history of allergies, the following suggestions may help you prevent allergies in your child: (1) breastfeed your infant for at least one year; (2) delay introducing solid foods until your infant shows definite signs of wanting solid foods; (3) begin with the less allergenic foods (rice, bananas, yellow vegetables); (4) avoid giving a mixture of food to your infant who is less than one year old because if he is allergic to the mixture, isolating the offending allergen will be difficult; and (5) withhold potentially allergenic foods (see the previous list) until your child is more than one year old.

Junk Food

Two types of food rightfully earn the title "junk food": foods that have artificial food colorings (mainly, red and yellow dyes) and cane sugar. This "table sugar" is processed so heavily that the few nutrients found in natural sugar are removed. This refined sugar is absorbed more rapidly from the intestines than other kinds of sugar and reaches a high concentration in the blood. This triggers the release of insulin which rapidly lowers the blood sugar, causing behavioral changes and often stimulating the person to eat again.

The child's developing brain is very dependent on a steady blood sugar as its prime source of energy. Fluctuations in his blood sugar can cause hyperactivity, fainting, irritability, depression, and aggression. Children with marked blood-sugar swings frequently have difficulty concentrating, and their learning is often compromised. Headaches, visual disturbances, and a general tired feeling are symptoms also associated with low blood sugar.

Not all sugar should be considered junk food since our bodies derive about 45 percent of their necessary calories from sugars, including the sugars that occur in the form of starches (grains and vegetables). The refined cane sugar or corn syrup, also called "dextrose" on some labels, is what I mean by "junk sugar." Nutritious sugars are the natural sugars such as the lactose in milk and the fructose in fruits. These sugars are absorbed and utilized within the body differently from how junk sugar is used. They cause fewer swings in blood sugar and, therefore, do not adversely affect a child's behavior. These sugars also contain small amounts of additional nutrients, such as vitamins and traces of minerals.

How can you know whether or not the sugar added to foods is junk sugar? Current label laws require contents to be listed in order of volume. If sugar is high on the list of contents, the food is very high in sugar. If the label says "corn syrup," "sugar," or "dextrose," the food is high in junk sugars. Natural sugars will be listed as honey or fructose.

Highly colored and highly sugared fruit drinks, soft drinks, and punches rank high among junk foods. Besides containing food colorings (which also may trigger behavior problems in some children) and junk sugar, these drinks contain very little, if any, actual juice, have limited nutritional value, and definitely should not be given to children.

CHILDHOOD OBESITY

An important quality in a Christian child is his ability to delay his gratification by controlling his impulses. Saying no to his appetite for food is one of the earliest forms of impulse control that a child can learn and that parents can model. In this section some causes of childhood obesity and how you as Christian parents can model appetite control for your child will be discussed.

Defining Childhood Obesity

At what point should you worry that your child is becoming too fat? If your child's weight is 10 percent greater than the average weight for his sex, height, and age, then he is overweight and potentially obese. If your child weighs 20 percent more than his ideal weight, he is fat or obese. Ten to 20 percent of all children are obese, making them candidates for many adult diseases.

What the mirror shows or what your child feels is often more important than what the scales or growth charts say. That is why the amount of excess fat your child has is more important than his actual weight. Doctors call this fat "skin-fold thickness," which is measured at different places on your child's body, and the changes in this fat can be used as a measure of weight loss or gain.

The fat-cell theory postulates that fat tissue increases by the size or number of fat cells. During his first two years, the critical period for fat cell development, a child's fat cells increase in number. Lesser spurts in fat cell number occur at seven years of age and again during adolescence. After growth is finished and a person has reached adulthood, his fat cells do not increase significantly in number; and thereafter any increase or decrease in fat tissue results from a change in the size of these cells.

If a child is overfed during infancy (or middle childhood or adolescence), the excess calories he ingests may produce an excess number of fat cells. Continued overfeeding will cause these fat cells to get larger. This results in a tendency toward obesity, which simply means that there are more fat cells to get fat. Once a child has too many fat cells it is very difficult for him to lose them. Weight reduction can occur only by decreasing the size of these cells. This theory gives rise to the concern that a child who has an excess number of fat cells may have to watch his weight all of his life.

Factors Contributing to Childhood Obesity

Perhaps the most important determinant of childhood obesity is the body type of the parents. There are three body types: ectomorphic, mesomorphic, and endomorphic. Ectomorphic eaters are lean and lanky. They can "eat everything and not get fat" because they accumulate much less fat tissue and seem to have a different metabolism. Some ectomorphs who overeat actually can have an excess amount of fat but, because of their lanky appearance, they do not appear fat. Ectomorphs are better able to gauge their food intake for their activity level. Mesomorphs are husky; they have a medium build or medium height and large bones. These people have a greater tendency toward obesity, carry excess fat much less attractively, and have more difficulty balancing their food intake and their activity level. Endomorphs have short and fat body types. They are most likely to produce obese children.

Heredity plays a very important part in the tendency toward obesity. According to statistics, overweight parents do produce overweight children. If both parents are obese, the probability of their having an obese child can be as high as 80 percent. If one parent is obese, there is a 40 percent chance of the child's being obese; and if neither parent is obese, they have only a 7 percent chance of having an obese child. Studies of adopted children show that they tend to follow the weight trends of their biological parents more than their adoptive parents, indicating that heredity plays a greater role in obesity than environment. Because of these hereditary factors, some children have a higher obesity potential than others, but whether or not they become obese depends on many factors in their environment.

Calorie balance. Weight control requires a balance of the number of calories a child takes in and the number of calories the child burns off. Children need calories for three basic purposes: to maintain their bodily functions, to grow, and to obtain fuel for exercise. Adult caloric requirements change only with exercise; whereas, children's caloric requirements are greatest during their periods of rapid growth spurts. If a child consumes more calories than he needs for growth and exercise, the excess calories are deposited as excess fat.

Appestat. Appetite control means that a child consumes just the right number of calories for her needs and that her appetite adjusts to her changing needs. There are many factors that affect a child's appetite control, or her appestat, and it is not completely known why some children cannot control their appetites.

249

Early feeding practices.   It is possible that early feeding habits may affect a child's ability to control her appetite. One of the early feeding habits that may affect eventual appetite control is breastfeeding. Whether or not breast-fed infants are less likely to become obese than formula-fed infants is controversial. There are many studies on this subject, and one can pluck from the medical literature any one of these studies that supports his own bias.

· In my opinion, breastfeeding does lower the risk for obesity for the following reason: breast milk changes to accommodate the changing needs of the infant. The fat content of breast milk changes during each feeding and also changes at various times of the day, usually being higher in the morning and lower in the evening. The nursing infant gets foremilk initially, which is low in fat, and with continued sucking she is rewarded with the creamier hindmilk that is high in fat and calories. When the infant has obtained sufficient hindmilk, perhaps the high-calorie milk signals her appestat that she is full, and she stops sucking when both her sucking needs and her appetite are completely satisfied. It is often difficult for a mother to tell whether a baby is hungry or thirsty. When breast-fed babies are thirsty, they may suck a shorter period of time and less vigorously to obtain the foremilk. The bottle-fed baby, however, does not enjoy the advantages of different milks for different needs. He gets the same high-calorie milk whether he is thirsty or hungry and the same high-calorie milk at each feeding.

As the infant grows older he needs less calories per pound of body weight; therefore, breast milk gradually decreases in fat and calories accordingly. Since there is general agreement that obesity is not healthy, it seems logical that the changes in the caloric content of breast milk are in accordance with God's design for preventing obesity in His children. Researchers who attempt to study the skin-fold thickness of breast-fed babies and of formula-fed babies have noted a difference in the feel of the fat. It is more difficult to measure the skin-fold thickness of breast-fed babies since they have a less well-defined line between their muscle and fat than formula-fed babies do. Some breast-fed babies do indeed appear to be very fat during the first year, especially babies who nurse "all day and all night." Nearly all of these babies lose their excess fat by the time they are two years old.

Another early feeding practice that may contribute to obesity is the early introduction of solid foods. This also is controversial, but the high rate of obesity in certain cultures that introduce solid foods early suggests that this practice may produce obesity in some children.

Temperament.   The child's temperament is also a factor in obesity. Children with quiet, placid personalities who enjoy more sedentary activities have a higher obesity potential. A vicious cycle develops; the less active a child is, the fatter he becomes and the less interested he becomes in physical activities. Fat children do not always eat more than lean children and some may even eat less, but fat children do eat more for their level of exercise than they need. Children with normal weight and appetite control reach a balance between exercise and appetite. As they exercise less, they eat less and vice versa. Obese children, however, do not achieve this balance. As they exercise less, they do not eat proportionally less. This imbalance between calories and exercise is an important concept about appetite control. More childhood obesity is caused by too little exercise than by too much eating.

Preventing Obesity

You can lessen your child's obesity potential by following these suggestions.

1. *Determine if your child is a candidate for childhood obesity.*

2. *Breastfeed your infant for as long as possible* and encourage infant-led weaning.

3. *Introduce solid food only when you are sure your infant needs solid food.* Introduce solids wisely and use these foods for nutrition only, not as fillers to hold your child through the night or to lengthen the interval between feedings. Choose foods that are high in nutrition but low in calories.

4. *Avoid the "clean plate syndrome."*   Many mothers feel responsible for how much their children eat. They often equate clean plates with effective mothering. You are responsible for what foods you offer your child, but allow her to be responsible for how much she eats so that she can develop her own appetite control.

5. *Discourage your child from eating to alleviate boredom.*   Children often turn to the refrigerator for satisfaction, but their appetites really crave more meaningful activities or interpersonal relationships. It is also more tempting for a parent or a baby-sitter to bribe a child with food than devote time and energy to feeding the child spiritually. Discourage your child from eating alone or nibbling in front of a television, and encourage him in activities that build his self-esteem. A child who feels right not only acts right but also eats right.

6. *Encourage impulse control and delayed gratification,* so that "each of you should know how to possess his own vessel in sanctification and honor" (1 Thess. 4:4). I believe a young child should be taught to fast, not to the extent that adults should fast because fasting may be medically unsound for some children. But chil-

dren can fast by giving up that second scoop of ice cream. When your child is old enough to have a good receptive language (usually by two years of age), he is old enough to understand no and to understand why his tummy needs discipline.

7. *Model good habits.*   As is true for all forms of discipline, modeling is very important for disciplining the appetite. If your child sees you overindulge, she most likely will overindulge. It is much easier for you to teach your child to discipline her appetite when she sees you fasting. Children are very quick to pick up the priority that food plays in your own gratification.

8. *Offer alternatives.*   Eating for enjoyment is one of the blessings God has given us, but overindulging this pleasure is wrong. If your child eats for pleasure and satisfaction too often, offer alternative forms of enjoyment such as favorite activities or places to go. Offer him any attractive activity that may get his mind off his stomach.

9. *Recognize the power of television commercials.*   Television commercials for junk food have contributed greatly to childhood obesity. Unfortunately, many children actually believe that commercials are true, especially when they see their parents eating or drinking what is advertised. These commercials teach children that food is a source of fun and entertainment rather than a source of balanced nutrition. Teach your child the real purpose God intended for food.

10. *Encourage a lot of physical activity for your child.*   Remember that if your child has a sedentary temperament, she is prone to obesity, especially if she has a high-risk body type. Exercise is very important for the sedentary child, especially if she is bored easily.

11. *Avoid blaming medical problems for your child's obesity.*   In the great majority of obese children, there are no underlying medical reasons for their excess weight. They simply eat too much or exercise too little or both. If your child generally seems well and is not unusually short, then a medical problem is unlikely. A short, heavy child always should have a complete medical evaluation.

A Sample Weight Control Program

Although obesity is an individual problem requiring an individual solution, there are key elements common to nearly all weight control programs. Try the following suggestions to cope with your child's weight problem.

1. *Determine how overweight your child is.*   For example, a child who is thirteen years old and is of average height should weigh 100 pounds. If your child

weighs 125 pounds, he is 25 pounds or 20 percent overweight; therefore, he is obese. Your doctor may measure your child's skin folds in the back of his arm or around his waist. These measurements help determine if the excess weight is primarily fat. They also serve as a basis for monitoring your child's body fat as his weight decreases.

2. *Determine why your child is overweight.*   By reviewing the factors contributing to obesity as outlined in the preceding pages, determine if she is overweight because she eats too much, exercises too little, or does both. Review her eating habits, her cravings, her level of physical activity, her hobbies, and her basic temperament. Review your family history. Are there many obese family members? Review the eating habits of the whole family.

3. *What is your child's motivation to lose weight?*   Does he really want to lose weight or do you want him to lose weight? Self-motivation is indispensable in any successful weight control program. How does being overweight affect your child's self-image, especially when he looks at himself in the mirror?

4. *Understand the mathematics of weight control.*   The average person needs to burn off slightly more than thirty-five hundred calories to lose one pound. Weight gain begins when your child consumes more calories than he burns off. It is important to remember that only a few extra calories a day over a long period of time lead to obesity. For example, an extra fifty calories per day, the equivalent of one small chocolate chip cookie, could result in an extra five pounds per year. To lose a pound of body fat, your child either must eat thirty-five hundred fewer calories or burn off an extra thirty-five hundred calories. A good weight control program will utilize both the eat-less and burn-off-more approaches.

5. *Count calories in various foods.*   To help you understand which foods provide the most nutrition for the least number of calories, study the following food facts.

Vegetables.   Salads are a dieter's best friend because they are relatively high in nutritional value but low in calories. Some vegetables are more nutritious than others; broccoli contains more protein per calories than most vegetables. Corn, lima beans, and potatoes are high in starch, and therefore, contain more calories than the same weight of other vegetables. Lettuce is a free food, meaning your child can eat as much lettuce as he wishes. Lettuce is very low in calories because of its very high water content. A large lettuce and tomato salad (with low-calorie dressing) is a good way to begin a meal.

Dairy products.   The caloric content of milk and other dairy products is determined mostly by the amount of fat they contain. One gram of fat contains twice the number of calories in a gram of protein or carbohydrates. Whole milk contains 4 percent butterfat; low-fat milk contains 2 percent; and skim milk has had most of the fat removed. Low-fat, unsweetened yogurt is a wise choice of dairy products for a dieter.

Meats.   The caloric content of meat also depends upon its fat content. Choose lean meat and remove its excess fat. Because lean meat has a high amount of nutrition for its calories, it is a wise choice of nutrition for the dieter.

Poultry.   Poultry has fewer calories than meats such as beef or pork because it has less fat. Removing the skin from poultry and broiling or baking it (instead of frying it) also lowers its calories.

Fish.   Fish is a very nutritious food because it also has few calories for its nutritive value and has relatively little fat.

Fruits and juices.   Fruit juices have more calories and less nutritional value than the same volume of vegetable juice. The fruit itself is nutritionally superior to fruit juice because the pulp content is preserved. Fruit juice is not very filling; therefore, some children drink an excessive amount of fruit juice, which may be a subtle cause of obesity. If your child is a compulsive drinker, dilute the juice to the limits of his acceptability.

Cereals and grains.   Avoid the "junk cereals" that are very high in sugars and calories but low in nutrition. Whole grain cereal is nutritionally superior to processed cereals.

Sugars and sweets.   Avoid these junk foods.

Oils and dressings.   Use low-calorie dressings. Avoid breading or frying foods in oil since this increases the caloric content of the food without adding much to the nutrition. Oils and dressings are very high in fat and calories; one tablespoon of mayonnaise may contain one hundred calories which is often the caloric content of the entire salad.

When preparing foods, trim the excess fat off meats and poultry. Fried foods are higher in calories than baked or broiled foods, and steamed vegetables are more nutritious than boiled ones because their vitamins are preserved in the cooking. Generally, the more natural and unprocessed a food is, the higher its nutritional value is.

Exercise and Weight Control

It is safer to increase a growing child's exercise than to impose strict diets. One hour of sustained exercise—running, swimming, fast walking—will burn off between three hundred and five hundred calories a day, which will reduce body fat by nearly a pound a week. A forced exercise program may be necessary for sedentary children until they build up their stamina and enjoyment of activity.

Change your child's basic eating patterns. Buffet dinners are a no-no for the compulsive eater. Use smaller plates and have the family bring them to the table already filled (the out-of-sight-out-of-mind approach). Cut food into smaller pieces and encourage your child to eat more slowly. Start each meal with a large salad with low-calorie dressing. Have your child eat in only one room, preferably the kitchen or dining room, and discourage his habit of nibbling in front of the TV or while talking on the phone.

Help your child improve his self-esteem. Feeling good about himself is an absolute necessity for any successful weight control program. Food is the most readily available source of gratification for a person with a low self-esteem. Urge your child to become involved in meaningful activities with his peer group. Help the older child emphasize academic achievements. Promote sports and team play. Take inventory of emotional stresses that may contribute to your child's low self-esteem and thereby to his eating habits.

Change Your Child's Behavior

A very important principle of behavior modification is called "shaping." Behavior modification is most effective when attempted gradually and step-by-step toward a final goal. Sudden, drastic changes in behavior—crash diets and too many changes too fast—are usually less effective than small but consistent changes. For teenagers, group therapy and individual counseling are often very helpful in weight control. These services are found in most major medical centers and are called "teen clinics."

Prompt your school to teach courses on good nutrition to children at the third-grade level, before the preadolescent and adolescent obesity stages. The menus in school cafeterias should emphasize low-starch diets. Vending machines should contain nutritious snacks and fruit juices rather than candies and sodas. There should be as many athletic programs for girls as there are for boys. School-age children need nourishing mid-morning and mid-afternoon snacks to prevent low-blood-sugar periods and to improve their learning and concentration.

Set goals. Since children are goal oriented, urge your child to determine how many pounds she wishes to lose within a certain period of time. How many pounds she should lose and how fast she should lose them depend upon her degree of motivation and upon how overweight she is. A safe and achievable goal for a growing child is a loss of one pound per week until the ideal weight is reached. This means a deficit of thirty-five hundred calories per week. Young children should not go on crash diets without professional counseling. A steady weight loss is not only safer for growing children but is likely to be more consistent. Slight modifications in eating habits are more likely to succeed than drastic changes in behavior patterns.

The cut-out-one-thing-a-day method is very successful for the slightly overweight child. The most successful diets are built upon a person's own food preferences, providing they are reasonably nutritious. Pick out one hundred calories' worth of junk food from your child's present diet, and if your child does nothing but eliminate these calories each day, she will lose ten pounds in one year. Since most children ingest only a slight excess of daily calories, this small change in eating habits may be enough to control their weight. I usually give the slightly overweight child a realistic goal, "You don't have to lose any weight, but don't gain any weight for one year." If your child continues to lose excess body fat as she gets taller, she really is losing weight.

If your child who is about 10 percent overweight cuts out one hundred empty calories daily (for example, one cola and one cookie), and does at least a half-hour of sustained exercises each day, he will burn off more than five hundred calories per day. This would result in a gradual weight loss of one pound per week. The maximum weight loss a growing child should be allowed is *two pounds per week* and this should not be attempted without professional dietary counseling.

Recognize your role. Parents, please do not feel that your child's weight loss is *your* responsibility. This may be true for the infant and young child but not for the older child and teenager. Your responsibility is to help your child increase her self-esteem and to create an atmosphere that is conducive for healthy eating habits. Also you should model and teach good nutrition by your own example at home. Your teenager's weight control is her responsibility, not yours. Prayer and support will do much more for your child's weight problem than constant nagging.

Parent-adolescent conflicts often arise when parents take a heavy role in their children's weight control programs. Leave the responsibility of weight control to your teenager and the direction of her program to her physician or dietary counselor. Direct your energies to your adolescent's emotional needs.

NUTRITION FOR THE YOUNG ATHLETE

Athletic children need extra-energy foods. An active teenage athlete may need an extra one thousand nutritious calories per day, the average number of calories burned off in two hours of sustained exercise. He should eat extra-energy foods that are primarily high-energy carbohydrates, such as fruits, fruit juices, and grains; vitamins and mineral supplements are not sources of energy. The young athlete should strive for a very balanced diet, and each day his diet should consist of six- to eight-ounce servings from the four basic food groups: (1) milk and dairy products (two servings)—yogurt and unprocessed cheese are good milk substitutes; (2) high protein foods and meats (two servings)—beef, fish, poultry, and eggs; (3) fruits and vegetables (four servings); (4) cereals and grains (four servings)—whole grain cereal, bread, pasta.

Your young athlete will need a lot of extra water, and the thirst mechanism is not always a reliable indicator of how much water is needed. Encourage your athletic child to drink water until he is no longer thirsty and then to drink two more glasses after that. Dehydration and poor nutrition can diminish the young athlete's performance.

Provide after-school snacks that have at least five hundred nutritious calories of primarily high-energy carbohydrates. Growing children, especially teenagers, may experience "down periods" of low blood sugar during the mid-afternoon or when school is out, and this certainly may affect athletic performance. Fruits, yogurt, and nutritious cookies are suggested snacks.

Iron-Rich Foods

Adolescent athletes need extra iron, males because of their growing muscles and females because of menstruation. If your child has low blood iron, his or her athletic performance may be minimized. The following foods are ranked according to iron content from highest to lowest: liver, beef, poultry, fish, prunes, iron-fortified cereals, raisins, beans, green leafy vegetables, and egg yolks. The iron in animal foods (beef, pork, poultry, fish) is absorbed more efficiently through the intestines than the iron in vegetables or egg yolks.

The Pre-game Meal

"What should my child eat before playing a big game?" is a common question. The pre-game meal should be low in fat since fatty foods stay in the stomach for a longer time, creating an uncomfortable feeling of fullness. Give your child a high-carbohydrate meal two hours prior to the game. I suggest the following pre-game meal: a lean meat or chicken sandwich (without mayonnaise), fruit and fruit juice, a salad, sherbet or nutritious cookies, and much extra water.

There is an old athletic axiom, "Sunday's game is played on Friday's food." A child can store up energy for a coming game by eating a high-energy, nutritious diet for several days before the game.

Crash Diets

I am often asked, "How much weight can my child lose without hurting himself?" If your child must lose weight to make the team, a crash diet and rapid weight loss will not help him. The body loses weight in two areas, from the lean body mass, or muscles, and from fat. Excess weight never should be dropped from a child's lean body mass but only from his excess fat. Most children's excess fat is at least 5 to 10 percent of their body weight; so, most children can lose 5 percent of their body weight safely.

A safe and steady weight loss for a young athlete is two pounds per week, which is best accomplished by two hours of sustained exercise each day plus a well-balanced diet that is completely free of empty calories or junk food. I advise that your child's weight loss program be supervised by a physician who provides proper dietary counseling and measures your child's skin folds at weekly intervals to be sure he is losing primarily fat and not muscle tissue.

CHAPTER 12

COMMON CONCERNS OF INFANCY

YOUR BABY'S BELONGINGS

Parents are often preoccupied with the preparation of their baby's room; they take a lot of time and go to great expense to fix it the way they want it. Perhaps the least important factor in caring for an infant is having her room equipped with all the latest baby paraphernalia because God has endowed mothers with the most important things needed to care for babies: arms, hands, breasts, eyes. It is more important to spend time and money preparing yourselves than fixing up a room.

Cradles and Rocking Chairs

Babies are accustomed to motion. They have been moving around for nine months. If you choose to have a separate sleeping place for your baby, I advise using a cradle instead of a crib, at least for the first six months. When your baby shifts his weight, the cradle will sway and often lull him to sleep. Many mothers find that they themselves become the newborns' "cradles." Many babies have to be put to sleep before they are put down, rather than put down to go to sleep. A mother who had been her baby's human cradle for many months told me a humorous story: "I was standing at a party, holding a glass of ginger ale and swaying back and forth from the habit of rocking my baby, when a friend came up to me and asked if I had had too much to drink." The human cradle wears out after a while so rocking chairs are a real must. A rocking chair is probably the most useful gift for a new mother, but before purchasing one, try it out. Be sure the arms are low enough to support the mother's arms comfortably while nursing. The breast and the rocking chair are a winning combination for mothering a baby to sleep.

Slings, Swings, and Other Things

I advise parents to use a sling-type carrier such as *The Original Baby Sling* to "wear" their babies on their chests or hips. I have personally studied the effects of baby-wearing: it makes life easier for the parents and keeps babies more content. Baby carriers bring your baby much closer to you than plastic infant seats and baby buggies. Plastic infant seats were originally designed for sick babies with heart problems who needed to be kept upright. They were not designed to be a substitute for a parent's arms. Although they are useful for some modes of travel and some activities (such as eating in a restaurant with a small infant), they are certainly second best to a sling or front/back carrier.

Wind-up baby swings are often useful for soothing the fussy baby when the "human swing" wears out. Babies more than three months old usually have enough head control to adapt to the swing, or their heads can be propped up with rolled towels. Mobiles to watch and rattles to grab are good toys to occupy and stimulate babies.

Tiny babies are more attracted to the colors of red and yellow, and they like light and dark contrasts such as black and white patterns on cards. Use the marvels of nature to attract and hold your baby's interest. Place your baby in front of a window facing a garden, trees, rain, or anything that is moving. These are God's mobiles and they are usually enjoyed by the curious infant.

Before you bring your baby home from the hospital, you will need to prepare his layette. The following chart will help you know what kinds of items and how much of them to supply.

Outfitting Your Baby's Layette

Supplies
- mild bath soap and shampoo
- mild laundry soap
- diaper pins (if using cloth diapers) 3 pairs
- diaper pail
- rectal thermometer
- cotton balls
- baby bathtub or molded bath aid
- diaper cream, zinc oxide
- cotton-tipped applicators
- rubbing alcohol
- petroleum jelly
- nasal aspirator with 2-inch bulb
- 8 oz. bottles for formula
- 4 oz. bottles for water
- bottle brush

Equipment
- bassinet, cradle, crib
- storage chest for clothing
- infant carseat
- baby sling
- changing table or padded work area
- portable bed
- diaper bag
- rocking chair
- vaporizer-humidifier
- night light

Linens
- flannel-backed rubber pads 4
- crib or bassinet sheets 2
- wash cloth 3
- baby blanket 2–4
- hooded baby towels 2

Clothing
- diapers (cloth) 3 dozen
- diapers (disposable)
- plastic pants (loose-fitting) 4
- receiving blanket 6
- lightweight tops (saques and/or kimonos) 8
- terrycloth sleepers and/or heavyweight saques 8
- booties 3 pairs
- sunhats 2
- warm hats 2
- sweaters 2
- undershirts (3–6 month size) 6
- socks 2 pairs

CARING FOR YOUR NEWBORN

Temperature of Your Baby's Environment

The smaller the baby, the more careful you need to be about changes in temperature. Premature babies and babies weighing less than five pounds may have immature temperature-regulating systems for the first few weeks; therefore they need to be kept warm. Full-term, healthy newborns, especially large ones weighing more than eight pounds, have body fat and mature temperature-regulating systems to adapt easily to an environmental temperature comfortable to an adult. A room temperature of about seventy degrees Fahrenheit is adequate for a full-term, healthy baby. What is more important than the actual temperature is its stability. Babies may not adjust well to marked temperature swings for their first few weeks.

Humidity in the room is important for two reasons: (1) it helps maintain the constancy of the heat, and (2) it keeps your baby's narrow nasal passages from drying out. A relative humidity of at least 50 percent is advisable. A dry climate or your home's central heating may necessitate the use of a humidifier or vaporizer to maintain this humidity. Signs that the humidity in his sleeping room is too low for your baby are persistently clogged nasal passages, snifflely breathing, and dry skin.

Clothing

The way you dress your baby is a matter of culture and temperature. As a general guide, dress your baby in the same amount of clothing you are wearing for a given temperature. Cotton clothing is preferable because it absorbs body moisture and allows air to circulate freely. Also be sure the clothing is loose enough to allow your baby to move freely.

Taking Baby Outside

If you live in a climate where the temperature inside and outside the house is similar, then a full-term baby weighing more than six pounds is able to go outside immediately after birth. By the time your baby weighs about eight pounds, he has enough body fat and his temperature-regulating system is mature enough to tolerate brief exposure to temperature swings, such as those experienced traveling from house to car and back. Babies less than six pounds may not tolerate marked changes in temperature; therefore, it is necessary to maintain some consistency of temperature by traveling from a heated house to a heated car.

Environmental Irritants

Cigarette smoke is the most commonly overlooked irritant to a baby's tiny respiratory passages. Studies have shown that babies of smoking parents have three times the number of respiratory infections found in babies of nonsmoking parents. Persistent nasal stuffiness and hacking coughs are the usual signs of irritation from cigarette smoke. I strongly advise parents to have a strict no-smoking rule in closed spaces such as a house or car, especially around children less than two years old.

Bathing Your Baby

The materials you need to bathe your baby are a small plastic tub or sponge form, several thick towels, a pair of white cotton gloves, cotton-tipped applicators, a mild soap, and an antiseptic solution.

Babies rarely get dirty enough to require a daily bath for cleanliness. It is usually enough to bathe your baby totally twice a week and wash her hair no more than once a week. Wearing cotton gloves will make it easier for you to hold your slippery baby. Rub some mild soap on the wet gloves, and use your gloved hands as a washcloth. Place a towel in the bottom of the sink or tub to prevent your baby from slipping, or use specially designed sponge forms. Cotton-tipped applicators are handy for cleaning the creases behind the ears and in the crevices of the navel. After your baby's bath, place her on a soft, padded surface to dry her off.

In reality, bathtime is playtime for both mother and baby. A baby loves the closeness of taking baths with you in your tub. Draw the warm water to just below your breast level, and allow your baby to float slightly nestled in your arms. Nurse her if she wants. This water ritual is relaxing for both of you, especially during a baby's fussy periods.

I generally discourage using powders and oils on a baby's skin because it is naturally oily and excess oil may attract bacteria. Powders, if inhaled, may be irritating to a baby's sensitive lungs. If you find that your baby's skin is becoming excessively dry, you may be washing her too often and rubbing too hard and thus removing much of the natural oils from her skin. Scented oils and powders may mask the natural baby scent mothers usually find so appealing. Babies love an oil massage *before* the bath. The beautiful ritual of massaging babies is described in Vimala Scheider McClure's *Infant Massage* (see Bibliography).

Care of the Navel

Your baby's cord will fall off sometime between one and three weeks of age. Twice a day, clean around the cord, digging deep into the crevices with a cotton-tipped applicator. Use the antiseptic solution your doctor recommends. It is normal to notice a few drops of blood when the cord falls off, but this will subside within a day or two. After the cord falls off, continue applying the antiseptic solution for a few days until the entire area in the umbilicus is dry.

COMMON MEDICAL CONCERNS OF BABY'S FIRST YEAR

The Health Care System

The most effective health care system set up in most locations throughout North America is the system of well-baby care. In this system your child is examined by your physician at periodic intervals, usually birth; two weeks; two, four, six, nine, twelve, fifteen, eighteen, and twenty-four months; two-and-a-half and three years; and once a year thereafter.

This schedule may vary according to the parents' needs and the baby's general health. The purposes of these periodic exams are (1) to check for actual or potential abnormalities in growth and development; (2) to note your child's nutritional requirements at various ages; (3) to discuss developmental and emotional changes; (4) to point out specific age- and stage-related needs; (5) to discuss your questions or adjustment problems; (6) to help your doctor get to know you and your child during the child's well state, which serves as a reference point for medical judgment when your child is ill; (7) to treat the illnesses or abnormalities that may be detected during examination even though your child appears well; and (8) to administer necessary immunizations.

Just as parents are developing intuition about their child in the early stages of parenting, the pediatrician also is developing an intuition about your child and about you as parents. It is very important for your doctor to know your child. Nothing is more frustrating for a doctor than to see the child only when he is ill. The doctor will feel he or she does not know the total child and is therefore at a disadvantage when it is necessary to make appropriate medical decisions. Scheduling periodic exams is the best preventive medicine, and it is also an economically wise investment in the long run.

Getting the most out of your visits to your doctor can be summed up by one word, *communication*. Shortly before your appointment, make a list of your concerns. Memorize this list, because I have found that new parents often forget to bring their lists. Being well prepared when you visit your doctor conveys that these visits are important to you and your child. If possible, both parents should attend these well-child visits since this also conveys the message of commitment.

Another kind of doctor's visit is for a specific problem. Because illnesses cannot be conveniently scheduled, your doctor will usually reserve some time during each office day for treating sudden illnesses. Please limit your discussion to the specific problem for which you brought your child to the office, since your doctor is probably fitting your child in between patients already scheduled.

A behavior or psychological problem may require a visit to the doctor. Since these visits usually require more time, request a long appointment and indicate to the receptionist the purpose of your appointment.

Praying for Your Child

If you have selected a Christian physician and your child has a particularly disturbing medical problem, ask your physician to pray with you for your child. This practice gives your child total Christian medical care. We are given clear instructions on how to pray for healing in James 5:14–15.

Sniffles

Sometime in his first few weeks you may think your baby has his first cold. These noisy, gurgling sounds are usually not colds (meaning an infection), but they certainly may sound like a cold and be a source of great concern. Babies do not breathe the ways adults do. Adults are able to breathe through their noses or their mouths, and their air passages are relatively large. Babies are predominantly nose breathers, and their air passages are relatively small. For these reasons, even a slight amount of congestion in the nose or throat may bother them. Sniffles in tiny babies are caused more by environmental irritants than by infections. The most common irritants are lint from blankets and clothing, dust, chemical fumes, and cigarette smoke. In fact, children of smoking parents do have more colds than children of nonsmoking parents.

Another cause of clogged nasal passages is very dry air, especially in the winter months that require central heating. As a general guide, when the heat goes on, so should a humidifier. A tiny baby cannot blow his own nose. You must do it for him, and the following suggestions will help you accomplish this.

Clearing your baby's nose.   Squirt a few drops of saline nose drops (available without prescription at the pharmacy) into each nostril. The drops often loosen the secretions and stimulate your baby to sneeze them toward the front part of his nose. Next, take a rubber-bulb syringe, called a "nasal aspirator," or a rubber ear syringe and gently suck out the loosened secretions.

When to clear your baby's nose.   Signs of a baby's obstructed nasal passages include frequent waking up, inability to sustain nursing (he needs his mouth to breathe), and breathing with his mouth open. If your baby sleeps comfortably with his mouth closed and he has not changed his nursing pattern, you do not need to clean out his nose even though he may sound noisy.

Sometime around his first or second month, your baby may experience what is called the "two-month cold." Again, this is probably not a cold. Babies often make more saliva than they are able to handle initially. As a result, the saliva collects in the back of their throats, causing noisy, gurgly breathing. You also may hear and feel a "rattle" in his chest, but the problem is not really in his chest. What you hear and feel is the air moving past the vibrating mucous in the back of his throat, producing sounds and vibrations like a musical instrument. These secretions are often too far back to get with a nasal aspirator, and the baby's problem is usually not in his nose anyway. Keeping a vaporizer running while he is sleeping often will thin these secretions. These throaty noises occur less when your baby is sleeping since saliva production usually lessens with sleep. These noises may continue during the first six months and may become more noticeable during times of teething. As soon as your baby begins to spend more of his time in an upright position and learns how to swallow the excess saliva, these noises gradually disappear. (See the section on colds later in this chapter for ways to recognize and treat actual infection.)

266

Eye Discharges

In a baby's first few months, discharging eyes are usually caused by blocked tear ducts. Most infants begin tearing by three weeks of age, and these tears should drain from the nasal corners of the eyes through the tear ducts. At birth, the nasal ends of these ducts are closed by a thin membrane that usually breaks open shortly after birth allowing the proper drainage of the tears. Often this membrane does not open fully, the tear ducts remain plugged, and tears accumulate in one or both eyes. There is a general principle of the human body that if fluid does not drain properly, it soon will become infected. As a result, the discharge from your baby's eyes may become persistently yellow, indicating that these tears have become infected in the region of the blocked tear ducts.

Treating blocked tear ducts.   Gently massage the tear duct which is located beneath the tiny "bump" in the nasal corner of each eye. Massage in an upward direction (toward the eye) about six times. Do this as frequently as you think of it during the day, for example, before each diaper change. If you properly massage the tear duct, this pressure on the fluid trapped within the ducts should pop open the membrane and clear the tear ducts. If you notice persistent tearing or yellow discharge from one or both eyes, mention this to your doctor during your baby's checkup, and your doctor will instruct you in the proper treatment of this condition. Blocked tear ducts usually clear up by six months of age. Occasionally, it is necessary for an eye doctor to open these ducts by inserting a tiny probe into them, but this should not be done until a satisfactory trial of massage and eye drops has been attempted.

Thrush

Thrush is a common yeast infection in the baby's mouth that looks like white cottage-cheese patches on the inner cheeks, inner lips, tongue, and roof of the mouth. This fungus infection seldom bothers the baby, and it is easily treated by a prescription which is painted on the white patches. The baby also may have a similar diaper rash which may need prescription medication. Sometimes the baby may transfer the infection to the mother's nipples during nursing, causing some tenderness, so that a prescription cream may be necessary to treat her too.

Common Skin Rashes

Normal baby "marks."   Most newborn babies have smooth, reddish pink marks on the back of the neck, on the forehead, between the eyes, and on the upper

267

eyelids. These are not really rashes but are areas of skin where the blood vessels are prominent and show through the baby's thin skin. These areas often become more noticeable when the baby cries. As your baby grows and accumulates more fat beneath her skin, her reddish areas become less noticeable and probably will disappear by one year of age.

Birthmarks.   The most common kind of birthmark looks like a small strawberry and is called a "hemangioma." It is caused by the proliferation of tiny blood vessels within the skin. It may not be present at birth but may appear within a baby's first few months. Hemangiomas gradually grow larger, begin to dry up by turning a grayish color in the center, and usually disappear within several years. Five percent of these hemangiomas are "rapid growing" and need to be watched carefully—they may require laser surgery.

Non-Caucasian babies often have bluish birthmarks on the skin of the lower back which look like bruises. These normal spots usually disappear with time but may remain until adulthood.

Milia are tiny, whitish, pin-head-sized bumps most prominent on the face, especially on the skin of the nose. This rash is caused by oily sections plugging the pores of the skin, but it disappears after gently washing with warm water and mild soap.

Newborn "acne."   Newborns often have a pimply, oily rash on the face resembling acne, which appears several weeks after birth. The increased hormone levels at birth cause the oil glands of the face to swell. The acne-like rash can be removed easily with gentle washings with warm water and a mild soap.

Seborrhea is a crusty, oily rash that appears behind the ears and on the scalp. In addition to washing with warm water, a prescription cream may be needed.

Cradle cap is a crusty, oily, plaquelike rash on the baby's scalp, most common over the soft spot. Cradle cap is best treated by massaging vegetable oil into the crusty areas and gently removing the softened scales with a washcloth or soft, fine-toothed comb. If this rash persists, a special shampoo and a prescription cream may be needed.

The skin, especially that of a newborn baby, enjoys high humidity. This is why most of these rashes seem to be worse during the winter when central heating dries the air. A humidifier in the baby's sleeping room often will lessen these rashes.

Prickly heat rashes are tiny pimples with red bases and clear centers. Prickly heat usually appears in areas of the skin where there is excessive moisture retention, such as behind the ears, between the neck folds, in the groin, and in areas where clothing fits tightly. This rash is treated by gently washing the area in plain, cold water or with a solution of baking soda (one teaspoon to a cup of water). Dressing your baby in lightweight, loose-fitting clothing also should soothe his rash.

Diaper rash.   Human skin, especially the sensitive skin of a newborn baby, was not designed to be in prolonged contact with wet cloth. Diaper rashes are caused by the chemical irritation of the ammonia formed by the urine and the mechanical rubbing of moist cloth on sensitive skin. The following suggestions are for the prevention and treatment of your baby's diaper rash.

1. Experiment with both cloth diapers and disposable diapers to see which one causes fewer rashes. If you use disposable diapers be sure to fold the edge of the diaper down so the plastic lining does not touch your baby's skin.

2. Change wet diapers as quickly as possible. If diaper rash is a persistent problem, change your baby when he wakes during the night also, or use double or triple cloth diapers.

3. After each diaper change, wash your baby's diaper area with plain water or mild soap, rinse well, and gently blot dry. Avoid strong soaps and excessive rubbing on already sensitive skin. A very red but not raised rash is often caused by an "acid burn" due to the acidic nature of your baby's stools (usually following a treatment with antibiotics).

4. Soak your baby's bottom in a baking soda bath (a tablespoon of baking soda in two quarters of water in his tub). After soaking the baby's bottom, give a "sniff test" to detect any smell of ammonia.

5. Allow the diaper area to "breathe." Avoid tight-fitting diapers and rubber pants which retain moisture. Reserve rubber pants for occasions where being a baby may not be socially acceptable. Place rubber pads underneath your baby to protect his bedding. Expose your baby's diaper area as much as possible to the air. While he is sleeping, unfold the diaper and lay it beneath him. In warm weather, let your baby nap outside with his bare bottom exposed to fresh air.

6. Creams and pastes are usually not necessary when your baby's skin is not irritated. Attempt to treat the diaper rash early before the skin breaks down and becomes infected. At the first sign of a reddened, irritated bottom, apply a barrier cream such as zinc oxide. Barrier creams also should be used during times when your baby has diarrhea, such as when he is teething or has an intestinal infection. Avoid cornstarch on the diaper area because it encourages the growth of fungi.

7. Fungus diaper rashes are red, raised, rough, sore-looking rashes that have tiny pustules and are resistant to simple forms of treatment. This yeast-infection kind of diaper rash is treated by a prescription cream and the measures noted here.

Fever

What constitutes a fever?   A rectal temperature greater than 100.5 degrees Fahrenheit (38 degrees Celsius) may be considered a fever. Most children have a normal oral body temperature of 98.6 degrees Fahrenheit (37 degrees Celsius), but normal temperature varies among children from 97 to 100 degrees Fahrenheit (37 to 38 degrees Celsius). Many children show normal daily fluctuations in body temperature. It may be lower in the morning and during rest and a degree higher in the late afternoon or during strenuous exercise.

What causes fever?   Fever is a symptom of an underlying illness, but it is not an illness itself. Normal body temperature is maintained by a thermostat in a tiny organ of the brain called the "hypothalamus" which regulates the balance between the heat produced and the heat lost in the body. A fever occurs when more heat is produced in the body than can be released, thus raising your child's temperature. Germs from infection within your child's body release substances into the blood stream called "pyrogens" (heat-producing substances) which cause a fever. Any time there is a change from normal body temperature, the thermostat reacts to bring that temperature back to normal; for example, when your child is cold, he shivers to produce heat. When your child is warm or has a fever, the blood vessels of his skin become larger (as evidenced by his flushed cheeks), and his heart beats faster. These mechanisms cause more blood to reach the surface of the skin and release the excess body heat. A child with fever also sweats to cool his body by evaporation and breathes faster to get rid of the warm air. In addition to having these general signs of fever, a child may have headaches, muscle aches, and general fatigue.

How to take your child's temperature.   You may take your child's temperature in three places: the rectum (rectally), the armpit (axillarily), and the mouth (orally). Rectal temperature is one-half to one degree higher than oral temperature, and axillary temperature is usually one degree lower than oral.

Rectal thermometers are easiest and safest to use on children less than five years old. Follow these steps to take your child's rectal temperature.

1. Use a rectal thermometer (one with a rounded, stubby end that is marked "rectal").
2. Shake down the thermometer with a wrist-snapping motion until the mercury column is below 95 degrees Fahrenheit.
3. Grease the bulb end with petroleum jelly.
4. Lay your child face down across your lap.
5. Gently insert the thermometer bulb about one inch into the rectum allowing the thermometer to seek its own path. Don't force it.
6. Hold the thermometer between your index and middle fingers (like a cigarette) with the palm of your hand and your fingers grasping your child's buttocks. By holding your child in this position you can hold the thermometer and keep your child from moving. Never leave a child alone with the thermometer in place.
7. Try to keep the thermometer in place for three minutes. The rectal reading will be within a degree of the true temperature after one minute.
8. Practice "feeling" your child's temperature by placing the palm of your hand on her forehead or by kissing her forehead so that you are used to telling when she has a fever. Then confirm it by taking her temperature with a thermometer.
9. Keep a temperature chart by writing down the time, your child's temperature, and the methods you have used to treat the fever.

A child more than five years of age will usually cooperate with having his temperature taken orally. Follow these three steps.

1. Use an oral thermometer (the oral thermometer has a longer, thinner shaft than the rectal thermometer and is marked "oral"). Shake down the thermometer as described in the paragraph on rectal thermometers.
2. Have your child lie or sit quietly and place the mercury end of the thermometer under his tongue, slightly to one side. Instruct him to keep his mouth closed and close his lips firmly but not hold the thermometer with his teeth. Allowing the child to open his mouth to breathe with the thermometer in place may make the temperature reading inaccurate.
3. Try to keep the thermometer in place with the mouth closed for two to three minutes.

If your child resists having his temperature taken orally, you might try to take an axillary reading. An oral thermometer may be used for an axillary temperature, but three to four minutes is required to achieve a stable temperature reading.

When to worry about fever.   Two kinds of infections cause fever: viral and bacterial. Viral infections are usually less worrisome and show the following features: (1) the fever comes on suddenly in a previously well child; (2) the fever is usually very high (103 to 105 degrees Fahrenheit); (3) the fever is easily brought down by the methods mentioned in the section on how to treat your child's fever; and (4) the child seems to feel better when the fever is brought down. When their children have viral infections, parents often say, "I am surprised the fever is so high because my child does not look or act that sick." The most common viral infection in the first year of life is called "roseola" which produces a very high fever (103 to 105 degrees Fahrenheit) for about three days, but there are no other symptoms and the child does not appear as ill as the high fever would indicate. After the fever breaks, a faint, generalized, reddish pink rash appears and lasts for less than twenty-four hours.

In a bacterial infection the temperature may not be as high as that of a viral infection, but the fever does not come down as easily with the methods recommended for treating your child's fever. Also when your child has a bacterial infection, he acts as sick as his high fever would indicate.

When to call your doctor about fever.   Remember, your doctor is interested in how sick your child looks and acts rather than how high the temperature is. If your child does not act particularly sick, administer all the recommended methods to lower your child's temperature before calling your doctor. How your child responds to temperature-lowering methods is one of the main concerns your doctor will ask you about. The younger the infant, the more worrisome the fever. Any fever in an infant less than four months old should be reported immediately to your doctor. If your child's temperature cannot be lowered by using the methods suggested in the next section, and if he is rapidly becoming more ill, call your doctor. Also call your doctor if obvious signs and symptoms associated with a fever, such as ear pain, severe cough, sore throat, any problems associated with urination, may indicate a bacterial infection.

When examining your feverish child, your doctor is attempting to determine whether the fever is caused by a virus or a bacteria. Bacterial infections need antibiotics; viral infections usually do not but may be treated by the methods indicated in the following section. Sometimes it is difficult to determine the kind of infection, and your doctor may perform some laboratory tests to help make this decision. Or your doctor may elect to wait a day or so before making a definite decision and request that you notify him of your child's progress.

Because of the common difficulty of determining the kind of infection, it is very important for you to report to your doctor if your child's general condition worsens; your doctor may have to revise his diagnosis. Viral infections usually last three to five days and gradually subside. Bacterial infections, however, usually worsen if untreated.

How to treat your child's fever.　　You can lower your child's temperature with two basic mechanisms: (1) giving your child medications, such as aspirin or acetaminophen, which reset her thermostat, and (2) using methods to get rid of excess body heat as described in this section. It is necessary to lower your child's thermostat with medications before using heat removal procedures. Your child's thermostat is set so that if her body temperature is lowered, her body is programmed to produce more heat and therefore raise her body temperature again. For example, removing a child's clothing and placing her in a bath with water cooler than her body temperature will signal her thermostat and cause her to shiver to produce heat and her blood vessels to constrict in order to conserve heat. The medications will reset the thermostat so that when the child's temperature is lowered by cooling, her body will not react to produce more heat. An example of this mechanism is evident in the way heat is regulated in your house. If your house is too warm, you lower the thermostat and then open the windows. If you open the windows first without resetting the thermostat, heat production continues and your house remains warm.

The most commonly used medication to lower a temperature is aspirin. Aspirin has two benefits for a sick child: (1) it lowers his fever, and (2) it helps relieve some of the general aches and pains that often accompany childhood illnesses. As with any medication, it is important to give your child the proper dosage. If the aspirin dosage is too low, it will be ineffective, and if it is too high, your child may become ill from aspirin overdose. The following dosage schedule is based on the most up-to-date research and is designed to be both safe and effective.

This dosage schedule is based upon giving your child aspirin every four hours around the clock. Since it is usually unwise to wake a sleeping child who has a fever, most children miss one or two doses each day, thus making the schedule slightly conservative. Children's aspirin, or baby aspirin, comes in one and one-quarter grain tablets (seventy-five milligrams). The dosage schedule is based on a child's age and is a rough guide for selecting a safe and effective aspirin dosage. If

Aspirin Dosage by Age

Age in years	1	2	3	4	5	6	7	8	9	10	11	12
No. of 1¼ gr. tablets given every 4–6 hours	1	2	2	3	3	4	4	4	5	5	6	8 or 2 adult aspirin

you wish to be precise, you may calculate your child's dosage by this method: five milligrams of aspirin per pound of body weight (ten milligrams of aspirin per kilogram of body weight) given every four hours. One adult aspirin, which is five grains, is equivalent to four children's aspirin.

Aspirin overdose. In order to avoid an overdose of aspirin, if you have given your child the appropriate dosage around the clock for forty-eight hours, check with your physician before administering any more. Current packaging laws have greatly reduced accidental aspirin poisoning in children. Even if a child younger than five years old ingested a whole bottle of children's aspirin, aspirin poisoning would be unlikely. As a rough guide, if your child does not take more than one baby aspirin per pound of body weight, he is unlikely to suffer any ill effects. If your child ingests any higher dosage than this, certainly call your doctor or your local poison control center. Adult aspirin preparations pose a greater chance of accidental poisoning than children's tablets, which means that you should take greater precaution with your bottles of aspirin than with your children's aspirin. If your child does take more than a safe amount of aspirin, call your doctor or local poison control center for instructions. When administering aspirin, it is usually best to give your child an increased amount of fluids to help wash the aspirin through his system.

Generally, aspirin is a safe and effective fever-lowering medication for most children. When used during certain viral illnesses such as chicken pox or the flu, aspirin has been incriminated as a possible cause of a serious brain and liver disease called "Reye's Syndrome." The cause-effect relationship of aspirin and Reye's Syndrome is still not proven, but at this writing it is recommended that aspirin *not* be used for these conditions. Acetaminophen should be used instead. *Acetaminophen* (Tylenol, Tempra, or Liquiprin) is a medication that lowers your child's fever as effectively as aspirin but is a less effective pain reliever. Acetaminophen is generally recommended instead of aspirin for the young child for the following reasons: (1) it is not linked with Reye's Syndrome; (2) it is also available in liquid form and therefore is easier to administer than tablets to the young child; and (3) it does not keep building up in your child's blood with prolonged usage and is less likely to produce an overdose with routine use.

The dosage of acetaminophen is the same as aspirin in a milligram-per-pound dose. Acetaminophen is available in the following forms: (1) drops: 0.8 milliliters equals 80 milligrams; (2) elixir: 5 milliliters (one teaspoon equals 160 milligrams); (3) tablets (chewable): one tablet equals 80 milligrams; and (4) adult tablets (regular strength): one tablet equals 325 milligrams.

The following dosage schedule of acetaminophen will help you determine the proper dosage for your child.

Acetaminophen

Age Group	0-3 mos.	4-11 mos.	12-23 mos.	2-3 yrs.	4-5 yrs.	6-8 yrs.	9-10 yrs.	11-12 yrs.
Weight (lbs)	6-11	12-17	18-23	24-35	36-47	48-59	60-71	72-95
Dose of Tylenol in milligrams	40	80	120	160	240	320	400	480
Drops (80 mg./0.8 ml.) droppersful	$\frac{1}{2}$	1	$1\frac{1}{2}$	2	3	4	5	—
Elixir (160 mg./5 ml.) tsp.	—	$\frac{1}{2}$	$\frac{3}{4}$	1	$1\frac{1}{2}$	2	$2\frac{1}{2}$	3
Chewable tablets (80 mg. each)	—	—	$1\frac{1}{2}$	2	3	4	5	6

Doses should be administered 4 or 5 times daily—but not to exceed 5 doses in 24 hours. (The above recommendations are for Tylenol. The dosage schedule for other brands of acetaminophen may vary.)

Other ways to lower your child's fever.   In addition to using aspirin or acetaminophen to reset your child's thermostat, the following methods will help remove the excess heat from your child's system.

1. *Undress your child completely,* or at most, dress him in light, loose-fitting clothing. This allows the excess heat to radiate out of his body into the cooler environment. Avoid the tendency to bundle up your child when he has a fever because this will only cause his body to retain heat.

2. *Keep your child's environment cold.*   Decrease the temperature in his room, open a window slightly, use an air conditioner or a nearby fan. A "draft" will not bother your child. This cool air helps remove the heat that is radiating out of his body. Yes, your child may go outside when he has a fever. The fresh, circulating air is good for him.

3. *Give your child a lot of extra fluids* when he has a fever because excess body heat causes him to lose fluids. Give him cool, clear liquids in small, frequent amounts.

4. *Give your child a cooling bath.*   If in spite of all these other measures your child's temperature remains over 103 degrees Fahrenheit (39.5 degrees Celsius), or if she continues to be uncomfortable with the fever, place her in a tub of water and run the water all the way up to her neck. The water temperature should be warm enough not to be uncomfortable but cooler than her body temperature. If the young child protests this tub bath and begins to cry, sit in the bathtub with her and amuse her with her favorite floating toys. Crying and struggling will only increase her temperature. Keeping your child in the cooling bath for twenty to thirty minutes should bring her temperature down a couple of degrees. During the bath, rub her with a washcloth to stimulate more circulation to the skin and increase heat loss. After the bath, gently pat your child dry, leaving a slight excess of water on her skin which will evaporate and produce a further cooling effect. Do not use alcohol rubs because they may produce shivering and toxic vapors. If your child's temperature zooms back up again, it may be necessary to repeat the tub bath.

Can fever be dangerous?   In most children, the fever itself is not dangerous. Fever does make children very uncomfortable, creating a general feeling of muscle aches and pains. The main reason for controlling high temperatures in young children is the danger of febrile convulsions. The young child's brain does not tolerate sudden temperature fluctuations and may react with a convulsion. It is not so much how high the fever is but how fast the temperature rises that causes convulsions. Most febrile convulsions can be prevented by using all the methods to control temperature just described. Febrile convulsions, while alarming to parents, seldom harm the child. The frequency and severity of these convulsions lessen as your child gets older and seldom occur in a child more than five years old.

Because a child with a fever is often uncomfortable, keep his body quiet and his soul at peace. Pray for your child, asking God to relieve his fever and the illness producing his discomfort.

Colds

What is a cold?   In medical terms, colds are called "upper respiratory infections" (URI), which means an infection of the lining of the air passages: nose, sinuses, throat, ears, and larynx. Germs, either viruses or bacteria, infect the lining of these air passages, and the tissue of this lining reacts by swelling and secreting mucous. The runny nose and the child's postnasal drip are caused by the accumulation of mucous. Your child may then sneeze and cough, which are his body's defense mechanisms, to clear this mucous. Swelling of the tissues accounts for many of the signs of colds: swelling of the nasal membranes causes a child to breathe noisily through his mouth; swelling of the veins and tissues beneath the eyelids causes a bluish discoloration; swelling of the tonsils and adenoids causes the throaty noises most commonly heard at night; swelling of the larynx causes the croupy, seal-bark cough. Most children have several colds per year. The school-age child is a very social being and "shares" her cold germs with other children. As the child grows, her immunity to various germs increases, and the number and severity of colds gradually decrease.

Although colds are, strictly speaking, caused by infections, allergies may also account for swelling and mucous secretion. The germs may settle in these secretions resulting in an infection. It is common for young children to have both allergy colds and infection colds.

When is a cold more than a cold?   The "common cold," as it is often called, is usually caused by a virus and subsides with the general measures mentioned here. However, it is important for parents to recognize when a cold needs a consultation with the doctor. The following general guidelines will help you decide when to take your child to a doctor for a cold.

Determine how much the cold is bothering your child. If your child is happy and playful, eats well, sleeps well, and is not particularly bothered by the cold, then it is mostly likely a viral infection. This cold is simply a noisy nuisance and probably will subside with proper treatment.

Check the mucous coming from his nose. If the secretions are clear and watery and your child is generally happy, his cold is most likely caused by a virus. If the discharge from his nose becomes thick and yellow or green and persists that way

277

throughout the day, and if your child becomes increasingly cranky and awakens more at night, he probably has a bacterial infection. Medical advice should be obtained. The eyes are often the mirror of the cold's severity. If your child has a persistently yellow drainage from his eyes, most likely he has an underlying sinus or ear infection and should be examined by your doctor. In my office we follow "Dr. Bill's rule": if your child's nose progresses from runny to snotty and his behavior progresses from happy to cranky, your child should be examined by a doctor.

When is a cold contagious?   If your child has a fever, snotty nose, and cough, consider him contagious and keep him out of the church nursery. Children are most contagious the first few days of the cold. It is not necessary to quarantine a child who has no fever, is not sick, and has only a clear running nose or slight cough.

How should you treat a cold?   General treatment of the simple cold is aimed at keeping the nasal discharge thin and moving. Secretions that become stagnant are likely to result in a worsening infection. Use a vaporizer while your child is sleeping. Do not add anything to the water in the vaporizer since an additive could irritate your child's respiratory passages. Give your child a lot of fluids to drink. Clear the nasal passages. Encourage the older child to blow her nose well and not to sniff the secretions back up into her sinuses.

Over-the-counter medications for colds are called "decongestants." They are designed to dry up the secretions and shrink the swelling of the lining of the respiratory passages. In my experience, these medications have had limited usefulness for children. If a child is given a high enough dosage of a decongestant to help the cold, he may experience the undesirable side effects of drowsiness or hyperexcitability, rapid heart beat, or nightmares. Dosages recommended on the package inserts are often so low as to be ineffective.

Decongestants are more effective for colds produced by allergies than for those produced by infections. Overuse of decongestants may, in fact, dry up the secretions to the extent that the child cannot cough up the secretions. Thus the cold worsens. Nose drops for a persistently runny nose that is really bothering the child may be effective, but they should not be used more than twice a day or for more than three days at a time. Most of these over-the-counter remedies are used in desperation to give the child some relief. It is best to check with your doctor before using any over-the-counter medication.

Antibiotics for colds.   Viral infections generally do not need antibiotics, but bacterial infections do. This is the judgment your doctor tries to make when examining your child for a cold. Your doctor listens to your child's chest and looks into his nose, throat, and ears to determine if there are any signs of bacterial infection. If there are not, your doctor may say to you, "This is a viral infection which does not need an antibiotic, and your child should get better by simply giving him fluids and cleaning out his nose. But call me if he gets worse." Keep in mind that you are going to your doctor primarily for consultation, not necessarily for medication. Do not be disappointed if your doctor "doesn't find anything." It often requires more judgment *not* to treat an illness with antibiotics than to treat one with them. Remember your doctor's closing statement to call if your child gets worse, since viral infections may progress to bacterial infections and a change of treatment may be necessary. If your doctor suspects your child's cold is caused by a bacterial infection, an appropriate antibiotic may be prescribed. Be sure to complete the entire course of the prescribed antibiotic.

Ear Infections

Because of the frequency and severity of ear infections in young children, you should have a full understanding of their causes and treatment. Children harbor germs in the secretions of the nose and throat to which they have not yet become immune. Because of the proximity of the nose and throat to the ears, germs commonly travel up the eustachian tube into the ear during a cold.

The eustachian tube in children often functions inadequately. The eustachian tube has two main functions: (1) to equalize the air pressure on both sides of the eardrum which allows the eardrum to vibrate freely and produce sound and (2) to drain the middle ear of fluid and germs which may collect during a cold. A child's eustachian tube is short, wide, straight, and at a horizontal angle, all of which allows germs to travel more easily from the throat up into the middle ear. As your child grows, the eustachian tube becomes longer, narrower, and at a more acute angle, thus making it more difficult for germs and fluid to collect in the middle ear.

During a cold, fluid accumulates in the middle ear. If the eustachian tube does not function properly and the fluid remains trapped, germs may cause an infection of the fluid within the cavity of the middle ear. The infected fluid accumulates behind the eardrum, presses on the eardrum, and produces intense pain. If the pressure from the trapped fluid builds up too much, this fluid may rupture the eardrum, and you may notice drainage of fluid outside the ear canal. This fluid resembles the secretions of a runny nose.

It is important for parents to be vigilant about recognizing the signs of a ruptured eardrum. Once the pressure is released, the eardrum ruptures, and the child feels better. But this is actually a false improvement; the infection still should be treated to allow the perforated area of the eardrum to heal. Continuous scarring of the eardrum can result in permanent hearing loss.

Ear infections often bother a child more at night. When she is lying down, the fluid presses down on her eardrum. A parent will often notice that his baby feels better when he holds her in an upright position or allows her to stand up in her crib.

How to recognize an ear infection in your child.　　The older child can tell you when his ear hurts, but it is often difficult for a parent to suspect an ear infection in a pre-verbal child. While some infants give no easily identifiable signs of ear infections, most show the following signs: your baby starts off with a clear, runny nose but is reasonably happy; the nasal discharge progresses from runny to thick; and your child's behavior moves from happy to increasingly cranky and irritable. Teething may be confused with ear infections, but when teething, your child should look generally well and his throat and nose secretions should not be persistently yellow or green. The combination of a discharging nose, with or without yellow drainage from the eyes, and increasing crankiness in the child should alert parents to the possibility of an ear infection, and a doctor should be consulted. Ear infections by themselves are not contagious. The child is contagious if he has a cold along with the ear infection.

Sometimes the fluid that builds up in the middle ear does not become infected and may not produce significant pain (this is called "serous otitis media"). This fluid will restrict the movement of the eardrum, thus diminishing your child's hearing. Even if only fluid is in the middle ear and there is no infection, most children show some change in behavior as a result of their diminishing hearing. This altered behavior may be the only sign to alert you of a middle ear problem.

How to prevent ear infections.　　Most children, because of the eustachian tube structure, will have occasional ear infections. The following suggestions may help lessen the frequency and severity of these infections.

1. Breastfeed your infant as long as possible. Breast-fed infants have fewer ear infections.
2. Control allergies. Allergies often cause fluid to build up in the middle ear which can get infected. Food allergies, especially those caused by dairy products, and inhalant allergies, especially those caused by cigarette

smoke and dust (such as that caused by stuffed animals in the bedroom), are the most common.

3. Observe your child's "cold pattern" and treat these colds early and appropriately. If your child has had previous ear infections and the usual sequence of events is first a runny nose, then a snotty nose, then crankiness, it may be wise to seek medical attention at the snotty-nose stage before the cold settles in your child's ears.

4. Some medications prevent the frequent occurrence of ear infection. Your doctor can recommend what is best for your child.

Treating ear infections. Most children can be grouped according to their type of ear infection: those with an occasional infection that clears up well with treatment; those with recurrent infections that need long-term treatment; and those with recurrent infections that do not respond to medical treatment but require surgical procedures.

The child with an occasional ear infection. After your doctor diagnoses an ear infection (otitis media), she will usually prescribe an antibiotic. The strength of the antibiotic and the duration it is to be taken will depend upon the severity of the infection and your child's past history of response to treatment. The healing of an ear infection usually goes through two phases. In the first phase your child should feel better within one or two days, and he may seem perfectly well within two or three days. During this time most of the germs have been killed by the antibiotic and the pressure of the fluid lessened somewhat so that your child's pain is nearly gone in the first few days. The second phase is that of gradual resolution of the fluid or drainage of this fluid from the middle ear through the eustachian tube. For this reason it is important to complete the prescribed duration of treatment. If you stop the antibiotics as soon as your child feels better, the remaining fluid in the middle ear may become reinfected, and the whole process must start all over again. It is also extremely important for your doctor to recheck your child's ear as soon as the prescribed antibiotic is finished. Your doctor may elect to continue a milder medication for a while longer if the infection is not gone completely. Partially treated ear infections are a common cause of permanent hearing deficits; therefore, follow-up checks are extremely important.

What can you do if your child awakens in the middle of the night with an earache? It is usually not necessary to phone your doctor immediately since antibiotics may take as long as twelve hours to have any effect and will not immediately relieve the pain. Try the following pain-relieving measures. Seat your child upright, and try to parent her back to sleep in that position. This often takes the pressure of the infected fluid off the eardrum and eases the pain. Warm some oil, such as olive oil, and squirt a few drops into the sore ear. Encourage your child to lie with the sore ear up, and pump the outer edge of the canal, trying to move the drops down toward the eardrum to relieve the pain. If your child has had frequent infections before, it is wise to keep an anesthetic ear drop for these middle-of-the-night earaches. Give him analgesics (aspirin or acetaminophen). These measures will often tide your child over until morning when you can consult your doctor, even though the child may seem to feel better by morning.

The child with recurrent ear infections.   Some children have one ear infection after another, occurring every few weeks. Parents are usually frustrated by the continued recurrence of these infections and the continued medical expense. Although children are usually resilient to recurrent medical illnesses, children with recurrent ear infections often begin to show deteriorating behavior such as chronic irritability. I call this the "ear personality," which is common in children with recurrent ear infections simply because they do not feel well or hear well. One of the main changes parents notice after these recurrent ear infections are treated appropriately is that their children act better. Remember, a child who feels right usually acts right.

Parents, take heart. There are ways to prevent these recurrent ear infections. The usual reason children have them is that the previous infection has never completely cleared up and the fluid remains behind the eardrum even though the germs have been treated appropriately with antibiotics. What usually happens is that the child has one ear infection and is treated for seven or ten days; he feels better, and then three or four weeks later he is back in the doctor's office with another ear infection because the fluid remained in the eardrum and became reinfected.

If your child's ear infections are occurring more frequently and lasting longer, your doctor may suggest a prevention regimen aimed at preventing the fluid from reaccumulating in the middle ear and at preventing the fluid which does accumulate from becoming infected. One such regimen consists of the following measures.

Strict allergy control.   Your doctor may take a history to determine what possible allergens, such as dairy products, cigarette smoke, animal dander, or dust from dust-collecting stuffed animals, may be affecting your child. These allergens should be removed from your child's environment.

Eustachian tube exercises are designed to pop open the eustachian tubes and allow the accumulated fluid to drain. Eustachian tube exercises and strict allergy control are designed to keep the fluid from accumulating in the middle ear.

Daily medication.   Usually a mild antibiotic keeps the fluid that does not drain from constantly becoming reinfected. These daily small doses of the mild antibiotic are often easier on a child's system than the periodic strong antibiotics.

This prevention regimen is extremely effective for the majority of children. Keeping a child free of ear infections for several months often allows the uninfected eustachian tube to grow properly and thus function properly; whereas, repeated infections further hinder the eustachian tube from functioning which results in more infections, and the cycle continues. These prevention regimens are used for periods of three to six months, and thereafter your child is taken off the medications to see if the infection recurs. Most children indeed outgrow these recurrent ear infections by age five.

Surgical treatment.   Occasionally a child will not respond to medical treatment of an ear infection. His middle ear will continue to have persistent fluid until it eventually becomes thick and gluelike, and it only can be removed by opening up the eardrum (called a "myringotomy") and draining out the fluid. Tiny plastic tubes are inserted surgically through the eardrums to allow the accumulated fluids to drain out, thus lessening the frequency of middle-ear infections and giving an immediate improvement in the child's hearing. In my experience, most children who have had their infections treated appropriately, who have been followed up appropriately, and who have been put on prevention regimens early and long enough have avoided surgical treatment.

At this point, let me caution parents against a common mistake in using the medical system. A child has a few ear infections, and a well-meaning friend or relative says, "Why don't you take your child to an ear specialist?" A better use of the current medical system both for you and your child is to stick with your child's physician who is trained primarily in the medical treatment of ear infections, is more familiar with childhood ear infections, and is less likely to recommend a surgical remedy. If your child has gone through the nonsurgical steps of treatment and the ear infections continue, your pediatrician then will refer you to an ear specialist. In this case the decision to administer surgical treatment for your child's ear infections is a combined decision between pediatrician and ear specialist, and your child will ultimately profit from this communication between his two doctors.

Parents, I cannot overemphasize the importance of being vigilant in treating your child's ear infections. Recurrent ear infections usually occur during a stage of speech development in the young child. If a child's hearing is lost periodically during these formative years of speech development, the child may show some speech delay and some permanent hearing loss. Even more noticeable are the chronic behavioral problems that occur with chronic ear infections. Poor school performance is also a common result of chronic ear infections in the older child.

Common Intestinal Problems

Some variations in children's stools are normal. The stools of a newly born baby contain a lot of swallowed amniotic fluid called "meconium" which accounts for the dark green, sticky, tarlike consistency. The newborn's stools are normally greenish brown for the first week or two, thereafter assuming a normal, yellowish brown color. The stools of breast-fed babies tend to be of a yellow, mustard-like consistency, tend to be frequent, and have a buttermilk-like, nonoffensive odor. It is normal for stools to show an occasional green color. They may be persistently green if the child's formula contains added iron. A sick child with a persistently green stool which is also extremely runny and mucousy may have an intestinal infection.

The frequency and consistency of stools vary considerably from child to child. Some babies have four to six stools every day; others have one soft stool every three to five days. Intestinal problems in a child are nearly always manifested by some outward sign, such as paleness, pain, and poor weight gain. If your child is generally well, it is unlikely that she has any serious underlying intestinal problem even though her stools may seem unusual.

A change in diet is often accompanied by a change in stool consistency. Some formulas are more constipating than others. Rice and bananas tend to be constipating foods; whereas, foods that tend to loosen the stools are corn syrup and most fruits and fruit juices, such as prunes or prune juice. It is common for stools to be loose during any condition that produces a lot of mucous in the throat, such as teething or a cold. Because antibiotics often change the kind of bacteria that normally reside in the intestines, it is common to have loose stools for a few weeks following a course of antibiotics.

Constipation refers to the consistency of the child's stools and difficulty in passing the stools, not to the frequency of the stools. Some infants and small children normally have bowel movements once every three to five days and if they do not appear uncomfortable, they are not constipated. A constipated baby draws his legs up onto a distended abdomen, strains, and becomes red in the face; he passes hard, pellet-like stools with much difficulty. Since the infant's rectum is often small, the passage of a hard stool may cause a small tear in the wall of the rectum called "rectal fissure." This fissure may produce a few streaks of fresh blood on the stool or a few drops of blood on the diaper.

When your infant strains to pass a stool, insert a glycerin suppository (available at drugstores without prescription) high into his rectum. Hold his buttocks together for a few minutes so that the suppository can dissolve. These suppositories look like little rocket ships, and for the tiny baby, you may need to cut the suppository in half and insert the pointed top end. If one formula appears to be constipating, try a change of formula. Also, give your baby extra water. Constipation in the breastfeeding baby is seldom a problem. Some mothers have found that cheese in their diet somehow can cause hard stools in their babies through the breast milk. It *is* a "normal" common occurrence for breast-fed babies (older than two months) to have a bowel movement only once every three to seven days, and when the stool finally comes, it is not hard at all, but more like a major mudslide! Unless the baby is uncomfortable (most are not), you don't need to worry. If the stool is hard, or baby is uncomfortable, follow the advice given on the use of suppositories, prunes, and/or extra water. Adding a tablespoon of corn syrup to eight ounces of formula also may soften your infant's stools, but do not add it more than once or twice a day without first checking with your doctor. By three months of age a baby is old enough to add some pureed prunes or prune juice to his diet.

Constipation in the older child commonly causes recurrent abdominal pain. Busy children often ignore the urge to defecate, and they allow the stools to remain in the rectum until they get hard. Because a hard stool is usually a painful stool, children choose to ignore the painful stimulus and further increase their own constipation. The longer a child is constipated, the weaker the rectal muscles become and the less the urge to defecate becomes, creating a vicious and long-standing cycle of constipation. Older children (ages five to ten) who are chronically constipated often will soil their pants. This embarrassing problem often presents itself as a "diarrhea" problem but is in reality due to the leaking of stools from lower intestinal muscles that have been weakened by chronic constipation. Paradoxically, treating the child with soiled pants as a constipated child may resolve this embarrassing problem.

You may treat constipation in the older child by following these suggestions.

Teach your child to respond immediately to her urge-to-go signal, not to hold on to her stools. Explain to her that not following this signal weakens the "donut muscles" around the rectum and will eventually cause her to have pain when she has a bowel movement. (The muscle surrounding the opening from the bladder and the muscles surrounding the rectum do resemble a donut and your child can understand this analogy.)

Your doctor may prescribe stool softeners or laxatives before bedtime to encourage your child to have a bowel movement the next morning. Some naturally laxative foods include fruit, prune juice, corn syrup, vegetable roughage, and bran cereal. Potentially constipating foods are rice, cheese, bananas, and chocolate. Remember that it takes four to six weeks to treat chronic constipation. The stools need to remain soft for that length of time in order for the intestinal muscles to regain their strength.

Diarrhea, meaning "liquid stools," refers more to the consistency of the stools than to the frequency. Infants and children normally have prolonged periods of loose stools due to some conditions already mentioned. When should you worry about diarrhea? The most frequent cause of problem diarrhea in childhood is the intestinal infection *gastroenteritis,* usually caused by a virus. If the intestinal lining becomes infected, it heals very slowly. During the healing process, the enzymes in the intestinal lining that help digest and absorb food do not function properly. This results in stools that are very frequent, watery, explosive, green, mucousy, and foul smelling. This kind of diarrhea is usually accompanied by cold symptoms and a generally unwell child.

Diarrhea becomes a worrisome problem when it leads to *dehydration,* a condition in which your child loses more water and body salts than he takes in. Signs of dehydration in your child are obvious weight loss; dry eyes, dry skin, and dry mouth; diminishing urine output; an increasingly quiet child (called "lethargy"); and often fever. No matter how frequent and loose your child's stools seem to be, if he is happy, bright-eyed, has wet eyes and mouth, is urinating well, and has not lost weight, you do not have to worry.

Treatment of diarrhea.   Your main goal in treating your child for diarrhea is to avoid dehydration. Decrease those foods that cannot be absorbed by infected intestines, and increase solutions containing extra salt and water which your child loses in the diarrhea. The following suggestions will help you accomplish these goals.

Weigh your baby without her clothes on the most accurate scale you can obtain. This is her base-line weight. Weigh her daily, preferably each morning before you feed her. If she has no significant weight loss, she is not becoming dehydrated. As a rough guide, if your child loses up to 5 percent of her base-line body weight (for example, a twenty-pound child loses one pound), she has experienced a significant amount of dehydration, and you should call your doctor immediately. Rapid weight loss should concern you more than slow and gradual weight loss. A twenty-pound infant's losing a pound of body weight over a period of two days is a much greater concern than his losing the same amount of weight over a period of two weeks. Infants usually appear very sick with a rapid weight loss but do not usually appear that sick if the weight loss has been slow and gradual.

Stop all solid food, dairy products, and formulas made with cow's milk. If you are breastfeeding, it is rarely necessary to stop even temporarily, since human milk is not nearly as irritating to infected intestines as cow's milk products. This is true also if your child is vomiting. Breast milk is easy on the stomach and nursing is comforting.

Give your child a clear fluid diet. These fluids should contain simple sugars, which are easy to digest in order to provide calories, and salts, which your child is losing in the diarrhea fluid. Make a sugar solution by adding one level tablespoon of ordinary table sugar to eight ounces of boiled water (do not boil the sugar solution because boiling may cause the water to evaporate and make the solution too strong). Flat ginger ale and colas are readily available sources of sugars. Fluids containing a lot of salt are called "oral electrolyte solutions" (Pedialyte, Lytren, and Infalyte are available at your pharmacy or grocery store without prescription). Do not continue these electrolyte solutions for more than twenty-four hours without checking with your physician. The sips-and-chips method of administering fluids provides your child small, frequent feedings (two ounces at a time) rather than a large feeding. In the older infant this is accomplished best by frequent sips of fluid and ice chips or juice popsicles. A clear fluid diet alone should not be continued more than forty-eight hours without checking with your physician, since this kind of diet continued too long may itself produce diarrhea, called "starvation stools."

After twenty-four to forty-eight hours, if your child is not losing weight and the diarrhea has lessened somewhat, add semi-solid foods such as rice cereal without milk and mashed bananas. Continue the regimen of small, frequent fluid feedings. As the stools continue to improve, gradually add applesauce, saltine crackers, gelatin, and yogurt. As your child's stools become more solid, so can his diet.

Resume milk or formula very gradually and only after you have seen much improvement in your child's condition. Resume the formula by diluting it to half regular strength. Gradually return to the regular strength over the next several days. Do not boil milk or give undiluted skim milk to a child who has diarrhea since these solutions are too concentrated and may worsen the dehydration.

If the diarrhea worsens after you have gone back to dairy products, go back a few steps and begin the regimen all over again. For a formula-fed child who is recovering from diarrhea, a soybean-based formula is often tolerated better than a formula made with cow's milk. Following an intestinal infection, it is normal to have a prolonged period of loose stools (I call this "nuisance diarrhea") which may last for several weeks or months. This is because the intestinal lining is very slow to heal in most children. If your child has persistent diarrhea, it is more important to focus on the total child than only on his bottom. If your child appears generally well and is not continuing to lose weight, you do not need to worry even though his stools remain loose.

When to call your doctor about diarrhea. After you have followed these steps and your child continues to lose weight, show signs of dehydration, be in increasing pain, or look increasingly ill, call your doctor for more advice. Before making your call, have the following information available: the frequency and characteristics of the stools; the degree of weight loss and over what period of time; details about any associated symptoms such as vomiting, fever, signs of a cold or increasing pain, or any signs of dehydration; and what kind of treatment you have been giving. Parents, do not be disappointed if your doctor decides not to administer medication to attempt to stop your child's diarrhea. Most diarrhea in childhood is best treated by dietary restriction and time. Narcotic medications, which are often used to control diarrhea in adults, are generally not safe for children.

Besides these methods of treatment, much prayer and patience are needed to cope with diarrhea in a young child, because this problem is usually a long-term nuisance. Vomiting and diarrhea occurring together are more worrisome than if one occurs without the other.

Vomiting in the young infant. Most vomiting in the first few months is simply regurgitation (spitting up) resulting from a temporary feeding problem, such as air-swallowing or overfeeding. This vomiting is not usually a medical problem and usually subsides when the infant sits upright, when he is between six and eight months. Milk allergy is also a cause of vomiting in the young infant.

Vomiting in the older infant and child is caused most often by an infection or an irritation of the stomach, called "gastritis." This condition is often accompanied by nausea, stomachache, and retching (dry heaves).

There are more serious causes of vomiting. In the tiny infant, projectile vomiting (vomitus coming out under great force for several feet), which persists with nearly every feeding and is accompanied by signs of weight loss, may indicate a condition called "pyloric stenosis." This condition occurs primarily in male infants two months of age and is due to the lower end of the stomach's being too narrow for food to pass through. The sudden onset of vomiting in a generally ill-appearing child, persistent green bile vomitus, accompanied by severe abdominal pain are signs that the intestines are twisted and obstructed. These conditions are surgical emergencies and require immediate medical attention.

How to assess and treat the vomiting child. If your child's vomiting is associated with other symptoms, such as severe abdominal pain, signs of cold, high fever, headaches, or increasing drowsiness, it is probably due to a temporary intestinal infection which can be treated by methods similar to those described in the section on diarrhea. Prevent dehydration by replacing the fluids he loses in his vomitus. Use the sips-and-chips method of fluid replacement. Popsicles made with frozen apple juice, flat ginger ale, or cola are the best means of getting fluids into an infant or a child very slowly. Popsicles also may be made with the oral electrolyte solutions described earlier. The sips-and-chips method allows the small, frequent feedings necessary if the intestinal lining of the stomach is infected. Allowing fluid intake in more than small, slow amounts can cause rebound vomiting, resulting in more electrolyte loss. Breastfeeding can continue.

Follow the same guidelines described under the section on diarrhea for noting signs of dehydration and for knowing when to call your doctor. Antivomiting medications are usually not effective in children. As with the treatment of diarrhea, mainly diet restriction and fluid replacement will prevent dehydration in the vomiting child.

Infectious Childhood Diseases

Since children are socially oriented, they tend to share infectious diseases. The following chart will help you identify these illnesses and treat them appropriately.

	Characteristic Features	Treatment and Precautions
Measles (red measles)	• begins like common cold: runny nose; severe cough; reddened eyes, sensitive to light • high fever (104°), lasts 5 days	• contagious from onset of symptoms until end of rash • preventable by vaccine • treatment: fever control, comforting measures

- rash: purplish-red, raised, begins on face, spreads to entire body, begins at height of fever, lasts 5 days

German measles (rubella)

- low fever (101°), mild cold
- rash: pinkish-red, faint, disappears by third day
- swollen glands behind neck
- differs from red measles: child not very sick, lower fever, fainter rash, less cough

- contagious from a week before rash to 5 days after rash gone
- preventable by vaccine
- avoid exposure to pregnant women
- treatment: comforting measures

Mumps

- begins as flu-like illness
- neck glands beneath earlobe markedly swollen and tender
- low fever (101°), headache, nausea

- contagious from onset of symptoms until swelling gone
- preventable by vaccine
- treatment: comforting measures

Roseola

- usually affects babies between 9 and 18 months of age
- sudden onset of high fever (103°–105°) in previously well baby
- lasts 3 days
- baby "not very sick"
- rash: rose-pink, faint, appears after fever gone, lasts 24 hours

- not considered a serious illness
- no vaccine
- not highly contagious
- treatment: comforting measures

Chicken pox

- low fever (101°–102°), generally unwell feeling
- rash: initially may appear on trunk as tiny dots resembling bites, rapidly progresses to blister-like vesicles on red bases; new

- contagious from 2 days before rash until all vesicles crusted over
- vaccine: available for special patients
- treatment: comforting measures

crops appear rapidly as old
ones form a crust

| Scarlet fever | • sunburn-like, red rash
• fever (103°) and sick child
• sore throat, swollen neck glands
• tongue white-coated or strawberry red same as strep throat with a rash
• rash: rose-pink, faint | • cause: streptococcus
• contagious for 24–48 hours after antibiotics begun
• treatment: antibiotics |

COMMON CHILDHOOD EMERGENCIES

Because children are active and curious, they are subject to bumps and scrapes. Be familiar with the following information to respond effectively in the event of a medical emergency.

Poisoning

If your child swallows a potentially poisonous substance, the following emergency steps should be followed:

Step 1. Encourage your child to drink lots of water to dilute the poison.

Step 2. Call your local poison control center. Their phone number may be found by consulting your local hospital or in the yellow pages. It would be wise to display the phone number of the poison control center in a conspicuous place such as on your telephone.

Step 3. Keep syrup of *ipecac* in your medicine cabinet. This syrup is very effective for inducing vomiting, thereby removing the potentially harmful substance. If advised to induce vomiting by your poison control center, give your child one tablespoon (three teaspoons) of syrup of ipecac in eight ounces of water or noncarbonated fruit juice. If vomiting does not occur within twenty minutes, give one more tablespoon of ipecac in juice or water. Be prepared for the vomiting by keeping your child in the bathroom or outside for forty-five minutes after the first dose of ipecac. It is important not to induce vomiting before consulting the poison control center because certain poisons may be harmful if vomiting is induced, and some substances may not require vomiting at all.

291

Head Injuries

God anticipated busy children would sustain many falls and knocks to the head during the normal process of growing up. For this reason He provided the skull as a helmet to protect the brain. The scalp is also subject to head injuries. Because the scalp is very rich in blood vessels, even a small cut on the scalp bleeds profusely. Also, blows to the scalp may break the underlying blood vessels, producing a large swelling called a "goose-egg."

First-aid steps for head injuries: (1) If your child has a cut or swelling, apply an ice pack and pressure for at least twenty minutes. This usually stops the bleeding and will reduce the size of the eventual goose egg. (2) Lay your child down in a comfortable place and begin a period of observation. If there is an underlying brain injury, it takes time for the swelling or bleeding in the brain to produce signs of internal pressure. The signs of a brain injury may not develop for several hours. Observe your child for the following signs.

1. *Is your child alert?*   Is he responding to simple questions? Does he seem aware of his name, where he is, where he lives, the names of mommy and daddy and brothers and sisters? Be prepared for your child's wanting to go to sleep after a head injury since sleep is the usual refuge of consolation for an injured child. Let your child fall asleep, but observe him every couple of hours for any change in breathing patterns or skin color. It is wise to wake your child every two hours at least to check his eyes and his balance.

2. *Can your child look at you straight in the eye?*   The eyes are the mirror of the brain, especially in a head injury. If your child looks at you straight in the eye, if his pupils are the same size in both eyes, and if he can see objects clearly, he is not likely to have an underlying brain injury. Ask your child to cover one eye and count how many fingers he sees. If he complains of seeing double, you have cause for concern.

3. *Is your child vomiting persistently?*   It is normal for children to vomit once or twice after a blow to the head; therefore, it is wise to feed your child only clear fluids following the injury. If your child shows persistent vomiting, even of clear fluids, your doctor should be called.

4. *Is your child walking steadily?*   If your child is off balance, especially if he is exhibiting weakness in one arm or leg, contact your doctor.

5. *Does your child have headaches?*   Some headaches are to be expected after a blow to the head, and they usually subside within a few hours. If your child's head-

aches increase in severity—especially if they are accompanied by some of the signs we have discussed—call your doctor. Do not give aspirin for head injuries since it may increase the bleeding. Acetaminophen is the preferred analgesic.

When should you call your doctor? If any of these five signs occurs, call your doctor immediately or take your child to your hospital. If none of the signs are apparent, you may wish to check with your doctor shortly after the accident for further instructions. If these signs of brain injury are not present, you do not need to rush your child to a hospital for skull X-rays. A period of careful observation and a medical examination are more useful than skull X-rays. Your doctor will advise you as to whether skull X-rays are necessary.

Choking

Infants and small children like to "mouth" small objects which can get caught in their throats and obstruct their breathing. Try the following procedure if your child starts choking.

Step 1.   If your child can talk, cry, or cough, her airway is not obstructed and you should not interfere with her own efforts to dislodge the material. If your child is breathing normally and is not panicky, give her emotional support and allow her cough reflex to expel the object.

Step 2.   If your child cannot speak or cry, is having difficulty getting air, is blue, or is losing consciousness, position her head-down and apply four hard blows to her back between the shoulder blades. If the blows to the back do not dislodge the object, administer four chest thrusts: with your child lying on her back on the floor, place your hands alongside the lower rib cage on both sides and quickly compress the chest downward and upward with the thrusts of your arms. If the chest-thrust procedure does not dislodge the object, repeat the four back blows.

Step 3.   While administering step 2, call to someone to summon the paramedics. It is wise to have your local paramedics' number displayed conspicuously on every phone in the house. In most metropolitan cities the paramedic system is now tied in with a simple 911, making it unnecessary to take time to look up a number. In many cities, the 911 system is automatically tied into a computer which gives the paramedics the name and location of the dialing phone. It is wise to check periodically to see if the 911 emergency system is operating in your community.

The Heimlich maneuver is another procedure for dislodging an object caught in the airway of a choking person. Most authorities recommend the combination of back blows and chest thrusts in infants under one year because of the possible

293

damage to abdominal organs with the Heimlich maneuver. For older children over three years the Heimlich maneuver is preferable and is performed as follows: stand behind the choking person and wrap your arms around her waist, making a fist with one hand and grasping the fist with the other. Place the thumb side of your fist toward the upper abdomen and compress with a quick upward thrust, repeating several times if necessary. This abdominal pressure is transmitted to the lungs, compressing the lungs and pushing the object up out of the airway.

It is not wise to use your finger to dislodge the object from the back of the child's throat unless you can see the object and are certain you can get your finger around it. Inserting a large finger in a child's small throat may push the object farther back into the throat or may cause the child to panic and suck the object into her lungs.

Swallowed Objects

Children are prone to swallow small objects such as coins. Most of these pass into the intestines and are eliminated in twenty-four to forty-eight hours without causing harm. Occasionally, objects such as a coin or hard candy may lodge in the child's esophagus, causing excessive drooling (because the child cannot swallow his saliva) and pain in the area where the object has become stuck. If these signs occur in your child, take him to the hospital or call your doctor for advice.

Convulsions

Most convulsions, in a previously well child less than five years old, are caused by fever and are called "febrile convulsions." These convulsions usually stop when you lower the fever by undressing your child and placing him in a tepid bath (see page 273 for ways to lower your child's fever). As long as he is breathing well and is not blue during these febrile convulsions, your child's shaking arms and legs do not harm him, and the shaking will gradually subside as the fever is lowered.

If your child stops breathing during a convulsion, is foaming at the mouth, or turning blue, place him in the prone position with his head down, allowing the secretions to drain out of his throat and his tongue to fall forward. This clears your child's airway, allowing him to breathe during the convulsion. If your child is showing signs of breathing difficulty during the convulsion, paramedics should be called immediately.

Burns

If your child is burned, the following emergency steps will lessen the pain and severity of the burn.

1. Immediately submerge the burned area in cold water for at least twenty minutes. Do not use ice packs or bare ice cubes on the burn since these may increase the damage to the tissue caused by the burn.
2. Cover the burned area with a clean cloth soaked in cold water until the pain of the burn subsides. Do not apply butter or oils.
3. Take your child to the hospital or call your doctor for advice on continued care of the burn.

Besides the above first-aid measures to alleviate the pain and minimize skin damage, the following suggestions will lessen the cosmetic scarring of the burned area.

1. Keep the burn covered with an appropriate antibiotic ointment, such as silvadene, prescribed by your doctor.
2. Do not break the blisters without your doctor's advice.
3. Wash the burned area twice a day under a jet of water such as a tap or shower and dry thoroughly with a clean cloth.
4. To prevent contracture of the burned area if the burn is over a flexion crease (such as the palm of the hand or the wrist), frequent stretching of the burned area should be encouraged.
5. As the burned area is healing, your doctor may need to remove some of the dead tissue to minimize infection. Some burns heal better with the open method (washed frequently and covered with an appropriate antibiotic ointment but without a dressing), and others need to be covered with a dressing. Your doctor will advise you which method of treatment is necessary.

Nosebleeds

Most nosebleeds in children are due to nose picking and injury to the tiny blood vessels lining the inside of the nostrils. They are more common in the wintertime, especially in homes with central heating, because the low humidity causes the inside of the nose to dry. If your child is prone to nosebleeds, running a humidifier or vaporizer during the months requiring central heating may be necessary.

Apply the following first-aid measures during a nosebleed.

Apply a ball of wet cotton into the bleeding nostril and pinch the nostrils together. Also, apply pressure for ten minutes to the upper lip just below the nostrils. This compresses the major blood vessel supplying the nose. Seat your child leaning slightly forward. After the nosebleed stops, leave the piece of cotton lodged in your child's nostril for several hours and then very gently remove the piece of cotton, being careful not to dislodge the clot and cause bleeding to recur. If using these measures does not stop your child's nosebleed, call your doctor or take your child to the hospital.

Nose Injuries

The nose contains tiny, soft bones and acts like a shock absorber which protects against jarring of the underlying brain. Nasal bones are easily fractured, and the following emergency measures will minimize cosmetic and functional impairment from a blow to the nose. Apply an ice pack to the area of swelling for at least a half-hour following the trauma. After this, if your child can breathe easily through both nostrils and if the nose is not crooked, the nose is likely to heal well without the fracture's having to be set. If signs of breathing obstruction or cosmetic distortion are present, consult your doctor immediately.

Eye Injuries

The two most common eye injuries in childhood are irritations from chemicals splashed into the eye and foreign bodies lodged in the eye. If your child splashes an irritant into her eye, immediately rinse out the eye for ten minutes. This is best accomplished by pouring a gentle stream of lukewarm water over your child's eyes from a pitcher. Foreign bodies (such as an eyelash or a speck of dirt) are most safely removed by a twist of moist cotton. If the foreign bodies are not easily removed by this method, seek medical advice.

Interrupted Breathing

Step 1.   Clear your child's mouth of any secretions or foreign bodies (see entry on choking in this section).

Step 2.   Employ mouth-to-mouth breathing. Place your child on his back and slightly bend his neck forward and his head backward in the so-called sniffing position. This is best attempted by kneeling alongside your child and placing one hand under his neck and the other on his forehead.

Fit your mouth snugly around your child's lips and nose. If your child is too large for you to make a good seal over his mouth and nose, pinch his nose and seal his mouth only. For a tiny baby, give four quick, gentle puffs (a puff is about the amount of air you can hold in your cheeks). For an older child, give enough air to

296

make his chest rise. Apply a breath every two to three seconds. Continue the mouth-to-mouth breathing until your child resumes breathing himself or until trained help arrives.

I strongly advise all parents and expectant parents to take a CPR course from their local Red Cross.

CHAPTER 13

COMMON DEVELOPMENTAL CONCERNS OF CHILDHOOD

TOILET TRAINING—A CHILD-CONSIDERED APPROACH

There was a time when a parent's effectiveness was judged by how fast he could hurry his infant through various dependency stages so that he was no longer a baby. A child should not be hurried through any developmental stage, lest he later exhibit diseases of unreadiness. The age at which children achieve awareness of their bladder and bowel functions varies tremendously. Rather than consider toilet training as your accomplishment to be mastered by a certain time, take cues from your child. Consider not, "When should *I* begin his toilet training?" but rather, "When is *he* ready for toilet training?"

Signs That Your Child Is Ready

Most children, especially boys, do not show consistent signs of bladder or bowel awareness until after they are eighteen months old. This is the age at which the nerves controlling urination and defecation become more mature. Also, at this age most children are so overjoyed at having acquired the skill of locomotion that they are too busy to sit still for anything, especially sitting on a hard toilet seat. The first half of this book was devoted to an important fundamental principle of child rearing: parents, know your child. Parents who really know their children will intuitively pick up signs of toilet-training readiness from them.

The usual indications of toilet-training readiness in an infant eighteen to twenty-four months old are (1) a desire to imitate Mommy's or Daddy's toilet functions; (2) signs that he is about to relieve himself—squatting down, grunting, a "quiet look in a quiet place" such as a corner; (3) signs of genital awareness, such as a little boy's holding onto his penis; and (4) the after-the-fact confession.

Some toddlers go through a stage when they resist any outside suggestions to modify their behavior, especially toilet training. In my experience, toddler negativity has been a highly overrated phenomenon and has been experienced less often in homes where parents practiced the principles of attachment parenting. However, this negative stage does indeed occur in some toddlers, and it is best to respect this and not frustrate everyone in attempts to toilet train during this passing stage.

A toddler often will want to imitate the toilet functions of his older siblings, which should be encouraged. In general, children are mood dependent when it comes to learning. If your intuition tells you your child is not at a stage in his or her development when he or she is particularly receptive to toilet training, back off a while. When you sense that your toddler is ready and willing for toilet training, you may follow these suggestions on how to begin.

1. *Give your child his or her own place to go.* Around two years of age, most children begin to exhibit a desire for order. They like their own shelves for their toys, their own drawers for their clothes, their own tables and chairs, and so on. They also like their own places for their toilet functions. Place an infant potty on the floor next to one of your toilets. Rather than place your infant on his potty chair, simply place the chair alongside your toilet, and wait for your child to accompany you when you go. If you catch your child during this "just like Mommy or Daddy" stage, he may sit on his potty chair when you sit on yours without any urging from you. If your child is not quick to get on his potty chair, you may want to place him on his potty chair when you sit on yours. Most children adapt better to a child-size potty chair than to the more threatening adapter on your own toilet seat. Another advantage of the potty chair is that it can be moved from place to place in the house or can be used in a car during a long ride.

Initially, your child may approach the potty chair with his or her clothes on. Allow your child to sit on the potty chair with his clothes on, sometimes reading a book or simply using the chair as a place to sit. Since imitation is a powerful motivator at this age, a child often will pull down his pants and sit bare bottom on the potty chair as he sees his older siblings or his parents do. This approach capitalizes on the internal motivation of the "I did it all by myself" stage.

2. *Remove the diapers.*   Although diapers seem necessary to protect apparel and furnishings from a baby's being a baby, diapers do diminish bladder and bowel awareness. Uncovered, children learn better how their body works—diapers prolong toilet training in some children. This is why toilet training is often more effective in the summertime when your child can be encouraged to run around the yard without diapers. Most children are not afraid when they see their excrement coming out of themselves, although some pediatricians have reported children's having a "fear of losing part of one's self" feeling. For the child who does not like to be completely undressed, remove his diapers but cover the rest of him with a long T-shirt borrowed from an older sibling.

3. *Teach your child words for his or her actions.*   Being able to talk about a skill greatly helps a child develop that skill. Teach your child appropriate words for toilet functions, which is actually one of her earliest forms of sex education. If you are uncomfortable talking about genitalia or toilet functions, the young child will pick up on your feelings. It is amazing how many different terms have been used to avoid addressing toilet functions and genitalia by their proper terms. Give your child appropriate names of his or her genitalia as penis, vulva, vagina. The terms *urination* or *defecation* may be beyond a child. Phrases like *go pee* or *go potty* are much easier. When you notice that she is exhibiting any of the before-mentioned signs that she is about to go, say to your child, "Let's go potty." In that way your child learns to associate the feeling he has to go potty with the phrase *Go potty.* Words make toilet training much easier, which is another reason to delay toilet training until your child is verbal.

4. *Encourage a toilet routine.*   Some children readily accept being placed on the toilet at certain times during the day. After breakfast in the morning is usually the best time to encourage a bowel movement. Some people have a gastro-colic reflex that aids in having a bowel movement after a meal, usually breakfast. Stated simply, the reflex occurs when the stomach is full; then the colon is stimulated to empty. Encouraging a child to have a bowel movement early in the morning also starts his day off with a clean slate, and avoids the tendency to ignore his bowel signals later on in the day when he is preoccupied with other activities.

When your child is verbal enough to understand toilet-training instructions, encourage him to respond immediately to his urge to urinate or defecate. Not following these urges predisposes children, especially girls, to urinary tract infections. Girls should be taught to wipe themselves from front to back after a bowel movement; they should not wipe from the rectum toward the vagina which may transfer bacteria from the stools into the vagina and increase the likelihood of urinary tract infections.

5. *Put your child in training pants.* After your child has achieved daytime dryness for a few weeks, she may graduate to training pants. They resemble ordinary underwear but are heavily padded in order to absorb the occasional "accidents" which are certainly to be expected as she is mastering her newly acquired skill. Do not punish or reprimand her for these occasional accidents. Teach her to wipe up her own little messes, not as a punishment, but to encourage her sense of responsibility for taking care of her body. Little boys often take great delight in spraying their environment, so they may need a little target practice to hit the toilet.

Dr. T. Barry Brazelton has reported a study of 1,170 children who were trained according to their own timetables by a similar approach. The average age for daytime training was twenty-eight months; boys took 2.5 months longer to complete training than girls. Eighty percent of the children were dry at night by age three, and only 1.5 percent of children who were trained by this method were still wetting their beds after five years of age.

Bed-wetting

Why does a child wet the bed? I want to emphasize that for the great majority of children, bed-wetting is *not* due to a psychological disturbance. For most children, the problem is due to immaturity of the bladder, not of the mind. In order to understand why some children wet their beds, let's first discuss how children normally achieve bladder control.

Infants usually empty their bladders by a reflex called the "bladder-emptying reflex." When the bladder reaches a certain fullness and the bladder muscles have stretched to a certain point, these muscles automatically contract and empty the bladder. Sometime between the ages of eighteen months and two years, most children become aware of this sensation of bladder fullness, which is their first step toward daytime bladder control. The child next becomes aware that he can consciously inhibit the bladder-emptying reflex and hold onto his urine. As a result of this conscious effort, the child's bladder-emptying reflex weakens, and the functional capacity of his bladder increases. When his conscious efforts overcome the bladder-emptying reflex, he achieves daytime bladder control, usually around two years of age. Nighttime control occurs when the child's bladder capacity increases and the bladder-emptying reflex becomes so weak that it is able to be overcome by unconscious inhibition of urination. Delay in bladder control, either daytime or nighttime, can occur if any of these steps is delayed: a delay in awareness of bladder fullness, a small functional bladder capacity, or a prolonged activity of the bladder-emptying reflex. Just as children mature at different rates, their components of bladder control also mature at different rates.

There is often a hereditary basis for bed-wetting which supports the theory that bed-wetting is a developmental delay in maturity. If both parents were bed wetters, the child has a 70 percent chance of being a bed wetter; if one parent was a bed wetter, the child has a 40 percent chance.

Parents of bed wetters mention that their children are very sound sleepers. In some children the messages from the bladder do not reach the mind because of deep sleep. In some children, bed-wetting may actually be a sleep disorder in which the loss of bladder control occurs as the child passes from one sleep stage to another. It is a known anatomical fact that children who wet their beds sometimes have functionally small bladders and must void more frequently. This fact plus the hereditary basis suggest that bed-wetting is usually not due to a psychological disturbance. In the majority of children, bed-wetting should be considered a developmental delay in one or more of the components of bladder control.

At what age should parents be concerned about bed-wetting? There is tremendous variation in the age at which children remain dry throughout the night. By three years of age, most children are dry at night; by six years of age 85 to 90 percent of children enjoy nighttime dryness. At six years of age 92 percent of girls and 85 to 90 percent of boys remain dry at night. By fifteen years of age approximately 1 to 2 percent of teenagers still wet their beds. Pediatricians usually consider bed-wetting after the age of six a condition meriting correction. What is more important is the age at which the child himself is concerned. Most children sincerely want to learn how to control their bodily functions and welcome suggestions from parents and physicians on how to remain dry at night. There are several ways to help your bed wetter.

1. *Avoid focusing on bed-wetting as a psychological problem* since for the majority of children this is simply not the cause. Understand the development of bladder maturity, and regard bed-wetting as a temporary developmental delay, a nuisance which you must understand, support, and parent as you did your child's other developmental stages. It is important for you to develop this attitude since

your child is likely to pick up on your thoughts and feel as you feel about his bed-wetting. If a child's bladder control mechanisms are simply not mature, outside pressure to force any immature system into functioning before its time is doomed to failure; it produces guilt and a secondary emotional disturbance that may aggravate the bed-wetting. Bladder control in young children is also affected by emotional stress. It is common for children to wet their beds during particularly stressful times.

2. *Early toilet-training habits may affect bed-wetting.* If a child is forced into early toilet training according to the norms of the neighborhood rather than her own developmental timetable, she will have a greater chance of prolonged bed-wetting. Children who are toilet trained according to their own developmental readiness tend to achieve nighttime dryness at an earlier age. This is another example of the basic principle mentioned throughout this book: a child hurried through any developmental milestone often will rebel later against whatever system hurried him.

3. *Teach your child the principles of bladder control* and explain to him why he wets his bed. Your child does not want to wet his bed. He dislikes waking up in a wet, odorous bed as much as you dislike constantly changing his bed and washing his sheets. Older children are painfully aware of the social stigma accompanying bed-wetting, and they do not need further negative attitudes from their parents. Explain to your child how his bladder mechanism works. Draw a simple diagram of a baseball as a bladder, and at the bottom of that ball show a donut muscle which opens and closes to help him hold onto his urine. Tell him that he is not a baby now but his bladder and his donut muscle have not grown up yet and he needs to work hard to keep his donut muscle closed at night.

It is important that your child does not feel he is a "baby in everything." I am not suggesting you ignore bed-wetting, especially in the child older than five or six, since it is a source of social embarrassment and certainly does nothing to help his emerging self-esteem. As you should do with other childhood behaviors, convey an accepting attitude toward your child. When your child's subconscious desire to hold onto his urine overcomes the full bladder's reflex to let go, he will enjoy nighttime dryness.

A child needs *motivation*. Encourage overnights at a friend's house and overnight camps. Encouraging him to take along his own overnight pad and sleeping bag may relieve some embarrassment. It helps to prepare the parents at his friend's house so that they can be equally understanding and supportive. Chances are they also have parented a bed wetter.

If your child is a prolonged bed wetter, make a special effort to encourage success in other fields of development such as academics or athletics. A bed wetter should be required to assist with the laundry and to strip his own bed, not as a punishment but as a means to convey to him a sense of responsibility for his bodily functions. Placing a large rubber-backed flannel pad on top of his regular sheet may cut down on the number of wet sheets.

4. *A positive reward system encourages nighttime dryness.* Persistent motivation often helps the child develop a subconscious inhibition of her bladder-emptying reflex at night. Daily rewards are more effective than a long-term reward such as a bicycle if a child is dry for a year. A calendar with a gold star or a coin for each day of dryness is often successful. For the older child who wets her bed, pray with her before bedtime, encouraging her to ask God to help her be dry that night. There is a fine line in each bed wetter between motivation and pressure. Try to sense how motivated your child is to stop her bed-wetting and how her bed-wetting affects her general self-esteem. Then gauge your own support level accordingly. Oftentimes a child who wets her bed is more motivated if she is accountable to a third person such as her pediatrician. A custom I have used for many years for a child who sincerely wants to stop wetting her bed is to have her call me at monthly intervals to give me a report on the number of dry nights on her calendar. You may discuss this approach with your pediatrician.

5. *Teach bladder exercises.* Some physicians recommend bladder exercises to increase the child's functional capacity and to increase the muscular control of his bladder during the day in hopes that they will carry over into his subconscious awareness of bladder control at night. Two examples of bladder control exercises are progressive urine withholding and the stop-and-go technique. Progressive urine withholding encourages your child to drink increasing amounts of fluid and to hold onto his urine for increasingly longer times. Theoretically this increases his functional bladder capacity and weakens the bladder-emptying reflex. In the stop-and-go technique, when a child has the urge to urinate, he is advised to start and stop the stream several times during urination. This exercises increases a child's awareness that he actually can control his donut muscle if he really works at it. Bladder control exercises are usually more productive for children who have difficulty controlling their urine during the day. I do not advise using these bladder control exercises without the advice of your physician.

6. *Restricting fluids after supper* is one of the oldest recommended practices for discouraging bed-wetting. In my experience this seldom does any good and is a bit uncomfortable for the persistently thirsty child. Food and drinks that contain caffeine should be avoided since caffeine acts as a diuretic and actually may contribute to bed-wetting. Teach your child to empty his bladder before going to bed. Little children, tired or in a hurry, often go to the toilet, dribble a little, and run off to resume play or go to bed. In order to encourage your child to empty his bladder fully before going to bed, encourage a triple voiding technique. Tell your child to grunt and empty himself three times, waiting a few seconds between grunts. This technique tends to minimize the residual urine left in the bladder when children void only once.

7. *The shake-and-wake method* is the old custom of waking your child before you go to bed so that she can urinate. If you go to the trouble to get your child out of bed, be sure you waken her completely so she can walk to the toilet on her own power. In order to clarify to your child that you are not taking the primary responsibility for her nocturnal toileting, ask her if she wants you to wake her up before you go to bed. If she is willing, then this practice may be worth a try.

8. *A bladder-conditioning device* is most successful for helping your child achieve nighttime bladder control. Several of these devices on the market are safe, effective, and inexpensive. The device consists of a pad that the child wears inside his or her underwear at night. The pad is connected by a wire to a tiny buzzer that fastens to the child's night garment. When one or two drops of urine hit the moisture-sensitive pad, a beep sounds and wakes the child so that urination can be completed on a nearby toilet.

The device operates on the principle that the stimulus of the child's own bladder-fullness sensor is not sufficient to awaken him fully but the stimulus of the beep alarm is. This beep simply reinforces the intensity of the bladder-fullness stimulus enough to wake the child. By repeatedly awakening when the stronger signal occurs, the child eventually becomes conditioned to awaken to the stimulus of his own bladder-fullness sensor. The device is well accepted by the child because it is his own device for his own problem, for which he takes responsibility. Some children try to play a "beat the beeper" game, attempting to get out of bed before the beeper goes off or with less and less urine reaching the pad. Relapses are common after this device is discontinued, and a second course may be necessary to achieve permanent success. Discuss the use of these bladder-conditioning devices with your doctor.

9. *Medications for control of bed-wetting* may be given to a child a half-hour before bedtime. No one is certain about how these medications work, but scientists believe they improve bladder muscle control and affect the state of sleep by allowing a child to be more aware of his bladder fullness. For most children, medications are less safe and less effective than bladder-conditioning devices. Relapses are also more common after the medications are stopped. In my opinion, medication should not be used to control bed-wetting until all other methods discussed here have been tried and your doctor makes the decision that your child's bed-wetting problem is having an increased effect on his general self-esteem.

SIBLING RIVALRY

Sibling rivalry is one of the oldest family problems, dating to biblical times when Cain killed Abel. The basis of sibling rivalry stems from comparison, one of the major determinants of human feelings and behavior. Consider yourself. You value yourself physically in comparison to the physical attractiveness of others; you have monetary worth in comparison to that of others. Even in school you were graded on a "curve," and you had a rank in class. Comparisons often result in feelings of inferiority because no matter what parameter you measure yourself by, there is always someone better than you in something. Accepting one's self is an adult goal often requiring years of maturing which, in fact, some adults may never reach. This self-acceptance can be more difficult for a child.

Sibling rivalry is a particularly sensitive problem because a child not only compares himself to other siblings but he also evaluates how his parents compare him to his siblings. This is a heavy load for children to carry. Since anger is the predominating emotion here, you may need to assess how much anger controls relationships in your family. Much of the rivalry you are experiencing could be generated by parental anger in all your dealings.

Another emotion that underlies sibling rivalry is love—the parents' love. Love, at least as the child feels it, may carry with it a fear of losing this love and the unwillingness to share this love with another child. Children cannot conclude that parents have unlimited, unconditional love for each child. When your second child comes along, your first child may imagine that some of your love for him is transferred to the other child. Instead of believing each child gets "one bag full" of love, he fears he has to share his one bag full of love and then his bag is only half-full (or less!).

How to Minimize Sibling Rivalry

Although sibling rivalry is a usual fact of family life, there are ways of minimizing it. There is no guarantee that your child will not get this "disease" at some point despite your immunizing her with preventive "medicine" early. You simply lower the risk. The following suggestions will help you lessen the feelings of rivalry between your children. These steps are directed at minimizing the feelings of inferiority and loss in the threatened child.

1. *Consider wise child spacing.*   Parents often ask how close together they should have their children. This very personal decision depends on your individual family situation. I believe sibling rivalry occurs less when children are spaced at least *three years apart* for the following reasons. By three years of age a child is probably weaned from the breast and has received her full potential of parental input that makes her feel right for that time of her life. The child is able to sense her parents' unconditional love by this time (but only if they are careful to actually demonstrate their love), mainly because she is more verbal in both expression and understanding. The three-year-old is able to verbalize her negative feelings about the new baby whereas a younger child only can express his feelings by his actions.

A three-year-old can become more involved in the care of the new baby. Temperament is an obvious factor—a high-need child may need a longer space.

Concerning child spacing, parents can take a tip from nature and from God's design. Most (but not all) women who are breastfeeding totally do not ovulate. In some cultures in which babies are breastfed exclusively for several years, siblings are usually born about four to five years apart. Although it is true that having children too close together is exhausting for the mother and encourages more sibling rivalry, some parents feel that this problem is outweighed by the child's having the constant companionship of a sibling near his age; therefore, they prefer to accept a greater degree of sibling rivalry in return for a closer relationship between children.

Parents should be aware of certain trade-offs in child spacing and sibling rivalry. Children who are spaced four to five years apart tend to squabble less, but they also may relate less to each other because they have fewer common interests. Children spaced one to two years apart may be more exhausting to parents and engage in more sibling rivalry, but they also tend to relate more to each other. Much also depends on the focus of the parents—how committed they intend to be in relationship with their children.

2. *Allow your first child to tandem nurse.* Once again, *do not wean your child before his time.* A sibling who supplants a brother or sister at his mother's breast is subject to rivalry. On the other hand, if your first child has been weaned, he may show a renewed interest in nursing. It is quite normal for a two- or three-year-old child to want to resume nursing temporarily when the new baby arrives. This is called "tandem nursing" and should be accepted willingly with a bit of humor. When our fourth baby arrived, our then three-year-old briefly resumed nursing, quickly became tired of it, and then satisfied himself by walking around sucking on two bottles for a few weeks.

3. *Practice attachment parenting.* Sibling rivalry is less likely in homes where parents have practiced the principles of attachment parenting for several reasons. First, the child feels right. A child who is secure in her love attachment with her parents may feel less threatened by a new arrival. Second, you know your child. Your intuition has been so finely developed with your first child that you will be more sensitive to the feelings that lead to rivalry among your children and you will anticipate circumstances that promote sibling rivalry. Third, you are role models. By practicing the parenting styles advocated in the early chapters of this book, you have modeled expected behavior for your child much as Christ modeled for His

309

disciples. By modeling love, gentleness, and touching, your child learns how big people treat little people, which is how she is expected to treat someone younger than herself. You may be surprised, but many children do not know what behavior is expected of them. If a child feels violent, she is apt to act violently to release her feelings.

4. *Pray with your child* asking God's blessing on the new baby. If your child is old enough to understand, place his hands on your pregnant abdomen, and invite him to pray for his brother or sister inside, reminding him that you really believe God especially listens to the prayers of little children. By teaching your child to pray for his sibling-to-be, you are beginning to model a relationship you expect from him later on, that is, siblings praying for each other. The value of encouraging your child to participate in your "pregnancy prayers" hit home to us during the birth of our fifth child when all our children were present. Within minutes after the birth, our four-year-old daughter, Hayden, put her hand upon the head of our newborn daughter, Erin, and exclaimed, "Praise the Lord. Praise Him!" Hayden simply carried over her feeling in prayer for the inside baby to the outside baby.

5. *Prepare your child for the new baby* as soon as your "bulge" becomes obvious. Let her feel the baby kick. By telling her this is just like she was when she was a baby, you help her identify with the baby inside you. Picture books help clarify misconceptions. Baby is not in Mommy's *tummy*, he is in Mommy's *uterus*. Show your child baby pictures of herself when she was a tiny baby.

Be sure to prepare your child for the time when you go into the hospital. She will probably be more interested in what is going to happen to her while you are gone rather than what is going on in the hospital. Tell her where she is going and who will take care of her. Market the whole idea of separation from you not as a loss but as something special: "Grandma will read you some nice books and do special things with you" (enumerate them). It is usually better to have a substitute parent take care of your child in your own home rather than to have someone care for her elsewhere. This will help alleviate her mounting suspicions that she is being displaced. If a bedroom shuffle is needed to make room for the new baby, do this well in advance of bringing the new baby home. Have her care-giver hold to the child's routine as much as possible when you are gone. While you are in the hospital, communicate with your child often by phone. Bring her to the hospital often to see you and the new baby.

As birthing becomes more homelike in the hospital, siblings are being wel-

310

comed into birthing rooms. In my opinion, most children can handle the birth experience by age three and sometimes even younger. Allow me to share with you a bit of pediatrician's intuition. I sincerely feel that if the older child watches and participates in the birth of the younger child, she feels a bond of love and protection for her younger brother or sister, and this bond may have lasting effects on the sibling relationship.

When the New Baby Arrives

Although these suggestions may minimize sibling rivalry, you should expect some ambivalent feelings in your child, especially if your children are less than three years apart. First, understand your child's position. Just when your two- or three-year-old has achieved a comfortable position in the family, someone else comes along to threaten it. It's very hard to sit back and watch a "stranger" become the focus of love from your parents when you still need that kind of attention yourself. It hurts, especially if you feel unloved as a result of losing that attention. Nearly every book on sibling rivalry explains the feelings of the displaced older sibling with a Hollywood-like analogy of a husband's coming home and announcing to his wife, "We have had so much fun together that I'm bringing home another wife and I expect you to share." Although this humorous analogy drives home the central point of sibling rivalry (one's position is threatened by sharing), it is not a realistic analogy. Having brothers and sisters is an accepted norm, and the child sees this as such (whether he likes it or not).

What Behavior Can You Expect from the Older Child?

Older children vary widely in their expressions of their feelings about new siblings. These feelings range from a "no hard feelings" acceptance to overt hostility and aggression. Some children sulk and retreat; other children lash out with biting and hitting in an all-out attempt to evict their new siblings; others show ambivalent behavior, one day hugging and kissing their new siblings (perhaps a bit "too hard"), the next day hitting them. Children seldom verbalize their feelings about new babies; they usually express them by their actions. The preverbal child is especially prone to physical aggression toward a new baby. Expect the older sibling to show regressive behavior, for example, the previously dry three-year-old may need to go back to diapers temporarily. Expect these anger-releasing antics from your "displaced" toddler.

311

How to Handle Sibling Rivalry

In controlling sibling rivalry, remember you only can control your children's actions, not their feelings. Here are some suggestions for handling sibling rivalry after the new baby arrives.

1. *Get your child involved with the new baby.*   *Involvement* is the key to the very young child who has ambivalent feelings. Encourage him to be Mommy's and Daddy's little helper, changing diapers, bathing the baby, or doing other similar tasks. This role of helper gradually should evolve to the role of *teacher*. Encourage the older child to teach the younger child. This will profit both of them. The older child will feel older and wiser as he "teaches" his little sister something. The older child also may become a source of developmental stimulation for the younger child. Babies often respond better to the sounds and faces of children than they do to those of adults; therefore, it is quite common for younger siblings to show advanced development. Using your older child as a teaching model is a real boost to his self-esteem and consequently may encourage desirable behavior toward his younger siblings.

If the new baby is fussy and you're having difficulty coping with her fussiness, bring in the reserve troops of older children. Let them assist you in trying various gentling maneuvers. An older child's ability to calm a fussy baby fosters a healthy, protective attitude and is a great preparation for his own eventual role as a parent.

2. *Make your older child feel important too.*   Well-meaning friends and relatives may make a great fuss over a new baby and shower him with a lot of gifts. Wise gift-bearing visitors *also will bring gifts for your older child;* but in case they don't, have a few spare, wrapped gifts waiting in reserve. Have a special gift for the new baby to "present" to the older sibling(s). And consider giving your older child a baby doll that wets, has diapers, and can be bathed. If you are breastfeeding, don't give the doll a bottle—you'll be amazed how readily your older child (boy or girl) will figure out how to "nurse" the baby doll.

3. *Get father involved.*   Father, take time to give special attention to the older child. Remember your older child is probably feeling she's lost a lot of Mommy's prime time. This is a realistic fact of family life because babies need more physical maintenance than older children. Dad can compensate for this feeling of loss by really getting involved with the older child and doing fun things with her so she feels what she has "lost" from Mom she has gained from Dad.

As the size of your family increases, each child continues to strive for his or her own identity but may have increasing difficulty finding it because of all the competition from within the family. Take some time out every day or every few days to do something special with each child individually. This special time helps satisfy each child's bid for equal time and gives each the feeling of individual worth.

4. *Encourage your older child to verbalize negative feelings.* The more he can do in words, the less he does in deeds. If he says, "I hate that baby," don't say, "No, you don't." If you deny his feelings, you're denying his right to feel emotions. It is better to express your understanding of these negative feelings and to pursue them and try to turn them into more positive feelings. Allow your child much time and space to approve of the new baby.

5. *Come down hard on physical aggression.* I strongly believe that any overture suggesting an older child is trying to hurt the younger should be dealt with immediately by whatever means necessary to convey the message that you will not tolerate the behavior. Not only can the baby be harmed physically from being hit or shaken, but this behavior models for the younger child that it is OK for an older child to hit a younger one.

Rivalry among Older Children

Part of the realistic expectations of parenting is that parents often will be called upon to referee squabbles among their children, to judge who is at fault, and to administer appropriate chastisement. The following behavior modifiers are designed to minimize rivalry among siblings.

1. *Encourage the older children to model for the younger ones.* It is a fact of life in families that older children are expected to care for, teach, and model for the younger children. For example, our seven-year-old Peter was having a problem with patience. He was quick to lose his temper and give up on a task if it became too difficult for him. We elicited the help of our thirteen-year-old Bobby to go over to Peter at these times of stress, lay his hand on Peter's shoulder, and say, "Peter, let me help you." As another example, one of our younger children was getting lax in his Bible reading. I asked one of our older children to engage in some brother-to-brother Bible study to model the importance of daily Scripture reading. In addition to a child's profiting from the modeling of another, it teaches family members to be concerned and aware of the needs of others. Admittedly this level of concern for one another's needs does not come easily to many siblings, and a little parental guidance is certainly necessary.

2. *Pray for one another.* A major part of your family devotions can be to encourage your children to pray for one another. In our family, one child may have the responsibility of praying for the prayer requests of his brothers and sisters, or each one prays for the one next to him and tries to remember throughout the day.

3. *Encourage expressions of love for one another.* The concept of love for one another can be a main focus of your family devotions. You may say, "I'm encouraging you to show acts of love for one another because this is what Jesus asks His disciples to do." Ask each of your children to show at least one act of love for another sibling each day. Hold them accountable for these acts of love by recording them in your prayer calendar during family devotions. This will not be easy, and your children will forget. With encouragement, this can evolve into a real habit and a powerful behavior modifier toward developing good feelings among siblings. One night as we had prayer time, our five-year-old shared that she felt no one in the family (except Mom and Dad) really loved her. We had a beautiful time together as we explored with her and her siblings how life had been going lately and why she had come to feel this way. We were all convicted and made a commitment that night to find ways for each of us to help this little girl feel the love we have for her. We were glad she was able to express her need.

4. *Minimize comparisons among your children.* This is often the basis for inferiority, which can turn into undesirable behavior among siblings. Praise a child for his accomplishments in relation to himself, not in comparison to a sibling. Each child should feel he is equally special in the eyes of his parents.

An excellent book on this subject is *Siblings Without Rivalry: How to Help Your Children Live Together so You Can Live Too* by Adele Faber and Elaine Mazlish (see Bibliography).

Child Spacing and Natural Family Planning

For a variety of socioeconomic reasons, couples may wish to limit the size of their families or wisely space their children. In this section the options of family planning open to Christian couples are presented, especially following the birth of a new baby. The term *conception control* is more accurate for the Christian couple than birth control since any method that prevents the birth of a baby after conception has occurred is not an option for them. The following information should help you make an informed choice.

Oral contraceptive—"the pill." Although it is perhaps the most effective method of artificial conception control, the pill is also one of the least safe. Many women experience side effects because the hormones contained in the pill interfere with their natural hormonal functions. As more and more information is known about the real and potentially harmful effects of the pill, this form of contraception is gradually becoming less attractive. If the pill fails to suppress ovulation, it then prevents implantation of the fertilized ovum. In this case the pill produces an abortion. Breastfeeding is usually not successful or advisable while you are taking the pill because of the hormonal interference (in some women the amount of milk produced will decrease even with the minimal dose pill) and the possibility of excessive hormones passing into the baby's system. The intricate workings of a woman's hormonal system is one of God's most remarkable creations. In my opinion, artificially manipulating these hormones in order to suppress ovulation or implantation is not only medically unsafe but is not in accordance with God's admonition to regard our bodies as temples of the Holy Spirit (1 Cor. 3:16; 6:19).

The intrauterine device (IUD).   The IUD is a coil-like device that is inserted into the uterus by a physician. There can be medical complications such as infection, perforation of the uterus, and hemorrhage. The real issue for the Christian is how the IUD works. The current IUDs are abortifacients, that is, they cause abortions by preventing the implantation of fertilized eggs into the uterine walls. Therefore, I do not recommend IUDs.

Diaphragm and spermicidal foam and jelly.   These methods are less effective and unattractive because they put a damper on the spontaneity of sex, and sometimes they cause allergy or infection. However, they are efficient methods of contraception.

Condoms.   Condoms are way down on this list of options. A condom alone is not always effective and should be used in conjunction with a diaphragm and spermicide in the female. Males often choose not to use condoms because they feel they lessen the pleasure of intercourse.

None of these methods of conception control is perfect. The pill and IUD are often medically unsafe or morally wrong, and the rest may be ineffective or unattractive.

Sterilization.   As a Christian physician, I am disappointed to see Christian couples decide upon sterilization without prayer and consultation. I personally believe that voluntary sterilization (unless for certain medical conditions) is unwise. Before considering tubal ligation or vasectomy, consider the following: You are making a permanent decision based on your lifestyle and your feelings *at the present time.*

315

You cannot predict how you may feel or how your family situation will be in the future. I have counselled many couples who wish to have sterilization reversed because their lifestyle, priorities, financial situation, or marital situation changed, even though at the time they made the decision they were "certain" they didn't want any more children.

The medical safety of sterilization, especially vasectomy, is open to question. Increasing scientific evidence suggests that some males, following vasectomies, develop sperm antibodies that may lead eventually to diseases of the immune system. Reported in *Medical World News,* September 25, 1988, a study at Boston University presented by the Society for Epidemiological Research showed that men who have vasectomies are three times more likely to develop prostate cancer than other men (prostate cancer accounts for 21 percent of all new cancers in American men and for 11 percent of all cancer deaths in American men). Similar results were reported in the *British Journal of Cancer,* March 1988.

Natural child spacing method. Scientific studies have shown that breastfeeding is a 95 percent effective method of conception control for at least a year after child-birth but *only if all the rules of the game are followed*. The act of suckling and the process of lactation results in a continuation of the hormonal state of pregnancy with the result that ovulation and menstruation do not occur. However, here a word of caution needs to be added. Breastfeeding is an effective method of contraception *only* if performed according to the techniques suggested in Chapter 10 and in Sheila Kippley's book, *Breastfeeding and Natural Child Spacing*.

1. Total breastfeeding-on-demand with a complete openness to night nursings and without the use of pacifiers or bottles.
2. Delayed supplements of solids and other liquids until the baby is six months old, and then only in minimal quantities.
3. Encouraging frequent, vigorous nursings without regard for the clock or the calendar.

In nearly every case where the mother has reported that "it didn't work," there was usually a breakdown in one or more of these requirements, usually the most common being not welcoming the baby into the family bed and discouraging night nursings. The amount of suckling stimulation necessary to suppress ovulation varies greatly from mother to mother, which is why some women conceive although they apparently follow all the rules. However, if couples follow the suggestions of the continuum concept of Christian parenting as discussed in the early chapters of this book, the wife is unlikely to conceive while breastfeeding until her menstrual cycle returns.

Studies have shown the following results in breastfeeding mothers: (1) the average length of lactation amenorrhea (no menstruation and therefore no fertility) is 14.6 months (the range is from two to thirty months); (2) 95 percent of these mothers do not ovulate before their first periods following childbirth and are not fertile until after their first periods occur; and (3) in 5 percent of mothers, fertile ovulation occurs before menstruation but usually not before the twelfth month.

Natural family planning method (NFP). These mothers who ovulate before their first periods are potentially fertile, even though they are completely breastfeeding their infants. Take heart though. There is still another method of conception control for these women, and that is the Natural Family Planning Technique. It consists of observing the following signs.

Examine your cervical mucous daily. At the midpoint of a woman's period she is fertile, and this fertility is heralded by the appearance of a stringy, egg-white type of mucous coming from the cervix. This mucous is readily detectable at the entrance to the vagina. The onset of fertility is also characterized by a slight rise in body temperature in the morning.

Complete details on fertility awareness by detecting the cervical mucous and increased body temperature are given in the references listed in the natural family planning section in the bibliography.

Natural family planning is a way of loving and not only a method of conception control. If this method is used correctly, studies have shown the combination of complete breastfeeding and fertility awareness to be nearly 100 percent effective. As a result, children can be spaced two to three years apart. One drawback to this method is that abstinence is advised when the woman is fertile, which is also usually at the height of her sexual interest. The dilemma could be solved by using a combination of diaphragm, spermicides, and condom during this fertile time but then it's no longer *natural* family planning with the element of trusting God to be the One who is ultimately in charge of blessing you with new life. NFP does require a certain amount of self-discipline for husband and wife—it is this element of sacrifice (see Rom. 12:1–2) that makes NFP so special in building up the marriage. I highly encourage you to learn more by reading *The Art of Natural Family Planning* by Dr. John Kippley. This technique requires a woman to understand how her own body works sexually and hormonally.

For more information on informed choices of conception control and Natural Family Planning, write to The Couple to Couple League, P.O. Box 111184, Cincinnati, Ohio 45211.

CHAPTER 14

DISCIPLINE AND SPIRITUAL TRAINING THROUGH AGE THREE

Father, I acknowledge You as the author of all discipline. I accept the responsibility You have given me to discipline my child. Your instructions are clear, but my spirit is weak. Discipline me that I may discipline my child and by so doing return him and his children and his children's children to You their almighty Father. Amen.

Parents have become accustomed to thinking about discipline as punishment—some external force that is applied to a child to keep him or her in line. Chastening is indeed a part of Christian discipline, but a minor part. (See Chapter 16 for how chastening differs from punishment.) If as Christian parents you sincerely want to discipline your child, your most effective discipline is to create such an attitude within your child and an atmosphere within your home that chastening seldom becomes necessary. But when chastening does become necessary, you must administer it appropriately. Dwell upon this thought for a minute: This may mean changing your attitude toward discipline so you consider how to avoid the necessity of chastening rather than considering how to chasten. In my opinion, too much emphasis is placed on the rod, especially by Christian writers. In the following section the concept of discipline will be built upon as a positive direction from within the child rather than an external force from outside the child. Christian parents will be taught how to chasten their children in such a way that they will see that the Christian approach to solving problems and healing relationships is a practical way of life.

LAYING THE FOUNDATION—DISCIPLINE BEGINS AT BIRTH

Parents usually begin to think about the how-tos of discipline when their children are about two years old because that is when most power struggles between parent and child begin. During their babies' fifteen-month checkup, parents may ask, "Can we discuss discipline now?" I often reply, "You began disciplining your child from the moment of birth." In reality, discipline is not one isolated part of the total package of child rearing. Everything you do with your child from the moment of his or her birth will play a part in discipline. All the previous chapters of this book have directly or indirectly led up to discipline. Explore now how you actually begin to discipline your child from the moment of birth.

Four basic building blocks form the foundation for discipline and spiritual training of the child: basing discipline on Scripture, providing a spiritual model, knowing your child, and helping your child feel right. God, our Father, has directed parents to do two things for their children: to teach and to discipline. *Teaching* and *disciplining,* as used in the Bible, are similar terms, but they differ in degree. *Teaching* means to impart God's Word to your children. *Disciplining* goes one step further—it imparts God's Word to your children to such a degree that His Word becomes part of each child's inner self, his inner controls, his base of operations. In short, to discipline a child means to instill a sense of direction.

Today's parents are bombarded with a flurry of theories and books on how to discipline. As a result, many sincere parents flounder in a sea of uncertainty. There is only one way for Christian parents to discipline their children, and that is God's way. Go to His Book and analyze His specific instructions on how to discipline your children.

Proverbs 22:6 is the master verse of Christian discipline: "Train up a child in the way he should go, And when he is old he will not depart from it." The book of Proverbs is noted for short verses with deep meaning. Dig into this verse now and discover what God is saying to you. *Train* means "bringing into submission." God is reminding you of your awe-inspiring responsibility to discipline your children. These are words of authority and commitment to get in there and work at it. In essence, God is saying: "Parents, take charge of your children." The instruction is the same for all ages, infancy through adolescence; discipline is a constant commitment until the child is ready to leave home.

There are various interpretations of the phrase, "in the way he should go." Does God mean he should go toward the general plan He has for all children to keep His commandments and follow His teaching? Or does God imply a more specific plan, one that is according to your child's inherent temperament and characteristics? Biblical scholars suggest the latter interpretation. Each child has an individual bent or "way" and an individual plan. What God is saying to you is to know your child, be tuned in to his individual bent, keep your radar system attuned to the direction he should take, and keep him focused in that direction *(which may not necessarily be the direction you want for him)*. This concept may be hard for parents to understand: "How do we know what destiny God has for our child?" The concept of knowing your child will be discussed in detail later on.

Some parents are disappointed when they really have trained their children, yet they seem to depart during the early teen years when they are deciding whether or not to accept their parents' values as their own. Parents, don't despair. For some children, there may be a longer time gap in the middle of the proverb: "in the way he should go . . . when he is old he will not depart." Some children temporarily stray from the way they should go, but because of an indelible Christian foundation imprinted upon them, they find their way again and do not depart from it.

The next biblical concept, and one which is very difficult for most parents to understand, is that within the child's nature is a bent toward good and a bent toward evil. It is up to Christian parents to unbend their children's tendency toward evil. The following Scriptures make this concept very clear: "I was brought forth in iniquity, / And in sin my mother conceived me" (Ps. 51:5); and "Foolishness is bound up in the heart of a child, / But the rod of correction will drive it far from him" (Prov. 22:15). Proverbs 29:15, "A child left to himself brings shame to his mother," also reinforces the concept that a child has an inherent bent toward evil. This concept is not in keeping with the secular view that a child should be left alone to decide for himself the way he should go. A child left without direction probably will wander. It is like throwing a child into a stream without first teaching him how to swim. If a child has not been trained to swim against the current, he will be swept along downstream by the prevailing current of the world.

In the preceding scriptural passages, God gave the following guidelines for effective discipline:

1. Make a commitment to discipline your child.
2. Assume authority; take charge of your child.
3. Know your child.
4. Recognize the evil bent in your child.
5. Expect a high probability of success if you follow these guidelines.

Now take these biblical guidelines and create an approach to effective discipline applicable to practical life situations. Consider the growth of the disciplined child, a child with direction, to be analogous to a tree's growing to bear fruit. The soil is the foundation of disciplined parents, and the trunk contains the principles of attachment parenting, improving the child's behavior. Evil influences bend the child one way and good influences bend the child the other.

PROVIDE A SPIRITUAL MODEL

Make Jesus Christ Lord of Your Lives

You cannot give to your children what you do not have yourselves. It is difficult, if not impossible, to impart a sense of direction to your children if you do not have direction. Your library may be filled with books about discipline, and you may preach many sermons to your children, but your example, what you are through the eyes of your children, will always be their best teacher.

Make a commitment that Christian discipline is a top priority. I will stress continually this term *commitment* because it forms the basis for all of parenting. You are well on your way to effective Christian discipline of your child if you love and fear your God and walk in His ways.

Know Your Child

To discipline your child, you must know your child. To train a child in the way he should go, you must know which way he should go. Almost all parents truly love their children; however, parents vary in the degree to which they *know* their children. The attachment style of parenting helps you to know your child better. For review, the essentials of attachment parenting are prenatal bonding, bonding and rooming-in at birth, father involvement in baby's care and spiritual leadership, unrestricted breastfeeding with infant-led weaning, a strong mother-infant attachment, nighttime parenting, gentling the high-need baby, unrestrained response to baby's cries, lots of touching, eye-to-eye contact, and focused attention, and daily prayer for wisdom to know your child.

What do parenting styles have to do with discipline? During my twenty years in pediatrics, I have noticed that parents who have practiced attachment parenting do indeed have fewer discipline problems with their children. Attachment parenting provides the best conditions for parents to really know their children.

I've noticed that parents who practice these attachment tips have the following characteristics as "disciplinarians": (1) they are more observant of their infants' actions; (2) they respond intuitively to their infants' cues; (3) they are more confident in the appropriateness of their responses; (4) the fathers are more involved in parenting; (5) they are sensitive to the feelings and circumstances that promote misbehavior; (6) they know how to convey expected behavior to their children; (7) they have more realistic expectations of childhood behavior in general; (8) they have a wider acceptance of what is normal for *their* children's behavior and are less provoked to anger; (9) they seek prayer and counsel when the going gets tough; (10) they learn the true meaning of giving of themselves; and (11) they enjoy their children more.

The family functions as a father-mother-baby *unit*. It is easier to discipline part of yourself because you know this self (baby) better. It's so beautiful to watch a mother, father, and baby who are in harmony with one another. Whenever I see this harmony in my office, I can't help feeling that surely this is God's design for the parent-child relationship. I believe God designed discipline to flow naturally from this inner harmony; discipline shouldn't be considered a list of methods of external forces suggested by some third-party advisor.

One day I was watching a mother respond intuitively to her child. The two were in harmony with each other. I said to her, "You're a good disciplinarian." Surprised, she responded, "But I don't spank my child." I went on to explain that "disciplinarian" implied the relationship of trust and harmony between her and her child.

Help Your Child Feel Right

Children who are the products of attachment parenting are easier to discipline because as infants they feel right, and infants who feel right are more likely to act right. This inner feeling of rightness is the beginning of a baby's self-esteem, and a child's behavior usually mirrors his or her feeling of self-esteem. This style of parenting also allows a mutual trust to develop between care-giver and child. Admittedly, the ease with which you can discipline your child is to a great extent determined by his or her temperament. However, a baby who has this inner feeling of rightness seems to have a greater receptivity to being directed as if direction, or discipline, reinforces this feeling. An inner feeling of unrightness within a child makes him less receptive to direction either from within or outside himself and accounts for the frustration of parents who state, "We just can't get through to him."

This next statement may surprise you, but I feel that the most important stage of discipline is the period from birth to one year of age. During this period you are developing sensitivity to your baby, getting to know him, maturing your intuition, and helping your baby feel right. This is the period in which you are maturing in your attitudes toward the whole of child rearing, and every little interaction you have with your baby carries over into discipline. Dr. James Dobson has made an important point that discipline is a balance between love and control. Being open to your baby during his first year allows this control to develop naturally during his second year. Before you can control your child (in the biblical sense of guiding him), you must first be open to him. Control will flow naturally from a foundation of knowledge of your child and openness to him. In the first few months you will find that being open to your baby means that you anticipate and respond to her needs promptly and totally. You are there for your baby unreservedly, giving her what she wants when she wants it, building love and trust. And all is well—no problem—harmony.

Around the third or fourth month there is a slight shift in the balance. Your baby can now become bored because developmentally she is ready for more than just being held and fed; she can become frustrated because her mind drives her to do things her body isn't ready to do yet. The cry that your baby uses to signal her boredom or frustration will be different from the hunger, pain, or "need to be held" cry, and you will still respond as quickly as possible but gradually you will learn that these cries don't require the "red alert" response from you. You don't have to drop everything the instant she signals; you find you can buy a little time (one or two minutes, then three or four) by using your voice to reassure that you are here and you are coming. Your baby learns she can wait, and you both learn just how long. This all happens gradually, without any calculation, but one day, when she's six months old, you realize that your responses are considerably slower now than they were at six days or six weeks. It would simply not be healthy if you were still trying to be so promptly and totally "there" for your six- to nine-month-old as you were in the first few months.

In the next stage of child development, the toddler years, you will build upon

324

this foundation toward widening the scope of Christian discipline, that of guiding the child.

DISCIPLINING THE CHILD
ONE TO TWO YEARS OLD

In the preceding section you learned how to lay the foundation for effective discipline in your infant's first year of life by (1) knowing your infant, (2) helping him feel right, and (3) seeing that he securely trusts you as his care-givers. Building a strong foundation on these elements in his first year gives you something on which to build a concept of disciplining him as a toddler. Without this foundation, discipline will evolve into a science of methods. With this foundation, you naturally and intuitively will guide your child instead of reacting emotionally to his actions.

By the time a child is twelve months old the roles of both infant and parent take on a new direction. In the first year, your role is primarily that of care-giver. This role certainly continues, but in the second year it broadens into the additional roles of authority figure and designer of your child's environment. In the first year your child's environment is mainly your arms, your breasts, and your bed. In the second year your child's environment widens through his acquiring two new abilities: loco-motion and speech. As the roles of parent and child take on a broader perspective, so does the concept of discipline. In the first year, discipline means primarily con-veying love and security to your infant and learning to know him. In the second year, discipline also requires guidance. The following discussion will center on two main features of guiding your child: (1) how to develop realistic expectations and knowledge of normal or usual toddler behavior in general, and of your child's be-havior in particular; and (2) how to modify your toddler's bent toward undesirable behavior and channel his energies toward desirable behavior.

At this point, take inventory of what your one-year-old is like as a person. When I ask parents to tell me about their child at the one-year checkup, they may say, "He is beginning to walk, he plays with blocks, he feeds himself," and so on. This is not the kind of answer I am hoping for. They have told me what the child *does*, not what he *is*. Other parents may say, "He likes to be held a lot; he is most happy when he . . . ; his favorite toy is . . . ; he loves to roll on his daddy's chest . . . ; his mood is generally pleasant, but he has his fussy times at the end of the day. I guess he is just tired. I've learned to handle these fussy moments." Those are the cue words I'm looking for: "he likes," "he feels," "I feel," "I know when he . . ." These parents have a head start toward effective discipline because they know their child.

Since discipline begins with knowing your child, use the following checklist to take inventory of how well you know your one-year-old:

- What makes your baby most happy, laughing and cooing?
- What makes your baby most unhappy, crying or sad?
- What parent-child play activity does he or she like best? (Playing peeka-boo, crawling on Dad's chest?)
- What are your baby's most noticeable cues that he or she needs something?
- Are you confident that you recognize and respond appropriately to your baby's cues, such as crying, gesturing, body tone, etc.?
- Does your response to your baby's cues make you both feel better?
- Does your baby feel right most of the time?
- Are you comfortable helping your baby feel right, such as comforting him when he or she is fussy?
- Do you enjoy being with your baby most of the time?
- Generally speaking, do you enjoy being a parent?
- Do positives outweigh negatives?
- Do you pray and seek counsel when problems arise either in your marriage relationship or in your parent-child relationship?
- Do you pray for your child daily?

This inventory is a general measure of how finely tuned your communication network is with your baby. If you have answered with more negatives than positives, please pray and seek counsel at this stage of your parent-child relationship so that you can make the subsequent stage of disciplining your toddler more effective.

Have Realistic Expectations of Normal Toddler Behavior

Many first-time parents do not have a clear understanding of what is normal or usual toddler behavior, and they may therefore interpret certain behaviors as "bad." Not understanding and accepting normal toddler behavior may lead to being harsh when you should be gentle, and restricting when you should be channeling. This is part of parental maturity that is necessary for effective discipline. The more children you have, the more your concept of normality will broaden and the more your acceptance level will widen. As a father of seven this is my first survival tip to you.

Locomotion widens your child's environment around age one. The ability to walk brings an insatiable appetite to explore. When his desire to explore matches his locomotor capabilities, he is in balance. When his desire to explore is greater than his capabilities to get there, he is out of balance. Also, when desire is greater than capability, his inner frustrations may be manifested by tantrumlike behavior. This imbalance results in *ambivalence,* one of the most normal and noticeable characteristics of a toddler. For example, watch toddlers in a park with limitless space to roam. A few will zip away from Mommy a long distance to explore. A few others will cling to Mommy because they seem threatened. Some toddlers will run off a short distance but will look back periodically to home base to be sure Mommy is still there.

A characteristic of child development, especially that of a toddler, is that the acquisition of a new skill compels the child to master that skill and use it to achieve other skills. Until your infant is able to crawl, she is a passive observer of the world around her and mostly dependent upon other people for stimulation and pleasure. Walking opens up new horizons for her and gives her an insatiable appetite to explore and uncover the secrets of the wide world. She sees that doors are to be opened, drawers pulled out, buttons pushed, knobs turned, and objects taken apart. She is a going concern from dawn till dusk, stopping briefly to refuel on food and love, only to jump down again and continue her independent research of the world around her. She succumbs to an occasional nap and does not yield to the enemy of sleep without a fight.

Your little navigator does not chart her course carefully. A toddler's explorations are directed more by impulse and trial and error than by calculation and reasoning. Toddlers are not willfully destructive or disobedient. They simply have not developed control systems to govern their intense impulses. The late Selma Fraiberg stated beautifully in her book *The Magic Years,* "Toddlers exhibit a declaration of independence but they have no intentions of unseating the government."

The second year is often presented in very negative terms. Some mothers say, "The terrible twos—I'll be glad when this stage is over." Any self-respecting toddler would disagree with these unfair words and would feel that he is simply misunderstood. The media has done toddlers a disservice. If all children really acted in the way they are portrayed, there would be many "only children." For parents, this is one of the most exciting yet admittedly exhausting stages of child development. Your toddler is really not a negative little person, he is very positive. He knows absolutely what he wants, and he is determined to get it at all costs. The no-nos come from his outside world. Perhaps this should be called the "negative stage of parenting" rather than the negative stage of the child.

Toward the end of the second year the development of language gives the toddler another avenue of communication with the world around him. The combination of language and locomotion gives the toddler a newly found power to use the world around him for his own needs or desires. For example, being unable to get the right peg in the right hole, our frustrated toddler runs over and tugs on Mommy's skirt, saying, "Mommy do it." When a child begins to use another person as a resource for a problem he cannot solve by himself, he has learned a vital educational skill. The toddler also will vacillate between "I do it myself" and "Mommy do it" followed by an incessant chain of "No!" and "Pick me up." This normal toddler behavior should not be interpreted as manipulation which needs restricting, but rather healthy communication which needs an appropriate response. If you respond to a toddler's cues appropriately and with direction, he is motivated to develop further his newly discovered powers. If this motivation is directed rather than restrained, the toddler feels right, he is further stimulated to continue developing these powers, and his self-esteem prospers.

The dilemma between disciplining and directing a toddler is arriving at a proper balance, exerting just the right amount of guidance and restraint without hampering the toddler's desire to learn. Rather than regard this stage as a permanent threat to your parental powers, consider it a passing developmental stage.

Now that you are more familiar with usual and normal toddler behavior, learn how you can guide and direct, or discipline, that behavior into desirable avenues. (See the Bibliography for books about normal childhood behavior.)

Be available on an as-needed basis. Your toddler needs your support while he works out the anxiety that is created by his internal ambivalence. You are still the pivotal point in his widening universe. As he makes his daily rounds throughout the house, he periodically checks on your whereabouts, and he is comforted knowing you are there.

Be observant of your toddler's behavior. Watch for his cues that he needs you, but also be willing to accept his need for his own space. Part of achieving parental maturity and becoming an effective disciplinarian is having your radar system so finely tuned into your child that you pick up his signals on your screen and store each bit of information. A child who has a consistently available and observant care-giver intuitively feels that someone he loves is in tune with him. Consider for a moment your relationship with your heavenly Father; what a feeling of strength and security to know that He is available and observant of your behavior and of your needs.

Consider Your Child's Environment

Respect your toddler's healthy curiosity by moving your valuable and breakable family heirlooms up a few feet. Bring them down in a few years when she is old enough to reason with. The out-of-reach and out-of-sight environment is certainly much easier on child and parent than a constant stream of "no-no" or "don't touch." Constantly saying no and frustrating the natural drive to explore only serves to produce anger in your child on a continuous basis. The toddler-on-the-loose precautions are certainly safer and less exhausting than a system that requires the ever-watchful eyes of a protective mother.

Also, consider size-related needs by giving your child child-size furniture. Having her own small table and chairs in a corner of your kitchen (where the action is) allows a young child to be comfortable sitting for a longer time, thus encouraging task completion and concentration. Since it is normal and healthy behavior for her to turn knobs, push buttons, and pull drawers, give your child her own things to turn, push, and pull. A curious toddler deserves at least one eye-level drawer in the kitchen that she can pull out, sort through, and fill with her own belongings. Place safety latches on cupboards that are off limits. Encouraging her to get into her own things will cause her to be less interested in the things she should not have.

Encourage "hands on" learning. Give your toddler things to carry, blocks to stack, things to pour, wagons to pull, safe places to climb, and objects to touch. A child's hands are tools she can use to explore and learn cause-and-effect relationships. For this reason, sensitive childhood development experts recommend that you do no hand slapping to discourage her touching things. Hand slapping to a curious toddler just beginning to reach out into the world is probably just as insulting as face slapping is to an adult. The more positive feedback she receives ("Thank you for bringing Mommy the clothes"; "Show me your car"), the less likely she is to want to touch the things that are off limits. (The concept of "me" and "mine" is important at this age too.) Create a positive environment, a get-into-things and a hands-on approach that respects the normal, innate curiosity of a developing toddler and makes negative discipline less necessary.

Take a few minutes here to dwell upon one basic goal of discipline, and that is to create an environment that does not create a conflict of wills. Creating a child-considered environment contributes to your maturity as parents who sincerely want to discipline your child. Learn to respect your child's different need levels at different stages of development. Rather than viewing discipline as a parental obligation to suppress your child until he is old enough to act like an adult, let your child act like a child so he can feel like a child. If you view discipline as guidance, you will regard a child-considered environment as guiding or disciplining your home environment so that the environment itself may discipline the child.

Be creative in high-risk situations that make discipline difficult. It is unrealistic to expect a curious toddler to walk down the aisle in a supermarket and not touch anything. I would be very suspicious of a young child who walked like an obedient soldier with his arms at his sides down the aisle of a supermarket and did not try to grab all those delightful things just begging to be grabbed. Keep his arms and hands full of things so he is completely "grabbed up." Let him help you grab things. After all, that is the model he sees—his mother is walking down the aisle grabbing things. Or keep him safely seated in the shopping cart (with a restraint strap) and carry on a conversation with him that lets him feel included in the shopping.

Replace "no-no" with "yes-yes" or simply "stop." One of the first words an infant says is *no* because *no* is one of the first words he hears. When an eighteen-month-old is sitting quietly and playing, nobody says anything to him. But let him start exploring and he excites everybody; he gets lots of attention. The child does not know intuitively, in most instances, which behavior is right or wrong, but he soon learns which behavior gets the quickest response from adults. And he learns behavior directly from the behavior you use toward him. Speak politely and gently even when correcting him, even though it is hard not to sound rude when you are irritated. And rather than grabbing a "no-no" from his hands, model asking for it ("Give it to Momma, please") and show him how to place it in your hand for you. If the object is dangerous, grabbing it may actually inflict injury. You can restrain his hand so that the scissors (or whatever) cannot do any damage while you are teaching him to hand it to you. These are matters of common courtesy—the way you would respect a friend. Behavior modification principles are especially applicable to a two-year-old who will naturally gravitate toward the behavior that gets him the most response (positive or negative). If a child likes the response he gets from good behavior, he will be inclined to repeat this behavior. Acknowledge him or catch him in the act of being good. Simply use more affirmative words in talking with your toddler and fewer negative words. If he is zeroing in on your valuable vase, rather than descend on him from above with an almighty "no-no," gently but firmly redirect his probing hands toward a safer object and quickly rescue the vase to higher ground.

Adopt the "why" principle. When your young child apparently misbehaves, train yourself to ask yourself, *Why is he doing that?* Is he tired, bored, hungry, or sick? Is he simply trying to get attention? Is he engaging in a power struggle? Is he trying to fit into a group but has not found his role? If you first approach your child's behavior by asking *why* he is doing something, rather than asking *what* he is doing, you will focus first on the child and second on the act. It is in such instances that knowing your child begins to pay off. In so doing you will understand better the feelings behind the child's behavior and be able to take effective steps to channel his behavior.

A good example of this in our family is our sixteen-month-old daughter. She playfully and gleefully begins to hit (aggressively touch) her mother on the head or face. Her mother expresses displeasure and asks her to "stop." Usually she doesn't, unless her mother picks her up and changes the situation. She is having fun and doesn't understand that it hurts. So her mother gives her something more appropriate to hit; she holds out her hand and says, "Gimme five." The hitting continues with great gusto, and both parties in the game enjoy it. Focusing on the why is good parental training for disciplining the older child when it is often necessary to focus primarily on the child's feelings rather than the action. (Don't ask your older child, "Why are you doing this?" but, "What are you doing?" It helps his ability to evaluate his behavior correctly if he can state *what* he is doing.)

Between twelve and eighteen months of age most conflicts occur between the child and his environment rather than between the parent and his child. Therefore, most of your authority and discipline are directed toward taking charge of your child's environment and thus indirectly setting limits for him. Even before your toddler has begun walking, you have covered electric outlets, locked your cupboards, removed breakable objects, covered sharp table corners, removed small objects that can be swallowed. Taking charge of a child's environment is an important part of disciplining him. A toddler's internal discipline operates at a very simple level. His behavior is directed toward what makes him feel good and away from what makes him not feel good. For example, a hand on a hot stove is not likely to be repeated, but a hand in a cookie jar is very likely to be repeated.

Toward the end of their second year together (eighteen months to two years), a parent's role shifts somewhat from environmental designer to educator and authority figure. The child's level of dependence is still high, and he is still quite ambivalent. However, at the end of the second year his behavior is usually directed less by impulse and trial and error and more by thinking and calculating. By this time he has learned cause-and-effect and how to manipulate his environment to get what he needs. For example, he begins to think of a footstool as the great equalizer to make him taller. He also knows that the cookies are in the cupboard. He puts the two together, figuring out that if he pulls the stool in front of the cupboard he can climb up and get the cookies.

The ability to calculate coupled with somewhat impulsive behavior usually leads to some power struggles between parent and child at this age. And this is where parents emerge as authority figures. A child must know who is in charge of his environment; the younger he is when he learns and feels who is in charge, the less traumatic this power struggle is to both parent and child. At this point let me impress upon you a very important consideration in disciplining your child: a child wants and needs limits. A child needs security and direction and becomes confused when he is without controls. Psalm 23:4 says, "Your rod and Your staff, they comfort me."

Develop Your Role as an Authority Figure

"No, no, no!" is a common parental outburst around the end of the first year, making parents cognizant of their emerging role as authority figures. Your role is an authority figure, taking charge of your child's environment. By creating a child-considered environment, you encourage your child's natural developmental curiosities to flourish while you protect her from harm until she has the wisdom and discernment to know her limits. Throughout Scripture are clear mandates to parents to take charge of their children (Prov. 19:18; 22:6; Eph. 6:4).

Authority does not mean that suddenly when she is two years old you decide to clamp down on your child. If you have laid the foundation of discipline in the first year, if you have fulfilled the conditions of attachment parenting, your role as authority figure will naturally evolve. The earliest condition that helps your role of authority figure evolve is your attitude of openness to your child's cues. Being open to your baby's cues and becoming "giving" parents do not mean you are losing control.

The first few years of parenting are similar to Christ's ministry. Jesus was clearly in charge of His disciples. He was a strong authority figure to them, but He was, first of all, a servant to them. He washed their feet (see John 13:5).

Parents who use restraint early and try to rear their children according to their preconceived ideas of how children *ought* to be (rather than how their individual children really are) are candidates for becoming ineffective authority figures later on. In my practice, I actually look for the cues of openness in parents during the first few months of their babies' lives so that I can counsel them more effectively about discipline.

Parents have a God-given right to expect obedience from their children. God's order for children is that they obey their parents: "Children, obey your parents in all things, for this is well pleasing to the Lord" (Col. 3:20). The biblical basis for authority is not only obedience but also respect for authority. "Honor your father and your mother," the commandment says. The term *honor* implies obedience plus respect. It is honor that you want from your children, not just obedience. Although obedience is owed to you, respect for authority is not an unconditional right of parents; it must be earned. The attachment styles of parenting will help you earn this honor.

Some parents may think that through the use of the *rod* (which they interpret to mean spanking), they can force their children to do what they want them to do, that is, to obey. However, the biblical basis for the word *obey* does not mean simply "to do as I say." It means "to hear intelligently," from the Hebrew root word *shama*. This implies that children need to be old enough and mature enough to understand what they are hearing their parents ask or command. It is difficult for parents to know how much their toddlers really understand. Most toddlers understand much more than they say because receptive language development is more advanced than expressive language. They understand the words for concrete objects they can recognize, such as *doggie, horsey, cat*, and so on. But they usually cannot understand abstract concepts or attitudes. They can say, "No, no" (it's easy to say and they hear it often enough), but they cannot understand how and why they are expected to obey. When they say "No" they don't mean "No, I *won't*" they mean "No, I *don't want* to." It is your job as parents to help them "want to" obey. This is known as motivating your child—it sets the stage for inner-directed discipline later on.

Toddlers may be incapable of completely fulfilling the biblical meaning of obedience, which is why spanking them before they are old enough to understand why they are being spanked would not be in keeping with the true biblical concept of obedience. Toddlers can be trained that a certain action warrants a certain response; this is negative training. Positive training uses all the steps of attachment parenting and the creatively designed child-considered environment to elicit the same response. For example you want your twenty-month-old to come get in the car to go shopping. You see he is busy with his trucks and will hate being interrupted.

Instead of just telling him to come, you motivate him by talking about something fun you'll do when you get there (see the doggies, ride the horsie). How much nicer for both of you than for you to have to pick up a kicking, screaming child and force him into his car seat.

Another example of positive training is to help a child leave an activity that he is enjoying when you have a time constraint. First, try to give him a five-minute warning so he doesn't have to cope with a sudden shift. Then if he is upset with having to leave his play, help him say, "Bye-bye trucks, see you later." Bringing closure to his play gives him a sense of control when he can say good-bye and look forward to a reunion. Parents who truly know their children will be able to choose which approach is in accordance with God's design for disciplining their individual children.

A child's parents can whip him into obedience, but they only can love him into developing an attitude of respect for them. *The American Heritage Dictionary* defines *respect:* "to feel or show esteem for; to honor." The couple who has practiced attachment parenting has earned their child's trust; they are appreciated as the source of his feelings of rightness. That child considers his parents worthy of esteem. It is imperative that a child respect his parents because this provides a basis for his attitude toward his adult world in general and toward any authority figure in particular. The more a child respects his parents' authority, the more readily he will respect God's commandments. If your child does not respect reasonable authority, you have a real problem that can have far-reaching consequences. The best way to teach respect toward parents is for parents to respect their child as a person.

DISCIPLINING THE CHILD TWO TO THREE YEARS OLD

The main elements of discipline in a toddler have been discussed: (1) your child becomes secure in her trust relationship with you and therefore feels right within herself; (2) you are in harmony with your child and really know her; (3) you have designed her environment appropriately to respect her curiosity yet protect her from harm; and (4) you have planted the seeds to help you become effective authority figures.

The two- to three-year-old is characterized by three interesting features: (1) mastery of expressive language; (2) increasing awareness of self; and (3) the beginning of social peer relationships. The two-year-old is learning to verbalize his feelings and demands, which enables him to hold the attention of adults and of his peers. He shows less tendency to act out his anxiety because he is able to express it with words. His developing language skills enable him to become a truly social person and enable him to manipulate (there is a positive aspect to this) his adult environment. This ability adds "bigness" to his concept of self.

A child's increasing ability to walk and talk her way into what she wants or feels she needs (the difference between a want and a need is as confusing to the child as it is to the parent at this stage) is a tremendous boost to her emerging but still fragile self-esteem. Bearing this in mind, you can effectively discipline your two-year-old. First, by recognizing that two-year-olds are driven to use their limited abilities to manipulate their environments and to improve their end of the parent/child communication network and, second, by responding appropriately to these drives for communication. An *appropriate* response is emphasized because this implies achieving a balance between responding in a way that further motivates her desire to improve her communication and increase her self-esteem, and responding in a way that is governed by reasonable restraint on what and how much she gets. This is the principle of *delayed gratification* which is so vitally important in discipline of the child at any age. (How to teach your child delayed gratification effectively is an important point discussed later.)

The development of a disciplined child is a continuum: how you discipline your child at one stage of development will carry over into the effectiveness of the next stage of development. If you have succeeded in setting appropriate limits and if you have seen outside control in your almost two-year-old, he will begin to show some inner controls of his own during the next year. By the time your child is two years old he can begin to show some inner control and become more certain of his limits because he has had the previous year to sort them out.

At this stage, stubbornness will occasionally rear its head (in some children more than in others), but there is generally less negativism on both sides. Most two-year-olds will become less clingy and obstinate, and at the same time, their parents become less restraining. By two years of age, most children have suffered enough bumps and bruises to have learned the limits of their home environments and therefore feel more comfortable and secure and in control of their own bodies. The behavior of the two-year-old becomes less impulsive, and he considers alternatives before acting. He has become increasingly aware of cause-and-effect relationships. The usual two-year-old is very egocentric. He sees things entirely from his own

335

point of view, and he tries to figure out how he can use the outside world to suit his own needs. Appreciate this as normal behavior at this age, a behavior that is not to be squelched but directed.

Since being egocentric and using expressive language to manipulate his environment is normal behavior for a two- to three-year-old, look now at what is appropriate parental response to this God-given behavior. First, the term *manipulation,* which unfortunately has fallen into disrepute, needs to be clarified. It has come to mean a method whereby a child wraps her parents around her little finger and dangles them as puppets in her exciting world of unending sensual (meaning the five senses) delights. "I don't want to feel manipulated" is a common parental feeling at this stage, which often leads you to overreact and misinterpret your children's behavior.

At this stage of a child's development there is healthy manipulation and unhealthy manipulation. A child sees her activities mainly as communication, not manipulation. A young child with a healthy self-esteem who feels good using all her primitive tools to communicate with her environment (people and things) will normally try to get everything she can to fulfill totally her insatiable appetite for pleasure. A two-year-old does not yet have enough inner control of what and how much of any good thing is best for her, and that is why she needs direction. Parents, avoid the tendency to overreact to the feeling, "I'm not going to let her manipulate me." This usually results in a power struggle in which your primary communication with your child will be negative (what you are not going to let her do) rather than positive (what you are going to let her do or have). When you direct her manipulation, she is encouraged to communicate her needs, and she feels right in communicating them. Put very simply, a child should always feel right in "asking and seeking and knocking." She should always feel that there is a tuned-in receiver for the signals she sends out. It is then up to you, striving for effective Christian discipline, to receive all of these signals and feed back to your child what, in your judgment, she should have and what she should not have. Let's call this "selective gratification." Here is where you begin planting the seed for one of the most important elements of effective discipline which peaks in the middle childhood and teenage period, and that is the concept of delayed gratification.

Unhealthy manipulation occurs when a parent, by being unavailable, unobservant, or uninterested, either ignores the child's signals and feeds back nothing to him or receives all of the child's signals and does not selectively process them, thus becoming overindulgent in giving the child everything he wants. Both extremes—

the child who receives nothing and the child who receives everything—are equally unhealthy.

How do you develop selective gratification of your child's demands? Follow all the principles: be available; be observant; know your child and the direction he should go; and, above all, pray, asking God for wisdom.

In addition to verbal language, body language is extremely important at this stage. Two-year-olds are very affectionate; this is the stage of open arms and "pick me up." Become a hugs-and-kisses family. The ability to give and receive affection is one of the most important behavior-improving influences in disciplining a child.

Encourage Good Behavior

Acknowledge your child's creativity.   Two-year-olds show varying desires and abilities to be creative. The skills of scribbling, stacking, finger painting, and modeling with clay are beginning at this stage. Your little architect takes great pride in her creative accomplishments and is eager to share them with you. No matter how haphazard it may seem to you, to her the page full of scribble is an artistic accomplishment, and she wants an approving response from her most trusted art critic. A positive response to your child's creative accomplishments at this stage becomes one of the most powerful reinforcers of positive behavior. If a child feels better from the response she gets from putting things together, rather than from tearing them apart, she is likely to continue the desirable behavior.

Maintain order in the house.   Between two and three years of age, children show an innate appreciation for order. A young child's developing brain is searching for organization, and this starts with organizing his belongings. Your role as designer of your child's environment increases to organizer of his environment.

These specific suggestions will help you provide order in your child's environment and use this order as a powerful enforcer of desirable behavior.

1. Instead of piling toys in toy boxes and corners, use low shelves with one-foot-square compartments, each containing one or two valued toys. Too many toys in places that are too small confuse the child who is already trying to sort out all the clutter in the busy world around him.
2. Give your child his own table and chairs. Child-size furniture improves his comfort and his attention span.
3. Use eye-level wooden pegs where he can hang his clothing.

This orderly environment complements the child's orderly mind and also encourages a sense of responsibility. One of the most common difficulties I see in children of all ages is the lack of an inner sense of responsibility. The development of a child's responsibility for his own actions begins with a sense of responsibility for his own belongings, and this should begin around two years of age.

Provide good nutrition. It may seem unusual to talk about good nutrition in regard to childhood discipline. However, you are on the offensive. Discipline is still being considered in the positive sense—what you can do to encourage desirable behavior. Good nutrition (or the lack of it) can have a profound effect on behavior. I recommend three feeding practices that may improve your child's behavior and therefore may contribute positively to your discipline relationship.

First, *breastfeed* your infant as long as both members of the nursing couple enjoy the relationship. I encourage mothers to think of breastfeeding in terms of years and not months. At this point you may ask, "What on earth has this to do with disciplining my child?" Early in this chapter on discipline you read about the importance of the young infant's developing a secure attachment and trust in his care-giver as a prerequisite for that care-giver's becoming an effective authority figure later on. Breastfeeding mothers simply spend more time with their children. Breast-fed infants eat more often, and they spend more time in their mothers' arms and derive more skin-to-skin and eye-to-eye contact. I am not saying that breast-feeding mothers love their children any more than bottlefeeding mothers, but I do feel that breastfeeding gives the mother a head start in knowing her child better, and the child is given a head start in feeling right. These two elements are basic to the foundation for effective discipline.

The second feeding practice I encourage you to consider is *nibbling.* This may sound like heresy, a blatant attempt to undermine the accepted custom of requiring a young child to sit still, consume three square meals a day, and eat nothing between meals. But consider the limitations of the young child, especially at two or three years of age. He does not have the attention span to sit still and finish a large meal. He is simply too busy. This often results in mealtimes becoming battles between parents and child instead of positive experiences. Medically speaking, it is better for a young child to nibble on nutritious foods all day long because he avoids frequent blood-sugar swings and the mood changes that often accompany them in an active child. This is why the behavior of young children deteriorates in late morning and mid-afternoon when they are the most hungry and their blood sugar is the lowest. See Chapter 11 for tips on feeding your toddler and young child.

338

The third practice that will improve your child's behavior is *avoiding junk food*. A description of junk food and its detrimental effects on your child's behavior are discussed in detail in Chapter 11.

Give Spiritual Training

Parents often ask, "At what stage of my child's development do I introduce the concept of God into discipline?" It is much easier to bring God into discipline at this stage if you have brought Him into your lives very early in your marriage. The pathway to successful Christian parenting is a series of personal relationships.

The first relationship is between you and God, by committing yourselves to follow His commandments and by acknowledging Jesus as your personal Savior and Lord. The second relationship is a dual commitment: you commit yourself to your spouse and to a lifelong Christian marriage, and you commit this relationship to God. You acknowledge Him as the supreme marriage Counselor from whom you will receive the necessary strength and wisdom to grow in a fulfilled Christian marriage. After you have committed yourselves to God as a couple, your next relationship is to commit yourselves to Him as parents. From the moment of conception, pray daily over your preborn child, acknowledging God as the architect and protector of your developing fetus. After birth, pray daily for your baby, asking God for wisdom to rear him or her according to His plan. Daily read God's Word aloud to your baby from his very early days. At around fifteen to eighteen months show him pictures and talk about Jesus. His own picture Bible would be a good way to start.

If you have brought God into your lives early in these relationships, you have laid a foundation for naturally imparting the concept of God to your child when he is two years of age. Without this foundation you will be less comfortable talking with your child about God because you do not know God's working in your own lives. It goes back to the basic principle that you cannot give to your children what you do not have.

How to Teach Your Two-Year-Old about God

Here are specific examples as to how you as Christian parents can introduce God to your child.

1. *Pray for your child.*   Thank God for your child every day. Ask God to watch over your child's development and to give you wisdom in rearing him in the way he should go. By the time your child is two years old, a spiritual feeding of daily prayer becomes as natural a part of child care as food for the body does.

From the day of the birth of our fifth child, each night before retiring I would lay my hands on my little daughter and spend a few moments in prayer. A few nights I went to sleep having forgotten to do this, but I would soon awaken with the feeling that as I lay down to sleep, I had forgotten to lay someone else down to sleep. I then performed my duty as spiritual leader of my home and put my hands on my little daughter, thanking God for the blessings of her day and asking Him to be with her during the night. I then retired with a comfortable feeling that we both would sleep better, because in the quiet of the night Someone who never goes off call is watching over us.

Daily prayer is vital to Christian family discipline. It becomes a discipline, a persistent spiritual habit by which the parent continuously prays, "Father, I invite You into our family; You are a trusted and vital family member (head of the family, in fact), and my day is not complete unless we talk to each other." By the time your child is two years old, she hears the words *God* and *Jesus* spoken in association with love and protection so that by the time she is three years old, she feels God's presence. A child's concept of God is very simplistic, and it is probably limited to a feeling: "Mom and Dad talk about Him all the time, He must be a very important Person; He loves me, He is a big Person." Such primitive concepts are vital to laying the foundation of the child's regard for God as the authority figure at a later age. One of the characteristics of toddlers' language skills is that they receive and understand much more than they say. They probably will understand more of the concept of God if they have been saturated with hearing about God from birth (Deut. 6:6–8).

One Christian mother confided in me that she feels her two-year-old knows Jesus. She had been praying with her child every night from the time he was one year old. When he was two the mother walked by her child's bedroom shortly after praying him to sleep and heard him saying, "Jesus . . . Amen." What went on in that two-year-old's absorbent mind in the few moments between "Jesus" and "Amen" only the child feels and God knows.

2. *Sing with your infant.*   Between the ages of one and two, babies can mimic the gestures of songs. For example, as early as nine months, our daughter Erin lifted up her arms at the cue of "praise Jesus." Following our evening meal prayer we have a custom of singing the following song.

> *Let's just praise the Lord, praise the Lord;*
> *Let's just lift our hands to heaven and praise the Lord.*
> *(Repeat, all the time lifting up your hands).*

340

Initially, Erin would simply watch this family praise. Eventually, she began raising her hands when we did. By fifteen months, as soon as the mealtime grace was finished, in anticipation of the praise song to follow she would raise her hands right on cue (sometimes reminding us to sing). Praising the Lord was being imprinted upon her heart even before she could grasp intellectually the real meaning of what was being sung. As we all joined hands, bowed our heads, and became quiet for prayer, she did the same. At seventeen months she was able to remind us to say the blessing by reaching for my hand on one side and her mother's hand on the other side. She knows we are supposed to do something special before we eat. Babies can sense praise to God long before they really understand it.

3. *Read to your child about God.* Two-year-olds (and even younger children) have a fascination for books. A Bible picture book and a loving parent's arm are a winning combination for holding his attention. Two-year-olds are able to understand the simple Bible picture books about Jesus. By reading to your child and showing him pictures about the life of Jesus, you are teaching him a vital message. He learns: "A Man in my picture book does all kinds of nice things, and my mommy and daddy talk about this same Man all the time. He must be a special Person." If you can convey to your two-year-old that one message, that Jesus is a special Person, you have done most of your job for laying the foundation for his deeper understanding of Christ and God in subsequent stages. In Deuteronomy 6:6 God said, "These words which I command you today shall be in your heart."

Discipline Undesirable Behavior

You should now know how to encourage desirable behavior in your young child as the basis for effective discipline. This should be your primary focus and consume the majority of your energy in disciplining your child. However, as Proverbs 22:15 says, "Foolishness is bound up in the heart of a child." Your child will get off the track at some time. There is in every child this bent toward disobedience and undesirable behavior. You don't have to teach them to disobey. To this reality God added, "But the rod of correction will drive it far from him." In this mandate, God has told parents very simply but very clearly, "Parents, take charge of your child; pick him up and get him back on the track; no matter what it takes to do the job, do it." (Pease see Chapter 16 pages 379–381 for further explanations of the "rod" verses.)

In discussing how to correct your young child's misbehavior, you need to understand an important point. Some children by their inherent nature have more foolishness than others. Some children take longer to get the point than others. There is an undesirable part of every child's temperament that God has allowed to be there from the moment of birth. We cannot reverse it. We can only modify it and channel it. Parents, do not look back and feel guilty and wonder where you have gone wrong. If you have been blessed with a high-need child who is endowed with a greater than average amount of foolishness, accept this and get on with realizing that your God-given role is to impart to your child above-average discipline.

Before discussing specific examples, there are general principles to consider in nearly all situations of correcting your child. The first principle is to recognize the vital ingredients of a strong foundation on which discipline by correction is based. A child must feel right within himself, and he must be secure in his trust and love relationship with his primary care-givers, usually his parents.

Based upon these fundamental feelings within the child, the second principle is that in every action toward disciplinary correction you want to convey two feelings to your child. (1) "I love you, my son or my daughter. You are very valuable to me and to God. You are a special person." (2) "Because I love you and because I am in charge, I will remain in charge until you are able to take full responsibility for your own actions."

The third principle is a simple concept of behavior modification, the principle of reinforcement. This means that behavior that is rewarded will continue and behavior that is not rewarded will not continue. Behavior that makes a child feel good will continue and behavior that makes a child feel bad will not.

The final principle in correcting your child is to pray and seek counsel if your disciplinary methods are not comfortable and are not working. If you base your disciplinary actions on the above considerations, you are not likely to go wrong.

There are several common undesirable behaviors in a two- to three-year-old.

1. *Whining.* Language is a newly found power for a young child, and it is only normal that he will use his God-given power to get what he wants. A young child quickly learns what kind of communication gets the quickest reaction from his parents. It is important that you are able to say no nicely—"I'm sorry I can't give you more." There is nothing to be gained by being rude in words or tone of voice or gesture. Not getting a cookie will cause him to feel angry—don't provoke him to more anger yourself. "Fathers, do not provoke your children to wrath" (Eph. 6:4). Take the example of the usual cookie jar struggle. Your two-year-old has already consumed his allotted number of cookies for the day. He has already been told, "No more." He decides to test the limits and ask for one more. His initial opener is

usually a feeble whining gesture toward the cookie jar. When your child opens his communication with a whine, it is usually a clue that he is uncertain of the response he is going to get. He really feels he is not going to get what he wants and probably shouldn't get what he wants. The whining child gets the anticipated negative response: request denied. Not willing to give up without a fight, his whining increases in loudness, hoping that you will give in to him just to get him off your back and out of your ears. At this point you may say: "Billy [address your child by name, because this raises his status as a person], Mommy knows that you want a cookie [you understand his position]. You have already had three cookies today, and I'm sorry, but I am not going to give you any more [he has been treated fairly, at least according to your rules, or for the older child, according to a mutually agreed-upon allotment]. My ears will not listen to whining [or God did not make Mommy's ears to listen to whining; the undesirable behavior is not rewarded]. Now come over and talk nicely to Mommy and help me slice these apples, and we can have some together after suppertime [desirable behavior is acknowledged and rewarded and delayed gratification is encouraged]."

If the whining is mild, not too irritating, and diminishing in degree, you simply may ignore this undesirable behavior since you said your ears do not listen to it anyway and the fire seems to be dying out (undesirable behavior unrewarded will stop). However, suppose Billy continues his increasingly irritating whining. Sit down next to him, put your hand lovingly on his shoulder, look him squarely in the eyes, and say, "I'm sorry, Billy, that I can't give you any more cookies. Now I'm going to set the timer for one minute. When the buzzer goes off, I expect you to start talking nicely with Mommy. Then we will have some fun. And if you do not, you will go to your room." You have conveyed expected behavior, given him a little time and space to sort it out, and conveyed the consequences of continued undesirable behavior which he is free to choose or not to choose. If at this point Billy stops whining, it is very important to follow through with the reward for desirable behavior and sit down and have some fun with him. He learns that it is more desirable to work with the family government than to overthrow it. Your sitting with him may be just what he needed.

Suppose the buzzer goes off, and Billy is still whining. More than the cookie is on the line in this illustration: your child's feelings are out of control and your authority is on the line. If you give in to your child simply to get him off your back or take the path of least resistance, you are out of God's will as a parent. You are also perpetuating this undesirable behavior and generally weakening your future stand when confrontations of higher priority than the cookie are at stake.

343

By three years of age your child should be able to comprehend most of a meaningful dialogue: "Billy, God gave you a beautiful voice that Mommy likes to hear. He doesn't want you to whine, and I don't want you to whine. Let's both kneel down and ask God to help you talk nicely to Mommy and not whine. Come, let's do this together." You turn a potentially negative disciplinary situation into a positive one. You have made your point and cleared the air of ill feelings. You also have gone one step further; you have conveyed to your child that there exists a support Person whom you value and whom you want him to value and that prayer is a valuable resource in times of need.

2. *Temper tantrums.* Two basic inner feelings in your child prompt most temper tantrums. First, a two-year-old has an intense desire to perform and act, but often the desire is greater than the capability. Facing this reality may lead to intense frustration that is released in a healthy, outward tantrum. This kind of tantrum needs loving support, gentleness, and understanding; guide the child toward successfully achieving the activity or channel her direction into a more easily achievable activity suited to her personality and achievement level.

The second cause of temper tantrums is hearing no just when the two-year-old's newly found power and desire for "bigness" propel her toward a certain act. Accepting an outside force contrary to her strong will is a difficult conflict she cannot handle without a fight. She wants to be big, but her world tells her and shows her how small she is. She is upset, but she does not have the ability to handle conflicting emotions with reason, so she copes with her inner emotions by a display of outward emotions, which are termed a *tantrum*. Think of your child's tantrums in terms of her newly forming sense of self and inner control becoming unglued. She needs someone to keep her from falling apart.

The most frightening temper tantrums are breath-holding spells. During the rage of a tantrum a child may hold her breath, turn blue, become limp, and may even faint. Breath-holding spells resemble convulsions; they cause the tantrum to become even more alarming to the already worried parents. Fortunately, most children who hold their breath resume normal breathing just as they are on the brink of passing out. Even those children who faint momentarily quickly resume normal breathing before harming themselves. These episodes usually stop when the child is old enough to express his anger verbally.

Temper tantrums can be exhausting and frightening experiences for both child and parent. Discipline mild tantrums just as you would discipline whining. In the

344

more severe temper tantrums the child is out of control, and he is confused about how to regain control, even if he wants to.

How are temper tantrums handled?   First, realize that you can't handle them; you only support your child when he has them. Temper tantrums reflect your child's emotions which *he* has to handle. Excessive interference deprives the child of the mechanism of releasing his inner tensions, but too little support leaves him to cope all by himself without the strength to do so effectively. What is the issue causing the temper tantrum? If he has chosen an impossible task and it becomes apparent he is not going to achieve it but won't give up, simply be on standby. Temper tantrums bring out the best in intuitive mothering. Keep your arms extended and your attitude accepting. Often a few soothing words or a little help ("I'll untie the knot and you put on your shoe") will put him on the road to recovery.

If the issue at stake is a power struggle of wills (for example, she wants a toy that she should not have), then the temper tantrum should be approached with the usual firm and loving double whammy of effective discipline: "I love you, my child, and I am in charge here." Sometimes, a strong-willed child will lose complete control of himself during a tantrum. When her behavior reaches this stage, simply hold her very firmly but lovingly and explain: "You are angry and you have lost control [you understand her position]. I am holding you tightly because I love you, I want to help you, and you will be all right [I'm in charge here]." You may discover that after a minute of struggling to free herself, a rigid child melts into your arms as if thanking you for rescuing her. My wife Martha ended one of our little daughter's tantrums on a spiritual note with, "Now let's pray together."

Temper tantrums in public places are embarrassing, and it is often difficult to consider your child's feelings first. *What will people think of me as a mother?* is likely to be your first thought. In this situation, if it becomes uncomfortable for both of you, remove your child to another room where he can have his tantrum in private. If the tantrum is based upon an inner frustration, then open arms and an accepting attitude will help defuse the child's explosive behavior. If the issue is one of defiance, again your authority is at stake, and all the levels of discipline mentioned in the example of whining should be carried out. Sometimes a child who is crying uncontrollably can't stop when you ask him to. He may or may not want to stop, but he literally cannot get hold of himself. If he wants to stop, an offer to pray with him for help from God is all that is needed for both of you. An in-arms prayer time is extremely comforting.

Sometimes tantrums can be so exhausting to parents that giving into the child seems easier because he probably stops his disruptive behavior immediately. However, keep in mind the principle that undesirable behavior, if rewarded, will persist. In addition to weakening your authority, rewarding temper tantrums will plant the seed in the child that aggressive and violent behavior will get him what he wants.

Tantrums often occur when parents impose unrealistic expectations on a child. Expecting a curious toddler to be a model of obedience in a toy store where he is surrounded by a smorgasbord of tempting delights may be asking too much. Children who are overly tired or hungry are especially prone to mood changes and temper tantrums, which may explain why many temper tantrums occur in the late morning or late afternoon when children are most tired and most hungry. Appropriately timed naps and the practice of nibbling (see Chap. 11 for tips for nibbling) may lessen the tendency for these tantrums.

Some tantrums occur when the child, during a high-need period, senses that her parents are not tuned in to her. She resorts to a tantrum in order to break through to them.

Most temper tantrums do not have lasting effects on the child. Fortunately, toddlers have a magnificent resilience for recovering from temper tantrums. They usually do not sulk for long periods of time, and a properly supported tantrum usually wears off quickly (but may leave parents worn out). Parents, take heart. The child's stage of temper tantrums seldom lasts long, and it is self-limiting for several reasons: his physical abilities eventually catch up with his desire for accomplishment; he does not like his inner feelings during a tantrum; and as soon as he develops enough language to express his emotions in words, his tantrum-like actions will mellow.

3. *Aggressive behavior against other children* (biting, hitting, scratching, pushing). There are as many theories about biting as there are teeth. Biting begins between the ages of eighteen months and two and a half years in a preverbal child and lessens when the child can communicate his feelings effectively with his tongue instead of his teeth. Because a toddler's mouth and hands are his first tools of communication, biting and hitting are to him forms of communication that are not intrinsically bad. The young child soon learns what is socially acceptable behavior by the response he gets from his victim or a nearby adult. If Isaac Newton had been a psychologist rather than a physicist, perhaps he would have worded his first law of child behavior: "For every undesirable action there is an equal and opposite reaction." The more quickly a young child can learn that undesirable be-

havior yields an undesirable response, the more quickly he will stop this behavior.

To stop a child's biting and hitting, consider these points. Determine the circumstances conducive to your child's biting, usually several children in a small space with a few toys. If your child shows aggressive activity with large groups in small spaces, your first disciplinary action is to design his environment and attempt to avoid circumstances that entice him to bite. In disciplining the biter, as with any undesirable behavior, consider first the feeling and the cause behind the action, rather than the action itself. Disciplining the biter is good training for you to think first why he is doing something rather than what he is doing. If considering the feelings within your child is your first step from which to proceed toward further disciplinary action, it is likely that your entire method of discipline will be more successful. Success is determined if the action stops and the child gains a learning experience.

Beware of falling into the trap of negatively reinforcing the biter. Biting attracts attention very quickly. If the child wants to be the instant center of attention, biting is sure to bring everybody running and set him apart as a special person. In some instances biting fulfills the craving in some children for attention, which reinforces their undesirable behavior. I feel that these attention-getting behaviors occur in a small percentage of biters and in these cases the "ignore it" advice may be applicable.

In general, however, do not ignore undesirable behavior in which one child harms another. Biting is not only hard on the tender little arms of unsuspecting victims, but it is also hard on parents. The parent of the biter is both disturbed and embarrassed, and the parent of the bitee is naturally upset that her child has been hurt. Negative feelings between parents may result. You can ease a potentially tense situation by discussing beforehand with the other parent that your child is a biter and that you are aware of his need for supervision. Biters always should be carefully supervised in groups. When a child bites, immediately remove him from the play group with appropriate admonitions such as, "Biting hurts, it is wrong, and you will sit in the corner or stay in this room until . . ." This isolation will teach the biter a valuable social lesson.

"Should I bite him back?" is certainly a valid question that a parent of a persistent biter may ask. No! Don't bite him back. Biting is an immature act, and you are a mature person. Therefore I am uncomfortable with the role modeling of a parent's biting a child. The biter already knows biting hurts by the reaction of the child who was bitten. If he really seems to not understand, or he is a younger "biter," you can encourage him to feel the effects of his own sharp teeth on his fleshy forearm. When your child's verbal skills improve and his emotions can be expressed better by language, his biting should subside (by three years of age). Biting in the child more than three years old who has good verbal skills is certainly of greater concern. In such cases professional guidance should be obtained.

The persistent aggressive behavior of an older sibling toward a young child must be stopped at all costs because of the principle of role modeling. Just as children look up to parents for affirmation of what is acceptable behavior, younger children look up to older children as their models. You don't want your one-year-old to learn that hitting and biting are behaviors to be modeled.

CHAPTER 15

DISCIPLINING THE CHILD THREE TO SIX YEARS OLD

By three years of age the child becomes aware of his total self—what he feels, what he is comfortable doing, and what he cannot yet do. He has mastered the art of using his parents as support resources and has defined his place in the family structure. By age three, the child has acquired language, motor, adaptive, and social skills. The combinations of these skills, his own basic temperament and intelligence potential, and parental guidance all come together at this stage to make up a definite person. The child who has learned these skills to his fullest potential during his first three years enters the three- to six-year-old stage ready to refine these skills. The child who has not achieved her potential in these skills during her first three years must continue to expend energy learning them; she is always trying to catch up. I do not believe that a child's basic personality (the sum total of her skills and feelings reflected in her behavior) is completely determined by this age, but it is certainly well on its way. The ability to change a behavior trait becomes increasingly difficult with advancing age.

The ages of three to six are generally smoother for both parents and child because the refinement of acquired skills usually produces less anxiety than the struggles to acquire these skills during the first three years. When you get your act together, you feel good about yourself, and I think this is true for three-year-olds too. The tantrums and other behavioral anxieties of the two-year-old were simply a manifestation of his struggle to get himself together.

By three years of age a child normally has developed enough language to communicate his desires and feelings effectively. He understands you and feels that you understand him. Since he is able to express his negative feelings with words rather than actions, his behavior generally becomes less impulsive and more directed. His abilities have finally caught up with his desires. Most three-year-olds have learned the important lesson of cause-and-effect relationships (child touches hot stove, child gets burned). This important milestone makes his exploring behavior less impulsive and more calculated and reasoning. Mastering language adds the finishing touch.

The attachment feeling that your child has for you enters a beautiful stage of social rapport. Your child is simply fun to talk with, to take walks with, and to play word games with. At this stage, your child may regard you as a close friend, a pal who is fun to be around. This relationship is normal and healthy as long as your roles of authority figure and spiritual trainer prevail. It is much easier to get the concept of discipline across to your child if he or she enjoys being with you.

Your child becomes aware of how much physical abuse his developing muscles and bones can handle comfortably. As he learns to protect himself from injury, the incessant no-nos of the previous stage gradually lessen. He may retain his desire for a pleasant bedtime ritual but will probably begin to treat you to an uninterrupted night's sleep; he also has better bladder control.

SPIRITUAL TRAINING OF THE THREE TO SIX YEAR OLD

The ages of three to six are critical for the spiritual training of your child because this is when he or she is most receptive to learning about God. In normal childhood development most children go through several stages of learning moral values. From three to six years of age, a child accepts the values of his primary role models, his parents. Your values are his values. At no other time in a child's life will his mind be so unquestionably receptive to your values. He is still operating on the simple principle that what is important to you is important to him. Sometime after six years of age, the child matures from being completely receptive to being selective of his parents' values.

This is a normal process of spiritual maturity in which your child inwardly transfers your values to his values. (This value-transfer concept will be discussed in more detail in the section on adolescence.) For this reason, this age is a prime time for spiritual training. The more values he accepts from his primary spiritual models during this stage, the greater the level of spiritual values will be from which he can select at a subsequent stage.

Parents, dwell upon this concept for a few moments. Appreciate the high level of responsibility you have at this stage to train up your child in the way he or she should go. Perhaps at no other stage of a child's development is the investment/return ratio so high.

A popular alternative to this viewpoint is that parents should remain spiritually neutral early in a child's development so that the child's mind remains open to decide for himself. Not only is this rather simplistic viewpoint contrary to Scripture (Deut. 6:6–8; Prov. 22:6), but experience has shown that it simply doesn't work. A child who is a product of spiritually neutral parents will most often, at best, turn out spiritually neutral himself. If you wait until your child is older to teach him about God, you are missing a period in his life when the ground is most fertile to sprout seeds. When he is older, you are planting the seed among thorns, and what little plants do happen to spring up may be choked out by the competition. The best time to get "in business" is at a period in your child's life when the competition is at the least.

Attachment parenting pays off.   The importance of laying the foundation for spiritual training during the first three years was affirmed by a mother who had a very high-need child. She persevered through all the steps of attachment parenting previously discussed in Chapter 8. One day we were having one of those "it is worth it" discussions, when she said, "I feel I am just beginning to cash in." This mother meant that the attachment style of parenting in those early formative years had built up a trust relationship between parent and child and the initial two goals of early parenting had been fulfilled: (1) knowing your child, and (2) making your child feel right.

The early investment of attachment parenting creates an attitude of giving within the parent and an attitude of receiving within the child. These attitudes form the foundation of the trust-and-authority relationship that makes your child more receptive to all forms of training, and thus, the third goal of parenting is reached: (3) leading your child to Christ.

Be spiritual models for your child.   I like to think of spiritual training as *spiritual giving*. Spiritual giving implies that leading your child to Christ flows naturally from your own walking with Christ rather than from someone else's list of how-to's. Just as the first goals of discipline will flow naturally from attachment parenting, your spiritual discipline of your child will flow naturally from your attachment with God.

This principle of spiritual modeling is beautifully illustrated in John 15:1–2, 4.

I am the true vine, and My Father is the vinedresser. Every branch in Me that does not bear fruit He takes away; and every branch that bears fruit He prunes, that it may bear more fruit. . . . Abide in Me, and I in you. As the branch cannot bear fruit of itself, unless it abides in the vine, neither can you, unless you abide in Me.

As spiritual leader of our family, I have adopted this passage as God's clear mandate for the relationship between us and our Father. We can extend this passage to signify the relationship between the spiritual leader of the family (usually, but not always, the father) and the children. If the parents remain in Christ and Christ remains in the parents, the parents become an extension of Christ to their children. When the children are older spiritually, they can develop direct relationships with Christ and abide in Him.

When your children accept the message of John 15:1–4 and accept Christ into their lives, you have achieved the goal of spiritual training. A child's accepting Christ directly as he gets older is much easier if he has first accepted Christ indirectly through his parents at an earlier age. Just as a mother who is one with her child is naturally giving her child her own milk, parents who are truly at one with Christ will naturally give spiritual milk to their children (see Heb. 5:12-13).

What about newborn Christians who have not laid this spiritual foundation during their first two years of parenthood? Is it too late? No! Just as early bonding with a newborn gives you a head start in parenting, an early spiritual foundation gives you a head start in spiritual training. The later you begin, the greater your commitment must be in order to catch up. As you are catching up in your spiritual growth, you probably will have to go through a long how-to stage before your spiritual training naturally flows from you into your child.

TEACHING YOUR CHILD ABOUT GOD

Your child's first three years of spiritual training basically teach him that God is an important Person. In the three- to six-year-old stage, this concept is carried one step further: God is an important Person because . . . At this point many Christian parents need help: What do I teach my child about God? How do I teach him? How much can my child understand about God at this stage?

Most of your teaching at this stage (and at every other stage) is in your example for your child. Remember, the three- to six-year-old is still operating from the basis that what is important to you is important to him. You can tell him a thousand times how important the Bible is, but if he seldom sees you reading and praying from your Bible, very little of your teaching actually will sink in.

Next, use one of the most powerful principles of learning: repetition. God used this principle in Deuteronomy 6 when He told people to saturate their child's environment with His Word. Not just a five-minute bedtime prayer or a one-hour Sunday school lesson. By example and repetition begin to teach your young child about God.

Very early in your child's spiritual training, set some goals. What do you want your child to learn about God especially at the three- to six-year-old stage? To answer this question, let's consult the Manufacturer's Handbook. God told us how and what to teach our children. The following Scriptures offer some basics to teach your child at this stage.

1. *"Love the LORD your God with all your heart, with all your soul, and with all your might"* (Deut. 6:5). In the New Testament Jesus reinforced the importance of this verse by repeating this concept. I emphasize this verse because Jesus emphasized it. When the teachers of the Law asked Jesus which is the most important commandment, He stated, "Love the LORD" (Mark 12:30). So, the first concept to teach your child is to love the Lord.

But how do you teach love to your child? To answer this question, open the Book again to Deuteronomy where God said that the next step is to make this love of God part of yourself: "And these words [to love the Lord] which I command you today shall be in your heart" (6:6). The next step is to "teach them [to love the Lord] to your children" (11:19). Get the concept of loving God into your child by any means. The more your child knows about Him, the more he will learn to love Him.

Our four-year-old Hayden told me she loves me more than she loves God because she knows me more than she knows God. It is certainly easier for a child to love his parents more than God because he can see and feel and hear his parents. But God is still an abstraction to a young child. Love related to how a child feels about his parents is usually a simple feeling such as, "I want to be near that person who does good things for me, who takes care of me, who makes me feel good, who is so big and strong and powerful that he can chop down trees and fix bicycles. I miss him when I am not near him." It is vitally important that a child love his parents whom he can see so that he can learn to love his God whom he can't see. A child's parents can help him know and love God by pointing out that God made everything and everyone because He loves us.

By using a picture Bible, a three- to six-year-old child can learn about Jesus more easily than he can learn about God. These two can gradually become one as your child matures. A young child can learn that Jesus loves little children (the song "Jesus Loves the Little Children" is a favorite at this age), that He protects little children, and that He is kind and gentle. Jesus is God's Son which makes him God too. Young children picture God as Michelangelo did—an all-powerful grandfather who made "Mommy and Daddy and me."

2. *Fear the Lord and walk in His ways.* In Deuteronomy 10:12 God said, "What does the LORD your God require of you, but to fear the LORD your God, to walk in all His ways." Your first goal as Christian parents is to teach your young children the concept of fearing God. Several times in Scripture the concepts of love and fear coexist. Usually by four years of age a child can understand that God is a powerful Person who makes rules (just as his or her parents make rules). The biblical term *fear* really refers to an awed respect for the power and wisdom of God. This concept of fear rounds out the concept of love. In reality how a child learns about God is paralleled with how he learns about his parents—to love and fear his parents (to have a healthy respect for his parents). Again, through the use of a picture Bible, the child less than six years can learn respect for the power of God as she grasps the biblical concept of sin. At this age the child can learn that the Person who loves also disciplines. If presented properly to a young child, the story of Adam and Eve, or of Moses and the Red Sea, and the New Testament miracles can convey to him the power of God—power to love, to heal, and to discipline.

Learning the concept of sin is a major turning point in the young child's discipline. The child less than six years old can grasp this simple notion of sin: "This big Person whom Mom and Dad call 'God' makes rules. I can't see Him, but He sees me. He knows when I do bad things even if Mom and Dad don't, but He still loves me anyway just like Mom and Dad do." You may introduce the teachings of the Ten Commandments to the child between four and six years old but keep them in simple, everyday terms: worship God in a special way on Sunday, obey your parents, be kind to your friends and don't hurt them, tell the truth, don't take other children's toys. By introducing to your child the concepts of fear, sin, and God's rules, you are laying the foundation of conscience building that matures in the next stage of development when he or she is between six and twelve years of age. The child less than six should be able to feel the beginning of a conscience, "I feel good when I do the right thing; I don't feel good when I do the wrong thing." Both your laws and God's laws should be consistently repeated and presented to the young child when he is most receptive to the concepts of right and wrong.

3. *"Love your neighbor as yourself"* (Mark 12:31). Jesus said this is the second greatest commandment after loving the Lord. One of the major milestones a three- to six-year-old has is the development of peer relationships. Three-year-olds show a desire to refine their social attitudes and show varying degrees of social readiness. The three-year-old evolves from parallel play patterns to a more cooperative play pattern of sharing other children's toys. The three-year-old becomes more comfortable in peer play groups of varying sizes, and it is in these play groups that some young children show behaviors of pushing and shoving until they have established themselves in the pecking order and learned what is socially acceptable behavior within the peer group. Demanding, possessive, assertive, and withdrawn behaviors are all realistic expectations at this age. The "law of the jungle" or "may the most assertive child win" is usually the most typical behavior needing modification in these peer groups.

Squabbles over toys are to be expected at this age because possession means ownership to a young child. If sharing is a major play problem for your child, ask children to bring a few toys of their own when they come to visit. Capitalize on your child's natural desire to play with another child's toys. As she grabs someone else's toy, another child will grab her toy. Have a rule that even though it is "her" toy when she is alone, in a play group, if a toy is put down, another child is allowed to pick it up and play with it. She will learn to give a toy to get a toy, and eventually, sharing can be the law of the jungle.

How much more meaningful it is to a child if the "love your neighbor" rule is introduced instead of the "may the most assertive child win" rule. At this stage, again with the use of picture books, show a child a picture of Jesus, saying he should love and be kind to the children he plays with. In the middle of toy squabbles it often helps to take a few minutes out and encourage children to put their arms around each other, saying, "Love each other. Jesus wants us to love each other." Young children need to learn that this is not a give-me-give-me world but that sharing and giving are the Christian way.

A common discipline problem facing you at this stage occurs when your child is acted upon aggressively and wronged. Should she be encouraged to fight back? In my opinion, it is healthy to teach children to be assertive but not aggressive. A child is assertive when he protects his own territory; a child is aggressive when she infringes upon others' territory. A parent often states, "I don't want him to grow up to be a pansy." Being assertive does seem to be within the realm of Christian discipline, and perhaps assertiveness toward the aggressor by the child who is transgressed upon is a valuable social lesson. Since Christ did stress meekness and the attitude of turning the other cheek, parents should teach their children that physical assertiveness should be followed by an act of love. In Galatians 5:14–15 Paul gave some guidance about handling aggressive behavior and squabbles: " 'You shall love your neighbor as yourself.' But if you bite and devour one another, beware lest you be consumed by one another!"

4. *Pray that the Holy Spirit will fill your child* (Gal. 5:22–25). The desired result in Christian discipline is to impress God's Word upon your child to such a degree that his or her entire behavior is directed by the inner power God has promised—the Holy Spirit. What a magnificent level of behavior on which to be! In Galatians 5:17–18 Paul reminded people of the bent toward evil that is present to varying degrees in everyone: "For the flesh lusts against the Spirit, and the Spirit against the flesh; and these are contrary to one another, so that you do not do the things that you wish. But if you are led by the Spirit, you are not under the law." After mentioning many common human sins, Paul went on to warn, "Those who practice such things will not inherit the kingdom of God" (v. 21). The ultimate goal of Christian discipline is for your child to inherit the kingdom of God, and a Spirit-filled Christian life is the best path to this kingdom.

Parents, pray daily for the Spirit to come into your child. It is humbling for Christian parents to realize that the fruit of the Holy Spirit mentioned in Galatians 5:22–23—love, joy, peace, longsuffering, kindness, goodness, faithfulness, gentleness, and self-control—will not develop in their children by their efforts alone. The earlier in a child's life you can pray these qualities into your child, the more effective your child's Christian discipline will be.

Teach your child to pray and to praise. Between three and six years of age a child learns to talk with God. This is the stage at which a child should know how to pray and why to pray. A child's attitude toward prayer at this stage can determine the attitude about prayer parents are all hoping their children will have—the desire to pray. The following specific guidelines will help you teach your young child to pray.

1. *Use short, simple phrases* containing ideas and terms that you want your child

to pick up: "Father . . . I thank You . . . I love you . . . I'm sorry . . . be with me . . . I ask for . . . I praise You." Most prayers of young children contain "give mes," but that is the nature of young children and certainly God understands this tendency. However, parents should teach their children to add the concept of praise and love and thanksgiving to their prayers in addition to what they ask for.

2. *Teach your child to pray for others.*   This custom makes their prayers less selfish and sets the stage for Christian fellowship at an older age.

3. *Pray often.*   Before going to bed and after getting up in the morning are the two most important times to pray with your child. You want your child to begin each day with God and end each day with God; and in between times he or she should pray as often as the need or desire arises.

4. *Pray spontaneously.*   Be vigilant for "openers": a child is hurt during play, a tantrum is out of control, or a child's behavior has deteriorated. Take advantage of these spontaneous occurrences, and take a few minutes to follow up by saying, "Now let's pray about this," or "Let's talk with God about this." This spontaneous prayer teaches your child that at any time during day and night he can and should talk to his heavenly Father.

5. *Encourage Scripture memorization.*   Give your child short, one-sentence memory verses and include the Scripture reference: "God is love" (1 John 4:8). Young children love the challenge of a memory verse, and their young minds are receptive to this exercise. Discuss the meaning of these verses with your child, then encourage him to relate the meaning back to you. Memory without meaning has limited teaching value to a child.

6. *Acknowledge answered prayer.*   Be sure to follow up on answered prayer requests with your young child. He or she needs to learn prayer power at this age. The follow-up of apparently "unanswered" prayer is more important for the older child, who can be taught better to pray according to God's will.

7. *Let your child hear praises.*   It is important for you to model praise and prayer for your child. If he hears sincere "thank You, Lords" and "praise Gods," he gets the idea that you are constantly walking with God, and he will want to walk with Him, too.

8. *Model prayer and family devotions.*   Children learn to pray as they hear their parents pray. Prayer demonstrates to the young child a sense of the reality of God; prayer gives her a sense of security that she is talking to Someone very important who hears her. Parents often learn from their children's prayers about the

people and things that are most important to them. This is one way parents can learn about the special problems and needs their children have. Older children's prayer requests are particularly telling since older children are more private about their needs.

Children enjoy using memorized prayers since the rhythm of these prayers appeals to them. Use memorized prayers as little as possible, since this kind of prayer from adults tends to be rattled off without sincerity. Children are very quick to pick up the vibrations that you are insincere and not at ease with prayer. Although the young child should be encouraged to pray among family members, some children do not welcome being put on the spot for a prayer performance, especially among strangers. It is more important that a child learn to focus his attention on God during prayer than on the group in which he or she is praying.

9. *Teach Scripture.*   A primary goal in your teaching Scripture at this stage is for your child to achieve a positive attitude toward the Bible. This is more important than how many verses he memorizes or how many stories he learns. Again, role modeling is your most effective Bible teacher. As your child sees God the way you do, he also sees the Bible as you do: "That big Book must be very important. Mom and Dad are always reading from it, praying from it, and talking about it. That Book tells us about important people who say and do important things. I want to learn about those people too." More than at any other age the three- to six-year-old is observant of his or her parents' values.

In the beginning when you teach your young child about the Bible, wait for openers. If your child sees you reading the Bible often enough he will eventually, and of his own free will, climb up onto your lap and ask you to read to him, too. This is especially true if you are reading the Bible as a family; he doesn't want to be left out. Capitalize on the interest he has initiated by inviting him with a very childlike reception such as, "Daddy was reading a neat story. Would you like to hear it?" After you have told him the story (pick one that is at his level, such as the baby Jesus story), say, "Would you like your own book about Jesus?" There are many picture Bibles written for all levels of child development. You may find that much of your Scripture-reading time is spent reading to your child out of his picture Bible. This is not wasted Scripture time for you, since you may be surprised at how much more you may learn about the Bible by getting down to your child's level, seeing God through his eyes, and giving simple answers to his questions. Jesus said, "Unless you are converted and become as little children, you will by no means enter the kingdom of heaven" (Matt. 18:3).

Play-acting is also a good way to teach Scripture to children at this age; they can dress up like various Bible characters and put on a family skit. Christmas and Easter are particularly valuable times for play-acting from Scripture. Children can dress up and participate in the event of Christ's birth. And, of course, you have all the little props, such as a doll for baby Jesus, a little wagon or crib for a manger, and an assortment of household animals.

Prescheduled time and structure for teaching prayer and Scripture to a young child are not as effective as spontaneous prayer and Bible reading when the opportunity arises. Young children live from moment to moment, neither thinking about the past nor anticipating the future. Prayer and Scripture teaching are much more meaningful when they are based upon a sudden event that occurs while you are simply having fun together. For example, a walk through a garden or the woods with your child will open up a variety of opportunities to relate God to nature. You may see a beautiful sunset and stop and say, "Bobby, let's thank God for the pretty red sky." After you have prayed, your child is likely to ask a simple question, "Did God make the sun?" which allows you the opportunity to talk about God and creation. When your child gives you a simple opener, reply with a simple answer. Don't exhaust him with long and complicated answers because he is likely to tune out and become less motivated to get into that subject again.

When teaching your child a certain scriptural passage, identify the central point. A child cannot take in multiple important points all at once and is liable to become confused. Remember, creating a positive attitude toward Scripture is your prime motive at this age, not the content of information. By consistently hearing a second language in the home, a child naturally picks it up. With consistent Bible teaching and by talking about God the way God told us to do in Deuteronomy 6:7–9, the young child takes on God's language as his "second language."

Christian parents who are sincerely trying to teach their children about God often wonder how much is sinking in and to what level. More often than not, if the message is taught sincerely and lived in role modeling, more penetrates your child than you probably think. For example, I heard my four-year-old daughter say, "I have Jesus in my heart." I asked her what that meant, and she responded, "I love Him." I said, "Is Jesus really in your heart?" and she surprised me by the answer, "No, but His Spirit is." I felt comfortable that she had in her "heart" what ought to be there based on her own level of spiritual development and understanding.

Parents, beware of the "floater"—the child who floats through your biblical teaching pretending to understand everything but actually perceiving very little.

Children pick up vocabulary very easily. They learn to talk a good game. I've heard the story of preschool children who heard a sermon about inviting Jesus into their hearts; one child said, "I have Jesus in my heart," and the other child said, "I have Jesus in my tummy." Probably the child who thought Jesus was in his tummy really had more of a concept of Jesus' being *inside* of him than the other child did.

For this reason it will help you to have a checklist to see where your child is in his or her spiritual growth by the age of six. This checklist is measured in relation to where you want your child to be. Periodically check where your child is in relation to the following goals.

1. To love and fear God.
2. To love our neighbors as ourselves.
3. To obey God and our parents.
4. To practice self-control.

TEACHING YOUR CHILD ABOUT JESUS

A child less than six tends to confuse the terms *Jesus* and *God* and is just as likely to say "Jesus made me" as "God made me." If you show him a "picture" of Jesus, he is likely to answer that the person is Jesus. Since there are no actual pictures it is not known what Jesus looked like. But I see no problem with this. Our children have many picture books and Jesus looks a bit different in each one. Our children have never been confused by this or even have mentioned it. They can always pick out which one is Jesus because He is the One the child is drawn to from the story in the text. If a child sees a picture of a grandfatherly-looking figure he is likely to answer that the individual is God. When teaching your child about Jesus, you should emphasize His humanity because children can relate to this. By your reading stories about Jesus, the child can learn that Jesus is kind, patient, and gentle and that He especially loves little children. Young children are more likely to view God as a disciplinarian, a father-authority figure who passes judgment on them.

A child less than six can grasp the concept that Jesus is the Son of God. He understands the concept of a son and that Jesus was a man, but do not confuse him with the concept of the Trinity at this age. It is more important for the child to be comfortable first with the humanity of Christ. Introduce the concept of the deity of

Christ later. Basically you want the young child to be concerned with what Jesus teaches, what He does for us, and what He tells us to do. Then later on when the child matures, he can be more concerned with who Jesus is. A six-year-old can grasp the fact that if Jesus is the Son of God, He must be God, too.

By first teaching the humanity of Jesus, you are teaching your child as He taught His disciples. First they learned that He was a powerful and righteous man. Only later did they come to see Him as the Son of God. Christ seemed to realize the difficulty that even adults would have grasping His deity, since He stated that revelation from His Father was necessary to grasp this concept: "Blessed are you, Simon Bar-Jonah, for flesh and blood has not revealed this to you, but My Father who is in heaven" (Matt. 16:17). At this point in the spiritual training of your child, pray that God will reveal directly to your child's receptive mind a clear understanding of what He wants your child to understand at this age.

When teaching your child about Jesus, relate His life to the real life of the child: Jesus was born as a baby. He grew up in a house, and He helped His earthly father work as a carpenter. When Jesus was older, a teenager (relate this age to a teenager your child knows, an older sibling or family friend), He taught people about His Father, God in heaven. When Jesus was a grown man, He told us the right things to do and the wrong things to do. Here mention the commandments in simple terms that the child can understand and emphasize the two great commandments of the New Testament: love God and love your neighbor. Teach your child that many people accepted what Jesus taught, followed Him, obeyed His commandments, and loved Him. Those people were called "Christians" because they were like Christ. Teach that Mommy and Daddy are Christians, and as he gets to know Jesus better and accept Him into his life, he will be a Christian too. At that point you may be fortunate to get a response of, "I want to be Christian too." This beautiful opener gives you the opportunity to tell your child what it means to be a Christian after he has given his life to Jesus and invitedHim into his heart. Tell him it means he (1) loves God; (2) learns about God by reading His Book; (3) loves his neighbor as himself (explain in child's terms); and (4) obeys God and his parents.

Once the child has reached this level of reasoning, he is ready to understand that being a Christian has both responsibilities and rewards. Jesus promised us that He would take us to heaven when we accept Him as our Savior. Read together John 3:16; 14:1–6; and 1 John 5:11–12. A young child is reward oriented: "I go to heaven because this is what Jesus promises, and He always tells the truth." His concept of heaven is most likely to be materialistic, simply because it is a place where everything is free and everyone feels good all the time. Come to think about it, some adult concepts of heaven are not much more mature than a child's.

The concept of salvation can be taught to a child sometime around the age of five or six. At this stage a child is going to wonder why Jesus was born and why He came here. This is the time to teach your child about the concept of sin. Explain to him (with the help of a picture Bible) that Adam and Eve sinned by disobeying God. At this point you are driving home the concept of disobedience. Adam and Eve, God's first children, did something wrong (they sinned), and as a result they suffered by losing the good things God had given them. Next you can introduce the concept that Jesus died on the cross to ask His Father to forgive us for all the sins we have ever done and will ever do.

The young child will have a limited understanding of repentance, but he does know that once he has "repented" (gone to his room for a while after doing something wrong), Mommy totally wipes the slate clean. This simple thought prepares the way for introducing the concept of how Jesus wiped the slate clean for everyone.

Remember that your child is "now" oriented. Teach mostly for the present, what Jesus means to him now and what he needs now at his stage of development. The best way to prepare a child for the future concepts of God is to meet his needs now.

The old axiom, "You learn by teaching," is especially true when you teach your children about God. A fringe benefit of teaching them is that your own beliefs are tested and your faith is strengthened. As you teach little children, you begin to see God through their eyes, just as they see God through your eyes. Perhaps in commanding you to teach your children, God also speaks to you through them.

This concept, that parents learn as they teach their children, is especially true for the parent who is a new Christian or who is sincerely trying to strengthen a weakened faith. The ideal is for parents to be rooted firmly in their Christian faith in order to impress Christian teachings upon their children. However, it is unwise to think, *I'll wait until I become the perfect Christian parent model, and then I'll teach my child about Christ.* For many Christian parents, spiritual growth is a slow and steady maturing process. A child cannot afford to wait for his parents to get their act together. The principle of Christian childhood education is very similar to the principle of childhood education in general as described by Dr. Maria Montessori. Dr. Montessori said that preschool children have what she called "sensitive periods" in which their little minds are most receptive to various types of learning. In my opinion, ages three to six are the years in which a child is most sensitive and receptive to Christian teaching. Parents, please don't miss this chance.

Some parents may sincerely feel that they are lukewarm Christians as adults because they had no in-depth Christian teaching during their own sensitive periods as children. Therefore, they are determined not to make this mistake with their own children.

Even though you are struggling to strengthen your Christianity with prayer and consultation, give your child your very best. As long as you are sincerely trying and praying for God's help, you will succeed. Be sincere. Avoid portraying Jesus as a mythical figure who will help keep your child on the straight and narrow path. Children outwardly seem to accept Santa Claus but inwardly and intuitively feel he is not real. If God is presented insincerely, He is likely to fade into obscurity just like Santa Claus and the Easter bunny. Give your child as much of the "real thing" as you can.

ESTABLISHING AND IMPROVING FAMILY DEVOTIONS

Through your modeling, your child will perceive that the Christian way of life is so attractive and feels so right that he or she cannot help realizing it is the right way to go. Family devotions are an important part of the spiritual training and devotional life of your child. However, for most families it is difficult to set aside an exclusive time of the day for the Lord. There is stiff competition for your time and also for the minds of your children. Family life is usually a series of "I gotta gos" or what Dr. James Dobson calls "routine panic." In our own busy home, we struggle with the concept of daily family devotions. This section will give you some practical suggestions on how to improve your family devotions.

The Lord must have priority in spite of all the protests: "But, Dad, the game is about to start on TV . . ."; "I'm late for . . ."; "Do we have to?" The first concept you need to convey to your family is the importance of family devotions. It's important to set aside some time each day for family worship. Throughout a child's life, he will be called upon to set priorities and to follow his conscience and God's commandments rather than his own impulses. The younger the child is, the better it is for him to learn that time with God has priority over any earthly commitment or desire. If you have introduced your child to family devotions and spent time in prayer and Scripture early on in childhood, these devotions will be received better when your child is older.

If you are just starting family devotions, the father must assume the role of spiritual leader and stress the importance of family devotions to his children: "God has blessed our family, and we must come together to thank Him; according to Matthew 18:20, God is with us whenever two or more are gathered in His name. We are going to take ten minutes after the evening meal each night to pray together as a family." With such an introduction you have told your children why family devotions are important, and you have modeled the concept that family devotions are important to you. Then you must rely on the Holy Spirit to make this time come alive. Spirit-filled prayer can be irresistible, so learn how to let the Spirit lead these devotions through you.

We have found that the best time for our family devotions is after the evening meal. Everyone is already gathered at the table, thus reducing the start-up time. A

364

pleasant evening meal should set the stage and attitude for the devotions to follow. This meal is often the only time in the day when all family members are together. It should be a happy time; a time when all family members are in tune with one another's happenings of the day. Mealtimes are for communication, not for correction.

On weekends and holidays consider having family devotions after breakfast. Starting the day with God sets the tone for the entire day. If interest in family devotions seems to wane, occasionally hold your family devotions as a part of a special outing such as to a local park. On family trips, devotions can be held during the car ride. The important thing is that your family does pray together, not where you pray together.

Parents, do not feel you have to convince your children that devotions are "fun." Children are already preoccupied with the idea that everything has to be fun. Devotions are sacred; early in their lives children should learn to delay their need for instant gratification. Family devotions are not in the same category as a family TV program.

Keep your devotions brief, approximately ten minutes to begin with, and increase their length according to the attention span and interest level of your children. As your devotions become more meaningful to your children, or in a time of particularly high need and when they are more attentive, the length of the family devotions can be increased. Consistency is more important than duration. It is more important to have them every night than to wait until there is enough time to have a "long" devotion. Avoid "squeeze" devotions. This special time with God should not be made to fit in between other commitments; other commitments should be made to fit around your family devotions. This level of priority is an important concept for your children to perceive.

How can you hold your child's interest? Many children, especially those younger than five years old, have short attention spans and like to fidget. To minimize this, insist on removing all toys and distractions from the devotion table. Giving everyone a "part" will hold the attention span of children. Even if your child who is younger than four years old appears to get nothing out of the devotions, persevere. If your child gets only one message—that family devotions are important because God is important to your family—then your efforts are worthwhile. Even if a young child does not actually understand all the words, he will perceive the attitudes of the prayers and phrases. Try to put the children's part early in the family devotions, which gets them involved right away. Ask your children to contribute suggestions on how to run the family devotions, and you may be amazed at what they come up with. Our seven-year-old Peter suggested that we take the phone off the hook during our devotional time, and we all concurred that it was a terrific idea.

Every family member could have a Bible, a notepad, and a pencil. The Living Bible, a children's edition, or a picture Bible is good for young children. You could maintain a prayer calendar to write down specific prayer requests, and later on, write down when and how they were answered—praise God for answered prayers. Family devotions could contain the following elements.

1. *Opening prayer.* The father, as the spiritual leader of the home, should open the devotions with a prayer. This prayer should remind the family of Jesus' promise, "Where two or three are gathered together in My name, I am there in the midst of them" (Matt. 18:20). An opening prayer could be, "Father, thank You that You are with our family during this special time. We thank You that You hear our prayers; open our hearts to Your message." Children often listen to cue words during prayer. This simple prayer conveys to them the presence of Christ within the prayer group, and it also conveys to your children the attitude of peace and tranquility they need in order to listen to the Lord.

2. *Scripture lesson.* Scripture can be incorporated into family worship in many ways. One way is to cover certain books of the Bible by reading sequential passages each night. However, we have found that the specific-topics approach works best for our family because it relates scriptural lessons to specific family needs. Specific topics tend to hold the interest of children better than sequential scriptural passages. If you choose this topical approach, you can list scriptural lessons that relate to the general needs as well as the specific needs of your family. Examples of these are love, patience, kindness, faith, prayer, obedience, charity, and sin. The family member who is assigned the Scripture reading for that devotion is given the Bible concordance and asked to choose several verses on the specific topic. The topic of love, for example, would give you enough scriptural passages for several weeks of devotions. Children seven or eight years of age or older can usually be given these verses to read to the family. Young children less than eight years of age may be given memory verses, since young children usually can memorize much better than they can read. Follow the Scripture reading or memory recital with a discussion of the meaning of the verse and its relevance to your family. The Bible is not only to be read and memorized: it is also to be understood and followed (2 Tim. 3:16–17).

3. *Sharing of needs and prayer requests.*   The father can ask if there are any prayer requests, and each family member can share his or her request with the group. Prayer requests serve many purposes. They convey to children that prayer is important. Christians should bring their requests and needs before other Christians, especially their own families. The ability to share a need sets the stage for a beautiful Christian family attitude. Sharing leads to caring, and caring leads to more *agape* love and more *phileo* love (as was described in Chapter 1) among family members. Learning to pray for others begins this way.

Prayer requests during family devotions allow an avenue of communication because some children feel less threatened opening up their hearts to God than to their parents or other family members. In our large family, the prayer calendar helps us take inventory of each child's specific needs. Children often have rather simple requests such as winning a ball game. They should be spared the heavy burdens that usually form the basis of adult prayer requests.

Acknowledge each prayer request. A parent can pray for all requests or encourage each child to pray for another child's need. Parents, encourage your children to care and pray for one another. Sensitivity to each other's needs, the "I care" attitude, is one of the most important dynamics for the Christian family. Remember the principles of modeling? Parents model for the children; older children model for the younger children. The modeling of attitudes and commitments to family devotions filters down from the older to the younger. If the interest of the young children periodically wanes, and it usually does, convey to the older children the responsibility they have to encourage their younger brothers and sisters.

4. *Praise for answered prayer.*   Periodically bring out the prayer calendar and thank God for answered prayer. Children need to learn the power of prayer and that prayer requests may not always be answered in ways they want them to be answered. What a wonderful way to learn that God, their Father, really does know what is best for them and meets their needs in ways they would not have expected or imagined or chosen.

5. *The closing prayer* should be offered by the father as the spiritual leader of the home. Fathers, assume authority in your prayers, for example, "Father, we have come before You as a family with love in our voices and in our hearts; we thank You for the love we have for You and for one another. Help us to care for one another and pray for one another's needs that we have shared in this special time together as a family. We bring our requests to You, Father, in full belief that You are present in this house to hear us and to help us."

367

SPIRITUAL TRAINING IMPROVES YOUR CHILD'S SELF-ESTEEM

A child's attitudes and behavior mirror his or her self-esteem. The first stage in developing your child's self-esteem is to practice the principles of attachment parenting during his or her first two years. The child receives the message that his parents love him and that he is important to them. In the period from three to six years of age you carry these principles of parenting one step further into your spiritual parenting. The child learns: "God loves me, I am important to God." The child who has sincerely invited Christ into her heart has a head start toward the development of a good self-esteem. The need for this continuum of love from parents, love from God, and love of self is especially true of a difficult or high-need child. The difficult child who has learned to feel and accept the love of her parents has a head start in receiving the love of God. This feeling can be reinforced by parents' instructing their children that God has made them in His image (Gen. 1:27) and that Christ shows special love for children (Mark 10:13–16).

A child who knows that the Spirit dwells within her and has a personal relationship with God her Father is well on her way toward developing Spirit-directed Christian living. This feeling that "God loves me" in the younger child gradually matures into the older child's feeling, "I'm right with God; I feel right; I act right." This feeling is the ultimate goal of Christian discipline—that righteousness means being right with God, based on salvation through Jesus Christ. Hebrews 5:13–14 states: "For everyone who partakes only of milk is unskilled in the word of righteousness, for he is a babe. But solid food belongs to those who are of full age, that is, those who by reason of use have their senses exercised to discern both good and evil." Matthew 6:33 states: "But seek first the kingdom of God and His righteousness, and all these things shall be added to you."

TEACHING IMPULSE CONTROL AND DELAYED GRATIFICATION

As Christian parents, you must help your children control their impulses and delay their gratification. It is not enough to instruct them in the teachings of Christ;

you must make practical, day-by-day applications. You need to teach them that they can't have everything they want. Today's children are growing up in a world where they are constantly being told of material things they need to "fulfill them." For a child to be fulfilled with the things of Christ, he must learn at a very young age to be able to say no to the things of the world, but this is difficult for a young child (and for many adults). The inability to control their impulses and to say no to their sensual desires is one of the main weaknesses that get many adults into trouble. Self-control is one of the fruits of the Holy Spirit (see Gal. 5:23).

By nature the young child is impulsive. He is also programmed to have his needs met consistently and predictably because they have been met in that way all during infancy. Fulfillment of needs is necessary for the feeling of rightness in the tiny baby and older infant.

As the infant matures into the child from three to six years of age, you will be more able to differentiate between his needs and his wants. Throughout Scripture, fasting is mentioned along with prayer as necessary to becoming a mature Christian. Fasting for a long time is medically unwise for young children who are prone to low blood sugar and behavioral changes. However, fasting to a young child can simply mean saying no to a certain craving. Teaching the child the spiritual basis for saying no adds a more meaningful dimension to the concept of fasting, which will not be very popular.

For example, you and your child are walking by an ice-cream parlor, and he makes the usual plea for an ice-cream cone with a double scoop. This opportunity falls into the category of "teachable moments" in which you might say, "John, I know you would like to have a double scoop ice-cream cone and I would like one too; but I have a neat idea. Let's talk about it. Sometimes Jesus asks us to give up something very special that we want because when we say no to having it we are stronger inside. Jesus calls this 'fasting.' I'm not going to have an ice-cream cone even though I really would like to have one. So why don't you have only one scoop, and we both will show Jesus how strong we are." Impulse controls start gradually. Rather than asking John to give up the entire ice-cream cone, start with one scoop and the next time he may volunteer to give up the entire ice-cream cone. Or you may say, "Let's wait until tomorrow for that ice-cream cone." The concept of tomorrow seems like an eternity to a young child.

The more you suggest delayed gratification for simple things, the easier it is to build up to major sacrifices and the more disciplined your child will become in controlling his wants. For the young child, simply giving up the fulfillment of certain cravings, such as ice-cream cones, is beautiful in the eyes of God. This helps the child accept the concept of true fasting more easily when he becomes an adult.

OTHER WAYS TO ENCOURAGE DESIRABLE BEHAVIOR

Disciplining your child is giving him or her a sense of direction. Spiritual training is the first and foremost step in discipline, but there are other ways in which you can design your child's environment to encourage his or her desirable behavior.

A primary behavior director is building a sense of responsibility and impulse control in the young child. When your three-year-old has accomplished most of the basic skills of childhood, she needs some direction about what to do with them. If her skills are not channeled in the right direction, she will deviate into trouble. This is often the last stage at which a child will voluntarily want to help Mommy and Daddy around the house. The three- to six-year-old does not often distinguish between work and play. In fact, to a young child, doing any task with a parent is play; doing it alone is work. Start building responsibility and impulse control with "play chores": helping Mommy and Daddy do dishes, sweeping the floor, picking up clothes (presented as the game "let's tidy up"). By involving the young child in household chores, you are helping him or her develop work attitudes and habits at a young age. In later stages, most children see work as somewhat undesirable, and they often rebel. Your main goal at this stage is to shape the attitude about work, not to get the floor clean.

As you encourage your child to work with you, gradually require him to do specific jobs on his own and hold him accountable for their completion. At this stage you are building on a principle in child discipline, the privilege/responsibility ratio: Increasing privileges means increasing responsibilities. When the privileges are unearned and multiply faster than the responsibilities, discipline is not balanced and the child is headed for trouble. Some people call this "spoiling" a child.

Wisely choose jobs for your three-year-old. Keep the task short, simple, and achievable. Be certain he can see immediately the fruits of his labors. A good choice is having him load a basket of laundry into the washer. The child gets his specific instructions, the task is short, he starts with a full basket, he quickly sees his accomplishment, and he is praised genuinely for the empty basket. Room tidiness should be required. Remember, from two to four years of age is a sensitive period for the concept of order. Child-level pegs for hanging up his clothes, drawers for storing, and shelf compartments for filing toys teach the child to respect an orderly environment. If you are not sensitive to the child's need for an orderly environment, she will drift off into the lazy custom of piles of toys and clothes all over the floor. The responsibility for her own belongings must be one of your non-negotiable mandates of housekeeping. Insist on a young child's completing the job well—putting away *all* her toys with your help if necessary—and then acknowledge a job well done. Remember the principle of positive reinforcement: desirable behavior, if rewarded, will continue.

CHAPTER 16

DISCIPLINE IN MIDDLE CHILDHOOD

So far this book has dealt primarily with the positive aspects of discipline, the instructing and training of your child in the way he should go within his world and toward God. You cannot stop at this, however. You need to know about the next part of discipline—correcting your child if he departs from the way he should go. For corrective discipline to be effective, you must first have the strong foundation of knowing your child, knowing that he feels right, and having Jesus Christ as Lord of your lives.

Also implied in positive discipline is a child's respect for parental authority: "Children, obey your parents in all things, for this is well pleasing to the Lord" (Col. 3:20). A child obeys (the Greek word translated "obey" in the Bible is *hupakouo,* which means "listen to") because she wants to. She obeys (listens to) her parents because she has respect (a reverent fear) for them. Remember, children are resilient and adaptable; children are able to pick up on Christian discipline at any age. If Christian parenting is new to you, openly share your newfound love of Jesus with your child, and she will respond with faith and love.

Having laid this foundation, you may find your child's behavior is desirable most of the time. However, all children have times when they do not go the way they should go and don't always obey (listen to) their parents. This is called a "bent toward evil" by some Christian writers and is mentioned in Proverbs 22:15, "Folly is bound up in the heart of a child." Some children bend more frequently and severely than others, and some children are more difficult to unbend than others, not because of the effectiveness of their parents' discipline but because of the strength of their bent. The behavior modification techniques described earlier do not guarantee the constant "goodness" of your child. They only lower your risk of having to use corrective discipline and increase its effectiveness when you do use it.

This bent toward evil is an important point for Christian parents to consider. It differs from the secular viewpoint toward children which believes that since children are basically good, they should be left to themselves to determine their direction. Christians believe, however, that unless children are disciplined toward good, they automatically will bend toward evil. I certainly don't believe children should be left to themselves. This approach is contrary to Scripture: "A child left to himself brings shame to his mother" (Prov. 29:15). However, the Christian concept of a child's evil bent also needs some clarification. Humankind (both adult and children) can be viewed as basically good. People are made in the image and likeness of God (see Gen. 1:26), and Jesus Christ paid the price for the sin of man. Perhaps this evil bent should be considered as having two causes.

First, every person has some undesirable character traits that often manifest themselves in outward behavior that is not all good. Original sin is present in every person born into the world, as a son or a daughter of Adam and Eve. Pride is the basic sin that caused evil. Strong-willed children are simply demonstrating this pride openly: "I won't give in." When a child is old enough to have a concept of self, he is old enough to be prideful and resistant to parental guidance, and that is what gets him into trouble.

Second, the evil bent in a child may be considered a susceptibility to temptation, a vulnerability. Because the child lacks the wisdom, experience, and discernment of an adult, the child is more vulnerable to temptation, which accounts for part of the evil bent.

CHASTENING VS. PUNISHMENT

Corrective discipline in the Bible is called "chastening" (Prov. 19:18), which differs from punishment. This important distinction separates Christian discipline from secular discipline. Christians follow a different Book. God's way to solve problems and heal relationships is not always the same and not always as easy as man's ways. Many books on discipline list "methods that work" (by "work" they mean methods that stop a certain misdeed), but what works isn't always right in the eyes of God. The Christian approach to solving discipline problems should be perceived by children as so right, so attractive, and so distinctive that they cannot help feeling the value of Christian discipline as a practical way of life.

The terms *chastening* and *punishment* differ in the following ways. *Chastening* implies a redirection of the child toward future, more desirable behavior, performed out of concern and love. It leaves a child feeling right. *Punishment* is retribution, a penalty for a past offense, which may not focus on a redirection toward future, desirable behavior. Punishment may be performed out of anger, without regard for the child's feelings, and does not always leave the child feeling right. Chastening redirects the child along the path he should go; punishment penalizes him for taking the wrong path.

There are three goals in a disciplinary action: (1) to promote desirable behavior, (2) to stop undesirable behavior, and (3) to result in a child's feeling right with himself, his parents, and his God. Punishment alone fulfills only one of these goals—it stops undesirable behavior, at least for the moment. Chastening carries punishment one step further, which is the level that God expects from Christian parents. By giving parents corrective discipline as a parenting tool, God is saying: "Parents, get into your child, find out what is going on inside her, find out why she did what she did, and how she feels as a result of her deed." Give your child the message, "I care and I'm going to mend whatever is causing you to act this way. I love you; I want you to feel right inside."

Perhaps the difference between punishment and chastening can be demonstrated best by a situation in my family. Remember, discipline problems are situation-specific; what applies to one family in one situation may not apply to another family in another situation. One Christmas morning our almost five-year-old daughter, Hayden, was excited as she pranced around dangling a set of sleigh bells. Suddenly our seven-year-old Peter let out a howl of hurt and indignation. His forehead had gotten in the way of Hayden's dangling bells. Peter assumed that Hayden had hit him on the head intentionally, so his howls of protest increased.

Hayden was vaguely aware that something was amiss, that her brother was hurt, and that her mother was giving her "a look," but she felt certain that she hadn't meant to do anything wrong. Martha, my wife, told her to stop swinging the bells around and to see if her brother was all right. She immediately stiffened and resisted her mother's command as Martha pointed out to her that the way she was playing with the bells was not safe when people were nearby because the bells are hard and hurt when they hit a person on the head. She went on, "So please come and tell Peter that you are sorry you hurt him." Hayden shook her head no and got an insulted look on her face, so Martha said, "You still must say you are sorry even if you didn't mean to hurt Peter, and you need to ask him if he is all right. You must care that he is hurting."

Hayden must have felt unjustly accused by my wife's looks and by her brother's howling because she continued to refuse to apologize. We told her she wouldn't be able to open presents until she had made things right with her brother. At this point my wife and I were in agreement on our stand that Hayden had not meant to hurt Peter but she still needed to say she was sorry for hurting him accidentally.

By this time the situation had become a conflict of wills. Hayden's pride was on the line, and she grew more and more resistant to apologizing. Our parental authority was on the line because we had previously been consistent toward expecting and demanding an apology and an "I care" attitude when one of our children hurt another child, whether or not it was accidental. This was also an act of defiance of reasonable parental authority for which a child must be chastened.

Our parental dilemma was how to punish, or rather to chasten, our daughter in this situation. We considered taking her to the bedroom and administering corporal punishment, but we simply did not feel right about this approach. Martha said, "I know her well and something inside her is not right. For one thing she usually does not have any trouble apologizing or forgiving." By now Hayden had gone into a state of near hysterics, crumpling up on the floor and crying out, "No, no, no!" At this point we realized a spanking was not the correct approach at this time. Our anger at her defiance disappeared as we understood we had a frightened little girl on our hands who did not know why she was doing the things she was doing. We sensed that there was more to this than her pride. She was undergoing an internal struggle that she did not understand.

I held her tightly in my arms to control her kicking and flailing, and I explained very calmly but firmly that she was going to have to ask her brother's forgiveness or she would have to sit on the couch and watch while everyone else opened their presents. This calmed her behavior somewhat, but she still refused to comply with our request. I could see that my wife was analyzing Hayden as only an intuitive mother can do. She later confided to me that she was also praying for the wisdom to correct the spiritual turmoil that was making Hayden act in a way that even she was not comfortable with. Martha was thinking of 1 Corinthians 13:4–5: "Love suffers long and is kind; love . . . is not provoked."

We both realized we had to reach Hayden at a deep level. My wife looked her straight in the eyes, and I put my hand on her shoulder. We explained to her that we understood how hard it is sometimes to say you're sorry. Martha told Hayden a story, "When I was a little girl, I refused to apologize to my sister, but my parents didn't know how to help me so I just stayed miserable all day in my pride and anger." We spoke to her in voices of caring authority. Hayden started to calm down and listen, and she soon muttered a tiny "sorry" to her brother. I encouraged her to expand on this apology by looking at him and touching his hand and saying, "I'm sorry, Peter, if I hurt you even though I didn't mean to." Her brother replied, "That's all right." (Always demand that the person apologized to completes the continuum by accepting the apology, thus creating more of a feeling of rightness and justice within the one who is apologizing.)

My wife then said to Hayden, "Now let's pray and ask Jesus to forgive you." She refused, to my surprise, because we have done this before many times. Then I realized she may not have understood why she was to ask Jesus for forgiveness. Actually it was not for the sin of hurting her brother because she hadn't meant to hurt him. We wanted her to pray about her screaming and kicking and defying her parents. So we explained to her, and she accepted that it was the right thing to do, but she said, "You pray for me, Mommy." Martha agreed to pray for her but still told her she would have to pray on her own, because Martha could sense her need for this confession in order to achieve the state of spiritual rightness inside her. I explained to her that as long as she refused to ask Jesus to forgive her she was separated from Him and from the rest of the family: that it would be as if she were outside the window looking in on us; we were all together but she couldn't be with us. My wife told her that we couldn't force her to say her prayer. But we told her that if she didn't pray and ask Jesus for forgiveness she wouldn't feel good about herself or about her brother and she would not feel close to Jesus at this time. We talked about how we loved her and how Jesus loves her even when she does bad things and He wants to help her. We talked about Jesus' wanting to live in her heart and that maybe she would like to welcome Him because we weren't sure she had ever asked Jesus into her heart in a way she understood. Then she looked at us with big wide eyes, and we knew we had found what she needed.

Early in this discipline dialogue, our other children were observing this conflict, and of course, they made the usual childish snickers as if feeling, "Boy, is she going to get it for defying Mom and Dad," because they knew that defiance is not tolerated in our household. As they saw how we were getting at the root of the problem and their sister was increasingly feeling more right, they began to be more interested and involved in what had become a family situation. At that point we all came together in a circle on the floor where Hayden was sitting and held hands. We prayed for Hayden, praising God for sending His Son, Jesus, to be born and to die for us and to save us from our sins. Also at that time, we took authority over Satan in Jesus' name (something we always do when we sense a spiritual battle). Hayden seemed to sense our firmness and strength in overcoming Satan. She then put her head on Martha's lap and willingly and eagerly repeated a few simple sentences asking Jesus to forgive her for her disobedience. She asked Him to come into her heart, in between quiet little sobs of relief and joy.

This incident took place several years ago and we have grown considerably in our parenting so that now as we look back we would be far less critical of her behavior, less accusatory and less pressuring of her. We have also learned that children sometimes need more time before they are ready and able to say "I'm sorry" and mean it. A child who is angry cannot apologize until the anger has been resolved. And we were still in a punishing mode—that is what we thought of first. Now we would not even consider a spanking.

This soul-searching chastening took about a half-hour; whereas, we could have handled the whole ordeal with a punishment of spanking which would have taken only a few minutes. If I had picked up Hayden and spanked her for her defiance, I would have accomplished only one thing: perhaps next time she would not be so defiant. I ran the risk of her still refusing to apologize after the spanking, and then what would I have done? Spank harder until she apologized out of fear? This would have left a feeling of not-rightness within the whole family and would have left her feeling a loss of self-esteem and a sense of embarrassment as she reentered the room to join the family. She also would have missed out on a spiritually significant event.

Chastening achieved the desired end—the apology—but it did so by directing her behavior from within, by understanding her and working through her own inner conflict in such a way that the whole family felt right. It made Hayden aware of how her own pride was a stumbling block to Jesus' coming into her heart. It increased her respect for the authority of her parents who were willing to take control and get to the heart of the matter by showing that "we care and we are going to stick by you; we care enough to give you our very best." It made her more spiritually aware of the forces of good and evil that can overtake a child, but some-one older and wiser took charge and led her in the way she should go. This method left every family member feeling right and increased the self-esteem of the offender because she won the battle over herself and temptation. She was a winner in the eyes of her brothers, rather than a loser.

Another benefit of chastening is that it models a kind of discipline for your children to carry over into their own eventual child rearing. Older children observe how their parents discipline the younger children and are very quick to pick up on how their parents discipline under pressure. We learned this when shortly after this encounter with Hayden, we saw our thirteen-year-old Bobby paging through the Bible concordance as if interested in finding a certain topic. I asked Bobby what he was looking up. He replied, "I'm looking up *forgiveness*."

The Biblical Approach to Spanking

To spank or not to spank is the subject of much emotional debate among child-care writers. It has produced controversial books, magazine articles, and TV programs, even legislation. Most (but not all) Christian child-rearing books highly favor spanking as an effective method of discipline. In contrast, Sweden has recently passed a law against spanking. Christian parents are naturally confused about all the mixed messages regarding the subject.

Let me state my opinion of spanking, which is based upon much prayer for wisdom, my own experience as a pediatrician observing what works and what does not, what God says in Scripture regarding discipline, and the opinions of Christian writers with whom I strongly agree.

The first point I wish to make is that it is absolutely wrong and against God's design to be mean and abusive toward a child or to strike a child out of frustration, hostility, or anger. The only reason some parents dare do this is that children are small and defenseless.

Second, spanking should not be the first resort in discipline. Parents ought to strive to create such an attitude within their children and an atmosphere within their homes that spanking is unnecessary.

Third, spanking should be reserved for major confrontations when a parent's authority is on the line, situations in which a child willfully defies reasonable authority, and other approaches are not getting through.

In this section on spanking I wish to present not only some clear guidelines based on my own opinion but also some basic scriptural and cultural considerations from which you can evolve your own philosophy on spanking based upon your own individual parent-child situation.

In regard to discipline in general, God has given us some guidelines. We have already discussed the meaning of Proverbs 22:6, "Train up a child." I like to think of the translation "initiate," instead of the word *train*, in connection with giving a child the right start. Discipline begins at birth.

Proverbs 22:15 states, "Foolishness is bound up in the heart of a child." This is sometimes very difficult for parents to understand. However, within the child's nature—as he matures—there is a bent toward good and a bent toward evil. It is up to Christian parents to unbend their child's tendency toward evil. The rest of that verse tells parents what they should do about it: "But the rod of correction will drive it far from him."

The book of Proverbs has more to say about the rod. It is here that the Bible seems to take a clear stand on spanking:

> *Do not withhold correction from a child,*
> *For if you beat him with a rod, he will not die.*
> *You shall beat him with a rod,*
> *And deliver his soul from hell (23:13–14);*
>
> *The rod and reproof give wisdom,*
> *But a child left to himself brings shame to his mother (29:15);*
>
> *He who spares his rod hates his son,*
> *But he who loves him disciplines him promptly (13:24).*

From the preceding verses it would seem that the Bible takes a clear stand in favor of spanking as the first mode of discipline because of the frequent use of the term *rod* in the Scriptures. I am uncomfortable with this interpretation of these Scriptures for several reasons.

First, while it is clear that the rod does appear to be an object to strike with, the term *rod* is also used in connection with the shepherd's staff: "Your rod and Your staff, they comfort me" (Ps. 23:4). The shepherd's staff was gently used to guide the wandering sheep along the right path. The rod was used to beat off a sheep's predators. This teaching is developed beautifully in the book *A Shepherd Looks at Psalm 23* by Phillip Keller, especially in chapter 8: "Thy Rod and Thy Staff, They Comfort Me." The original Hebrew word *shebet* means "a stick" (for punishing, writing, fighting, ruling, walking). Proverbs 13:24 could be translated: "He who spares his *ruling* [authority] hates his son, but he who loves him disciplines [it doesn't say *punishes*] him promptly." Remember, the book of Proverbs is written in the form of poetry where words often have symbolic meanings. In other Old Testament books there are uses of the word *shebet* that are obviously symbolic.

Second, references to the rod are found primarily in the Old Testament. The Old Testament's basic approach to justice, and probably also to discipline, was different from that of the New Testament. For example, in the New Testament Christ modified the eye-for-an-eye system of justice (see Matt. 5:38) with His turn-the-other-cheek teaching (see Matt. 5:39–44). In the New Testament, Christ preached gentleness, love, and understanding, as did Paul: "Shall I come to you with a rod, or in love and a spirit of gentleness?" (1 Cor. 4:21). In the New Testament, Christ did not overturn the laws of the Old Testament but simply fulfilled them to a higher level of spirituality and understanding: He stressed discipline and direction from within the child rather than direction by force from without. Let me suggest that, taken in the context of the total Bible, the total child, and what is known about child psychology and development, spanking is not appropriate. I feel that what God is saying in these Scripture references is simply: "Parents, take charge of your child and bring him into submission to your authority. Since the child can be brought into submission just as well (or better) by other means, spanking should not be used."

Reasons for the Anti-spanking Movement

There are three reasons why the anti-spanking philosophy has grown in popularity throughout the past twenty-five years. First, the unwillingness to spank children in the seventies was a natural spin-off from the general movement toward a greater awareness of the feelings and dignity of the child. I feel it is a natural consequence of the childbirth-without-violence philosophy, which has indeed enriched people's regard for the dignity of a newborn as a feeling person. The same feelings that changed child-birthing practices carried over into child-rearing practices. A growing number of parents began practicing concepts similar to those of attachment parenting. To these parents, spanking became synonymous with hurting and violence. Therefore, spanking was naturally foreign to their whole thinking about the parent-child relationship. They became more interested in alternative methods of discipline and were willing to put an enormous amount of energy into those methods. They wanted their children's behavior to be directed by a feeling from within rather than by an external force. Parents who have shied away from spanking for these reasons are to be commended, and as long as they adhere to God's primary message of getting the job done their views about spanking should be respected. If you feel a conflict in your feelings toward spanking, pray and ask God to give you the wisdom to clarify those feelings based upon the preceding Bible passages.

The second reason for the anti-spanking movement, and one with which I have no sympathy, is the carryover from the permissive approach to discipline. A child left to himself will find his own way, according to this approach. The Bible is clearly against this doctrine (see Prov. 29:15 and 22:6). A child left to himself will depart from you and will not respect your authority. I feel that parents who do not spank because they follow this general permissive attitude simply show a lack of concern and lazily shirk their responsibility as authority figures. They will be held accountable here on earth for the outcome of their children and after death by the judgment of their Lord.

The third reason spanking is gradually losing favor as a discipline technique is the belief that spanking is the forerunner of child abuse, which has reached epidemic proportions. If a child's behavior is spank-controlled throughout childhood, he is very likely to continue this miserable parenting practice with his own children. Role modeling is an extremely important concept underlying our parenting practices. The role modeling of spanking is indeed a concern. When a child sees you spank another child, or when he himself is spanked, the role-modeling concept he picks up is that it's all right for a big person to hit a little person.

Remember, one of your goals of discipline is to create an attitude within the child and an atmosphere within the home wherein spanking is seldom if ever necessary.

For the most part, children who are the products of attachment parenting are easier to discipline for the following reasons.

1. They love and trust their parents so deeply that they willingly submit to parental authority. They can handle the concept of submission because they view authority as love and security, not as infringement upon their rights. Consequently, they are less defiant; and defiance is what usually gets children spanked.

2. These children know what behavior is expected of them because their parents have taken the time and energy to convey the behavior they expect as well as the consequences of misbehavior.

3. Because their parents have taken the time and energy to carry out the suggestions for encouraging desirable behavior, the children have less opportunity to deviate into situations that may get them spanked.

4. Children are motivated to please their parents because they have

learned there are positive rewards and feedback from their parents when they are pleased—the principle of reinforcement of desirable behavior.

5. Parents depend more on encouragement and discipline rather than on rewards and punishment.

6. Older children who have been reared in this style of parenting are motivated to relate with and please God, their heavenly Father, as they have learned to please in their relationships with their parents.

7. Since children are fun oriented, young children soon learn that their worlds are much smoother and that they actually have more fun when they live according to the rules set by their parents and by God.

The end result is that their parents have achieved the goal of effective discipline—an attitude within their children and an atmosphere within their homes that promote desirable behavior. The children have direction from within themselves. They are motivated toward desirable behavior because they enjoy the right feelings this desirable behavior promotes. They are so accustomed to feeling right that they naturally avoid situations that make them not feel right. They are on their way toward having Christian consciences.

I admit that this level of discipline is not easy to achieve in some children. It takes much more time and energy to create this attitude in your child and this atmosphere in your home than it takes to go to the rod. This is especially true of the strong-willed or high-need child. Disciplining the high-need child is one of the paradoxes of parenting. Most parents who attempt to spank-control their high-need children usually report, "I'm spanking more and getting less results. Spanking seems to be hurting me more than her."

Today's children are generally spanked less than children were years ago. I feel this is a natural consequence of more sensitive parents. For example, suppose you were to ask a parent, "What would you do if your three-year-old were making an unruly nuisance of himself at a family gathering?" Parent A might respond, "That's simple, I would take him in the other room and redden his bottom; I'll bet he would never act that way again, and it didn't hurt the way I turned out." Parent B might respond, "First, I know that she doesn't settle down in crowds. Second, I would have told my child beforehand what behavior is expected of her. For example: 'We are going to Grandma's house where there will be lots of your cousins to play with. I expect you to play outside, to be careful not to pick up any of Grandma's vases, and to come in when you are called.' And then I would ask my child to repeat what I had said to him." Parent B might also add the reminder: "I will have to take you into the other room and spank you if you do not do what I ask." (He would carry through on the spanking if necessary and follow the spanking with a sign of love and an explanation of why he was spanked.) Parent C might say, "If he seemed to be getting into trouble, I would first go through my checklist. Is he tired, hungry, bored, etc.? If he 'forgot' after I had reminded him of the rules, I would take him upstairs and help him take a nap, or take him outside for some father-son time together, maybe have a snack. He responds beautifully when I take the time to understand him."

Let me offer an opinion about the approaches taken by Parent A, Parent B, and Parent C. Parent A went directly to spanking as the first resort. I feel he showed lazy parenting, exhibited his power more than his authority, and did nothing to strengthen the respect or love relationship between parent and child. Parents B and C, on the other hand, took time and energy to follow a wiser approach to discipline:

1. They conveyed to the child what behavior was expected of him or her and took the time to be certain that the child understood.
2. They considered the child's needs and feelings and made an effort to channel the child into some play activities that would encourage desirable behavior.
3. If the child showed undesirable behavior, the parents put time and interest into understanding what the feelings and circumstances were that prompted the behavior. They focused on the child rather than on the undesirable actions.
4. Parent B carried out the admonition of spanking if it seemed necessary, but he also followed the spanking with a sign of love. Parent C is programmed not to spank.

Parents B and C conveyed *both* love and authority to the child. The child knew what behavior was expected of him or her, and the consequences of misbehaving: the result was a greater respect for the authority of his or her parents. Parent B may seem like a last-resort spanker (save your "big guns" till last) which some Christian writers are against (because the child was just waiting for the "big guns" anyway). I don't think so. The big guns won't be needed in most situations. Parent C's approach requires the most investment of time and energy—he'll know his child even more.

When You Should Not Spank

There are times when you absolutely should not spank your child.

1. *Do not spank in anger:* "In your anger do not sin" (Eph. 4:26 NIV). The

384

emotion of anger in itself is not wrong. However, God told people not to allow any of their actions to be motivated by anger. He also said that anger should be justified and short-lived. This admonition applies especially to actions toward children. If you are a parent easily provoked to anger, be on guard against this reaction. Do not spank to release your anger or vent your frustration. Don't wait until you're angry to try to pray. Ask the Holy Spirit to convict you ahead of time about these moments. Develop a stoplight in your emotions which consciously says, "Wait, take time out for a minute, pray, and examine your motives for spanking. Let your hostility settle down." When your thoughts are not clouded by anger, you can usually come up with a more effective means of discipline than spanking. If your primary motive is to avenge your anger, then hold off. Pray for guidance to act according to God's will. "If any of you lacks wisdom, let him ask of God, who gives to all liberally" (James 1:5).

For example, your three-year-old sits down to breakfast—her mind is full of fantasy, her attention is short, and she is thinking about everything but her food. Oops! There goes her glass of milk all over Mom's clean kitchen floor! You are naturally angry. You just washed that floor. Should you spank? No! This is an example of childish irresponsibility rather than willful defiance. Your child did not spill her milk deliberately. This is an accident. Don't be afraid to show that you are angry; children need to know that parents have feelings too. But keep your anger in line with reality. If you explode, you'll have to apologize. Follow your statement of dismay with, "I understand that this was an accident," then add an admonition, "but I expect you to be more careful when you sit at the table." You may also follow with a logical consequence of not refilling her glass of milk if this is a recurrent problem.

Take that same child and the same glass of milk. Suppose you notice the glass of milk is getting closer and closer to the edge of the table. You ask your child to move the glass away from the edge because it may fall and break. (A creative mother shared with me, "I put a large circle on the table with red tape and instructed my child that his glass must stay in the circle.") She defies your admonition and deliberately pushes the glass toward the edge of the table; as you predicted, it falls and breaks. In my opinion, she deserves chastening. This is an act of willful defiance. This testing the limits of authority is a classical childhood ploy. Much more is at stake here than milk spilled on the floor; your God-given authority is at stake. Your child expects to be chastened. What do you accomplish by disciplining her? (1) You impress upon her who is in charge; (2) you show that defiance will always be corrected; and (3) you contribute to the shaping of her future behavior—

the more readily she conforms to parental authority, the more readily she will conform to the authority of God in particular and other authority figures in general. Also, she is more likely to follow her own conscience once the appropriate inner authority has been developed.

Here are some alternatives to spanking in this situation. A logical consequence of this on-purpose spilling would be to calmly ask her to help clean up the mess as you talk about what she was feeling—you want to understand and help her understand why she acted that way. Was she feeling angry or jealous (left out) or resentful (crabby inside)? This kind of behavior is a red flag that the child and the family need professional help. A further consequence is that you will assume she does not want any more milk since she pushed it away on purpose. A negative reinforcement could be used here, such as she is now asked to leave the table and sit in a "time out place." If you do this without anger, she will be more likely not to resist. If you are both angry, you will need to cool off so you can help her cool off before proceeding, or whatever you do will be perceived as punishment and no learning will take place. She can come back to the table when she can apologize, and she may need your help doing that. She may need you to pray with her.

2. *Do not spank babies and young children.* In fact, some biblical scholars who have researched the use of the term *rod* in the Scriptures conclude that Solomon was probably referring to the use of the rod for older children, not infants and toddlers. They believe the rod was reserved for particularly wicked deeds and that the child was old enough to understand the meaning of the spankings. I agree with these interpretations, but if you are spanking more and more as your child gets older, then there is a breakdown in your parent-child communication and in your approach to discipline. Professional guidance should be obtained.

Do not spank if you have a weak parent-child relationship. The principles of attachment parenting are necessary foundations before spanking should ever be considered. Otherwise I feel you are imposing a heavy burden on a fragile foundation which, with continued stress, eventually may lead to a shaky structure (self-esteem) that eventually may crumble. If you have built a solid foundation of love and trust with your child, an occasional swat "to clear the air" will not damage this relationship, but it will not improve it either.

These guidelines for discipline are generalizations. Only when you have gone through the more positive steps for effective discipline and your child still defies reasonable authority would spanking be a consideration. (1) You have followed the principles of attachment parenting, building up a secure love-and-trust relationship;

(2) you have clearly defined to your child what behavior you expect of him, and he understands what you expect; (3) you have tried alternative methods to no avail; (However, be aware that when you run out of alternative methods, you will usually revert back to the way you were dealt with as a child, no matter how convinced you are that you would never do that. I encourage you to make a life-long study of discipline and correction [see books listed in the bibliography] so that you don't spank just because you did not know what else to do.) (4) your child willfully defies reasonable authority, and your authority and your relationship with your child are on the line; and (5) you have prayed for guidance for the best method of discipline for your child in a given situation, and your conclusion is that a spanking is in the best interest of your child's inner direction and your authority relationship.

Parents sometimes consider spanking in life-threatening situations. For example, your three- to six-year-old is told not to ride his tricycle into the street. If he does, the tricycle will be put in the garage for one week (logical consequence), and he will be spanked. He rides into the street. This child has neither respect for your authority nor a sense of safety. Parents want to leave an impression on mind and body that will make repeated offenses less likely. Failure to carry through on what you said you were going to do will weaken your future authority relationship and lessen your child's respect for you. An example that is often given is of the child who runs out into the street (life-threatening situation.). A child must be taught to respect danger. He must not be left with access to the street until he is old enough to understand. You must be with him, teaching him, until you *know* he is safe. You want him to be able to stop and look both ways before crossing. You also want to have a rule that until he reaches a certain age he must come and ask you first, so you can watch him. You want him to learn to look at the street. You don't want him to learn only to look back at you to see whether you are about to hit him.

How to Develop Spanking "Wisdom"

There are so many variables and so many different parent-child relationships that an absolute dictum of "spank" or "don't spank" is not possible. Here are some general guidelines to help you develop your own attitude about spanking.

1. *Pray for wisdom* to know whether spanking in general is a proper chastening for your child. Disregard all opinions you have heard about spanking lest they cloud your judgment. Open your ears to God's direction, asking Him for an inner sensitivity to spanking in general and in specific circumstances. For our own family, we have concluded, after much prayer, that (1) we will not let unacceptable behavior go

unchastened; (2) we are committed to create an attitude within our children and an atmosphere within our home that spanking is not an option; (3) spanking in general is a poor option in all the methods of discipline; and (4) if, in certain circumstances, spanking seems to be the wisest direction, then we are open to using spanking as a form of chastening, not as a punishment. In short, we are programmed against spanking our children. We don't want to spank our children, so we are going to devote a lot of time and energy to utilize alternatives to spanking. This has been a healthy approach for our family. Other parents may choose another viewpoint.

2. *Consider if there are specific risk factors* in your family that affect your attitude toward spanking.

Parents who are most likely *not* to abuse spanking
- have practiced the principles of attachment parenting all along so that they know their children and their children feel right,
- have children whose temperaments are generally easy-going,
- were not spank-controlled as children, and
- are truly walking with the Lord.

Parents who may spank inappropriately
- have generally shaky parent-child relationships,
- were abused as children,
- have high-need children,
- find that spanking does not work,
- are prone to impulsive anger, and
- are not walking with the Lord.

If you have any of these risk factors that might hinder you from spanking appropriately, I suggest you examine your entire parent-child relationship according to the principles already discussed and examine your relationship with God. Some parents simply cannot handle "the rod" wisely. The earlier you accept this and seek help toward alternative means of discipline, the better off your parent-child relationship will be. The product of abusive spanking is anger; the cause of abusive spanking is also anger. An angry child will grow to be an angry adult.

Your child will pick up on your motives for spanking. Are you spanking him for *his* own good or for *your* own good? If you are a parent easily provoked to anger, be on guard. A child spanked in anger will retaliate in anger. This is the main reason parents say, "He's so stubborn; the harder I spank him, the worse he gets."

3. *Spank soon after the offense.*   It is important to cool down but a spanking should be given as soon as possible after the offense (Eccl. 8:11) and by the person whose authority is at stake. Don't say, "Wait till your father gets home and then you'll get it."

4. *Help the child accept the spanking.*   To help avoid a struggle, explain the whole spanking sequence to your child at a time when she is not just about to have a spanking. You should not have to drag her kicking and screaming off to her "execution." If she resists her spanking, she is also being defiant or else she feels unjustly treated, which means you may need to reexamine your decision.

5. *Explain to your child why you are spanking him.*   Some parents may not agree that a child needs to understand why he needs to be chastened. These parents may equate explanations with apologies which they interpret as weakening their position. But an appropriately administered spanking should not alienate the spanker and the spankee. A wise parent conveys to his child that the spanking is done out of love and out of a God-given duty. "For whom the LORD loves He chastens" (Heb. 12:6) is a good scriptural reference to support your position. Hebrews 12:11 states, "No chastening seems to be joyful for the present, but grievous; nevertheless, afterward it yields the peaceable fruit of righteousness to those who have been trained by it." Spanking done as a chastening, not as a punishment, can be effective in some situations. An excellent discussion of the difference between chastening and punishment and how spanking is to be handled if chosen as a form of chastening, is found in Jack Fennema's book *Nurturing Children in the Lord* (see Bibliography).

6. *Encourage a confession* (see James 5:16; 1 John 1:9). Confession of wrongdoing is very therapeutic. A child is seldom going to welcome a spanking, but understanding and acknowledging he was wrong help him accept the discipline. When a child sees the fairness of a correction, he usually respects the authority figure administering the spanking. Incidentally, he struggles less, which makes spanking easier. "Johnny, did Dad tell you not to ride your bike out into the street? . . . What did you do? . . . You disobeyed me, right? . . . You were wrong, and you could have been hit by a car. . . . You agree that you deserve a spanking?" Johnny will probably manage a few feeble yeses during this interrogation. This little dialogue allows Johnny to feel and release guilt and helps to shape his conscience. This helps him recognize

his feelings when he has done wrong and accept a very real fact of life that wrong deeds will be chastened.

7. *Choose a proper instrument for the spanking.*   To readers who absolutely disdain any form of spanking, consider the following: I have repeatedly stated in this book that we are programmed against spanking in our family. I have spent most of the discipline chapter teaching parents how to develop alternatives to spanking. Therefore, my position on spanking is clear. However, as a pediatrician for twenty years, I am painfully aware that spanking may lead to child abuse. This section is written primarily to parents who have already made up their minds to spank their child and need guidelines to avoid physical and emotional abuse. There are two schools of thought on what to spank with—a neutral object (a stick, a wooden spoon, etc.) or the hand. Proponents of the neutral object feel that the hand, as part of the parent, is a tool for loving and learning and not an object to be feared. This concept is a carry-over from animal behavior psychology. Pet owners are advised never to use the hand to strike with but to use sticks to discipline their pets. Animals shy away from the objects they are struck with. If you want your dog to fetch your morning paper, don't use a rolled-up paper for discipline or he will learn to hate rolled-up papers.

Some parents associate a stick with "beating" and a hand with spanking; they feel better using their hands. By using your hand you will feel the force of your strength. Other parents feel that if they program themselves away from using their hands to spank, they are less likely to hit their children reflexively out of anger. Having to get the neutral spanking object allows them more time and space to cool off. I am more concerned about the attitude of spanking than the choice of the instrument.

Let me suggest using neither the hand nor a clublike object such as a wooden spoon. A switch is a more appropriate spanking tool. Use a thin, very flexible stick such as a willow branch. The best switch is one that inflicts stinging pain but no injury to the child's bottom. Most cases of child abuse I have seen were inflicted by an angry person behind a heavy hand or a wooden spoon.

Spanking is traditionally administered to the child's buttocks. I feel it is very important to respect the child's sense of modesty and never bare the buttocks. If a child is still in padded diapering, he or she is too young to be spanked anyway. To spank a child anywhere else on his or her anatomy is to risk injury. For example, above the buttocks are located the spine and the kidneys, below are the more bony areas. The face and head must never be struck due to the delicate structures and the emotional insult and trauma that would be caused. A young child's hands never should be spanked because the hands are the tools of exploring.

8. *Follow up after spanking.*   An appropriately administered spanking should leave *both parent and child feeling better. An inappropriately administered spanking will leave an angry child and a parent who feels guilty.* To avoid bad feelings all around, follow the spanking with an expression of love. The child may be hesitant to ask for forgiveness or to admit he got what he really should get, and you may not know what to say. Saying "I'm sorry" or "I didn't want to spank you" is confusing to the child. He gets mixed messages: "If you didn't want to spank me, why did you do it?" Or "If you are sorry, then you did something wrong." Of course, if the spanking was done in error, before you had all the facts, you *must* make a sincere apology to your child. Never be afraid to admit you were wrong. This is the best way to teach a child to say *he* is sorry. End a spanking with, "Now let's pray together," after the crying has subsided and you have gathered the repentant child into your arms.

Your prayer should include an expression of love for your child and an acknowledgment of God as your Father and of your accountability to Him for chastening your child out of love. Use Hebrews 12:5–11 for a prayer model after spanking: the prayer for forgiveness and a thanks for forgiveness. During the after-spanking prayer, your child should pick up that you (and God) forgive him. Both you and your child should emerge from a spanking with a clean slate.

OTHER METHODS OF DISCIPLINE

The Feedback Technique

You should try to understand your child's position before administering any chastening that requires a judgment on your part. Why did your child do what he or she did? Which child started the fight? As has been said before, you can control your children's actions, but you cannot control the feelings that prompted these actions.

One of the ways of learning about these feelings in your child is called the "feedback technique." In this technique, a parent in the position of authority conveys the message, "I care." He then carefully listens to the child and discerns what the child is feeling or trying to express. Then he feeds back to the child what he thinks the child felt. For example, your frustrated three-year-old throws a toy at her brother. She is angry, losing control, and she needs understanding and support, in addition to chastening, for her actions. Begin by formulating in your own mind what she is feeling and then say to her, "You are angry and this is why you hit your brother. . . . I understand. . ." The feedback technique is even useful for your toddler whose ability to understand words and concepts usually is more advanced than her ability to speak. Your toddler may not be able to express her feelings verbally, but she will usually be able to understand your verbal expression of her feelings. This technique is also effective for the older child or adolescent who does not like to listen to your opinion of her behavior until she feels you truly sympathize with her feelings. Nothing is more frustrating to a teenager than a parent's long tirade or reprimand before the parent attempts to understand her position. When you begin your discipline methods with the feedback messages of "I care," "I understand," you help your child be more willing to accept your authority and your advice. (See the Faber and Mazlish book, *How to Talk So Kids Will Listen and Listen So Kids Will Talk,* listed in the Bibliography.)

Natural and Logical Consequences

Understand natural and logical consequences. The principle of consequences for misbehavior is one of the oldest biblical forms of corrective discipline. Natural consequences is a form of corrective discipline in which the punishment is automatically built into the act. For example, a child touches a hot stove and gets burned; you can be sure he will not touch that stove again. Psalm 7:15–16 is a good biblical example of natural and logical consequences for an adult.

> *He made a pit and dug it out,*
> *And has fallen into the ditch which he made.*
> *His trouble shall return upon his own head,*
> *And his violent dealing shall come down on his own crown.*

Logical consequences is a form of corrective discipline in which the person in authority, usually a parent, makes a rule and clearly points out the consequences for breaking this rule. The implication in this discipline is that if a child chooses to break the rule, he also chooses the consequences. If you see your child heading for the wrong path, you can point out to him, "You are making a poor choice," letting him realize his responsibility for his own actions and giving him a chance to reconsider before the consequence is actually upon him. In this form of discipline the "punishment" closely fits the misdeed. God frequently used logical consequences in the Old Testament, such as the law of restitution: if a man stole a sheep or killed it, he replaced it with four sheep. Sports utilizes logical consequences. A football team plays according to the rules, and the penalty for breaking the rules is agreed upon beforehand.

Withdrawing privileges is a form of logical consequences. The most classical biblical example of this is Adam and Eve. They disobeyed the rules of the garden, and God took away their garden.

Logical consequences is a very effective form of discipline for older children, especially in large families, in order to get the busy household running more smoothly. For example, "Your bike is to be put on the porch every evening after you are finished riding it. If you forget, the bike will be put in the garage for one week."

The Family Council

The family council is a form of corrective discipline that is a must for large families and is an effective way to use logical consequences. In our family, one of the ways we use the family council is to sort out problems. In a large family everyone must have certain responsibilities, and with maturity come increasing privileges and a proportional increase in responsibilities. Every so often when the list of "I forgots" gets too long and our household regresses from busy order to ordered chaos to disordered chaos, I call the troops together around the dining room table for a family council. I list the behaviors and responsibilities expected of them and make sure each child understands the list. I then convey to each child the consequence of not doing the jobs or of continuing certain undesirable behavior. For example, anyone who grumbles puts a dime in the "grumble box," or gets an extra job; any teen who habitually dawdles in the morning and is not ready when the carpool driver arrives either walks to school or misses school that day (which also has its consequences); the car cannot be used until it is cleaned out; and if toys are not put away according to the rules, they get put up for a week.

DISCIPLINING THE HIGH-NEED CHILD

In some respects, all children are strong-willed but some have stronger wills than others and I call them "high-need" children. Because parenting these high-need children can be a very complicated subject (see *The Fussy Baby* in Bibliography), I will attempt to help you understand why your child has high needs and why the usual techniques or methods apparently don't work.

The high-need child is impulsive. He has great difficulty saying no to himself and even more difficulty saying yes to you. He is driven. The high-need child very often has higher than average intelligence. He is not satisfied with average teaching or learning. In short, an above-average child requires above-average parenting. He will require above-average teaching at school, and he requires above-average teaching about God at home.

Parents, take heart. There is light at the end of the tunnel. In parenting, there is what I call the "investment return ratio." In all children, the more parental energy invested, and the earlier and more consistently it is invested, the greater are the returns. For the high-need child, the investment return ratio is even greater; more needs to be invested but more is returned.

If a bank had an investment plan for a high-need child, the manager would say to you, "Your child will need an above-average college. You will need to invest more, invest earlier, invest more consistently, and invest for a longer time. You will be tired from working extra hours. The dividends will be slow in coming and may not arrive for a long time. You may not always be aware that it is paying off. The investment has a greater risk because if it is not kept consistently high, the value of the stock will fall more sharply. However, if it is kept up, your rewards will be beyond all expectations." These creative children, if properly parented and prayed for, usually turn out to be a great joy to their parents and to God.

You will need to show more love and apply careful correction to your high-need child. Each parent must work out the proper ratio of behavior modification to correction. On the surface it may appear that the high-need child needs more correction and less behavior modification, but for most high-need children, the opposite is true. This concept is best illustrated by a situation I had in my office when counseling the parents of high-need two-and-a-half-year-old Johnny. Johnny had been an energy-draining baby who demanded constant motion and physical contact in order to be settled, and even that did not always work. After two and a half years, the parents were worn out. Unfortunately, Johnny arrived at a time when his father was very busy trying to get ahead by working longer hours. As Johnny demanded more, his mother gave more, and his father managed to escape from the entire situation by working longer hours. The situation deteriorated into a high-need child who did not feel right, a tired mother who also did not feel right, and a father who became more successful in his corporation than in fathering his child.

394

One day the father said to me, "You know, I'm spanking Johnny more and more, but I'm just not getting through to him." I then asked the father, "Are there times when you notice you don't have to spank Johnny as much?" The intuitive mother quickly volunteered, "On days when he and Johnny have a lot of one-on-one fun time together, Johnny is the most wonderful child." In discussing this situation further I discovered that both parents, who were themselves labeled by their parents as strong-willed, were gifted children and turned out to be high achievers. They completed the strong-willed continuum by producing their own strong-willed (high-need) child. It's interesting that heredity often does play a factor, which supports my feeling that many high-need children do not have behavioral problems but are instead intelligent, gifted children who need high-input parenting. I advised these parents to put the rod to rest for the time being, discussed the need-level concept with them, and advised the father to redirect his priorities.

The high-need child's impulsiveness is usually what gets him in trouble. Impulse control is very hard for the high-need child and for his parents because, as has been stated, these children have such high need levels. I do not mean that their high needs can be satisfied by material things. These children need focused attention from their parents, a lot of touching and gentling, a lot of playing with, building with, reading with, talking with. A high-need child needs to learn that she can't have every toy she sees or every ice-cream cone she wants. She needs to be put in her place if she is hurting another person in some way, such as biting or scratching. The control of aggressive behavior and of the "I wannas" is much easier for parents if they have practiced selective gratification early in the child's life. In an increasingly materialistic world of instant turn-ons and instant entertainment, impulse control is a high-priority objective for parents of all children, but especially of high-need children.

DISCIPLINING THE CHILD SIX TO TEN YEARS OLD

During the first five years of your child's life, you should create a total Christian home so the following values are instilled in him or her.

- God is important to Mom and Dad.
- God seems to enter into everything we do as a family.

- God loves me; I am a special person in God's sight.
- God disciplines me through my parents when I do wrong.
- I feel right when I act right, and I do not feel right when I act wrong (the beginning of conscience).
- I fear God (in the sense of awed respect for God).

From this foundation, he can develop the primary goals of middle childhood: to increase his self-esteem and to accept your Christian values as his own Christian values.

Between ages six and ten your child will either accept and develop your Christian values or question them and evaluate alternative value systems. How much of your Christian values he accepts or rejects depends on two variables: (1) the depth and consistency of Christian teaching in your home and (2) how susceptible your child is to competitive value systems. From this, it follows that your main objective during this stage is to saturate his environment with Christian values that enhance rather than weaken the values you instilled in him during his earlier years. The next objective is to protect him from those outside influences that compete with and may seriously weaken the Christian values taught at home. Although your child may live in a strong Christian home, he is not exposed to a totally Christian world. The big secular world out there often fails to steer him in the way he should go.

Your central focus is to emphasize the factors that help your child grow internally toward his or her commitment to a Christ-centered life. You can achieve this by continuing to model strong spiritual principles—the concepts of God, family devotions, daily prayer, prayable situations, and teachable moments—and by continuing to carry out Christian principles of discipline discussed earlier. Continuing to provide this spiritual home model for your child gives him a strong, outer protective shield that wards off attacks from competitive value systems.

Teach your child to put on the protective armor of Christ (Eph. 6:13–17). A young child's armor is very thin, like a semi-permeable membrane that is unable to filter selectively those things that add to or take from her spiritual growth. Strong and consistent home spiritual training helps the child strengthen her protective armor.

Your values are in direct contrast to non-Christian philosophies that encourage parents to expose their children to all the influences of the "real world" and to let them make their own decisions. I strongly oppose this approach. A young child does not have the wisdom and discernment to be able to follow those things that are of God and turn from those that are not of God. A child left to himself is in trouble (see Prov. 29:15).

Think of the instruction and protection a child receives when participating in Little League sports. In these activities the child undergoes proper coaching which builds strength from within. The child is equipped with protective clothing and is allowed to compete only with players of his or her own age and weight in order to reduce the likelihood of physical injury. Parents should do even more to instruct and protect their children in regard to influences that cause spiritual injury.

Getting to Know the Other People in Your Child's Life

As your child grows into a social person, he becomes involved in many activities outside the home. He is confronted by a wide variety of value systems from other authority figures. They are called "persons of significance," and they include teachers, coaches, pastors, Scout leaders, and so on. Before you entrust your child to the authority of any of these persons, be sure you have a clear understanding of their personal values and of what they will be teaching your child. Impress upon these persons the values you wish your child to be taught.

One of the strongest influences on a child more than five years old is her peers. She depends on them for acceptance. This is one of the strongest arguments for the wisdom of home schooling. During this peer-dependency period a child senses the norms of the children she knows, and she begins to accept or reject those values. Children, especially those younger than six or seven, do not have the wisdom and discernment to make a judgment about the peer values that run contrary to those of her parents. Faced with a choice, she may turn her back on the values taught by her parents. Parents often have less control over the effects of peer pressure than they do over the influences from older persons of significance. Although it is no guarantee, it helps to know the values of the parents of your child's peers before encouraging their friendships.

You may protest, "But, doctor, isn't this causing my child to lead a sheltered life?" Yes, it is. I feel God is very clear in His directive (see Deut. 6:7–9) that parents should instill Christian values into their children so deeply that they develop the wisdom and discernment to reject competitive value systems. Until the child has reached the age when he has these abilities, parents should shelter him from, or rather filter out, any person or activity that endangers his spiritual growth. There is no benefit in thrusting the young child out among the thorns of the world until he is able to protect himself. Parents never can protect their children fully from competing influences, of course, but they certainly can minimize them. Many times you will be called upon to turn a spiritually dangerous situation into a teachable situation.

When your child is confused by a competing value system, seize the opportunity to explain why what the other person said or did is not in accordance with God's plan. After you have explained this fully to your child, ask her the leading question, "How do you feel about this? Would you feel right or wrong if you did . . . ?" Encouraging your child to express his judgment about an alternative value system is one of the ways you can take a running inventory of how she is accepting your value system.

Helping Your Child Build Self-Esteem

In keeping with the idea that the child who feels right acts right, you should help your child build his self-esteem during this stage. In the first few years of life a child's self-esteem is determined primarily by how he feels his parents feel about him, but in middle childhood his self-esteem is determined primarily by how he feels others feel about him. Dr. James Dobson in his book *Hide or Seek* (see Bibliography) has emphasized the important fact that physical attractiveness is one of the prime determinants of a child's self-esteem in today's society. Abilities in sports and in academics are the next yardsticks by which a child's self-worth is measured. A child who is considered the ugly duckling of the crowd, is uncoordinated in sports, and is not a whiz at academics is going to be troubled. The older child can take some consolation in the realization that he is loved by God, but the child at this age level is deeply affected by where he fits into his peer group.

If you have a child who is not obviously blessed with one or more of these "measures" of success, you should help him become involved in some activity in which he can succeed and gain recognition. Involvement and recognized success are vital to self-esteem development at this stage. Your ability to know him in the early years of his development really pays dividends now. Parents who truly know their children know their strong points and weak points; therefore, they are more able to create environments that allow their strong points to flourish, and they can protect them against attacks on their weak points. Whether it is sports, music, academics, gymnastics, or crafts, it is vital for every child to receive recognition that he is good at something. If you have difficulty recognizing what your child is good at, here is a tip: children are most likely to be interested in what they are most comfortable doing. Allow a child to pursue and develop his own interests; do not force him to excel in something you are interested in. If your child succeeds at something and receives recognition for her success, her self-esteem is so boosted that it is likely to carry over into success in other fields.

Let me suggest a social aid that is particularly useful for the shy child who has difficulty winning friends. Encourage your child to invite friends over to your home. Create an atmosphere that makes him feel comfortable bringing another child home to play and to stay overnight. His home becomes his castle. He is king of the hill automatically. He is more likely to play a better game if the game is played in his own ball park.

The Christian Edge

The incidence of problems with low self-esteem seems to be increasing in children, especially during the ages of preadolescence and adolescence. I believe one of the main reasons for this epidemic is that today's children are constantly being bombarded with the importance of physical attractiveness, athletic skills, and academic aptitudes. They are struggling constantly for acceptance in these three areas, and if they don't achieve it, they are really in trouble. Today a child has many more choices of direction and many more relationships outside the home that will either accept or reject him. In the past, the extended family was a child's primary relationship until he was ready to leave home toward the end of his teens. There was no doubt that he was strongly loved by nearly everyone around him. As parents seem to be giving up more and more of their responsibilities to institutions outside the home, children are required to measure up to more and more relationships outside the home, which I feel is the basis for the current diseases of low self-esteem.

Christian families have an edge on overcoming this self-esteem problem in children. If you rear your child in a Christ-centered family and strive to develop the inner circle of Christian commitment as described here, your Christian child can feel the constant love of God. Parents, drive home to your children the fact that Christ loves them; He gave up His life for them. This is a very difficult concept to convey because children are more influenced by the concrete relationships they see on earth, and God is still an abstraction to many children. However, the child between five and ten years of age can achieve this inner awareness of the love of God. Your child's acceptance of Jesus as his or her personal Savior will be the most lasting preventive medicine against diseases of low self-esteem. Most of the peer relationships a child will form throughout his life will be temporary and fleeting; the love relationship a child has with his parents and with his God will be a lasting relationship.

Helping Your Child Develop a Christian Conscience

Usually children younger than six are unable to discern right from wrong by the reasoning process. The young child learns what is right or wrong by the response he gets from a certain action. If he gets a desirable or pleasurable response to a certain action, such as when he obeys his parents, he is likely to continue this "right" behavior. If he gets an undesirable or even painful response from an action, he is less likely to repeat this "wrong" action. Because preschool children lack the insight into the basic rightness or wrongness of an action, it is very frustrating to try to reason with them. As a result, corrective discipline in the preschool child is usually in the form of chastening, consequences, or correction. As a child becomes older (usually around six years of age) he is more able to reason and, therefore, more able to be reasoned with. Parental discipline gradually shifts from the corrective measures of consequences and correction to the more guiding measures of counseling.

Ephesians 6:4 is the key verse for this focus on discipline methods. Let's look at this verse in three different translations:

> *Fathers, do not exasperate your children; instead, bring them up in the training and instruction of the Lord* (NIV).

> *And you, fathers, do not provoke your children to wrath, but bring them up in the training and admonition of the Lord* (NKJV).

> *And now a word to you parents. Don't keep on scolding and nagging your children, making them angry and resentful. Rather, bring them up with the loving discipline the Lord himself approves, with suggestions and godly advice* (TLB).

Paul summarized the entire parent-child discipline relationship in his epistle to the Ephesians:

> *Children, obey your parents in the Lord, for this is right. [Paul carried this thought a step further in Col. 3:20: Children, obey your parents in all things, for this is well pleasing to the Lord.] "Honor your father and mother," which is the first commandment with promise: "that it may be well with you and you may live long on the earth." And you, fathers, do not provoke your children to wrath, but bring them up in the training and admonition of the Lord (6:1–4).*

This scriptural passage says it all about discipline, especially discipline of the school-age child. Carefully analyze it to determine exactly the relationship God expects between parent and child.

"Children, obey your parents." This is a natural law between parents and their offspring. "In the Lord." Here God raised this natural law of obedience to a Christian level. Parents are God's representatives (their authority is from Him in the chain of command) so that a child's obeying his parents implies obedience to God and fear, or awed respect, of the Lord. You have learned earlier that how a child learns to obey and respect his parents at an early age often determines how he learns to obey and respect God at a later age. This probably presupposes that the child is walking with the Lord as much as possible at his particular age and level of understanding. "For this is right" ties in to the feeling of rightness I describe repeatedly throughout this book, a feeling a child receives when he is walking with his parents according to God's design for the parent-child relationship and walking with the Lord according to the commandments of the Lord.

"Honor your father and mother." Commentators on this verse feel God purposely used the word *honor* instead of *love* to elevate the significance of this commandment. The term *honor* implies love, respect, and obedience. "Which is the first commandment with promise." In the rest of the Ten Commandments God gave simple statements but did not attach any promise or reward if people keep the commandments. Here, Paul referred to the fact that God attached a promise to this commandment, and the promise is "that it may be well with you and you may live long on the earth." The fact that God made this promise to children who honor their fathers and mothers elevates the importance of the commandment. As I was reading this verse an awe-inspiring idea occurred to me: although this commandment is given directly to children, we can infer from this that parents must be honorable, and also be spiritual models for their children. If you fail to give your children models to honor, are you not also robbing them of the promise that God has given them for honoring their parents?

Paul completed this continuum of parent-child discipline by advising parents, especially fathers, to merit honor from their children: "And you, fathers, do not provoke your children to wrath." God here advised fathers not to be so unjust and harsh with their children that they cannot honor their parents and cannot obey their authority. Instead of angering or exasperating their children, fathers are advised to bring them up "in the training and admonition of the Lord." This sums up the Christian discipline God expects you to give your children. *Training* implies both instructive and corrective discipline, the two main forms of discipline we discussed in the discipline of the preschool child. *Admonition* implies counseling and is derived from the Greek word which means "training by word of encouragement, a reproof for the purpose of improvement." The last phrase of this verse, "of the Lord," is usually interpreted to mean such discipline and admonition that the Lord would exercise on His children.

Parents, use Ephesians 6:1–4 as your model for discipline. These verses are full of suggestions and insight into the parent-child relationship. Meditate on them and study them.

As your child becomes older and develops more insight for his or her actions, your discipline will shift from corrective discipline to admonition or counseling, although there is usually need for both instructive and corrective discipline at all ages. The elements in counseling the older child are similar to those mentioned earlier for chastening the younger child: confrontation, acceptance, confession, and healing or covenanting.

1. *Confrontation.* When your child does a certain undesirable action which, in your judgment, is not in accordance with the Christian values in your home, confront him or her with the action. A model for confrontation is given in Matthew 18:15, "If your brother sins against you, go and tell him his fault between you and him alone." It is in the confrontation part of counseling that a Christian parent has the edge. Only a parent who is honored by his child is truly able to counsel his child. Confrontation from the honored parent toward the obedient child is also done in a position of genuine love for that child. The love must flow from the parent during the confrontation and be felt by the child who receives the counsel. A confrontation done out of love should strengthen the child-parent relationship rather than weaken it. Christian confrontation means more than exposing the offender's deeds; it implies discerning his spiritual needs and restoring the offender.

2. *Acceptance.* After you confront your child in love, help him accept the confrontation. The older he becomes, the less willing he may be to accept confrontations. He may see them as direct attacks on his need for independence. If you have previously laid the foundation of respect for your parental authority and have given your child the "I care" message in the initial confrontation, your child may be more open to accept your counsel. One of the most frustrating situations in counseling your child is his tuning you out; he may be standing next to you, but his mind and spirit are somewhere else. If this happens, you may need to add physical touching (put your arm around his shoulder) and insist on eye-to-eye contact as you are talking to him.

3. *Confession.* Confrontation and acceptance should be followed by your child's confession of his wrongdoing. If your child feels threatened or regards confessing as a weakness, pray with him about the following scriptural passages, reminding him what Scripture says about confession: "If we say that we have no sin, we deceive ourselves, and the truth is not in us. If we confess our sins, He is faithful and just to forgive us our sins and to cleanse us from all unrighteousness" (1 John 1:8–9). James 5:16 reminds your child of the healing property of confession: "Confess your trespasses to one another, and pray for one another, that you may be healed. The effective, fervent prayer of a righteous man avails much." Proverbs 28:13 is a warning for those who do not confess: "He who covers his sins will not prosper, / But whoever confesses and forsakes them will have mercy."

Confession is one of the earliest helps toward conscience building. In order for your child to confess that he has done wrong, he must first make a value judgment that his action was indeed wrong. A child's conscience is like an internal computer, and each value judgment of right or wrong becomes a bit of information stored into his computer for later retrieval. If a parent lets wrongdoings go uncounseled, the child is deprived of a bit of information to store in his conscience. Each act of biblical counseling is stored in the child's memory for later retrieval. I am not suggesting that you confront your child for every little offense, for sooner or later the overcounseled child will turn off his receiver. If each act of counseling carries with it the "I care for you, my child" message, this tuning out is unlikely to happen. For the child "who always seems to be in trouble," biblical counseling will give the message that his parents will never give up on him.

Listen to your child. Don't be too quick to judge the rightness or wrongness of an action before you understand his position. The older the child, the more sensitive he is to attacks on his own position. Nothing frustrates a teenager more than the feeling that his counselor does not genuinely understand his position. A child does not expect his parents to agree with his position, but he does expect them to listen. The Bible gives us clear counseling about the importance of listening: "He who answers a matter before he hears it, It is folly and shame to him" (Prov. 18:13). James 1:19 is good counsel for parents about judging too quickly: "Let every man be swift to hear, slow to speak, slow to wrath."

4. *Covenanting.* The final step in the counseling process is covenanting, which implies a commitment on the part of the child not to repeat the wrong action and a commitment on the part of the parents to stand by the child to help him redirect future behavior.

Our eight-year-old son, Peter, is usually a well-disciplined child, for which we continually praise the Lord. One day, however, he lost his patience and in a defiant tone of voice yelled at his mother in one of those "I won't do it" situations. I immediately stepped in and took charge by calmly but firmly taking Peter by the arm, looking him squarely in the eye, and confronting him by saying, "Peter, you have lost control of yourself. I will not tolerate your talking to your mother that way for two reasons; she is your mother and I love you. Come on outside; we need to have a little talk about this."

I next elicited an acceptance and confession from Peter that he was wrong in showing this outburst of disrespect for his mother. In order to make a spiritual lesson out of this counseling, I brought in the commandment of "honor your mother" and discussed the meaning of the term *honor*. During the acceptance and confession of this wrongdoing, I brought out some of Peter's feelings that prompted his action. "Peter, why did you speak to your mother that way, and how did you feel about it after you lost your temper?" Peter then defended his position by pleading his case that he felt what his mother was asking him to do was unfair. I listened to Peter as he defended his position, and the more he talked, the more he began to realize he was indeed wrong. But he was still a bit uneasy about outwardly admitting it. While a child is struggling for a confession, it is important to convey a sensitive understanding of his position without being manipulated into agreeing with him.

Following the confession and acceptance that he was wrong, we made a covenant, "The next time you feel like being disrespectful to your mother, I want you to think immediately about what we talked about today. If it helps, go into another room where it is quiet and ask God to help you control your temper. Now, Peter, I am going to say something very important to you and I want you to understand it. I absolutely will not tolerate your shouting at your mother, and I am going to do whatever it takes to keep you from doing this. Do you understand me, Peter?" [Allow ample time for your child's response, and if you are not getting it, repeat your admonitions until he does respond.] "I am going to help you help yourself, Peter. God has given you to me, and some day I am going to have to answer to Him for how I disciplined you. I am going to keep riding herd on you when I see you losing your cool, Peter, because I love you, and I am your father." [You may bring in Heb. 12:6, "For whom the LORD loves He chastens."] "Now let's pray together and then go tell Mommy you are sorry for shouting at her." This episode ended with Peter's apologizing in the accepting arms of his mother.

A child's conscience is her inner policeman which tells her what she ought to do and what she ought *not* to do. One of your prime goals as a Christian parent is helping your child build a Christian conscience. Christian parents are evangelists in their own homes, proclaiming the gospel to their children and instilling into them a clear understanding of right and wrong based on both common sense and God's love. When their children are old enough to walk in faith, they should carry with them the inner voices of their teachings that will continue to direct them in the way they should go.

During the first few years of your parenting, the following fundamentals lay the foundation for the development of the Christian conscience, which begins sometime around the age of six.

1. Follow the early principles of Christian continuum parenting, which lead to a feeling of rightness within the child.
2. Develop the methods of effective Christian discipline, especially the positive reinforcement of desirable behavior and negative reinforcement of undesirable behavior.
3. Constantly encourage impulse control.
4. Use chastisement as your primary method of corrective discipline.
5. Give your child a clear understanding of what is right and what is wrong by counseling him and by deepening his knowledge of Scripture.

The imprint you have made upon your child during her early formative years now becomes a part of her. It is as if she takes you with her as she ventures into the world. After you have laid this foundation, you can build her conscience primarily by reinforcing all of the principles mentioned here as long as she remains under your influence. I cannot overemphasize the importance of keeping constant vigilance over your child in order to help her develop impulse control and in order to counsel her through undesirable behaviors.

In my opinion much of the literature of child psychology goes overboard in sacrificing principles of good discipline simply to avoid making the child feel "guilty." I do not share this philosophy. Throughout this book I have stressed that a child who feels right, acts right, and vice versa. If a child acts wrong, he needs to feel wrong. If he acts contrary to the commandments of either his parents or God, some little voice inside ought to say, "You should not have done that." As a result of this voice of conscience, the child does not feel right (in other words, he feels guilty). A child who is accustomed to an internal feeling of rightness does not like to feel wrong, and this feeling of guilt is an extra incentive for him not to repeat the actions that make him feel wrong. There is too much concern that guilt will damage a child's self-esteem. On the contrary, guilt feelings, if properly handled, actually can boost a child's self-esteem because these feelings serve to keep future behavior in check. However, excessive guilt is not part of God's design and needs to be dealt with and healed through Christian counseling.

At this point I would like to offer a word of encouragement to parents who are hurting because they feel that their child is in trouble and is not developing a conscience. Don't give up; hang tough. Every time your child goes off the track, pick him up and put him back on it. As I mentioned earlier, every time a child's undesirable action is redirected by a person whose authority is respected, you are moving one step closer to helping him develop his own discipline from within.

My dear Christian parents, an unfortunate reality is that many obstacles in the world compete with your child's conscience. It seems that God foresaw the difficulty parents would have in competing with these alternatives, and He promised you help through the Holy Spirit. Parents, daily ask God to fill your child with the Spirit, which is the ultimate directive of a Christian conscience. First Corinthians 2:15 states that the spiritual man (meaning the Spirit-filled man) makes judgments about all things. He has spiritual discernment or a Spirit-directed conscience.

Teaching Your Child to Be a Servant

John 13:4–17 tells the story of Jesus' washing His disciples' feet. Verses 14 and 15 state, "If I then, your Lord and Teacher, have washed your feet, you also ought to wash one another's feet. For I have given you an example, that you should do as I have done to you." This is explicit instruction from the Lord that Christians must learn to serve one another. The best way for this ministry of service to become part of a Christ-centered life is for it to begin at home. Of course, children experience the way they are served by their parents, and your attitude ought to be one of serving. But children need to learn it for themselves in the way they can care for one another and for older people in the family, parents and grandparents. Job lists can be presented in this way to bring a spiritual dimension to daily chores. Special needs of family members can be great opportunities for service—push great-grandmother in her wheelchair; spend time keeping baby amused so Mom can relax; make brother's bed to surprise him; and so on. The possibilities are endless, and so are the blessings.

CHAPTER 17

CHRISTIAN SCHOOLS

"**W**hen should my child start school?" is a common question parents ask. There are many studies on childhood education which yield conflicting advice, leaving parents who want the best for their children to flounder in a sea of uncertainty. In today's educated society, the school you choose for your child is a major influence on his or her self-esteem. Therefore, where and when to send your child to school are decisions that should be made with much prayer and consultation. I am not a professional educator, but as a pediatrician I see children daily who have been positively or negatively affected by their school experiences, and I will share with you what I have learned from my observations.

WHEN TO SEND YOUR CHILD TO SCHOOL

When deciding if your child is ready for school, ask yourself, "How will school contribute to my child's self-esteem?" Parents should program themselves to consider the effect of school on their children's self-esteem first and on their academic performance second. This may sound like heresy and a reversal of priorities to some parents who make education a top priority in their child's life. As a Christian father of seven children, I too make education a top priority, but I am much more concerned about how my children feel about themselves as individuals than about how they feel about themselves as students. I have observed that a child who feels good about himself or herself as a *person* has a much greater chance of performing well academically. On the other hand, a child with a low self-esteem is less likely to do well in school. In my experience, low self-esteem contributes more to learning problems than specific learning disabilities do.

In this section I will use the term *starting school* to mean "starting school outside the home." Parents who have followed the continuum concept of Christian parenting really started their child's education at his or her birth.

There are two opposing schools of thought about when children should start school. The first believes no child is too young for school. Japanese schools and writers have popularized the advantages of early childhood education. They base their philosophy on the fact that the most rapid development of a child's brain occurs in the first three years. Therefore, this is the period in which a child has the greatest capacity for learning. For example, a young child can easily become bilingual simply by being exposed to two languages simultaneously from early infancy.

Teachers who evaluate these early educational programs vary greatly in the conclusions they draw. Some teachers say children do not necessarily show a higher academic achievement if they begin their formal education early. Some teachers, especially music teachers, report that children pushed into learning before their time often exhibit burnout by the age of eight or ten when most children are beginning to learn music.

One of the best-known advocates of early childhood education was Dr. Maria Montessori who pointed out that a growing child has "sensitive periods" or stages in which his or her developing brain is most receptive to certain types of learning. I am a strong advocate of the Montessori philosophy of teaching because it is geared to a child-considered environment. A child educated by this method is encouraged to succeed at his or her own rate—*not in comparison with other children*. Work and play are synonymous; a child *learns how to learn,* and learning becomes a joy to the child's absorbent mind (a complete description of the advantages of the Montessori method is given in my first book, *Creative Parenting*). It is important to point out that Dr. Montessori developed her philosophy of education for underprivileged children who were neglected in their homes. There is nothing in the Montessori philosophy or method of education that cannot be done just as well by a caring parent in a child-considered environment at home. (See the Bibliography for suggested readings on early childhood education.)

An opposing school of thought to these "early starters proponents" is the growing home school movement which advocates teaching your child at home until he is about ten years of age. This movement was popularized by Dr. Raymond Moore in his book *School Can Wait*. The movement to bring education back into the home arose from the same concerns that brought birthing back into the home and babies back on to their mothers' breasts. These movements are a tip of the iceberg of a new breed of parents, especially mothers who are no longer content to allow strangers to tell them how to birth, feed, and educate their children. The main reason I am sympathetic with this tendency to bring education back into the home is parents are beginning to place a higher priority on a child's character traits and Christian values than on early reading, writing, and arithmetic.

Another reason for the growing popularity of home schools is the concept of peer dependency. I have mentioned that by middle childhood your child begins either to accept or reject your values. How many of the values he accepts or rejects depends on the degree of competition your child receives from alternative value systems. Parents who would like to teach their children at home have made the decision that the options of education in their community are unacceptable because the schools' value systems compete with that of the home. These parents also have the real concern that the child's self-esteem actually may be lowered by attending school outside the home, rather than increased. Parents who are considering delaying school entry usually have two major concerns: (1) "Will my child be socially deprived?" and (2) "Will he be academically behind?" Dr. Moore claims that his studies show children who are taught at home tend to become social leaders when they are eventually placed into school systems at the age of ten. They also tend to be academically ahead of those children taught in the usual school system, which is probably due to the fact that they receive much more one-on-one teaching than children in the average overcrowded classroom.

The age at which you send your child to school and whether or not you educate him at home depend upon *your total family situation*. What is important is that you base your decision upon whether school will be an extension of your family's Christian values and will contribute positively to your child's self-esteem. You do have choices in education just as you had choices in childbirth. Consider what is best for your individual child in your individual family situation regardless of what are the norms of the neighborhood. If, after much prayer and counsel, you have decided to teach your child at home and delay school entry, expect to get some flack from your friends and/or family. If you decide to set up your own home school, suggestions for various activities and curricula are offered in the books listed in the Bibliography under the section on "education."

There is an excellent book titled *Summer Children: Ready or Not for School* (see Bibliography) which explores the reasons why every child under the age of five years, six months should wait a year before starting kindergarten. The authors, one of whom has a doctorate in education, another a school psychologist, have done their own research and have reviewed extensive data from other researchers. They feel that what is now expected in kindergarten is simply too much, too soon, for too many, often resulting in learning disabilities as the child progresses through school.

If you decide to enroll your child in a kindergarten or first grade at the traditional age of five or six, your next decision is whether or not to send your child to a Christian school. Parents, I strongly encourage you to do so if the logistics of your community and your finances permit. Sending him or her to a Christian school can give your child a head start toward a Christ-centered life. However, you should be just as selective in choosing a Christian school as you were in choosing a pediatrician. While a Christian school is no guarantee that your child will be surrounded only with committed Christians, it simply lowers the risk that your child will be exposed to persons of significance who will compete with your Christian values.

I object to the philosophy of exposing a young child to a public school because it prepares him more for the real world. For what or for whom are you ultimately preparing your child, for the world or for Christ? Exposing your child to all of the options so that he can choose his own path is not only scripturally unsound (see Prov. 22:6), but in most cases, a child left to himself will not choose the path to Christ without some direction from persons of significance around him. Even in a Christian school your child will be exposed to varying levels of commitment to Christ. There will be deeply committed Christian children from deeply committed Christian homes who will minister to your child, and there also will be children from lukewarm Christian or non-Christian homes to whom your child can minister. For example, one day a nine-year-old attending a Christian school confided in me, "My mom and dad sent me to a Christian school hoping that some of the Christian teachings will rub off on me and just help to keep me out of trouble, but they really don't believe in Christ."

Another reason I object to public schools is the exposure your child will get to the religion of secular humanism and New Age philosophy. An excellent book on this subject is written by Johanna Michaelsen, *Like Lambs to the Slaughter* (Eugene, OR: Harvest House, 1989).

HOW TO GET THE MOST OUT OF YOUR CHILD'S SCHOOL

Choosing your child's school is only the beginning; you need to keep your finger on the pulse of the classroom. Don't leave all of your child's Christian teaching to his or her teachers. I strongly maintain that a child's primary Christian education must come from the home and must be complemented by the school and the church. Visit the classroom frequently. Become deeply acquainted with your child's teachers to the extent that you honestly know what their values are. The school is only as good as the parents behind it, and the standards of any school are only as high as the parents demand.

Show your child's teachers you value their profession and regard them as an extension of your home. A suggestion that will help you convey this is to invite each teacher at least once a year to your home for dinner and an evening discussion of how you value your child's education. Pray for your child's teachers asking God to give them the wisdom to discipline and nurture your child in the ways of the Lord. Convey to your child's teachers that you are praying for them. One of my greatest joys as a pediatrician is hearing the parents of one of my little patients tell me they are praying for me.

Keep your eyes on the classroom and be involved in the daily activity of the school. The attitude and atmosphere of a Christian school should carry out the admonition of the Lord in Deuteronomy 6:6–9 in which God tells us to saturate the child's environment with instructions about Himself. A Christian school that is living up to its name should encourage an atmosphere of love for one another, making its Christianity self-evident and a model for non-Christian schools.

A Christian school should focus more on how a child feels than how he learns. Unfortunately this is not always the case. In order to justify their existence, perhaps Christian schools have become defensive trying to compete with the public school system. Many Christian schools are so preoccupied with how their children compare academically with children in the public school system that they lose sight of the basic fact that all Christian psychologists teach: A Christian school should be more prepared than a public school to help the child who fails to learn, because he probably has a fragile self-esteem. Unfortunately, most Christian schools are not equipped to meet the needs of special children.

Have a proper attitude about homework. A typical complaint I hear from parents is, "My eight-year-old refuses to do his homework, and each night it becomes a hassle to get the work done. I am tired of getting on my child's back to complete his assignments." Because this is a common problem, let me offer an opinion about homework for the elementary school child. I believe children below grade six should not have homework or should have no more than twenty minutes of homework a night. I base this opinion upon the observation that homework is a negative experience for most young children. Also, I feel the main objective in sending a

411

child to school in the early elementary school years is to develop a positive attitude toward learning; a secondary objective is to impart information. The homework hassle often creates a poor attitude in the child about school in general, and this may interfere with his total educational experience.

Unless a child has a specific learning problem that requires remedial help at home, both teachers and parents should set up the educational schedule at school so that the child has enough time during the day to complete his assignments. If homework is assigned, it should be in the form of a creative project that the parents and child can do *together,* and it should not just be filling out a workbook or carrying the same routine classroom teaching into the home. Because of the demands of the educational system of children and the demanding work schedules of parents, there is diminishing time at home for spiritual training and for parents and children simply to enjoy each other. This is especially true for parents who work long hours, for single parents, and for parents who send their children to day care after school.

The two most common reasons children give me for not doing their homework are "It's boring" and "I'm tired." These are justifiable complaints. For example, if a child is learning about plants in school, his homework should not be reading and writing about plants (which should be done at school); his "homework" should be his own garden. In the later elementary school years a certain amount of homework discipline may be necessary to prepare the child for the increased demands of high school.

HOW TO GIVE YOUR CHILD AN EDUCATIONAL ADVANTAGE AT HOME

Home education for the young child practices the principles of Christian continuum parenting. Since parents who practice these parenting styles know their children better, they know intuitively how to educate them. The child who is a product of this level of parenting *feels right*. The child who feels right is more likely to learn right because this child is at peace with himself, and his mind is therefore more receptive to learning. As Hannah waited to wean Samuel from his home to his education at the temple, so must you decide when your child is ready to be weaned from the security of his family to an education outside the home. The concept of home learning I wish parents to appreciate is what I call the "educational continuum." A young child who is exposed at his own comfortable pace to an enriched environment of meaningful activities that enhance his God-given skills *feels more valuable as a person*. The more the absorbent mind of the preschool child is exposed to an environment of learning, the more he wants to learn. The more the outside world becomes interesting to him, the more he becomes interesting to himself and to others. The fulfilled child enjoys learning because he enjoys the good feeling that results from having his curiosity satisfied. Parents who have created a home environment that allows their child's individual talents to flourish at his own individual pace have given the child a real educational advantage. When the child begins a more formal schooling outside the home, gaining information will be given priority over attitudes about learning.

What about the child who is the product of a less stimulating environment? If her parents do not stimulate her curiosity and if she has no model to imitate at home, she is without direction. If her curiosity is not satisfied, she becomes less curious. If she is not challenged, she becomes less motivated. An example of an unstimulated child is the child who is parked for many hours each day in front of the television set to be pacified and entertained. This child resigns herself to a lower level of fulfillment. She becomes passive and uninteresting, to herself and to others. A dull and wasted child becomes an unhappy child. The result of this break in the natural educational continuum is that the child's desire to learn operates at a lower level. Because the unfulfilled child has not developed a joy of learning and a positive attitude toward learning in her earlier years, while her interest and curiosity were at their peaks, she is suddenly overwhelmed with information when she enters kindergarten or the first grade. She then may become less interested in learning, may rebel against the system, and is prey to being classified as having a learning disability. The following suggestions will help you stimulate your child's educational environment. (See Bibliography for further reading on this subject.)

1. *Select toys appropriate for your child's age and stage of development.* Choose toys that teach as well as amuse and that demonstrate the cause-and-effect relationship.

2. *Enrich your child's language studies.*   Studies have shown that *active language* input (the child is being directly talked with) is one of the prime determinants of personality and educational development.

3. *Read to your child.*   Children love to read *with* others. I emphasize *with* because children enjoy books well before they have the ability to read. When you are reading with your child, try to relate the pictures in the book with scenes in real life

413

so that your child's mind does not become confused by too much picture-book fantasy. Books are often the entree to what I call "expansion" learning. Use his books as an opener and expand on certain themes. For example, if your child points to a tree in the book, expand on his interest by taking him outside and showing him a variety of trees. You may even climb up into the tree or watch the birds in it. These short periods of spontaneous learning are often more meaningful than large blocks of planned teaching.

4. *Give your child a large pad of paper, a variety of crayons, and some rulers.* The blank sheet encourages more creativity than coloring predesigned figures. Arts and crafts stimulate a child's fine motor development, creativity, and sense of accomplishment. The young child loves recognition for his or her artistic creations even if it is a simple blob of watercolors on a sheet of paper. For this reason, display your child's primitive artwork around your house, such as on the refrigerator door. This is a real boost for your child's desire to create. She feels that Mommy and Daddy are interested in what she makes; what she makes must be pretty good; therefore, she must be pretty good.

5. *Build things with your child.*   Expensive "designer" toys are not necessary for giving your child an enriched environment. Children three years old and younger enjoy building things. A simple set of blocks and canister-like containers in your kitchen are good starter toys. Older children love to build with scrap lumber. I feel every family ought to have a pile of scrap lumber outside the house for a child to build with.

Let me share with you an example of how you can get a lot of mileage out of simple and inexpensive toys. One Christmas when our first two children were five and seven years old we decided to buck the commercial Christmas and not succumb to filling our home with a bunch of plastic toys. I went down to the local lumberyard and filled our station wagon with end cuts of scrap lumber. The night before Christmas I dumped the lumber on the basement floor with a couple of hammers and boxes of assorted nails. Our children still remember that pile of lumber as one of their best Christmas presents. It lasted several years and encouraged creative carpentry (just like Jesus' carpentry!).

6. *Music should play an important role in your child's education.*   Infants and children are usually very attentive to good music. Studies show that young children are usually more attentive to classical music, perhaps because the orderly nature of classical music fits in with the developing order in a child's mind. Make music lessons available for your young child and encourage him to develop a musical skill

414

according to his own interest and talent levels. Accomplishing a musical skill contributes greatly toward a child's total fulfillment. Music also provides a form of family entertainment. Some of the happiest families I have seen are families that sing and play music together for both enjoyment and fellowship. Music is also a beautiful vehicle with which the young child can learn to praise God.

7. *Use God's world of nature as one big textbook for your child.*   Your backyard, the woods, the beach, the mountains, the sky, the sun, the moon, the stars are all fascinating to a child. Tiny bugs and insects are also interesting because children are fascinated with smallness and minute detail. Plant a little garden with your child so that he can see what God allows to develop from a tiny seed nourished in fertile soil. Not only do gardens fulfill a child's sense of accomplishment and of reward for efforts, but they also provide a natural opportunity for you to discuss God's creation and the origins of life.

8. *Provide opportunities for your child to develop awareness of his or her body.* Gymnastics, sports, and artistic dance such as ballet will help your child develop and appreciate the body God has designed for him or her.

These suggestions are just a few of the many activities that *fulfill* a child. I have strong feelings that parents should help their child develop his talents and creativity so that he is able to stimulate, satisfy, and amuse himself *from within*. The fulfilled child is able to derive satisfaction and avoid boredom by reading a book, creating an art or craft, playing a musical instrument, devising a game, or engaging in an exchange of humor (humor plays a very important part in the educational development of a child). One of the reasons parents should strive to help their child be fulfilled from within is that today's child is surrounded by a world of instant turn-ons and gratification from the use of material things. Many children become preoccupied with passively entertaining themselves and feel they need to be constantly amused or they will get bored. A child who needs to be entertained passively or who needs a material gadget for fulfillment is susceptible to being unfulfilled as an adult.

WHAT ABOUT THE CHILD WHO FAILS TO LEARN?

The term *learning disability* is a relative term. The American educational system grades children on a bell-shaped curve, and most children in the middle of this curve can function adequately within the system. However, children at either end of this curve may have great difficulty learning within the system *as compared* to the other children. The current system of school entry and grade progression is based upon a child's age rather than his mental maturity. About 10 percent of grade school children experience varying degrees of difficulty learning all the subjects according to the methods used in the present system. Children who learn within the present system have "learning abilities"; those who do not learn within the present system are labeled as having "learning disabilities." Not only does a child with this label not measure up to the expectations of the educational system into which he or she has been placed but, what is more important, the child does not learn *as compared to the other children*. Continued exposure of a fragile child to comparison gradually leads to diseases of low self-esteem. A child with a disability in academic performances may eventually have an even greater "disability" in his or her self-esteem. Because a child's academic performance and his self-esteem are so intimately related, it is often difficult to determine whether how a child learns is a result of how he feels or whether how he feels is a result of how he learns.

Intuitive parents and teachers can and should be alert to a child's maladjustment to school. If you have met your child's teachers and have kept abreast of her classroom situation, you are likely to foresee her reaction to this new environment. Knowing your child's teachers, or parent substitutes, enables them to know your child better.

The high-need child is indeed a candidate for developing school problems. Just as the high-need child needs above-average parenting, he also needs above-average schooling. Parents who have trained this high-need child according to principles of Christian attachment parenting have developed a wider acceptance of his behavior. Some of these high-need children do not indicate their temperaments until they enter school, primarily because a school has a narrower range of acceptance than the home and a child is made to conform to a system that does not know him. Also, the high-need child receives more one-to-one input from his parents at home.

If you have identified your child as a high-need child, select a school that is sensitive to his individual needs. The mismatch between child and school is one of the most common causes of learning disabilities. This mismatch should be called a "teaching disability" rather than a "learning disability." Many children designated as having learning disabilities are actually brilliant children who learn quickly and become bored by the classroom situation. Because they are labeled "dumb," they feel dumb and eventually act dumb. Children are very quick to feel and act according to the labels they perceive the persons of significance around them have given them.

There are specific signs of impending school problems. Boredom is usually the earliest sign. A child becomes bored with himself and bored with his performance at school. Another sign is diminishing enthusiasm. While it is unrealistic to expect a child to jump out of bed and rush off to school without an occasional grumble, most of the time your child has some spark of enthusiasm about going to school. Most children have an inborn desire to learn. If presented properly, learning should be enjoyed by most children most of the time.

Watch for the slow adjuster. Most children are very resilient and adaptable to the transition from home to school or from one grade to another. However, some children do not adjust to change easily and need a higher level of sensitivity during these transitional periods. This is why most behavioral problems appear at the transition from one developmental or educational stage to another. The high-need child often has trouble being compliant.

School phobias are another sign of impending school problems. If your child presents an increasing number of vague physical complaints that occur with regularity the night or morning before school and subside on weekends and holidays, suspect that a fear of leaving home or attending school or both may be the underlying causes of these physical complaints.

Behavioral problems are often related to poor school performance. Children are generally very vulnerable to any attacks on their self-esteem and protect themselves at all costs. A child who does not receive strokes from academic performance usually will seek alternative methods of recognition in school, such as being the class clown. Undesirable behavior in the classroom often carries over into undesirable behavior at home.

A step-by-step approach to helping your child who fails to learn is discussed in detail in my book *Creative Parenting*. I cannot overemphasize the importance of getting at the root of poor school performance. I would have to rate the diagnosis of school problems as the most mismanaged problem of childhood. In my experience, most school problems ultimately are traced back to diseases of self-esteem. Some children do indeed have specific learning disabilities that prevent them from learning in the way most children are able to learn; however, today's school system is more ready to diagnose and treat these problems.

Exercise much prayer and consultation to get at the source of your child's learning problem. Your main "treatment" is to focus more on how she feels rather than on how she learns. Rather than devoting your attention to activities that relate directly to your child's learning, concentrate on having *fun* with your child. Direct most of your energy toward activities that contribute to her general self-esteem with the view that any improvement in her sense of well-being is likely to carry over in her ability to learn.

CHAPTER 18

SEXUALITY EDUCATION FOR THE CHRISTIAN CHILD

"When do I start talking to my child about sex?" is a common question parents ask. I reply, "You begin giving sexual messages to your child the minute he or she is born." In this section, I will use the term *sexuality* which implies not only the physical aspects of sex education but also the emotions and attitudes accompanying these physical changes.

MODELING IS THE FIRST STEP IN SEXUALITY EDUCATION

The attachment philosophy of child care I have advocated throughout this book is the earliest form of sexuality education. The principles of Christian continuum parenting imply that you are a touching family. Early in your child's life you convey a very special sexual message to him, "We love to *touch you;* you are a special person." This results in a feeling of rightness. It is vitally important that a child feel right about himself or herself as a *person* in order to feel right as a "he" or a "she." If you have modeled touching and loving your child, he is more likely to grow into a touching, loving person. The ability to give and receive affection is one of the greatest gifts you can encourage in your child.

The display of affection between husband and wife is another form of sexuality modeling. Watching Mom and Dad embrace is especially important for the older child. This conveys a feeling of stability within the family in a world where the child sees families breaking apart all around him. Also encourage the show of affection between siblings. Siblings are not usually running over with affection toward each other, and parents usually have to foster an attitude of closeness between them. Love for others is the hallmark of a Christian. Young children cannot see the feelings of love between their parents, but they can see their actions and draw their own conclusions. Become a hugs-and-kisses family.

BASIC PRINCIPLES IN SEXUALITY EDUCATION

Genital Awareness

Very early in infancy a child begins the normal and healthy exploration of body parts beginning with thumb sucking and finger play. Genital awareness usually begins sometime in a child's second year, and the initial pulling and poking progresses to awareness of genital sensitivity and the pleasure of self-stimulation. How you react the first time you see your little boy pulling on his penis or your little girl poking into her vagina is probably one of the earliest sexuality messages you convey to your child about his or her genitalia. It is important that a child not perceive his genitalia as "bad." Genitals are part of him or her and should not be called "bad body parts." Genital play does not betray any underlying psychological disturbance any more than thumb sucking does. In fact, a child's ability to use his or her own body parts for self-stimulation is considered by some researchers as evidence of his or her basic security. Children raised in institutions often show less exploration and satisfaction with their own body parts than children raised in the secure home environment.

Your attitude toward toilet training is the next sexuality message you convey to your child. During toilet training, a child develops increased awareness of genital sensation and of the function of his body parts. Your attitude toward toilet training must communicate to your child that what these body parts do is basically good.

Gender Identity

Gender identity is usually understood by age three when children begin to call each other "boys" and "girls." Little girls and boys become aware that they look different and urinate differently. Little girls may wonder where their urine comes from since they do not have penises. Correct this confusion by showing your little girl where the urine comes from, emphasizing that she has the counterpart of a penis so she will not be preoccupied with not having one. Your little boy may wonder why girls do not have penises and he may wonder if he will lose his penis. Proper instruction can certainly minimize this confusion. If you find your child developing confusion and embarrassment, correct this immediately. It is important that this developing sexual person be proud of the body he or she has been given, and it is important that he or she respect the privacy of another person's sexuality. The concept of not touching another child's private areas can be understood by the age of four.

Parents may contribute to genital confusion by using inappropriate terms for genitalia. Not only are these slang terms confusing to your child, but they also convey a subtle message that you are embarrassed about these body parts. The terms *penis, scrotum, vagina,* and *vulva* can be understood by a three-year-old.

Appropriate gender behavior is usually apparent by age three. Boys are generally more aggressive and enjoy rougher play than girls at this age. How much of this gender behavior is an inborn genetic difference and how much is acquired by parental influence are interesting matters. Certainly, both genetic and cultural influences contribute to early gender identity. It is a known fact that girl infants are gentled more than boy infants. Parents are more likely to roughhouse with boys and play more quietly with girls. In my office, I often fall into this gender trap with my patients by eliciting a hug and a kiss from a little girl and a handshake or a "give me five" from a little boy. I remember my own ridiculous reaction the first time I saw my three-year-old son playing with a doll; fortunately, my wife's wisdom saved the doll from immediately being substituted with a football. These parental-play instincts are probably healthy. In my opinion, unisex attitudes are unhealthy, unchristian, and unscriptural (Eph. 5:22–25). I do believe that programming aggressive behavior in boys may contribute to the much higher incidence of their behavioral problems. The sexes should be gentled equally, and the show of affection and tenderness should be encouraged as equally as the manifestation of assertiveness and physical activity.

It is normal for four-year-old children to shift from one sex role to the other, alternating between dolls and footballs. For some children sex role adaptation is uneasy and prolonged, and they are labeled "tomboys" or "sissies." It is healthy for a child to adapt to his or her sexual role at his or her own pace.

Proper role modeling can help a child seek his appropriate gender behavior. Confusion and dissatisfaction with gender roles is a common cause of sexuality adjustment problems in the older child and adult. Parents, remember you are bringing up someone else's future mate. It isn't fair to leave your child's sexuality education to your son's future wife or to your daughter's future husband.

Young children are quick to perceive the different roles played by mothers and fathers. Although role definitions are less distinct in today's society, I feel it is important to give your children sexual role models. Children often will parent as they were parented. For example, women are likely to breastfeed if they were breastfed. One woman explained why she was still nursing her toddler, "My mother breastfed me until I was two years old."

Women are also more likely to pursue careers outside the home if their mothers did. This trend seems to be balanced by earlier and greater father involvement in infant care. Although the traditional role models of mommies having babies and daddies working are probably foremost in a child's mind, it is important for him to see his father heavily involved in caring for his siblings and his mother. It is unrealistic for a young boy to perceive his father as someone who is always outside the home. One man confided to me, "My image of my father when I was a young boy was getting up in the morning and looking out the window and seeing my father's back and his briefcase as he left for work."

Parents, do not minimize the memories that your child can have of his early sexuality experiences. Most children can remember pleasant experiences from as early as three years of age. What is disturbing is that children can remember often traumatic and unpleasant experiences from an even earlier age.

Where Babies Come From

Sometime at the age of four or five your child may raise the long-anticipated question, "Where do babies come from?" You are now called upon to begin your child's formal sexuality education. The following suggestions will help you begin to teach your child about the miracle of birth.

Expose your child to the births of animals. For example, encourage your child to watch the family pet give birth to her offspring. This is the most natural way to communicate that babies come from inside mommies.

Expose your child to the birth of a sibling. Unfortunately, in our society the mother is usually separated from the rest of her children when she is giving birth. One of the most eye-opening events in our family was the birth of our fifth child which was attended by all our children, aged four to fifteen. Our four-year-old daughter, who had been prepared and told what to expect, was keenly interested in our family event, and at no time did she seem squeamish or upset. Taking part in and witnessing her mother give birth to her sister certainly conveyed a more realistic view of birth than the usual fairy tales about storks. I strongly encourage parents to allow their children to witness the births of their own brothers and sisters and recommend *Children at Birth* by Marjie Hathaway and Jay Hathaway (Academy Publications, 1978) or *Birth Through Children's Eyes* by Sandra Van Dam Anderson and Penny Simkin (Seattle, WA: Pennypress, 1981) for reading material on this subject.

Watch for openers. Children do not usually ask directly, "Where do babies come from?" They are more likely to give you an opener by looking curiously at a pregnant woman or by showing interest in the new baby a friend's mommy just brought home.

Use correct terms and facts. Babies come from Mommy's uterus, not from her tummy. Use books and visual aids to enhance your instruction but not to substitute it. Suggested books to teach the concept of birth to four- to six-year-olds are *How Babies Are Made* by Andrew C. Andry and Stephen Schepp (Time-Life Books, 1979) and *Being Born* by Sheila Kitzinger (New York: Putnam, 1986). For the older child, do not simply give him a book and ask him to read about sex. Be sure you have read the book yourself to see that both the sexual facts and the sexual *values* meet the standards you have set within your own family. If you do suggest that your child read a certain book, explain why you are suggesting it and invite him to discuss it with you after he has read it.

Give short, simple answers to your child's questions. Give him just as much information as he asks for and satisfy his curiosity at his own pace. Too much detail confuses the young child. Young children think in the concrete, not in the abstract, and are prone to misinterpret statements. *Be sure you understand what your child is asking.* Parents can misinterpret their children's questions easily. This is best illustrated by an old story in which a five-year-old boy asked his daddy at the dinner table, "Daddy, where did I come from?" In response to this dreaded question, both mother and father struggled uncomfortably through a long, involved, and overly anatomical description of the birth process. The five-year-old, by this time yawning and losing interest, replied, "Johnny next door came from Ohio, and I wanted to know where I came from."

After a child understands that a baby comes from inside Mommy, the next logical question will be, "How did the baby get there?" The age at which children show interest in the details of sexual intercourse varies from four to eight years old.

Girls seem to understand the process earlier than boys because they understand what a vagina is. When describing the functions of sperm, egg, testicle, ovary, and uterus, it is best either to draw pictures or use books with simple illustrations. The process of intercourse is one part of sexuality education in which the "solid food is for the mature" advice should prevail. Use wisdom and discretion to teach your child according to his or her level of interest and understanding. Being able to present sexuality to your child comfortably and accurately has the fringe benefit of enabling broad communication with him or her in the future. It conveys to your child that you are an open, accurate, and willing resource of information, and it sets the stage for a more meaningful dialogue by the time your child is a teenager. It is better for children to get proper sexuality education from their parents than to get patchy and often inaccurate information from their peers. Sexuality education is too valuable to be entrusted to the playground.

Dirty Words

Children learn very early that certain words have shock value to adults. Young children often use slang words not because of the meaning these words have but for the reaction they get. A four-year-old who utters a four-letter word is guaranteed to stop everyone around him in his tracks. Obscene language and swear words are the undesirable part of a child's vocabulary to which he is naturally going to be exposed in his quest for the accepted norms of society. The role of Christian parents is to lay down *beyond any doubt* the accepted norms within the Christian household and to make clear that any language outside those norms absolutely will not be tolerated. This approach implies that parents model for their child language that is acceptable. If a child hears a parent use a "dirty" word or a swear word, then this word falls into the norm. Explain *why* a certain word is not acceptable so your child will understand why it is offensive to you and to others. Using the name of God in vain certainly should not be tolerated within any Christian household, and your child should be taught very early that this commandment is directly from the Lord.

SEXUALITY EDUCATION IN MIDDLE CHILDHOOD

The period of middle childhood is often described as a time of "normal homosexuality." Boys tend to stick with boys and girls stick with girls, and gender lines are seldom crossed between the ages of eight and ten. Comparing genitals between members of the same sex is common at this age, especially among boys: "I'll show you mine if you show me yours." This period is also called a "latent" or "dormant" period because in many children there seems to be a decrease in the rate of growth and in sexual interest. While this may be a latent period for your child, it should not be a latent period for you. This is an important time for providing correct sexual information and for forming sexual attitudes for adolescent sexuality. This is the age when you are competing with the sex education your child gets outside the home. Being comfortable with and interested in presenting proper sexuality education to your child at this age avoids the "blind leading the blind" approach of street-corner sex education. Children often become very private about their bodies at this age and become increasingly uncomfortable with parental nudity. When you sense these feelings of modesty, develop discretion about your personal nudity.

Most children in the middle childhood and adolescent ages are just as uncomfortable being approached with sexuality education as their parents are uncomfortable approaching them. For this reason, it is important to create the proper setting for sexuality education. Don't suddenly pick a night and get it over with by announcing, "Tonight we are going to talk about sex." Children are very mood dependent when it comes to most forms of learning, especially learning about sex. When your child gives you a cue that he is interested and receptive to some meaningful parent-child dialogue about the topic, plan a special outing that allows you and your child to communicate freely. If you already have created a series of these special times together, your child may give you a few openers of his own.

SEXUALITY EDUCATION IN SCHOOL

Sex education in school is a controversy that faces most parents when their children are about ten years old. Parents certainly have a right to know who is teaching their children what and when, and the school needs to be sensitive to the parents' feelings. I always have maintained that a school is only as good as the parents behind it. The main problem with sex education is that it is impossible to separate sexual facts from sexual values. Even in Christian schools, the value systems of parents vary greatly; therefore, it is hard to agree on a curriculum of sex education in a particular school. Opponents of sex education in schools feel that information fosters interest and encourages more sexual activity. They also legitimately fear that their own values will be undermined. Advocates of sex education in schools suggest that at least adolescents be given a better understanding of sexuality in order to make more responsible decisions about their own sexual behavior.

The real facts are that today's adolescents are more sexually active than previous generations were, but their sexuality education is no better. However, I am uncomfortable with the attitude that the responsibility to correct this deficiency belongs to the school. Unfortunately, like so many other government programs, the school must assume responsibility because many parents are not doing their job at home. Ideally, the information and attitudes of sexuality education should be taught and lived at home. The school should be an extension of this home education by providing a dimension the home cannot provide, such as group discussion. Group discussion about adolescent sexuality is the main benefit of sexuality education in the schools. Perhaps this discussion on sexuality education would be presented better at your church than at your school. Since a developed and agreed upon set of sexual values is often the number one controversy, parents are more likely to agree upon a set curriculum and values within their church than within a school, which usually has a wider range of value systems.

The following suggestions can help the home, the church, and the school work together to impart not only accurate sexual information but, more importantly, Christian attitudes about sexuality.

Keep your eye on the classroom. Be involved in selecting the curriculum and be sure you know the basic values of the person or persons who will be teaching the class. It is amazing that absolutely damaging instruction can get into our school systems. I remember reviewing a proposed curriculum for sex education for a high school. In the section on birth control, abortion was presented as an accepted norm and abstinence was presented way down on the list of birth control. Parents ought to examine thoroughly all parts of the curriculum down to every chapter and verse. If a course doesn't meet your moral standards, you can refuse to allow your child to attend.

Sexuality education should be presented as part of a general biology course, such as "how the body works," and should not be marketed as a sex education course.

Sexuality education never should be lumped with discussions of alcohol and drug abuse. Sexuality is a normal, healthy part of Christian living; drugs and alcohol are not.

Group discussions should be encouraged. General topics focusing mostly on the anatomy and physiology of the reproductive organs may be taught with boys and girls together in a class, and with group discussions encouraged. More personal elements of sex education such as menstruation, hygiene, and wet dreams are taught more comfortably in separate classes of boys and girls.

Schools need to reject the message that everybody is sexually active. Just at the age when an adolescent is attempting to formulate his own values and make decisions, some sex education courses send him mixed messages: premarital sex is not advised but everybody is doing it. This may indeed be true in many schools, but in many schools and homes traditional Christian values are still adhered to and everybody is *not* doing it. Schools should make a special effort to present premarital abstinence as the norm.

Parents, pray and be vigilant, keeping your finger on the pulse of the classroom. If you blindly turn your child over to peer dependency and the value system that prevails in his or her school, you run the risk of creating an adolescent with a low sexual self-esteem. Sexuality education should encourage the development of a sexually informed and sexually responsible adolescent whose emotions are under the control of his or her God-fearing Christian values. If your child is in a public school that violates your values, take an active part in changing the sex education course. (See Bibliography for suggested reading on this subject.)

DATING AND RELATING

"When should I allow my teenager to date?" is another common question from parents. Because dating readiness varies among teenagers, I will offer some general suggestions that will help you decide when your teenager should be allowed to date. It is tempting to follow the crowd to avoid being called old-fashioned, but, parents, cling to your Christian beliefs; the crowd is not going in the right direction. I would suggest you not be old-fashioned if the "new fashion" were working, but it isn't.

Teenagers are more sexually assertive and active than ever before. Diseases of sexual irresponsibility are rampant: teen pregnancy, venereal disease, and divorce. Men and women are remaining single longer than ever before. In many cultures, men and women date late and marry early; in this culture they date early and marry late. I feel God did not design males and females to be in close contact in the single state for so long. Since today's educational and economic systems encourage marrying later, it stands to reason that there should be some modification of the present unrestricted dating practices, certainly in Christian homes. Parents, in today's sexual climate, without God's help, it is totally unrealistic to expect teenagers who are going steady to adhere to sexual abstinence. God did promise He would not let people be tempted beyond what they can handle and that He would provide a way out in order that they can stand up under temptation (see 1 Cor. 10:13). He also said to "flee sexual immorality" (1 Cor. 6:18). It is on these foregoing considerations that I base the following suggestions for Christian dating practices.

What Is a Date?

To many parents, the term *date* is one of those four-letter words that remind them of the social and sexual maturity of their adolescents. It implies some sort of contract, an agreement between two members of the opposite sex to be together for a certain occasion. There is a certain "I'm yours" commitment to the term *date*. In Christian teaching, dating is considered a preparatory stage for mate selection. The young teenager may not have such a sophisticated view of dating.

Mixed-group activities, particularly church group activities, should be encouraged for children before their teenage years. Properly chaperoned mixed parties encourage boys and girls to enjoy one another as individuals before the attraction between the sexes is physical. These mixed-group activities encourage children to learn how to relate to both sexes in the "comfort in numbers" setting.

The next stage of boy-girl activities is *group dating*, in which boys and girls in their early teens attend properly chaperoned activities as couples. This is the initial form of dating. Depending on the individual circumstances, group dating should be a healthy stage of sexual maturity for the young adolescent. Group dating brings the adolescent out of himself or herself and should have a maturing effect on the otherwise egocentric teenager. This may be the first time the adolescent acknowledges any other person to be as important as himself. The next stage of dating is *single dating*, which today usually means a boy and a girl and a car. This is a level of dating that is of most concern to parents. The following discussion pertains to single dating.

When Should My Teenager Be Allowed to Date?

The age of dating readiness is as variable as the age of puberty. The desire to date usually parallels the puberty level of the adolescent and his or her temperament. One of our boys showed interest in dating at thirteen, another at seventeen. The next variable is the responsibility level of the teenager. Some are more responsible at an earlier age than others. Impulse control is another variable. A teenager who has proven he is able to control his impulses in nonsexual matters is more likely to be able to control his impulses in sexual matters. What is the level of Christian conscience development in your teenager? Dating is a higher step on the privilege-responsibility ratio. These are the reasons dating readiness cannot be defined absolutely by age alone.

Parents, do not be reluctant to assert your authority on permission to date. This is one of the final steps in the long continuum of discipline and is another example of where your God-given authority is on the line. Teenagers intuitively expect parents to act as their authority and wisdom in giving permission to date. The following is a common scenario. Mary is a freshman in high school. Tom, a senior, invites her out on a single date. Mary does not feel ready but feels peer pressure to begin dating. Mary consults her dad, who says no. Mary then says to Tom, "Sorry, my dad won't let me date yet." Dad is the scapegoat, and Mary is off the hook. Mary later confides in her dad, "Thanks, Dad, I really didn't want to go anyway." Like so many stages in childhood discipline, the child (in this case, the teenager) expects the parent to assume the authority in circumstances when he cannot say no himself.

Parents, don't be too quick to allow your teenager to fling himself or herself into the habit of constant dating in which all of the adolescent's time is spent with members of the opposite sex. Healthy dating should have a positive effect on the adolescent's self-esteem. However, in the most healthy progression of sexuality development, it is vitally important for an adolescent to be comfortable relating to members of the *same* sex in order to develop a healthy relationship with the opposite sex.

What about Going Steady?

This level of dating is the accepted dating style in most high schools. Going steady is a real boost for a teenager's self-esteem. Most of these going-steady infatuations are short-lived and many teenagers will go steady many times during their high school and college years.

If at all possible, encourage your teenager to date around. Many teenagers go steady because they are more interested in the security of a relationship than they are interested in their dates as people. This level of commitment deprives a teenager of the ability to mature his or her own personality by learning to relate to many members of the opposite sex. It is also unrealistic to expect a teenage boy and girl who are constantly together to continue sexual abstinence very long.

There is a healthy progression in a relationship between the two sexes: (1) the personal level, (2) the affectionate level, and (3) the physical level. It is important for an adolescent to experience a variety of personal and affectionate levels, but going steady encourages his dating relationship to be spent at the physical level. If you sense that a steady dating relationship is developing for your teenager, discuss it with him in a dialogue that is caring and wise.

What about Predating Counseling?

Discussing dating with your teenager follows the same formula as administering any other disciplinary action with your child; you may not agree with each other but you need to understand where each other is coming from. Approach your teenager with love, and use Scripture as the basis for your discussion. To make a case for sexual purity, cite 1 Corinthians 6:12–13, Ephesians 6:13, and Romans 8:9. Your teenager may not protect himself with the values he grew up with, but it is important he feels you will remain his friend in the face of disappointment.

What about Dating a Non-Christian?

The Bible takes a clear stand on the issue of relationships with non-Christians: "Do not be unequally yoked together with unbelievers. . . . what part has a believer with an unbeliever?" (2 Cor. 6:14–15). Christian dating practices should contribute to the spiritual growth of both parties. I advise parents not to allow their teenager to date anyone who is not growing as a Christian. The concept of "missionary dating" (dating to bring someone to Christ) is a potentially dangerous practice and parents ought to discourage it. Most teenagers are still growing as Christians themselves and do not have the spiritual control to overcome their sexual impulses. Dating another Christian is certainly no guarantee of sexual purity, but it does add one more important restriction to the teenager's new sexuality. Since dating is a prelude to marriage and since marriage to a nonbeliever is an extremely foolish and risky proposition, eliminate this possibility by urging your teenager to date only Christians.

Christian parents should impress upon their dating teenagers the responsibility they have for influencing the sexual maturity of their dates. The teenage boy has the responsibility for influencing how the teenage girl views men in general, and the teenage girl influences how the teenage boy perceives women.

Teenage Sexuality

Teen pregnancy is one of today's most common medical problems, and it is currently reaching epidemic proportions, even among Christian teenagers. In the past few years in the United States, at least one million teenage girls have become pregnant each year.

Teenagers are sexually active and become pregnant for many reasons. Some teenagers do not fully understand their sexuality and deny that they are candidates for pregnancy. Their sexuality education often has been inadequate and their precautions ineffective. Sexually active teenagers do not use contraceptives reliably. They may feel that contraceptives delete the spontaneity of sex, or are conscience-pricking reminders that they are sexually active—or they simply forget to use them. In my experience, one common characteristic underlies many teen pregnancies—a poor self-image. The teenage girl who has a poor self-image may feel pregnancy proves her femininity and fulfills a need. A teenager may also form a sexual alliance to fill a void in his or her life because of lack of success or identification at home or at school. A teenage girl may become sexually active following a family divorce or the death of her father, or if she has a chronic medical illness, she may use pregnancy as proof of her health.

Attachment parenting can bolster your teen's self-image and can reinforce the values he has learned in your home, thereby minimizing the risk of teen pregnancy, but other preventive measures are available to you. Involve your teenager in extra-curricular activities. A teenager who is involved in school activities, sports, and church activities is less likely to seek sexual activities as a means of gratification. Also, be aware of the message your teenager receives from the secular world. For example, the health department provides booklets from Planned Parenthood entitled *Eight Popular Ways for Having Intercourse . . . That Most Smart Teenagers Would Use, The Perils of Puberty,* and *So You Don't Want To Be a Sex Object.* A proper sexuality education is the best way to prevent your teenager's being influenced by organizations such as Planned Parenthood.

Another "parental contraceptive" is to insist on Christian dating practices. The sexual urges of teenagers have not changed throughout the past generations. They have always had these urges which were designed by God. What has changed is that today's teenagers are surrounded by many models and persons of significance who encourage them to become sexually active. Because the competition for children's values is increasing, your responsibility to teach them Christian values must also increase. If they do not get these values at home, they are vulnerable to the shallow values of the secular world. Get your child used to a *higher standard of loving* inside his home so he will expect the same away from home. However, dating a Christian is certainly no guarantee that your young person will not be tempted or even pressured to be sexually active. It is important that you convey the importance of chastity in the life plan God has for your child. In our family we discuss this openly and use teachable moments to reinforce our values, having a feel for the pulse of our teen's social life. A good book we have used with our older teens is Josh McDowell's *Why Wait?* (see Bibliography).

Contraceptives

Whether or not to prescribe contraceptives for a sexually active teenager is a difficult dilemma for a physician. Prescribing contraceptives implies he or she is condoning a sinful act. On the other hand, an unprotected sexually active teenager most likely will become pregnant. There is only one prescription available to the Christian physician: I believe Christian doctors should share the duty of counseling teenagers to exercise sexual purity.

Teenage Pregnancy

Premarital pregnancy should bring out the best in Christian love between parents and their child. If you are presented with this family crisis, convey to your son or daughter, "We care and we are going to help." You can accept your teenager as a person who is in trouble and needs help without condoning his or her actions. Your teen probably feels guilty enough and is embarrassed to talk to you. A concerned third party, such as your pastor or your physician, can bring you together in this time of need.

Your teenager is now faced with several difficult decisions. As a Christian doctor, I advise teenagers to carry their babies to term and insist that they have adequate medical care during their pregnancies. Teenagers who receive good prenatal care are no more susceptible to medical problems during pregnancy than any other age group, but the danger of teenage pregnancy has been popularized because most teenagers do not have proper prenatal care and are more likely to suffer obstetrical complications.

The teenage couple who carry a baby to term must decide whether to raise the baby or give it up for adoption. Although this decision is very difficult, *it is their decision to make alone.* The great majority of forced teenage marriages end in divorce; there is a high incidence of child abuse among the children of teenage parents; teen parents usually deprive themselves of further education and are relegated to the status of welfare roles. My heart goes out to the pregnant teenage girl who, following much prayer and consultation, decides to raise her baby alone. I feel the church should extend the same Christian caring to this mother and child that they extend to widows and orphans.

Teenage Abortion

The third option that is often presented to your pregnant teenager is that of abortion. This option is not open to a Christian teenager. Because abortion is commonly presented by the humanistic social planners, I feel it is necessary to go into some detail in presenting the Christian attitude toward abortion. Because of the impact of current abortion laws on today's youth, I have chosen to face this problem head-on as a concerned Christian physician and parent rather than evade the subject because it is too "touchy" to be presented in a baby book. Abortion is not a religious issue, it is a human issue that has far-reaching implications on the physical and moral development of today's youth. Whether your personal opinion is pro-life or pro-abortion, consider the following Christian principles in deciding that abortion should not be available to the pregnant teenager.

The basic concerns I have about abortion are *the act* and *the attitude* of abortion. The act of deliberately aborting a fetus, no matter how you rationalize it, is the act of taking a human life. Since taking a human life is wrong, the obvious solution to this dilemma is to define the fetus as "not a human life," and this is exactly what the Supreme Court has done. In 1973, the Supreme Court proclaimed that "the fetus is not a person; legal personhood does not exist prenatally" (Rowe *vs*. Wade, January 23, 1973). When many states disagreed with the federal decision, the states' opinions were termed *unconstitutional* by the federal government. In no other moral blunder has a decision of so few affected the lives of so many. In this historical decision, the federal government not only usurped individual states' rights, but it also deprived a segment of this population unable to defend themselves of the right to life.

To understand how ridiculous this court decision was, consider what this "nonperson" can do. As early as one month after conception, this nonperson has a beating heart; by a month and a half, brain waves can be measured on his developing brain; by two months, he can grasp an object placed in his hand; by three months he has a functioning brain, can urinate, defecate, sleep, see, hear, and feel pain. All of his limbs and organs are formed by three months, and they mature throughout the remainder of the pregnancy. Only because immaturity forces him to derive food and oxygen from his mother does he give up his right to personhood because a court has so ruled. It is interesting that the absence of brain waves and a heartbeat is accepted as medical death but the presence of a heartbeat and brain waves are not accepted as "medical life."

When the abortion-on-demand laws were liberalized, the fetus could be killed legally *at any time before term*. Occasionally an aborted baby is born alive "by mistake," and nothing is more embarrassing to the abortionist than delivering a live baby. In a few court trials where a baby has been killed after delivery, the abortionist was legally acquitted on the grounds that the baby was "intended to be an abortion." Just how far can the law be stretched, and where will it end?

These abortion-on-demand laws give the mother and society the right to kill a baby because the baby is either inconvenient for the mother or unsuitable for society. The advocates of abortion claim that abortion is an issue of women's rights and that women should have complete control over their bodies. If the fetus were like an inflamed appendix whose continued presence in the body would jeopardize the health of the mother, then it should be removed. The fetus has committed no crime. Therefore, should the fetus forfeit his or her right to life?

Abortion is marketed as the answer to the teen pregnancy problem and the medical profession has been lured into this mess by feeling obligated to provide a "service" to meet the growing demand. Since the rise in the pregnancy rate among teenagers parallels the easy availability of abortions, could it be that the abortion-on-demand laws are actually contributing to teen pregnancy and encouraging teenagers to be less sexually responsible? It is unfortunate that even members of the medical profession have allowed themselves to be followers instead of leaders on this issue. When I graduated from medical school, I remember taking the Hippocratic oath: "I will not give to a woman an instrument to produce abortion." I feel that the Supreme Court's decision approving abortions on demand in 1973 was one of the most disastrous moral turning points of this century. Since 1973, more than twenty-seven million unborn children have been destroyed by abortion. Not only is the number of abortions performed annually increasing, but they are also being performed on older and older fetuses. An example of this was the grizzly discovery in California of seventeen thousand aborted babies in a garbage container. A coroner's autopsy determined some of these babies weighed as much as four to five pounds.

The attitude of abortion has even more far-reaching effects on our youth than the act itself. At the very age when teenagers are attempting to grow into responsible people, they learn that they can amend one irresponsible act with another irresponsible act: "I'll simply get an abortion." Pro-abortion propaganda has programmed the vulnerable minds of our youth to rationalize that it is not really a person that is being scraped out and flushed. The subtle moral message is, "Don't think about what *it* is, think about how you are going to get rid of it." The abortion-on-demand laws are the first inch in the yardstick of a complete disregard for the God-given dignity of human life. Feticide (killing the unborn), which is what we really should call abortion, is listed in the public high school sex education programs along with the pill and the IUD as an accepted form of birth control. Since feticide has been marketed as an accepted form of controlling birth, the next logical step is to regard infanticide as an acceptable form of controlling life. A recent example of this is the case of Infant Doe, a Down Syndrome newborn who was born with a closed esophagus so that food was not able to reach his stomach. If given proper intravenous nourishment, this baby could easily have survived until an operation was performed to correct the deformity of his esophagus. Despite offers made to adopt Infant Doe, the courts upheld the parents' decision to withhold any medical treatment. The baby was allowed to die after seven days of thirst and starvation. Infant Doe's tragic death convinces me that our world is moving toward the philosophy that only those persons who have the health and ability to speak out are those who have the right to life.

The abortion-on-demand laws also convey the attitude to developing youth that there are no absolute laws of right or wrong. The concept of rightness or wrongness is relative to what is convenient to a particular person's circumstances at a given time. Abortion is a classic example of this moral confusion: if a fetus is killed by an assailant, this is called "murder"; if a fetus is killed by an abortionist, this is called "choice."

What Does the Bible Say about Abortion?

One of the most beautiful Scriptures that attest to the personhood of the fetus is Psalm 139:13–16:

> *For You have formed my inward parts;*
> *You have covered me in my mother's womb.*
> *I will praise You, for I am fearfully and wonderfully made;*
> *Marvelous are Your works,*
> *And that my soul knows very well.*
> *My frame was not hidden from You,*
> *When I was made in secret,*

And skilfully wrought in the lowest parts of the earth.
Your eyes saw my substance, being yet unformed.
And in Your book they all were written,
The days fashioned for me,
When as yet there were none of them.

God's involvement in fetal development is again stated in Jeremiah 1:5: "Before I formed you in the womb I knew you; / Before you were born I sanctified you; / And I ordained you a prophet to the nations." Exodus 21:22–25 states that even the "life for a life" penalty could be imposed upon someone who struggled with a woman causing damage or loss of life to her fetus. Genesis 2:7 gives further support to the God-given personhood of the fetus: "And the LORD God formed man of the dust of the ground, and breathed into his nostrils the breath of life; and man became a living being." This passage indicates that it is God's breath of life, the soul, that gives personhood to a living being. Luke 1:44 says that Elizabeth's unborn child leaped for joy at Mary's greeting, suggesting that fetuses feel emotion. Perhaps the most compelling passage supporting the sanctity of human life is in Exodus 20:13: "You shall not murder."

Complications of Abortion

Not only is abortion against God's law, but the high incidence of medical complications following abortions also suggests that abortion is against the natural law of the woman's body. Women who have abortions are more likely to experience sterility, premature births, miscarriages, obstetrical complications, and severe psychiatric breakdowns in subsequent pregnancies. Even with preabortion counseling, guilt may reappear years later when a woman reassesses her past life. All of these complications have far-reaching implications for parents of pregnant teenagers who should be aware that teenagers are able to obtain abortions *without their parents' consent*.

What Can Christians Do about Abortion?

It seems to be a fact of American political life that those who shout the loudest get the best results. In the early seventies, the pro-abortionists shouted the loudest and got the aforementioned disastrous results. It is now up to Christians to shout for repeals of the abortion-on-demand laws and to enhance attitudes toward life so that abortion doesn't influence legislators to approve the selective killing of the handicapped, the aged, and the infirm, as well. Become an active supporter of prolife organizations such as the American Life Lobby (P.O. Box 490, Stafford, VA, 22554; phone, 703-659-4171) and the National Right to Life Committee (419 Seventh Street NW, Suite 402, Washington, DC, 20004; phone, 202-638-4396).

There are right-to-life organizations in every major city throughout the United States. Support prolife political leaders. Ask prospective candidates what their previous voting records are on abortion-related subjects and what their voting attitudes will be. *Support prolife physicians.* When selecting your obstetrician, come right out and ask the doctor if he or she performs abortions. If the answer is yes, be sure to impress on your doctor that the reason you are switching doctors or are choosing another one is that you did not feel right trusting the life of your baby in the hands of a doctor who regards human life so ambivalently that he or she feels the option to sustain or destroy it.

Let me close this section on why abortion is not an acceptable option of birth control by quoting from Proverbs 6:16–17: "There are six things the LORD hates, seven that are detestable to him: . . . hands that shed innocent blood" (NIV).

CHAPTER 19

CONTROLLING ELECTRONIC INFLUENCES ON YOUR CHILD

The Twenty-Third Channel

The TV set is my shepherd. My spiritual growth shall want.

It maketh me to sit down and do nothing for His name's sake because it requireth all my spare time. It keepeth me from doing my duty as a Christian because it presenteth so many good shows that I must see.

It restoreth my knowledge of the things of the world and keepeth me from the study of God's Word. It leadeth me in the paths of failing to attend the evening worship services and doing nothing in the kingdom of God.

Yes, though I live to be one hundred, I shall keep on viewing my TV as long as it will work, for it is my closest companion. Its sound and its pictures comfort me.

It presenteth entertainment before me and keepeth me from doing important things with my family. It filleth my head with ideas that differ from those set forth in the Word of God.

Surely no good thing will come of my life, because my TV offereth me no good time to do the will of God; thus I will dwell in spiritual poverty all the days of my life.*

*Life Messengers (Seattle, WA), used by permission.

TELEVISION

The average child will have watched fifteen thousand hours of television by the time he is eighteen years old. During this time, he will have witnessed eighteen thousand murders and three hundred fifty thousand commercials. Children do not distinguish between learning and entertainment; they learn from everything they see. Most children tend to accept much of what they see on television as being realistic; they are not yet able to distinguish fantasy from reality easily. Therefore, children are likely to learn and remember new forms of aggressive behavior by watching the kind of violence presented in the mass media. By repeated exposure to violence and aggressive behavior, their emotional sensitivity is gradually lessened. A direct relationship exists between the amount of violence a child watches on television and the aggressive behavior he demonstrates. Violent television programs do not relax children or leave them with a good feeling. They create anxiety.

Children also learn unchristian attitudes toward sexuality from TV. Most of the love relationships portrayed on TV are mutually exploitive rather than mutually fulfilling as Christian marriages should be.

Watching television is a passive event. At the stage when you are attempting to teach your child inner fulfillment and impulse control, he learns he can simply push a button and achieve instant gratification without using either his mind or his body. Watching television also fosters a short attention span and poor physical and mental health. More than half the commercials on television advertise foods of questionable nutritional value that are highly sugared and artificially colored and that have detrimental effects on a child's health and behavior. Children younger than eight do not distinguish between program content and commercial content. For example, they may feel that the hero with whom they identify also endorses the products in the commercials.

By watching television, children are made to believe that what they drive, drink, smoke, and wear is what really counts. They hear these messages at the time when they are looking for ways to build up their self-esteem. Children younger than ten actually believe most commercials. And advertisers are masters at producing catchy slogans which may remain in a child's mind for a long time. For example, it is common to hear or see a three-year-old singing a television jingle over and over again.

Television presents a world of bright and beautiful people of athletic excellence and of wealth and power, attributes which the child is quick to perceive as respected most by the world. The child who does not see herself as having any of these important characteristics may lose herself in the world of fantasy and imagine herself like her heroes on television. But down deep she may feel she never can be like them. Since building self-esteem is one of our prime goals as parents, TV becomes a competitive teacher.

A Christian Parent's TV Guide

In my family we have wrestled with this electronic prophet of competitive values for a long time. At times we have even considered getting rid of it, which may be unfair and unrealistic. Try the following suggestions to achieve a balanced diet of television watching within your Christian home.

Do not allow indiscriminate TV watching. Convey to your children why indiscriminate TV watching cannot be tolerated within a Christian home. Show them that uncensored television directly opposes God's mandate to parents in Deuteronomy 6:6 and Ephesians 6:4. Convey to them, "I care about what goes into your brain. This is part of my responsibility as your parent for which I will be held accountable by God my Father." You would never allow a stranger to visit or entertain or teach your children without your participation. Why be permissive with television? I have placed this scripture verse above our TV set: "I will set before my eyes no vile thing" (Ps. 101:3).

Be selective. Screen the screen. Select which programs your child may or may not watch just as you would approve or disapprove of a book or movie. To help you preselect which programs your child may or may not watch, become involved in organizations that encourage the wise use of television. See the Bibliography for more resource material on discriminate TV watching. There are many entertaining and educational programs on television. Children's horizons can be broadened enormously by this electronic media if it is used correctly and wisely. One particular area of programming parents need to screen more carefully is Saturday morning cartoons. Admittedly this is a time when parents are likely to want the TV to act as a baby sitter. Sit down and watch the programs your children are being exposed to week after week—you will see sorcery, witchcraft, spell-casting—things all condemned in Scripture (Deut. 18:10–12). Many cartoons are offensively violent. This is a time when a good library of videos can provide the alternative—there is a selection of delightful Bible cartoons, Christian musicals, and adventure stories to choose from.

Watch TV as a family.   Neither you nor your children should be allowed to tune into the tube and tune out the rest of your family members. Use commercial time as a time to discuss the messages of the program. If the program or the commercial is contrary to your family values or principles of good health, point out to your children how misleading the message is. This helps them be selective and develop a sense of judgment. No matter how caring and how selective you try to be, occasionally a part of a program may portray unchristian values. Take this opportunity to explain to your children why these values are contrary to the law of God. You may even compare some of the values mentioned on television with specific scriptural passages, again teaching your child that in your house it is the Word of God that will be followed.

Video cassette recorders are a great help in preselecting television programs. A VCR enables you to edit out certain parts of a program which in your opinion compete with the Christian values that prevail in your home.

Alternatives to TV Watching

Having fun as a family does not always mean having some third party entertain you. Family games and activities, such as charades and Bible quizzes, and family projects, such as decorating a room, building a tree house, and planting a garden, are family activities that are much more meaningful than passive TV watching.

Once our TV was broken for six months. During this quiet time, we noticed a marked increase in interpersonal relationships within the family. Our children were playing games and building things together, and we were doing more creative activities together as a family. We read aloud to one another and enjoyed Christian classics. During this experimental period I heard fewer "I'm bored" complaints from our younger children as if they had resigned themselves to a more creative attitude, knowing that the little box was not around to pacify them. I must confess, my own love of sports allowed the tube to be fixed, but later we all agreed we were better off limiting its use. We find our sensitivity heightened when we happen to catch an offensive show. Things that did not bother us before are now offensive to us.

How Much TV Should My Child Watch?

What your child watches on TV is much more important than *how long* he watches TV. I certainly feel the Lord will not bless the home in which children spend more time watching television than they do reading Scripture and praying. If you allow your child to watch one hour of television per day, which I feel should be the maximum, challenge him to read the Word of God for at least half that long or even ten minutes, plus time for prayer. Parents, take charge of the television as part of your mandate to "train a child in the way he should go."

OTHER ELECTRONIC INFLUENCES

Computers and Video Games

As parents, you grew up B.C., before computers, so it is difficult to understand the impact of the personal computer on your children. The computer probably will have at least as much influence on a child's life as television has since its beginning forty years ago. It is unrealistic for parents to deny the influences of the personal computer. If the child of tomorrow is going to compete in the world of tomorrow, he probably will have to join the computer age rather than ignore it. The term *computer literacy* probably will be as important in the future educational system as the term *reading readiness* is in today's system. Christian parents should be aware of the influences computers can have on their children.

Is the computer becoming a substitute for your child's meaningful interpersonal relationships? Be vigilant to his seeking fulfillment from his computer rather than from God's Word.

Like so many matters in today's materialistic world, the issue of computers and video games is mainly that of balance. As long as children are taught to *use* machines and to *love* people and God, then they have a proper perspective. As they begin to love machines and use people, they are susceptible to drifting farther and farther away from God.

On the subject of video games, in ten years the number and kinds have mushroomed an incredible amount. PacMan and sports games have been replaced by every type of spectacle imaginable. Many of them are steeped in occultic practices sometimes so subtle that you may not even realize it. Mostly it is blatant and offensive, dealing with sorcery, witchcraft, interpreting omens, and casting of spells. Active participation is encouraged in these things that are condemned in Scripture (Mal. 3:5, Deut. 18:10–12). Be sure you screen video games carefully; take the time to sit down and watch or play with your child so you can teach him or her to discern. Video magazines need to be watched carefully, also. The illustrations are often frightening and inappropriate especially for younger children.

Rock Music

Appreciate the profound effect music has on your child. The average teenager listens to thirty-two hours of music per week, and rock fans are the fastest growing category of music consumers.

Where does rock music fit into the Christian lifestyle? There are two schools of thought on the inherent goodness or evil of rock music. Defenders of rock propose all music is strictly a matter of personal taste; there is nothing inherently unchristian about rock and the lyrics give moral value to a song. Opponents of rock feel the beat of rock music is potentially satanic and erotic. They feel that rock attempts to mesmerize the masses and to provide models of alternative lifestyles to the Christian home.

As a Christian parent, you can arrive at a workable system which respects your God-given responsibility to your child and also respects your child's individual taste for music. Although I have had no in-depth formal education in music appreciation, I feel every individual has a sensitive note that music will touch. If music strikes an individual's note and leaves him feeling right, then that music is right for him. If the music causes disharmony, cacophony, and disorder instead, the music is wrong for that person. The earlier you begin teaching music appreciation to your child, the more finely tuned his or her ear will be.

Your ultimate goal is for your child to make a personal judgment about the intrinsic artistic value of music and to determine whether different kinds of music give him a feeling of rightness within him or an unpleasant feeling of unrightness. Throughout the Bible, especially in the Psalms, worshipers were encouraged to make music to the Lord, and there was a feeling of rightness for having done so. Very early in his childhood, begin playing Christian hymns and classical music for your child in your home. Music lessons during middle childhood add further appreciation for the order of music. By the time he is a teenager, the appreciation of artistic music you will have imparted to your child will be his best defense against the mediocrity that prevails in most of today's rock music.

Listen to the music your teenager enjoys and discuss it with her. It does not suffice to say, "Julie, turn that horrible record off, I can't stand it." This dogmatic and judgmental approach may be unfair and fails to teach your child to be discriminating about the music she selects. Your child probably is thinking, *What's wrong with this music? Is it bad or does Dad simply not like it because it's not his taste?* Take some time out, sit with your child, and listen intently to the record. Write down the lyrics and discuss them. For the great majority of musical pieces, the lyrics give the song its moral value, not the actual beat. Many times teenagers are not even aware of what the lyrics are saying or implying. By taking time to go over the lyrics with your teenager, you are conveying the message to him, "I care about what goes into your mind." This also takes discipline about music out of the realm of personal taste and adds a dimension of credibility to your judgment concerning the basic goodness or badness of a musical composition. Analyzing the lyrics of a song also equips your teenager to be selective and to look beneath its outer shell for some subtle messages that may be unchristian. For example, the entire rock culture is based on a "me first" fulfillment at all costs, using other people and the pleasures of the flesh. Secular rock music allows models and persons of significance to influence your child's mind and compete directly with the Word of God.

What if your teenager says, "But, Dad, this is a *Christian* rock group"? To most teenagers the term *Christian rock* means only one thing: the lyrics are Christian. It follows, therefore, that if you believe only the lyrics give moral value to a song, then this Christian rock should be accepted into your home.

One of the occupational hazards of parenting a teenager is to be open to his taste in music and not to impose your own upon him unless you have been trained in certain principles of music appreciation. I realized this when I accompanied my teenage son to a Christian rock concert. Although my own musical tastes were offended, I noticed Christian messages were reaching the ears and hearts of teenagers who might not have been reached in any other way.

There are signs that rock music, even Christian rock, is becoming unhealthy for your teenager. One of the most justifiable fears parents have in letting rock music in their home is that their child will model the lifestyle of the composers. Many a teenager's room is papered with record covers and looks like a shrine to these musical idols. The lifestyle of most rock stars bothers parents more than the music. One scriptural reference you may discuss with your child is Luke 6:45: "A good man out of the good treasure of his heart brings forth good; and an evil man out of the evil treasure of his heart brings forth evil. For out of the abundance of the heart his mouth speaks." If you see your child idolizing these rock stars, you have a Christian responsibility to cast these characters out of the house.

Watch for escapism. Because of the widespread marketing of earphones and miniature radios, children literally can escape from the world and blot out all family interruptions or interaction. Too much of this seclusion is not a balanced diet for the developing teenager.

In summary, it is my opinion that rock music of which either the lyrics or the advertised lifestyle of the composers are definitely not Christian should not be allowed in your home. That which relays a Christian message and is sung by Christian people may be allowed into your home. I urge you to guide your teenager in selecting her music as you would guide her in her selection of movies, TV programs, and books.

Movies

The only real way to protect your children from inappropriate movies or videos is to see them yourself first, or ask a trusted, like-minded friend for his opinion. You may want to take the same approach with the music your children listen to: When they bring a movie or tape or CD home, listen to it first, or at least watch the film or listen to the music with them. This way you can discuss the film or music with your children and point out how it measures up to God's Word. You can also have an understanding with your children that you will turn off the movie or music at your discretion.

Families and children are increasingly interested in and aware of movies. The popularity of VCRs has brought the attraction of cinema into our homes. It is necessary to realize that the rating system for movies (G, PG, PG-13, R, and the new NC-17) is not a reliable indicator of a movie's suitability. I have seen one or two R movies that were less offensive than some PG movies. It is usually a mistake to let your children see anything but a G movie without parental guidance. If your children are going to watch a movie at a friend's party, be sure to ask the host or hostess what movie will be shown so you can determine ahead of time how to handle the invitation.

The bottom line in controlling the electronic influences in your child's life is to step in, after prayer and counsel, and call a halt to any influence which in your opinion is competing with your child's walk with Christ.

CHAPTER 20

HELP!
I'M A
SINGLE
PARENT

The plight of the single parent is one of the most difficult social problems. Single-parent households are the fastest growing category of all family units. Approximately one out of every two children will spend some part of their childhoods under the care of a single parent. In 1980 in the United States, one million children were being reared by single teenager mothers, and twelve million children under eighteen were living with a single parent.

Although a growing number of women have become single mothers by choice, the following discussion is directed primarily to the parent who is single as the result of divorce.

THE EFFECTS OF DIVORCE
ON YOUR CHILDREN

To understand better the impact of divorce on children, examine some of their feelings. The extent of these feelings will vary depending upon the age of the child, the state of the home before the divorce, and how the divorce was handled by the parents.

447

Insecurity

The family structure was set up by God so that the child could feel secure in having his needs met appropriately and consistently. Children feel secure in a familiar structure, even though that structure may be a bit shaky. Following a divorce, that structure is removed, and the present and future security of a child is threatened. He or she experiences feelings of uncertainty and loneliness. Young children tend to worry, "Now that Dad has gone, will Mother go, too?" Because the custodial parent, usually the mother, is undergoing a post-divorce adjustment, the capacity to parent is diminished. Most children have so many needs that one parent alone has a difficult time meeting those needs. All these elements work together to intensify the child's insecurity.

Depression

The child of divorce becomes depressed mainly because he feels a sense of loss and a sense of uncertainty about his future care, but the many changes following a divorce also affect him. These may include the loss of a parent's presence in the home, a move to another home or town, the loss of friends, a lessening in financial status, and the stigma of "Mom and Dad are divorced." Although the stigma of divorce is no longer as socially upsetting as it once was, most children perceive that living in a divorced home is not the accepted norm.

Depression manifests itself in different forms according to a child's age and personality. There may be overt signs of depression such as withdrawal, sadness, and multiple psychosomatic complaints (headaches, tummy aches, tiredness). A child may compensate for his depression with "acting-up" behaviors—becoming the class clown, getting into trouble, forming sexual alliances. Some children remain silently depressed and say nothing about the whole situation.

Anger

Children of divorce usually live in a household (or two households) in which anger and resentment persist for several years. A home in which anger predominates diminishes the parent's capacity to be an effective parent and also has a negative effect on a child's developing personality. An angry home will often produce an angry child, and an angry child usually becomes an unhappy and depressed child.

Weakened Self-Esteem

Insecurity, depression, and anger all have a weakening effect on a child's self-esteem. A child with a poor self-esteem is less able to bounce back from the effects of divorce. All of these have a cumulative effect on the child who has no support resources to handle it.

Role Model Loss

Children accustomed to the traditional mother-father, husband-wife models must adjust to new parental figures. Because both the custodial parent and the absentee parent are now pursuing (either by choice or by necessity) careers outside the home and are coming to terms with their own postdivorce adjustments, the child's expectations of what the traditional mother and father are like are shattered. Not only are his models gone at home, but an older child often gets conflicting messages from his parents. This is particularly true of the absentee parent who may pursue an unchristian lifestyle which confuses the child who has been taught traditional Christian values. A confused child is susceptible to renouncing the Christian values he has been taught and to departing from the way he should go.

Faith Crisis

The effect of divorce on a Christian child may be even more devastating than for a non-Christian child because in the Christian world, divorce may be considered more a failure than it is in the non-Christian world. The Christian child may therefore become more embarrassed about the divorce. He may turn more closely to his faith or withdraw entirely and pursue an alternative lifestyle. (See the section on the role of the church in divorce for further discussion of the effect of divorce on a Christian child.)

Are boys and girls affected differently by divorce? Although they vary widely in determining how divorce affects either sex, some studies suggest that boys are generally more affected than girls. The reason for this is probably that society encourages boys to suppress their feelings. Boys are discouraged from crying and expressing their sorrows and may choose to vent their stored-up anger in other ways. Girls are more likely to talk freely about what they feel.

Male and female children of divorce differ in their sexual identity problems. Male children of divorce have a higher incidence of homosexuality. Female children of divorce have more sexual problems. Girls often form inappropriate sexual alliances and also marry at a young age to father figures. These sexual identity problems usually result from a loss of appropriate role models.

What happens to children of divorce as they grow older? One cannot generalize or predict accurately the effects of adverse circumstances on a child. In general, however, children of divorce suffer in all areas of life. They have lower academic achievements, more trouble with the law, lower self-esteem, and more problems with sexual identity than children of intact families. But God made children to be resilient, and some children have an immense capacity to bounce back from this family crisis and compensate by actually becoming high achievers. These are tough children. It is interesting that some of the most influential people in the world have come from broken homes.

Effects at Various Stages

1. *Feelings in the preschool child (three to five years).*   Preschool children do not usually verbalize their feelings, but they show their resentment by regressive behaviors reflecting insecurity and a sense of loss: thumb-sucking, bed-wetting, whining, temper tantrums, aggressive behaviors, and sleep problems (caused by a fear of awakening and seeing Mommy—or Daddy—gone too). Because of the fear of losing his other parent, the preschool child may cling to his father or mother, crave attention, and not let him or her out of his sight. The young child may also blame himself for the divorce and feel, "I was bad." After the loss of one parent it is common for the preschool child to want to sleep with the custodial parent. This need should be respected during the post-divorce adjustment period.

2. *Feelings of the school-age child (five to ten years).*   Children at this age are more likely to verbalize their feelings and bombard their parents with questions: Why did you divorce? When is Daddy (Mommy) coming back? Children do not accept the finality of divorce, and they fantasize about various ways of reuniting the family. Depression and sadness are part of the grieving process as they come to terms with their loss. The older child usually tries to figure out a reason for the divorce, who the bad guy is, and what is going to happen to him now, especially if there are many changes in lifestyle following the divorce. The child at this age may become angry at one parent or the other. The older child often becomes more sensitive to the loneliness of the custodial parent and may assume the role of friend and companion to the parent. These are healthy roles as long as the compassionate child is allowed to ventilate his feelings while attempting to comfort the grieving parent. Psychosomatic complaints (headaches, stomachaches, fatigue, vague aches

and pains) are common during this age and are either attention-getting complaints or real pains related to the body's reaction to the combined stresses. Anticipate a few visits to your child's doctor during the first year following a divorce.

3. *Feelings of the adolescent.*   Adolescents are confused. The Christian values they have been taught and the role models they have respected are now weakened. The adolescent may become judgmental about who is at fault and begin to see his parents as individual persons, not as a couple. For this reason, adolescents are very perceptive about how each parent adjusts after the divorce and what lifestyles they choose to pursue. They become particularly judgmental about dating and sexual activities of the parents; therefore, both the mother and the father should exercise some discretion about sexual pursuits. Do not expect your adolescent to warm up immediately to your dates. Because adolescents themselves are going through identity crises, they are particularly vulnerable to the effects of divorce. Adolescents do not usually view divorce as improving the family situation unless there has been excessive physical violence during the marriage.

Whereas the young child is old enough to know what is going on but not old enough to have enough compensatory skills, the adolescent has more support resources to help him cope. Teenage girls may form premature sexual alliances shortly after the divorce because of a need for emotional support and sexual identity. Yes, the adolescent girl is susceptible to pregnancy shortly following the divorce of her parents. Adolescents experience a loyalty dilemma over which parent to support. The way in which this dilemma develops depends upon how each parent reinforces the problem or discourages the adolescent from choosing sides.

Divorce is tough on children of all ages. I do not think it is any tougher at one age than at another; it is simply tough in different ways because children's needs vary at different ages. As the Lord "hates divorce" (Mal. 2:16), so do children of all ages hate divorce.

COMMON PROBLEMS FOR THE CUSTODIAL PARENT

If the custodial parent is the mother, she may face the conflict between the continuing role of mother and the additional role of worker outside the home. After a divorce it is common for children to increase their demands on the mother's energy and time, and these increased demands come at a time when the mother is also trying to redirect her own life. Most often the mother pursues a career outside the home, for financial reasons and for a psychological boost to her already weakened self-esteem.

Some mothers feel that even though they are not forced to work for financial reasons, it is necessary to pursue some career outside the home for fulfillment as a person. This decision should be made with much prayer and counsel. A custodial mother who is continually unhappy and unfulfilled as a person will not be an effective single parent. Although her primary role will still be that of a mother, it is important for her to do what she has to do for her own individual fulfillment.

My heart goes out to those mothers who are suddenly faced with the dual role of primary breadwinner and loving mother. It is tough to leave one's child in the care of another person, work all day to earn a living for the family, return home from the exhausting world of work, and have energy left over for complete organization of the household. I sincerely believe that God gives a special strength to single mothers who are required to do more than their share.

Discipline

Following a divorce, household routines often become disorganized and discipline relaxed. This is unfortunate because the post-divorce adjustment period is a time when organization and consistent discipline are most needed. This is also a dilemma because the custodial parent may be using so much energy for his or her own adjustment that little is left over for discipline of the child. The following suggestions may help you cope with this dilemma.

As soon as possible after the divorce (or even before), call a family council with your children to give them a clear understanding of the future organization of your home. Even though the home has been severely changed, you are still a family and family life must go on. Older children will have to accept some increased responsibilities. This is a non-negotiable fact of single-parent family life. The assignment of specific tasks can be negotiated at the family council. Make a list of the new responsibilities to be shared, and let each child have some choice in his or her contribution to the family. Most single parents find it necessary to run a tight ship. Try to achieve some balance between the increased responsibilities that are put upon your children and the emotional support you give them. Too many increased responsibilities too soon may make the already angry child further rebel and resent the divorce. If you increase both your expectations of your child and your show of love for him or her, your child is likely to respect the recent changes in discipline. To avoid the usual confusion of a tight ship at home and a loose ship at Daddy's (or Mother's) house, try to arrive at an agreed-upon level of discipline that will be maintained consistently at each home.

Conflicting Models

A common problem in divorced homes is that children may see alternative lifestyles in their parents' houses. A typical after-divorce scenario is that one parent adopts a free-living lifestyle that he or she demonstrates in front of the child. The child understandably becomes confused. The values he learned from his custodial parent do not match those of the missing parent.

What does a mother do when a child comes to her and asks, "Mommy, is it right for Daddy to be living with another woman?" Mommy is caught in another dilemma. God expects the mother to encourage the child to continue to love his father, yet what the father is doing is clearly wrong. In this case I believe that the mother is obligated to give her child an honest answer: "No, what your father is doing is wrong." When explaining this kind of conflict to your child, try to separate the act from the person: "What Daddy is doing is wrong, but Daddy is not a bad person. You still should love him and pray for him every day that he will again walk with God and do what is right." Taking this approach fulfills your obligation as the spiritual leader of your home and yet, at the same time, encourages your child to love his father.

This problem of conflicting models is intensified further if the child spends prolonged periods of time with one parent, such as during the summer. If this is the case, the custodial parent should spend a great deal of time preparing the child to cope with the alternative lifestyle. If this situation is true for you, intensify your efforts to model Christian values in your own home. Also equip your child with the armor of God. Tell her you will be praying for her each day, and advise her to pray and read Scriptures daily. It would be wise to pick out certain passages of Scripture to serve as a source of strength and direction when she is exposed to alternative values in the house of your ex. (The term *ex* seems cold and final, but really says it all in conveying the anger and resignation that divorced parents often feel.) Encourage your child to call you whenever she feels her faith weakening or is having difficulty accepting these alternative values. Teach your child to go into her father's house not in judgment but in love and strength and prayer.

HELPING CHILDREN COPE

Once the decision to divorce is final, the way parents handle the divorce is of primary importance. Parents should do all they can to ease the pain for their children.

Tell Them What Is Happening

Parents, do not underestimate your children's ability to understand. Even toddlers have a feeling of not-rightness when one parent is missing. Tell your children a few weeks before the separation occurs, which allows time for questions and feelings to come out during the remaining time the family is intact. Both parents can continue to support the children's adjustment and anxieties. Be specific. Tell your children the reason for the divorce in language and detail appropriate to their age and level of understanding. (Details of marital infidelity serve no useful purpose and should be withheld from them, however.)

It is important for children to feel reassured that they are not the cause of the divorce, that they are still loved, and that they still will have a Mommy and a Daddy, although Daddy (Mommy) will not be living with them. At this point, your children, egocentric as they are, probably will be more concerned about what will happen to them than what will happen to you.

The custodial parent needs to define what changes will occur within the household: Mother will get a job. You will not live in the same house. Children need to be reassured that family life will go on, that family life has not been completely destroyed, only severely changed and adjusted.

It is important for the non-custodial parent to define what his or her continued role will be in the children's care. This is probably one of the most confusing feelings for children, who at the time are really not sure how much of their parents they will be losing. This is also a dilemma for parents since early in the divorcing period they may not have answered this question in their own minds. Be as specific as possible with your children. Tell them where you are going. If possible, take them to your new home. Leave a phone number and convey one big message: "I am still your Dad (Mom), and I am easily accessible to you" (if, indeed, you will be so accessible).

After telling your children about the impending divorce, don't be too quick to judge the true meaning of the impact of this crisis on them by their initial reactions.

Initially your children may be noncommunicative as they work out their ambivalent feelings concerning this devastating news.

Visiting Rights

During a divorce, parents often are preoccupied with their own "rights." Remember, a child has rights too—a right to two parents. The term *visiting rights* is a superficial term since it implies more fun and entertainment than a relationship. The term *parenting rights* is more realistic and implies more of a commitment to a relationship. Tell your child how often you plan to visit. The younger the child, the more frequent your visits should be. Ideally, visiting a young child should be like his feeding schedule—small, frequent visits on a demand basis. The absentee parent should realize that scheduled parenting is an unrealistic way of life for both you and your child. Weekend parents often schedule lots of fun things, corrective discipline is often lax, and the relationship is that of a "Disneyland parent." This kind of parent-child relationship is not a balanced diet for the growing child. Focus more on giving of yourself than on things; focus more on loving your child than entertaining him or her.

Scheduled parenting is particularly unrealistic for the older child who may have planned his own activities with his own peer group during the weekend you have planned; thus, he will regard your visiting rights as infringing upon his own rights to social development. For the older child, a more flexible, spontaneous, and unscheduled time with the absentee parent respects his busy life, and he should be consulted in working out a visiting arrangement. For example, the father may call up and say, "I would like to be with you tomorrow. What would you like to do?" These visiting dilemmas are not all negative. Parent-child communication may actually improve following a divorce because this may be the first time the child has the parent's undivided attention. Although the concept of quality time is also an artificial relationship, it is really the best the absentee parent can do.

To minimize confusion between the fun-and-games lifestyle with the absentee parent and the more realistic lifestyle in the home of the custodial parent, it would be wise for the absentee parent to point out this artificial relationship to the child by saying, "Johnny, I hope you realize how much I love you and want to spend this fun time with you on weekends. Because I do not have as much time with you as your mother does, we will be doing lots of fun things while we are together. But because I love you, I feel you should understand that life is just not like that all the time. When you are at home with your mother, I expect you to obey and help your mother with the household chores, to complete your homework and do well in school. You know, Johnny, I hope you realize that it is much easier for me than it is for your mother. I can do all my social activities and get my work done during the week so that on the weekend I have time to spend with you. Your mother doesn't have it that easy. She works during the day and is tired at night and may often need the weekends to catch up on some activities that she needs for herself. I want you to realize, son, that if you were living with me and visiting your mother, I would expect the same things from you as what your mother expects at home." You are conveying to your child a more realistic situation.

Make Few Changes

The concept of multiple losses is one of the most difficult problems to cope with. The child has already lost perhaps the most important relationship in his life—a two-parent home. If at all possible, try to keep your child in the same house, the same school, and the same church so that he is not forced to make too many changes too soon. If changes are necessary, try to ease into them gradually; allow the child to adapt to one new relationship at a time.

Protect Your Child

Do not let your child be caught up in the crossfire of hostility between two angry, divorcing parents. Do not use your child as a spy or as a carrier of messages. Above all, do not make derogatory remarks about your ex to your child. This only further confuses the child who is trying to sort out his own ambivalent feelings. Consider that the stress of divorce on a child is second only to that following the death of a parent. A confused child is less able to cope with this stress.

Be vigilant for signs that your child is not coping with the divorce, such as depression, acting-up behavior, prolonged anger, the "quiet child" not bothered by anything, poor school performance, fear of forming close friendships, inappropriate sexual alliances, and gradually diminishing self-esteem.

Persons of Significance

Because the child has lost the important model of the intact two-parent home, it is important to help her compensate by surrounding her with other models. These persons of significance could include a pastor, a teacher, a coach, a Scout leader—anyone who models for your child the Christian person you want her to be. In a single-parent family, the parent must choose the persons of significance very wisely because the child needs extra help to understand what values are important and which standards should be followed.

ROLE OF THE CHURCH

Divorce may be particularly devastating to a Christian couple because they not only have failed a social relationship but they may feel they also have failed a Christian relationship. Divorce is also particularly devastating for the Christian child, since all the ideals he has been taught about the indissolubility of the Christian marriage have been shattered in his own home. For these reasons Christian parents and children may need more support than non-Christians. Unfortunately, this support is not as great as it should be within the Christian community, especially toward divorced parents. Christians often support the parent who is single because of the death of a spouse, but they may reject a parent who is single because of divorce.

It is also true that a divorced parent does not often seek the fellowship and support within his or her own church because of this feeling of being a failure within the system. A widow or widower has the same practical need but does not feel blamed for being single. A parent single by death may not "feel single"; a parent single by divorce may. Divorced women may have difficulty returning to a state of their own identities, and they may be prone to feelings of loneliness. In some cases parents and children of divorce need more ministering than widows and orphans.

The Bible contains clear instructions that churches and Christian homes should act as extended families to the single parent and the children of single-parent households: "He administers justice for the fatherless and the widow, . . . giving him food and clothing" (Deut. 10:18); "Bring out the tithe of your produce of that year. . . . and the fatherless and the widow who are within your gates, may come and eat and be satisfied" (Deut. 14:28–29); "The LORD watches over . . . and relieves the fatherless and widow" (Ps. 146:9); and "Pure and undefiled religion before God and the Father is this: to visit orphans and widows in their trouble" (James 1:27).

It is extremely important that divorced parents feel their church family has not failed them. The church can help the child of divorce compensate for his loss by taking an active part in his spiritual training. How a child handles a loss or a handicap depends on his degree of compensation. The church family can bring a child closer to God and surround him with Christian models and persons of significance who give the child the message: "We care, and we will not fail you."

Churches often have singles-only Sunday school classes. A word of caution: don't be too quick to suggest to the divorced or widowed parent, "You may want to join the singles class." That parent may not be ready to feel single and may not wish to be ostracized from the fellowship of his or her couples' class and the friends made previously as part of a couple. He or she likes to feel welcomed into couples' activities because of his or her individuality.

The church family also can assist the custodial parent and the children in their grieving process primarily by helping them toward forgiving the absentee parent. Prolonged and stored-up anger is probably one of the greatest obstacles to the post-divorce adjustment. The sooner the custodial parent overcomes this anger and truly says, "I forgive," the sooner he can pull the remaining household together and get on with family life. The most important determinant of how children adjust to divorce is how soon the custodial parent gets both his spiritual house and his earthly house in order.

A message from the church family to parents and children of divorce should be, "We care; we love you as persons, whether single or married; we realize that caring for children takes more than one parent; and we will help you in the material and spiritual care and feeding of both yourself and your children."

I have not been exhaustive of the many challenges that face parents today, but my prayer is that you know *Christian Parenting and Child Care* is your ally—you are not alone. You have the support of Christian organizations and Christian parents who share your commitment to building a home for God. Above all, you have the promises of Scripture and the continual guidance of our heavenly Father.

As you continue to parent your child and train him in the way he or she should go, remember that your reward will be great, both in this life and in the life to come. I am excited for you; I know that soon you will know your child, will help him or her feel right, and will lead him or her to Christ.

Bibliography

The following books and reference sources are arranged according to their major subjects, although many of them cover a wide range of topics on parenting. Please bear in mind that when recommending a book, *I am not necessarily endorsing every statement made in it*. I have chosen to recommend those books which, in my opinion, contain important messages that will contribute to your growth as Christian parents. Not all of the books on the following list are specifically Christian, but they are not non-Christian either. I have also chosen those books most in accordance with the philosophy of attachment and feeling right that I have continually advocated in this book.

Abortion

Schaeffer, Francis A. and C. Everett Koop. *Whatever Happened to the Human Race?* Westchester, IL: Crossway, 1983.

Written by the late renowned Christian philosopher and the former surgeon general of the United States, this book is a real must for understanding the issues surrounding abortion, and it exposes the rapid but subtle loss of human rights.

Swindoll, Charles. *Sanctity of Life: The Inescapable Issue*. Dallas, TX: Word, 1990.

Besides the sanctity of life, Swindoll examines abortion after the fact and makes a plea for morality and the resolve to be strong.

Wilke, Dr. J. C. & Mrs. *Abortion: Questions and Answers*. Cincinnati, OH: Hayes Publishing, 1989.

If you could choose only one book this should be it: a reference manual with questions and answers on all the aspects of abortion.

Breastfeeding

Breastfeeding Organizations. La Leche League International, Inc., 1-800-La Leche, P.O. Box 1209, Franklin Park, IL 60131.

This organization not only teaches better mothering through breastfeeding but teaches better mothering in all aspects of parenting and child care. There is a local La Leche League in every major city in the United States and throughout the world. Write for a free catalog of their breastfeeding publications which contains nearly one hundred books and booklets on all aspects of parenting.

Breastfeeding Your Baby: A Mother's Guide.
  A one-hour video produced by Medela, Inc., (the breast pump company) in cooperation with La Leche League. William Sears, M.D., Jay Gordon, M.D., celebrities, and breastfeeding experts instruct and encourage; families speak on breastfeeding's benefits. Available through La Leche League.

Bumgarner, Norma Jane. *Mothering Your Nursing Toddler.* Franklin Park, IL: La Leche League International, Inc., 1982.
  Not only does this book extol the virtues of nursing the toddler and not weaning the child before his time, it is a beautiful account of attachment mothering.

Kippley, Sheila. *Breastfeeding and Natural Child Spacing.* The Couple to Couple League International, Inc., P.O. Box 111184, Cincinnati, OH 45211.
  This book discusses the concept of natural mothering and how it can postpone the return of fertility.

Torgus, Judy (editor). *The Womanly Art of Breastfeeding.* Franklin Park, IL: La Leche League International, Inc., 1987.
  The authority for the breastfeeding mother, this book not only deals with the joys and problems of breastfeeding but also affirms the profession of attachment mothering.

Childbirth

Brewer, Gail Sforza and Tom Brewer, M.D. *What Every Pregnant Woman Should Know: The Truth About Diet and Drugs in Pregnancy.* New York: Viking-Penguin, 1985.
  The importance of good nutrition in pregnancy. Relationship of toxemia and diet in pregnancy.

Dick-Read, Grantly. *Childbirth Without Fear.* (5th ed.) Edited by Helen Wessel. New York: Harper and Row, 1984.
  This is a classic book on natural childbirth which demonstrates how laboring women can overcome the fear-tension-pain cycle.

Evans, Debra. *The Complete Book on Childbirth.* Wheaton, IL: Tyndale House, 1986.
  This book is valuable for the original and beautifully expressed concepts on marriage and birth. Her information on breastfeeding is insufficient and I do not completely agree with her attitudes toward pain and childbirth. Readers will want to balance this book with others on Christian childbirth and breastfeeding.

Korte, Diana and Roberta Scaer. *A Good Birth, A Safe Birth.* New York: Bantam, 1990.
  This basic guide to childbirth options helps expectant parents negotiate to get the kind of birth experience they want. Also provides insight into recent trends in childbirth.

MacNutt, Francis and Judith. *Praying for Your Unborn Child: How Parents' Prayers Can Make a Difference in the Health and Happiness of Their Children.* New York: Doubleday, 1989.
  A beautiful and insightful guide to praying for your baby during each stage of pregnancy, from conception to delivery. The authors show how parents who surround their unborn infant with love, prayer, and serenity will profoundly affect their child's personality and well-being.

McCutcheon-Rosegg, Susan and Peter Rosegg. *Natural Childbirth the Bradley Way.* New York: E. P. Dutton-Penguin, 1984.

An updated guide to pregnancy and childbirth. Step-by-step preparations are provided for the couple looking for a totally natural, drug-free birth.

Nilsson, Lennart. *A Child Is Born*. (Rev. ed.) New York: Delacourt, 1990. Also published by Life Education, reprint no. 27. Canaan, NH: Media International.

A series of unprecedented photographs of the development of the embryo, from conception to birth, the book will help you realize the true miracle of fetal development and how a Supreme Architect is certainly in charge of this development.

Noble, Elizabeth. *Having Twins: A Parent's Guide to Pregnancy, Birth and Early Childhood*. Boston, MA: Houghton-Mifflin, 1991.

A veteran childbirth expert tells how to carry healthy babies to term.

Odent, Michael, M.D. *Birth Reborn*. New York: Random House, 1984.

A beautifully illustrated description of birth at Pithiviers in France, using explicit photography to help demonstrate how birth is best achieved in the modified (standing) squat position and also with the aid of tubs. The description of how birth can be a normal, safe, and confident part of life encourages couples in planning the birth they want.

Wessel, Helen. *Natural Childbirth and the Christian Family*. Bookmates International, Inc., Apple Tree Family Ministries, P.O. Box 2083, Artesia, CA 90702-2083.

A must for all parents who are taking prepared-childbirth classes. Mrs. Wessel, a mother of six, adds a Christian perspective to the childbirth-without-fear techniques described by Dr. Grantly Dick-Read.

_____. *Under the Apple Tree*. Fresno, CA: Bookmates International, Inc., 1981. (See above for address to write for booklet.)

An absolute must for Christian parents-to-be. Mrs. Wessel discusses the scriptural basis of marriage, birthing, and early parenting practices; it should be read and studied by husband and wife together.

Discipline

Craig, Sydney. *Raising Your Child Not by Force but by Love*. Philadelphia, PA: The Westminster Press, 1973.

This book, written from a Christian perspective, helps parents gain an understanding of discipline as a *positive* concept. It has great insight into the feelings of children and the effect of our discipline (good and bad) on their feelings. It also gives insight into why we get angry with our children and alternative ways of expressing and managing anger.

Crary, Elizabeth. *Without Spanking or Spoiling*. Seattle, WA: Parenting Press, 1979.

Alternatives for parents to recognize and attain their personal goals in childrearing.

_____. *Kids Can Cooperate: A Practical Guide to Teaching Problem Solving*. Seattle, WA: Parenting Press, 1984.

Teaches children skills to solve conflicts themselves.

_____. *Pick Up Your Socks . . . And Other Skills Growing Children Need*. Seattle, WA: Parenting Press, 1990.

Teaches children responsibility skills.

Faber, Adele and Elaine Mazlish. *Siblings Without Rivalry*. New York: Avon, 1987.

Help your children live together so you can live too.

_____. *How to Talk So Kids Will Listen and Listen So Kids Will Talk*. New York: Avon, 1982.

Communication skills for parents: how to listen and deal with feelings; alternatives to nagging and punishment.

Fennema, Jack. *Nurturing Children in the Lord*. Phillipsburg, NJ: Presbyterian and Reformed Publishing, 1977.

A study guide on developing a biblical approach to discipline, this is an excellent book for Christian parents who wish to base their discipline on scriptural principles.

Kesler, Jay. *Too Big to Spank*. Ventura, CA: Regal, 1978.

This is a practical guide for parents to help them discipline and build self-esteem in their teenager.

Leman, Kevin. *Making Children Mind Without Losing Yours*. Old Tappan, NJ: Revell, 1984.

Should have been titled *Helping Children Mind* by Dr. Leman's own admission. A practical, common-sense approach to discipline based on action (but rarely spanking) not words. Called Reality Discipline, it teaches children to be accountable for their actions. Only one area of concern: Dr. Leman advises parents to leave their young babies at home so they can get out now and then. I encourage couples to get out together and take baby too.

Narramore, S. Bruce. *Help! I'm a Parent*. Grand Rapids, MI: Zondervan, 1972.

This book applies both psychological and biblical principles in arriving at a systematic approach to discipline.

Stewart, Blaize Clement. *The Loving Parent: A Guide To Growing Up Before Your Children Do*. San Luis Obispo, CA: Impact, 1988.

A secular book dealing sensitively with issues such as obedience, lying, stealing, cheating, anger, and sexuality.

Divorce

Hart, Archibald D. *Children and Divorce—What to Expect, How to Help*. Waco, TX: Word, 1982.

Written by a Christian psychologist, this realistic and helpful guidebook helps divorcing parents understand their children's feelings and help them cope.

Smith, Virginia Watts. *The Single Parent*. Old Tappan, NJ: Revell, 1979.

This very sensitive Christian guide to the plight of the single parent offers sympathetic understanding and practical advice on the dilemma of achieving personal fulfillment and rearing a child for Christ.

Education

Elkind, David. *The Hurried Child, Growing Up Too Fast, Too Soon*. Reading, MA: Addison-Wesley, 1989.

Offers insight and advice on the burden of stress on modern children who are "forced to bloom."

Harris, Gregg. *The Christian Home School*. Brentwood, TN: Wolgemuth & Hyatt, 1987.

A good starter book for families considering home school.

Macauley, Susan Schaeffer. *For the Children's Sake: Foundations of Education for Home and School.* Westchester, IL: Crossway, 1987.

The daughter of the late Christian philosopher Francis A. Schaeffer, who grew up in Switzerland and L'Abri Fellowship, writes about the wonderful, life-enriching, joyous experience education can be for your child, in your home and in your school.

Montessori, Maria. *The Discovery of the Child.* New York: Ballantine, 1967.

A good explanation of the Montessori philosophy of education, this book defines the needs and offers practical education suggestions for the various sensitive periods of the child.

Moore, Raymond S. and Dorothy N. *Home Grown Kids.* Waco, TX: Word, 1981.

A practical handbook for teaching your children at home, this book calls attention to the fact that education is still the prime responsibility of the parent. The educational suggestions are provocative and well worth considering; however, I do not agree with some of the authors' suggestions on early child care, especially much of their nutritional advice.

Uphoff, James K., June E. Gilmore, and Rosemarie Huber. *Summer Children—Ready or Not For School.* J. & J Publishing Co., P.O. Box 8549, Middletown, OH 45042. (See page 409 for description.)

Marriage

Crabb, Lawrence Jr. *How To Become One with Your Mate.* Grand Rapids, MI: Zondervan, 1982.

This is a small, very readable excerpt from *The Marriage Builder,* by Lawrence Crabb, on oneness of body and spirit in the marriage relationship. Looking to Christ to fulfill our needs enables us to minister to our mates.

Harley, Willard. *His Needs, Her Needs: Building an Affair-Proof Marriage.* Old Tappan, NJ: Revell, 1986.

Identifies the ten most important marital needs of husbands and wives and teaches how those needs can be fulfilled.

Wheat, Ed, M.D., and Gloria Okes Perkins. *Love Life for Every Married Couple.* Grand Rapids, MI: Zondervan, 1980.

How to fall in love, stay in love, rekindle your love.

Media

Farah, Joseph (editor). *Between the Lines.* 325 Pennsylvania Ave., SE, Washington, DC 20003.

A biweekly newsletter covering the politics and morality of the news media and entertainment industry.

Lappe, Francis Moore. *What To Do After You Turn Off the TV.* New York: Ballantine, 1985.

For other information concerning media write:

Christian Leaders for Responsible Television
c/o American Family Association
P.O. Box 2440
Tupelo, MS 38803

Mother-Infant Attachment

Fraiberg, Selma. "Every Child's Birthright." In *Selected Writings of Selma Fraiberg,* Louis Fraiberg, editor. Columbus, OH: Ohio State University Press, 1987.

Kaplan, Louise. *Oneness and Separateness: From Infant to Individual.* New York: Simon and Schuster, 1978.

A beautiful discussion of the inner workings of the child as he goes from oneness to separateness. Dr. Kaplan explores some of the theory of the benefits of mother-infant attachment and the consequences of premature detachment.

Klaus and Kennell. *Parent-Infant Bonding.* Saint Louis, MO: C. V. Mosby, 1982.

This book discusses results of studies which suggest the positive benefits of mother and baby remaining in close contact with each other immediately after birth.

McClure, Vimala Schneider. *Infant Massage.* New York: Bantam, 1989.

Teaches parents to discover the joys and benefits of massage for their babies and for themselves. Photographs illustrate each step of the process. Massage promotes bonding, reduces tension and fussing, and aids in physical development. I highly recommend this book.

Montagu, Ashley. *Touching: The Human Significance of the Skin.* New York: Harper and Row, 1986.

The classical treatise on the importance of the skin as the largest organ of human sensation. Dr. Montagu discusses at length the psychological benefits of skin-to-skin contact.

Natural Family Planning

Kass-Annese, Barbara, R.N., N.P., and Hal Danzer, M.D. *The Fertility Awareness Workbook.* New York: Putnam, 1981.

A concise, how-to book on natural family planning. Good illustrations and diagrams.

Kippley, Sheila. *Breastfeeding and Natural Child Spacing.* Cincinnati, OH: The Couple to Couple League International, Inc., 1989.

This book discusses the concept of natural mothering and how it can postpone the return of fertility.

Kippley, John and Sheila. *The Art of Natural Family Planning.* Cincinnati, OH: The Couple to Couple League International, Inc., 1989.

To be used either on your own or as part of an instructional program, the book teaches the sympto-thermal method of fertility control. Part One explains the "why" of NFP; Part Two the "how to." My favorite chapter is entitled "Marriage Building with NFP."

New Age

Kjos, Barit. *Your Child and the New Age.* Wheaton, IL: Victor, 1990.

A solid explanation of various aspects of the New Age influence in schools and media, with practical suggestions on what parents can do. Issues such as counterfeit spirituality, values clarification, New Age globalism in schools, mind manipulation, distortion of imagination, pagan sentiments in toys, TV, movies, reading material, and music.

Michaelsen, Johanna. *Like Lambs to the Slaughter: Your Child and the Occult*. Eugene, OR: Harvest House, 1989.

Information parents need to have to help their children survive or avoid the subtle and not-so-subtle New Age influences in the world today.

Parenting and Child Care

Cahill, Mary Ann. *The Heart Has Its Own Reasons*. New York: New American Library, 1985.

This book encourages mothers to stay home with their children and gives practical and timely suggestions on how that can be managed financially.

Campbell, D. Ross. *How to Really Love Your Child*. Wheaton, IL: Victor, 1978.

This book, written by a Christian psychiatrist, discusses the importance of touching, eye-to-eye contact, and focused attention. It offers practical tips on how to convey your love to your child.

——————. *How to Really Love Your Teenager*. Wheaton, IL: Victor, 1981.

Encouraging guidance for parents struggling to understand and express love to their teens. Picks up where *How to Really Love Your Child* leaves off.

Crook, William G. and Laura J. Stevens. *Solving the Puzzle of Your Hard to Raise Child*. New York: Random House, 1987.

Parents of high-need children need the information in this book concerning the effect on behavior from improper or inadequate nutrition. Tells how to improve the child's diet and, therefore, his behavior.

Dobson, James. *Hide or Seek*. Old Tappan, NJ: Revell, 1979.

In my opinion this is the best of Dr. Dobson's many books. It deals with the extremely important issue of how to build self-esteem in your child.

——————. *Preparing for Adolescence*. New York: Bantam, 1980.

An excellent text for parent and pre-teen to share, with an accompanying study guide for your child. I've used it as each of our first four approached their teen years.

Noble, Elizabeth. *Having Twins: A Parent's Guide to Pregnancy, Birth, and Early Childhood*. Boston, MA: Houghton, Miflin, 1991.

A veteran childbirth expert tells how to carry healthy babies to term.

Sears, William and Martha. *The Ministry of Parenting Your Baby*. Elgin, IL: D. C. Cook, 1990.

Helps parents prepare for their baby's first year of life.

Sears, William. *Becoming a Father: How to Nurture and Enjoy Your Family*. Franklin Park, IL: La Leche League International, Inc., 1986.

——————. *Nighttime Parenting*. New York: New American Library, 1987.

Practical tips for parenting your child to sleep.

——————. *Creative Parenting*. New York: Dodd-Mead, 1987.

This five-hundred-plus-page book is a secular version of and a suggested companion to *Christian Parenting and Child Care* and covers all of the important medical concerns in more detail. Includes a large section on child development, accident prevention, and safety around the house.

——————. *The Fussy Baby*. New York: New American Library, 1987.

This book describes what I call the "high-need baby" and presents a style of parenting that meets their special needs.

_____. *Growing Together: A Parents' Guide to Baby's First Year*. Franklin Park, IL: La Leche League International, Inc., 1987.

This book describes the month-by-month development of babies from birth to one year.

Sex Education

Andry, Andrew & Stephen Schepp. *How Babies Are Made*. New York: Little-Brown, 1984.

This is the perfect starter book for teaching the reproductive process to your children. Illustrated with paper sculpture, figures are realistic and simple. Begins with plants and animals, and tastefully illustrates humans, for ages 3–10. Ends with the mother breast-feeding her baby.

Kitzinger, Sheila and Lennart Nilsson. *Being Born*. New York: Grosset Dunlap, 1986.

The same magnificent photos of Nilssons's *A Child Is Born* combined with poetic text about conception and birth make this book timeless. Adults as well as children are drawn to it, even though it is written for children.

McDowell, Josh and Dick Day. *Why Wait? What You Need to Know About the Teen Sexuality Crisis*. San Bernardino, CA: Here's Life Publishers, 1987.

A very frank look at the situation challenging teens and the biblical perspective on what God wants for their lives in regard to chastity.

Sexuality

Evans, Debra. *The Mystery of Womanhood*. Westchester, IL: Crossway, 1987.

A biblical perspective on being a woman, finding the inner beauty of femininity, handling stress of daily living, fertility and childbearing, sexuality in a healthy marriage, and living with a cyclical nature.

Penner, Clifford & Joyce. *The Gift of Sex: A Christian Guide to Sexual Fulfillment*. Waco, TX: Word, 1981.

A comprehensive and joyful guide to sex for Christians.

Sleep Problems

Sears, William. *Nighttime Parenting*. New York: New American Library, 1987.

Practical tips for parenting your child to sleep.

Thevenin, Tine. *The Family Bed*. New York: Avery, 1987.

This book brings back an age-old concept in child rearing and advocates children sleeping with their parents or with other siblings as a way to solve bedtime problems, create a closer bond within the family, and give children a greater sense of security.

Your Child's Devotional Life

Blitchington, Evelyn. *The Family Devotions Idea Book*. Minneapolis, MN: Bethany House, 1982.

This book is full of practical ideas on how to conduct meaningful family devotions.

Chapin, Alice. *Building Your Child's Faith*. Nashville, TN: Thomas Nelson, 1990.

    Simple, fun ideas for teaching children how to pray, worship, and discover the Bible.

Haystead, Wes. *Teaching Your Child About God*. Ventura, CA: Regal, 1981.

    This is an easy-to-read book with practical advice on the spiritual training of the child at various stages.

Index

About the Author

William Sears, M.D., is a pediatrician in private practice in San Clememte, California and is Clinical Assistant Professor of Pediatrics at USC School of Medicine. Dr. Sears received his pediatric training at Harvard Medical School's Children's Hospital in Boston and Toronto's Hospital for Sick Children, the largest children's hospital in the world.

He is a monthly columnist in *Christian Parenting Today* and has published articles on child care in *BabyTalk, American Baby, Parenting, McCall's,* and *Redbook.* His first book, *Creative Parenting,* is the only baby book to receive endorsement from both the president of the largest pediatric organization in the world— The American Academy of Pediatrics—and the world's largest parenting organization—the La Leche League International. He and his wife Martha, a registered nurse, are the parents of eight children.

Dr. Sears' other books include *Creative Parenting, Nighttime Parenting, The Fussy Baby, Becoming a Father, Growing Together, 300 Questions New Parents Ask, Safe and Healthy, Ministry of Parenting,* and *The Baby Book.*